Constructing a Colonial People

Constructing a Colonial People

Puerto Rico and the United States, 1898–1932

Pedro A. Cabán

Westview Press
A Member of the Perseus Books Group

Copyright © 1999 by Westview Press, A Member of the Perseus Books Group

Published in 1999 in the United States of America by Westview Press, 5500 Central Avenue, Boulder, Colorado 80301-2877, and in the United Kingdom by Westview Press, 12 Hid's Copse Road, Cumnor Hill, Oxford OX2 9JJ

Find us on the World Wide Web at www.westviewpress.com

Library of Congress Cataloging-in-Publication Data
Cabán, Pedro A. (Pedro Angel)
   Constructing a colonial people: Puerto Rico and the United
States, 1898-1932 / Pedro A. Cabán.
      p.   cm.
   Includes bibliographical references and index.
   ISBN 0-8133-3903-0
   1. United States—Foreign relations—Puerto Rico.   2. Puerto Rico—
Foreign relations—United States.   3. United States—Foreign
relations—1897-1901.   4. United States—Foreign relations—20th
century.   5. Imperialism—United States—History.   I. Title.
E183.8.P8C33   1999
327.7307295—dc21   99-28134
                                                                              CIP

The paper used in this publication meets the requirements of the American National Standard for Permanence of Paper for Printed Library Materials Z39.48-1984.

10   9   8   7   6   5   4

To Pedro Cabán Caribe and
María Hernández Jiménez

Contents

Tables

Acronyms

AFL	American Federation of Labor
BIA	Bureau of Insular Affairs
FLT	Federación Libre de Trabajadores
LDC	less developed country
NAM	National Association of Manufacturers
PRFAA	Puerto Rico Federal Affairs Administration
PUR	Republican Union Party
UP	Unión Puertorriqueña
USDCL	U.S. Department of Commerce and Labor
USDS	U.S. Department of State
USDW	U.S. Department of War
USICPR	U.S. Interdepartmental Committee on Puerto Rico

Acknowledgments

When I set out to write this book I had in mind something very different from what you are reading. Originally I was going to write a lengthy study on the political economy of Puerto Rico's post-World War II development. I had planned to write a brief section on the formation of the colonial state to give the historical context for the contemporary analysis. However, after reviewing virtually all the available secondary literature on the first three decades of U.S. colonialism I was struck by the absence of a comprehensive study of the state in Puerto Rico. Similarly, the issue of how this colonial state, as well as the federal government, undertook the mission of Americanizing Puerto Ricans required further examination.

I have had the good fortune of having intellectual support and substantive input from a number of good friends and colleagues over the years. In particular, I am indebted to Steve Bronner, whose penetrating observations continually challenged me to clarify the broader theoretical and comparative derivatives of the Puerto Rican case. My work benefitted substantially from my friendship and professional association with Jorge Rodríguez Beruff, Humberto Garcia Muñoz, Haroldo Dilla, and Armando Fernández. Over the years I have had the good fortune of having worked closely with Frank Bonilla and Arcadio Díaz Quiñones, two eminent Puerto Rican scholars of our time.

I am grateful to Robert Alexander, Luis Martínez Fernández, José Morales, and Oscar Zanetti for reading portions of the work and for their constructive comments. During various stages in my research and writing, Sherrie Baver, Nilsa Burgos, Juan Manuel Carrión, James Dietz, Jeff Frieden, Juan Manuel García Passalacqua, Tom Holloway, Robert Kaufman, David Lewis, Pablo Maríñez, María Milagros López, Theodore Lowi, Howard McGary, Edgardo Meléndez, Gil Merkx, Mark Naison, Edward Ortiz, Angel Israel Rivera, Bruce Robbins, Francisco Scarano, Anna Marie Smith, Neil Smith, William Solomon, Caridad Souza, Andy Torres, and Carmen Whalen gave of their time to discuss and evaluate my ideas. To each my thanks for their interest in my work.

Projects such as this take some time to take shape. I am grateful to Douglas Chalmers, who influenced my early thinking on the comparative dimensions of Puerto Rican political and economic change. During my 1992–1993 fellowship year at the Rutgers University Center for Critical Analysis of Contemporary Culture I received much needed critical insights and commentary from Neil Smith,

Susan Gal, Bruce Robbins, Briavel Holcomb, John McClure, Michael Shafer, Gerard Aching, Cora Kaplan, and Edward Ramsamy.

I owe a debt of intellectual gratitude to Angel Quintero Rivera, whose pioneering work on Puerto Rican political economy continues to have an impact on the contemporary scholarship. My thanks to Juan Valdés Paz, Rafael Hernández, and Isabel Jaramillo, for the productive and pleasurable hours we spent in Cuba discussing the comparative colonial experience of Cuba and Puerto Rico. I am grateful to Karina Cespedes, Daniella Hott, and Monica Licourt for their research assistance. My thanks to the librarians at Rutgers University, Betsy Fetzer and Peter Stern, and specially Kevin McGuire, who was tireless in his pursuit of materials I needed to complete this work. My editors at Westview, Leo Wiegman and Karl Yambert, were enthusiastic supporters of this project and moved quickly to get the manuscript into print. I am grateful to both. Much of the research for this book was generously supported by the Office of the Dean of the Faculty of Arts and Sciences at Rutgers University. In particular I offer my special thanks to Richard L. McCormick and Richard L. Foley.

My fifteen-year-old daughter, Jennifer, not only voluntarily stayed away when her dad had to work, but she read and commented on parts of the manuscript. I owe my greatest debt of gratitude to my compañera for life, Rosalie Morales Kearns. She has been a steadfast source of encouragement and intellectual support. I am fortunate she is a talented professional editor who always found time from her demanding schedule to assist in the completion of this book.

Introduction

The United States and Puerto Rico

Since 1493 Puerto Rico has been the colonial property of empires, and its people have been subject to the laws of these nations. Puerto Rico's experience under U.S. rule is of more recent vintage. On December 10, 1898, representatives of the vanquished Spanish empire were compelled to sign the Treaty of Paris, by which it formally relinquished sovereignty over Cuba and ceded Puerto Rico, the Philippines, and Guam to the United States. The treaty established that the "civil rights and political conditions of the natural inhabitants of the territories ceded to the United States will be determined by Congress." In fact, in the intervening century not only Congress but also the executive branch and the federal courts have determined the political and economic conditions of the people of Puerto Rico. This unilateral and arbitrary authority to determine the political conditions of Puerto Rico is the essence of colonialism. Colonialism has been and continues to be an essential element of the Puerto Rican condition and identity.

This is a study of the first three and one-half decades of U.S. colonialism in Puerto Rico. I examine in considerable detail the ambitious campaign of social engineering, institution-building, and capitalist development the U. S. government instituted in that strategic island. The United States achieved a measure of success in effecting important changes in its new colony, and it did so without provoking civil unrest and violent opposition. However, it never did completely achieve the goal of remaking the colonial subjects in the image of the colonizer. Moreover, within three decades colonialism had degenerated from a carefully conceived program of territorial administration and institutional modernization to a system of rule by absentee corporations, incompetent colonial administrators, and indifferent local political parties. Even seemingly well-meaning officials could not halt the process of political decay and pauperization that afflicted the prized possession. By 1932 Puerto Rico was on the verge of social collapse, and the very legitimacy of the colonizing mission was at risk.

This is also a study of accommodation and resistance by Puerto Ricans to the transformative campaign engineered by the new colonial power. Although I focus almost exclusively on the Puerto Rican colonial experience, I do so in the context of an evolving United States policy toward its other possessions and Cuba. I begin with the rather conventional premise that the United States acquired its overseas

1

territories as part of a hemispheric, if not global, strategy of commercial expansion and foreign investment. However, the United States had specific plans for Puerto Rico: The new possession would be converted into a stable strategic enclave in the Caribbean. From this enclave the United States could project its military influence in the region and exert its growing commercial and industrial strength. Puerto Rico had a dual role in the imperial designs of the United States: It was a naval outpost charged with protecting the Panama Canal, and it was a transit point for the expansion of U.S. business into Latin America. Puerto Rico's key economic and political institutions would have to be transformed for the country to carry out these tasks. The most dramatic and enduring changes were effected in the economic and political spheres—capitalist development and state-building.

Class Structure and Economic Transformation

U.S. corporate investments in Puerto Rico increased rapidly after Congress passed the Foraker Act in 1900. This legislation established a colonial state that was the motor force behind Puerto Rico's transformation. Following a practice employed by European colonial powers, U.S. officials designed policies to encourage national capital to invest in the colony. Laws were enacted specifically to protect the property and privilege of U.S. business and citizens. Tariff, fiscal, and monetary measures and abundant cheap labor converted Puerto Rico into an investor's paradise.

For all colonial societies the process of capitalist development has been "more or less abrupt, more or less brutal and effected by more or less direct means" (Crow, Thorpe, et al. 1988, 31). Puerto Rico's experience was no different; the society and economy were literally reconfigured during a relatively brief period of three decades. The spread of capitalism transformed the social class structure and the nature of political struggle in Puerto Rico. But the trajectory and speed with which development took place was also conditioned by the existing class structure and political conditions. Capitalist development is not a mechanistic and invariant process, and it does not necessarily follow that other modes of production will simply and uniformly disintegrate when confronted with capitalism's superior productive forces. Whether existing modes of production in these societies decompose, endure, or are incorporated into the emerging capitalist sector varies across societies. How any given society responds to foreign economic penetration, particularly externally induced capitalist development, is historically specific and will be conditioned by a number of factors.

Drawing on Chile's history of agrarian capitalism, Zeitlan and Ratcliff postulate that "capitalism is profoundly conditioned by the historical forms of land property and the types of agrarian classes it confronts in its development" (1988, 146). This observation is particularly relevant for understanding Puerto Rico's capitalist development during the first two decades of U.S. colonialism. Puerto

Rico underwent profoundly unsettling economic changes and experienced a marked dissolution of the social organization of daily life. But some sectors of local capital gained in the frenzy of economic growth, whereas others were consumed by it. The country's class structure was literally reconfigured within one generation. In addition a single industry, sugar, virtually monopolized Puerto Rico's productive resources. The change in sovereignty precipitated economic and social turbulence that generated resistance as well as accommodation among the disoriented colonial subjects.

The actions of organized political forces and the ideologies that guide their activities are of vital importance in explaining the trajectory and particularities of capitalist expansion in any given society. What follows is a series of considerations on how class structure and the political representation of class interests bear on the question of the barriers that foreign capital confronts, or can confront, as it attempts to assert its dominance in a relatively underdeveloped society of the kind Puerto Rico was at the turn of the century. These considerations will frame much of the discussion in this book.

Resistance to foreign economic penetration will be strong if the productive forces of the country are under the control of a unified national political elite. Such resistance is particularly strong if the country has well-developed trade relations with powerful nations who are reliant on its agricultural exports. Under these circumstances foreign firms will pay substantial political and economic costs to acquire control of local resources. The more developed capitalist production relations are in the colony, the more determined local firms will be in politically resisting the entry of foreign capital. In a society in which capitalism predominates, a proletariat will have formed. Despite its antagonism to the national property-owning class, the proletariat will resist the profound social dislocations and economic disintegration that result from large-scale direct foreign investment. However, such society-wide resistance requires a coherent nationalist ideology that convinces workers that foreign capital threatens the dissolution of their material and social conditions.

The political solidarity of the local property owners and their capacity to lead other sectors in resisting foreign financial and commercial domination are very real impediments to capitalist development. If, however, the principal capitalist sector has not achieved a position of unquestioned social and political dominance, its capacity to marshal other strata and classes to resist foreign penetration is tenuous at best. A society is more vulnerable to foreign capital penetration if conflict and marked political cleavages divide its capitalist class. Some sectors, particularly those that are in a subordinate position in the national economy, may seek cooperation with foreign capital to gain access to capital, markets, and technology. The extent to which societies are characterized by diverse labor regimes, land tenure systems, and modes of production also bears directly on the challenge that foreign capital confronts as it seeks to appropriate command of the local economy. Limited proletarianization, extensive artisan production, non-wage labor forms of agrarian employment, and peasant and household-based production divide the producing class socially, ideologically, and materially. These divisions and the lack of political organization facilitate the development of a wage-earning labor force in service to foreign capital. Under these conditions the formation of nationally based opposition movements to colonial domination is a formidable task.

The type of direct foreign investment also influences the likelihood of the investing firms encountering resistance or accommodation. Investments in productive activities that threaten to displace local capitalists will be resisted. Similarly, foreign firms that appropriate locally controlled land and labor resources will also be resisted by local firms. On the other hand, if local capitalists can collaborate with foreign capital and gain materially by assuming a subsidiary role in the emerging economic order, opposition to foreign firms will be reduced. Local firms engaged in agricultural export production benefit from the processing, marketing, and distribution capabilities that technologically advanced foreign firms can supply. If direct foreign investments generate demand for locally produced inputs, local firms will also work with the foreign corporations.

All or most of the conditions that affected the level and type of resistance to colonialism and capitalist penetration were present during the first three decades of U.S. rule. The competing economic interests of domestic capital and the diversified labor regimes help explain why the country's productive structure was virtually demolished and reconstituted during the first two decades without provoking a unified national resistance.

Puerto Rico: Sugar Bowl and Gateway to Latin America

U.S. empire builders saw Puerto Rico as the gateway to Latin America and as the Malta of the Caribbean. So it is not surprising that within weeks of acquiring Puerto Rico, the United States moved decisively to dismantle the governing apparatus left by the Spanish and to substitute its own institutions. Policies were enacted that rapidly set into motion the country's transition to twentieth-century capitalism. Given Puerto Rico's importance to the realization of U.S. economic objectives in the hemisphere, the new colonizer chose to invest heavily in Americanizing the small island nation and converting it into an enclave of the metropolitan economy.

Puerto Rico and the Philippines were the first densely populated overseas territories the United States acquired through war and conquest. Because these territories were so densely populated the United States did not have the option of relocating the indigenous people and replacing them with its own citizens. Instead colonial policy was designed to Americanize these people into loyal colonial subjects and to convert the overseas possessions into large-scale producers and exporters of sugar and other agricultural products. U.S. officials presumed that the Americanized colonial subjects would form a cheap and disciplined labor force available for hire by corporations engaged in export production. Favorable tariff and fiscal policies inflated the profitability of the sugar industry and encouraged massive investments in this sector. By developing the sugar industry in Puerto Rico, as well as in Cuba, Hawaii, and the Philippines, the United States sought to break its dependency on European beet sugar and achieve self-sufficiency in this high-energy, cheap source of food. Shortly after U.S. forces defeated the Spanish, the occupying military government began to transform Puerto Rico's economy. As it dismantled the antiquated agrarian economy, the U.S. governor generals energetically fostered investments and modernized the country's transportation and communications system. The policy aim was to incorporate Puerto Rico into the metropolitan network of investment and trade.

Capitalist expansion under colonial management followed a dynamic and a logic that engendered both confrontation and adaptation among the colonial subjects. But in general, metropolitan commercial and manufacturing capital confronted only limited barriers to its expansion in Puerto Rico. The process of economic incorporation and political transformation was accelerated in 1900, when Congress passed the Foraker Act. This law established a colonial state apparatus that directed Puerto Rico's economic transformation and that relentlessly pursued the campaign of Americanization. Aided by favorable policies, corporations with superior financial resources were able to readily penetrate Puerto Rico's economy. By the 1920s U.S. corporate investments in sugar, tobacco, and needleworks dominated the economy. By this time the small island of Puerto Rico was satisfying 14 percent of the U.S. sugar market.

Identifying Allies in the Colony

In order to quickly effect Puerto Rico's institutional and economic transformation, U.S. officials relegated the established political leadership to a subsidiary role in the governing process. Colonial authorities also identified those domestic elites and popular forces that favored annexation and forged alliances with them. Puerto Rico's divided and antagonistic property-owning classes made such real and potential alliances possible in the wake of Spain's departure. As U.S. officials expected, local merchants and landowners who stood to gain materially from the change in sovereignty were ready to promote Puerto Rico's incorporation into the metropolitan economy. Although numerically insignificant in 1898, the labor force increased rapidly with the influx of investments. Workers needed to be organized and socialized into the U.S. brand of trade unionism. (The American Federation of Labor (AFL), then under the leadership of Samuel Gompers, took a key role in this process.) Finally, those sectors of society that dared challenge colonial policy had to be neutralized.

Public perception of the United States began to change from welcome liberator to insolent meddling bully after 1900. The groundswell of support for the

U.S. presence in Puerto Rico dissipated, and specific sectors of collaboration or resistance came into being. Elaborate, shifting scenarios of political struggle and deal-making characterized the relations between colonial officials and the local political leadership. Puerto Rico's political parties and nascent labor organizations represented the interests and objectives of competing economic and political forces. Intense material, ideological, and political differences divided the property-owning classes and alienated the laboring classes.

The political parties proved unable or unwilling to build national alliances to confront U.S. colonial rule. As I will explain later, the two dominant political parties, the Federal and Republican Parties, represented distinct class interests. The Federals relentlessly pursued home rule and attempted to block many institutional changes proposed by colonial officials. The Republicans, in contrast, were loyal apologists for U.S. rule and believed in an extended period of colonial tutelage to prepare Puerto Rico for statehood. Puerto Rico's agricultural workers and artisans harbored an intense antipathy toward the dominant economic and political force, the *hacendados*. Colonial officials exploited these intense divisions and prevented the crystallization of effective opposition to its rule. This lack of unity was to no small degree the outcome of a historical process of class and political rivalries that preceded the U.S. invasion.

Politics Before 1898:
Divided Loyalties

Before Puerto Rico's acquisition by the United States, two political forces vied for the attention of the Spanish Cortes: the Autonomist Party of Puerto Rico (founded in 1887) and the Spanish Unconditional Party (founded in 1891). These parties mirrored the traditional split between the Creole and Peninsular social forces, forces that competed for supremacy during the South American wars for independence. The Autonomist Party, one of whose most active leaders was Luis Muñoz Rivera, articulated the interests of sugar planters, coffee and tobacco *hacendados*, the *pequeña bourguesia*, artisans, small merchants, and professionals. These sectors were unified in their struggle to wrest political autonomy and more liberalized commercial arrangements from Spain. The Autonomists challenged the inflexible system of colonial rule that subordinated Puerto Ricans to the dictates and needs of the Spanish crown and capital. Spanish mercantilism had impeded Puerto Rico's economic development. Moreover, Spain systematically opposed the efforts of Puerto Rico's leading economic sectors to ascend to political leadership of the country. But unlike the Puerto Rican Section of the Cuban Revolutionary Party, which was conspiring to achieve independence through armed struggle, the Autonomists sought reform. Although not revolutionary, the Autonomists were an economically progressive force which aspired to eliminate the colonial policies that blocked the development of the country's productive forces.

During the last three decades of Spanish rule the *peninsulares,* resident Spanish merchants, controlled most of Puerto Rico's commercial trade. They held the mortgages on much of agricultural land and plantations, and through credit and debt held in check the political activities of the native-born *hacendados* (Rowe 1902, 352).The Unconditional Party represented these sectors that were both the product and beneficiary of Spanish colonialism. The *Incondicionales* campaigned for Puerto Rico's annexation into the Spanish body politic.

Under intense pressure from the United States and faced with a disastrous war of attrition in Cuba, Spain on November 25, 1897, reluctantly issued proclamations establishing autonomous governments in Cuba and Puerto Rico. Whereas the Cubans rejected the overture, the Autonomist Party accepted the measure as the crowning culmination of its efforts to achieve self-rule for Puerto Rico. Frustrated by their failure to preserve Puerto Rico's colonial status and feeling betrayed, the *peninsulares* disbanded the Unconditional Party on April 2, 1898.

Praxedas Sagasta, the president of the Spanish Council of Ministers, had proposed the Autonomous Charter for Puerto Rico in return for the Autonomist Party's support for his Liberal Party government in the Spanish Cortes. Muñoz Rivera and Rosendo Matienzo Cintrón accepted the *quid pro quo* and convened a general assembly of the party in which it was decided to disband the Autonomist Party and establish a Puerto Rican chapter of the Liberal Fusion Party of Spain.

The leadership's decision to disband the Autonomist party was strenuously resisted by sectors of the professional strata of the party. Opposed to the *hacendados* who had dissolved the Autonomists, the dissident professionals wanted to extract more concessions from Spain. Moreover, they were not about to accede to the *hacendados'* plan to impose their dominance over the society with the assistance of the Spanish Liberals (Figueroa 1971, 2:73–131; Rosario Natal 1989, 123–136).

José Celso Barbosa, Manuel Fernández Juncos, José C. Rossy, and other prominent professionals in the Autonomist Party resigned, and with their followers founded the Partido Autonomista Histórico in March 1897, vowing to oppose the pact with Sagasta (Ribes Tovar 1973, 368). This sector broke with the social order based on the culture of the *hacienda* and openly opposed the Spanish colonial regime (See Díaz Soler 1960,1:119ff; Quintero Rivera 1977, 29–30, 56).

Spain inaugurated the autonomous government on February 11, 1898, and appointed a six-member cabinet (Todd 1953, 133). On July 17, 1898, Spanish governor general Mejías convened the first and only session of the Autonomous Parliament of Puerto Rico. A week later, on July 25, 1898, U.S. armed forces invaded Puerto Rico, landing in the port of Guánica. Puerto Rico's only too brief experiment in self-rule was abruptly terminated.

In 1899 the Liberal Party was reorganized as the Federal Party under Muñoz Rivera's leadership. In the same year José Celso Barbosa disbanded the Partido Autonomista Auténtico and established the Republican Party. These two political parties were the dominant political forces for almost two decades. They initiated the enduring division between Puerto Ricans who aspired for autonomy under the protection of the United States (Federals) and those who wanted annexation as a state of the Union (Republicans).

The Colonial State

When Congress passed the Foraker Act in 1900, it established the first legally constituted overseas colonial administration in U.S. history. Congressional debates and Supreme Court decisions leave no doubt that the United States did not intend to incorporate Puerto Rico into the Union. Puerto Rico was a territorial possession subject to the plenary powers of Congress. The United States designed a structure for colonial administration without the involvement of the subject population. This colonial state was neither representative of nor accountable to the colonized people. It was set up to administer the colony, promote economic growth, preserve political stability, and legitimize colonial rule. Although it is formally nothing more than a bureaucratic extension of the metropolitan government, the colonial state has not been simply a regulatory and enforcement agency. Over time its functions have changed as the colonial state has gained relative autonomy to mediate the content and direction of social and economic change. It is also a dynamic actor that promotes fundamental changes in the economy. State agencies have granted incentives, subsidies, and tax holidays to attract foreign investors, financed the development of the physical infrastructure, facilitated access to cheap labor, maintained the requisite industrial and social peace during periods of economic change, lobbied aggressively in Washington for favorable legislation for U.S. firms, and undertaken a host of other activities in the interests of attracting and retaining foreign investments.

The colonial state has performed these tasks more adequately during certain historical periods than during other periods. When it has failed to respond to the shifting demands of an ever more complex and sophisticated political economy, its powers and structure have been adjusted. As noted earlier, the conditions under which these changes have taken place and the consequences for economic growth and colonial legitimation are also central concerns of this study. On one level the colonial state resembles the state in advanced capitalist economies. Admittedly it lacks autonomy in the international sphere, and the laws it passes can be rescinded by Congress. Nonetheless, it is the repository of significant local power, and consequently political parties have fought to control its legislative, executive, and judicial branches. Its centrality as an arena of political struggle is not surprising, since the colonial state is a key actor in promoting economic change, is the principal employer, and is the conduit through which federal funds liberally flow into Puerto Rico. But state presence is not solely confined to the colonial state. The federal government operates a number of agencies and maintains a sizable military establishment. Thus two state systems operate coterminously: the colonial state apparatus that is under the management of local political forces, and the civilian and military agencies of the United States.

The Colony on the Verge of Collapse

I examine Puerto Rico's economic history from 1898–1917. The United States enacted by the end of World War I virtually all the legal and economic changes to encourage direct foreign investments and Puerto Rico's rapid incorporation into the metropolitan economy. A detailed economic discussion of the period from 1917–1932 is beyond the scope of this book and does not necessarily provide additional insights into the process of constructing a colonial people. But some understanding of the economically determined political dynamics of the period is necessary.

By the late 1920s U.S. officials knew the troubling reality that Puerto Rico's people were among the poorest and most sickly in the Caribbean. The development of a vast sugar and tobacco complex and exploitative needleworks industry had created a labor force that was reliant for its survival on the growing foreign corporate presence. Unemployment and underemployment accelerated as the contingents of displaced small-scale agricultural producers and subsistence farmers entered the labor market. Capitalist development was profoundly destabilizing for many Puerto Ricans as they discovered that their economic survival had become a function of the capacity to find work in highly saturated labor markets. The federal government and colonial authorities charged the giant absentee sugar corporations, which amassed huge fortunes but paid miserly wages, with responsibility for the labor conflict, social deterioration, and political instability that threatened the colonial enterprise.

By the early 1930s it seemed that the very process of Americanization was generating its antithesis, the formation of a nationalist vision of Puerto Rican identity and the emergence of political forces committed to promoting this identity. Unrestrained market forces had precipitated a social and economic crisis that ultimately convinced the metropolitan state to intervene to save its crumbling Caribbean colonial possession. Years before the New Deal arrived in Puerto Rico, the federal government transferred funds to the island in the hope of ameliorating the intensity of human immiseration and imparting some stability to the troubled island.

The period from 1917 to 1932 was marked by political confrontations and bitter recriminations between U.S-appointed colonial officials and Unión Puertorriqueña (UP) members who wanted to reform the colonial regime. Republicans who ardently supported Americanization and were proponents of statehood challenged the UP. Large-scale protests and violent clashes took place between workers who, with increasing militancy and organizational skill, struck major centers of production and fought the local constabulary. During this period the political sphere was highly volatile; temporary alliances were established between the warring political parties, severe ideological and personality clashes ripped the parties apart, new political organizations surfaced and died. Nationalist Puerto Ricans organized a party that repudiated the established leadership and demanded U.S. evacuation of Puerto Rico. The political volatility of the times did not seriously threaten U.S. control over Puerto Rico, but it did seriously compromise the task of Americanizing the colony.

The Chapters

This reexamination of Puerto Rican political economy raises and attempts to satisfy a number of analytical and theoretical questions about the U.S. colonial experience. What I attempt to do is theorize Puerto Rico's institutional development during the first three decades of colonialism. Chapter 1 examines how economic transformation in the United States and the nation's changing role in the global economy factored into the decision to wage war on Spain. Puerto Rico's particular economic and strategic function within the emerging empire is examined in the context of new technologies of commerce and war and U.S. aspirations for regional hegemony. Puerto Rico's forceful acquisition was part of a U.S. global drive to assert itself commercially and to propagate its political institutions and cultural values regionally. But Puerto Rico quickly assumed importance as an offshore platform on which to implement and fine-tune a doctrine of capitalist development, institutional modernization, and cultural transformation.

In Chapter 2 I discuss the economic, political, and legal changes enacted by the military governments in Puerto Rico. I look at how the governor-generals negotiated the initial stages of Puerto Rico's transition from a Spanish colonial backwater into a forward base for U.S. commercial expansion into Latin America and a strategic nodal point in the Caribbean. I explicate the underlying logic of the colonizing mission—what colonial officials referred to as "Americanization." The campaign to reconfigure Puerto Rico's institutions had both political and economic components. The War Department initiated Puerto Rico's institutional transformation during this time, emphasizing public instruction, infrastructure modernization, legal and judicial changes, and professionalization of the constabulary. Congress relied heavily on the work of the military regimes in developing the Foraker Act, the defining piece of colonial legislation.

During the brief period of military rule from 1898 to 1900, the major political divisions that were to influence the contours of elite reaction to U.S. colonialism were forged.

Chapter 3 discusses some of the economic forces and strategic considerations that influenced the formation of colonial policy for Puerto Rico, as well as the other territorial possessions. U.S. imperialistic aspirations had to contend with the array of powerful domestic economic forces. The interplay of domestic and international influences is the backdrop for understanding the development of a territorial policy that was unprecedented in U.S. history. The chapter concludes by examining the logic and properties of the colonial state that Congress developed and imposed on Puerto Rico.

In Chapter 4 I take a close look at the Executive Council and examine this unique institution's role in promoting capitalist development and institutional transformation. This extremely powerful institution, which has been overlooked in the historiography of Puerto Rican colonialism, was responsible for designing and implementing the Americanization campaign. I examine the council's role in the ideological, coercive, and developmental spheres. The Executive Council helped set into motion Puerto Rico's transition to an export platform economy dominated by absentee sugar and tobacco corporations.

What kinds of resistance and accommodation did the new colonizers encounter as they set about to systematically and thoroughly transform Puerto Rican society? To what degree did the existing political forces retard or facilitate this process? These are the central concerns I address in Chapter 5. I look at the history of conflict and accommodation between the political parties and the colonial state from 1917 through 1932. Intense ideological, social, and material cleavages shaped the dynamic of party politics in Puerto Rico and factored into the strategies colonial officials used to promote Puerto Rico's Americanization. It was during this period that the foundations of the modern Puerto Rican political party system was established.

Chapter 6 examines how the very process of institutional and economic transformation engendered new complexities that complicated the task of colonial management. In 1917 Congress replaced the Foraker Act with the marginally more liberal Jones Act. This act is best known for conferring collective citizenship on Puerto Ricans. Here I discuss the background of the Jones Act, as Puerto Ricans of all political persuasions mounted a relentless offensive to liberalize the colonial regime. Growing antipathy to colonial rule fed U.S. perceptions that independence was gaining adherents and that change was necessary. The Jones Act was a war measure passed on the eve of U.S. entry into the European war and designed to ameliorate the growing chorus of discontent in the colony. The politics of how this act came into being is a central concern of this chapter. The Jones Act was welcomed as a liberalization of the colonial regime; it was, however, of no consequence for Puerto Rican women, who continued to be deprived of the right to vote. I discuss how Puerto Rico's suffrage movement orchestrated an effective political campaign to compel the local legislature to enact voting rights for women.

In Chapter 7 I discuss the Federación Libre de Trabajadores and the Socialist Party. Agricultural and industrial workers went on strike by the scores of thousands, and their actions disrupted production and trade. The seeming inability of the FLT and the Socialist Party to impose discipline on the hungry workers led colonial officials to intervene directly in the sphere of industrial labor relations. Initially a politically marginal force, by 1917 the Socialist Party was emerging as a vital political actor. By the mid-1920s widespread poverty and disease, political conflict, labor unrest, and the emergence of a militant anti-U.S. nationalist party combined to place at risk the legitimacy of the colonial enterprise. This context allows an understanding of why the federal government chose to reassess its policy of benign neglect and directly intervene to respond to the growing crisis of legitimacy.

Positioning the Study

Much of the scholarship on the first thirty years of U.S. colonialism in Puerto Rico examines the trajectory of capitalist development without providing an adequate analysis of the altered institutional context that was essential for this process. This work is a historically grounded interpretation of the evolution of U.S. colonial policy in Puerto Rico that attempts to overcome this limitation in the otherwise excellent scholarship on the period. By examining the elements of a clearly formulated and comprehensive program of institutional transformation, state building, and capitalist development, I interrogate the sophistication of U.S. colonial policy. I also set the context for a work in progress, in which I am assessing how and why the U.S. fundamentally altered its colonial policy from 1932 through 1952.

One of the strengths of the book is that I make extensive use of and incorporate into the narrative the written word—and thus the public thinking—of the key agents of the period. Many quotations from men and women who shaped the institutions of colonial Puerto Rico inform this analysis with a particular detail and complexity lacking in other works on Puerto Rico. I situate the evolution of colonial policy by reference to moments of historical significance, particularly the emergence of the United States as a global economic power and its drive for empire. I examine the new scholarship on U.S. expansionism during the Progressive Era and the normative/ideological constructions that rationalized a national program of territorial expansion and colonialism at the end of the century. In so doing, I have sought to place the Puerto Rican experience in the broader, and more interesting, context of the corporate and political restructuring that was unfolding in the United States during the Progressive Era.

This study is implicitly informed by a historical materialistic framework, but I do not fall into the trap of relying exclusively on economistic explanations for political behavior. Political forces, whose relationship to materiality has to be explicated and not presumed, clearly influence the contours of the colonial project. One thing I attempt to do is to develop a historically grounded explanation of why the United States set about to acquire Puerto Rico and remake it in its own image. Concretely, I have tried to develop a global/national context for studying the political economy of colonialism at the turn of the century. I do so by examining—in general terms and by reference to the seminal secondary literature—the reconfiguration of United States capitalism at the turn of the century. I look with particular attention at the intellectual forces that were influencing the formation of a new vision of a national identity and civilizing mission, as well as the theoretical foundations for imperialism and militarism. What I seek to do is link the strategy of global expansion—which is rationalized in terms of the white man's burden of civilizing the poor, sick, wretched masses of the newly acquired territories—with specific policies. I examine the evolution of colonial policy during three decades in the context of shifting policy concerns, strategic considerations, and economic motivations of the metropolitan state and capital. I try to bring out the links between conceptual foundations of policy, the concrete program, and the colonial subject's response.

My work also seeks to engage some of the explicit and underlying assumptions in development theory. Although everyone appears to be celebrating the long overdue burial of development theory, I think reports of its death are greatly exaggerated. The concerns that informed modernization and development theory of the 1960s and 1970s continue to be prevalent, and are in fact the implicit normative forces that drive much of the current work. Puerto Rico was undergoing a transformation that parallels with remarkable accuracy changes that have taken place in many less developed countries, (LDCs). The links between institutional transformation, economic modernization, and political stability still form an important component of development discourses. These are links that I examine in detail, and from which I postulate a series of mid-range conceptualizations. Theorizing and research on the mechanisms through which developed countries impose secular, universal, and scientific belief systems on people who are tradition-bound, parochial, and so forth, is a focus of current development-related work.

The relationship of Western ideas and thought to the rationalizing impulses of capitalist development is still the dynamic that informs much of the analysis of development in LDCs. Policymakers contemplated very specific and clearly enunciated rationalizations for crafting Puerto Rico, and to a lesser extent Cuba and the Philippines, into societies that resembled their images of what the United States was. These powerful men of the era were engaged in articulating a discourse of development whose similarity to current theorizing in postcolonial studies should be examined. I think this work makes a modest contribution to the postcolonial literature. It is, after all, an examination of the complex interactions and mediations of an imperial culture and the myriad of indigenous cultural, discursive, and political practices that manifest themselves in both resistance and accommodation to that imperial culture.

An understanding of Puerto Rico's colonial past is essential to explaining why that small island nation continues to be a colonial possession of the United States as we enter the third millennium. Since 1989 Congress has periodically considered legislation to effect a change in Puerto Rico's political status. In 1997 the House and Senate introduced legislation and held hearings on a proposed referendum to allow residents of Puerto Rico to express their preferences regarding the political status of the country. The work I have written synthesizes a great deal of the policy literature and provides a historical context for understanding congressional action on Puerto Rico's political status. Past imperial practice and colonial response identifies the range of possible choices that are available to U.S.

policy makers as they debate Puerto Rico's decolonization as we enter the third millennium

Finally—and I owe a debt of gratitude to Theodore Lowi for this—my work is relevant for understanding recent practices of globalization. The imposition of new forms of economic organization is invariably mediated by local political structures and practice. Increasingly research and theorizing are being directed to understanding the challenges that emerge in non-Western or non-capitalist countries as a result of the profoundly disruptive consequences of globalization. Although this study concentrates on a historical moment almost a century ago, it elucidates the remarkable similarity between the particular practices of globalization at that time and the contemporary moment. I directly engage a critique of market capitalism and demonstrate that official pronouncements of its beneficence were, then as now, at odds with practice.

1

U.S. Imperialism
and the New Colonial Era

The advent of the United States of America as the greatest of world-Powers is the greatest political, social, and commercial phenomenon of our times. It is only when we look at the manifold manifestations of the exuberant energy of the United States that we realize how comparatively insignificant are all the other events of our time.

—*William T. Stead, 1901*

Extending the Empire Overseas

Economic dislocations and political disorders during the last decade of the nineteenth century convinced policymakers and important business interests of the need for the United States to acquire external commercial markets. But in the context of late-nineteenth-century European imperialism the development of markets was not necessarily a benign process of investment and trade. The corollary of the imperative for market expansion was a militaristic drive for territorial acquisition. Overcoming economic crisis and fear that the commercial opportunities necessary to overcome this crisis would be lost moved the United States to war. The country pursued war against Spain in 1898 to defeat the aging empire and wrest control of its last remaining colonies in the Caribbean Sea and Pacific Ocean. On these strategic insular possessions the United States built naval bases and cable and coaling stations, from which it launched a campaign of economic penetration into Latin America and China. Puerto Rico, more than any other former Spanish possession, was the hapless victim of an explosive U.S. drive to assert military and naval hegemony in the Caribbean.

In the context of growing late-nineteenth-century European commercial interest in Latin America and German aspirations for a Caribbean naval base, Puerto Rico quickly emerged as a potentially important asset to the United States. Its strategic value rose as a direct consequence of U.S. commercial expansion into Latin America in the early twentieth century. German war plans in the early 1900s to establish a naval presence in the Caribbean only heightened U.S. resolve to retain colonial control over Puerto Rico. Once the Panama Canal was operational, Puerto Rico's strategic significance escalated further. Puerto Rico was important to the U.S. for other reasons as well; it served as an experimental station for colonial administration and was a laboratory to design and test the campaign to Americanize a subject people. Puerto Rico was envisioned as a cultural bridge that would serve to link North and South America. By 1932 Puerto Rico had been transformed into an invaluable outpost of the empire and an important agricultural asset that supplied the United States with 14 percent of the sugar its people consumed. The reasons for Puerto Rico's annexation and its role in the emerging commercial empire of the United States are the themes of this chapter.

The U.S. empire's hemispheric political and economic objectives in the late nineteenth century decisively influenced the colonial policy it devised for Puerto Rico. However, Puerto Rico did not figure prominently in the public debates or newspaper accounts during the period leading to the outbreak of war with Spain in 1898. Puerto Rico was scarcely mentioned in debates in Congress or the Spanish Cortes and seldom referred to in the diplomatic exchanges of the period (Carr 1984, 33). Before the outbreak of war only a small group of naval planners and policymakers realized the potential strategic significance of Puerto Rico. Nevertheless, once Spain was defeated, the island's fate as a colonial possession of the United States was sealed. Puerto Rico was simply too small and too vital for the United States to allow it an independent existence. Senator John T. Morgan, the chairperson of the Senate Foreign Relations Committee, had expressed this position in June 1898, barely a month before the U.S. invasion of Puerto Rico: "The ability to sustain an independent government is more questionable because her population cannot increase in so limited an area to the strength that is essential to independent statehood. Her geographical position is too important to distant nations, to admit of her separate independence" (Morgan 1898, 643).

A sovereign Puerto Rico, lacking a military capability and led by a political elite with close economic and cultural ties to Spain and France, was unacceptable to the new empire. The defenseless island nation could fall prey to an aggressive European state and be converted into a base from which to challenge U.S. naval dominance and jeopardize the new empire's commercial interests.

International Trade, the Canal, and Empire

In the closing decade of the nineteenth century the United States was an emerging global power that was preparing to compete militarily and commercially with European nations. During the 1880s European industrialized states rushed to carve out spheres of influence and colonies in Asia and Africa. Japan was also asserting its imperial ambitions. Paul Reinsch, a political economist whose writings on colonial administration influenced U.S. policy makers, dramatically described the situation: "All are straining every nerve to gain as large a share as possible of the unappropriated portions of the earth's surface. Wherever sharp methods of competition are necessary to accomplish this object, they will be employed. By rapid preemption the available area is becoming exceedingly limited, so that the eyes of the civilized world are already turned to the South American continent for further fields of exploitation" (Reinsch 1900, 66).

Of particular concern to the United States were the heavy investments by Europeans in Latin America at the turn of the century. Reinsch apprised his readers that through banking relations and the merchant marine British and German capitalists had achieved "the conquest of South American trade." According to Reinsch, "Geographically and politically the United States would seem to have a decided advantage in the competition for this trade, but there are no direct banking relations and very few direct sea communications between North and South" (Reinsch 1900, 35). Latin America was an attractive alternative to Asia precisely because its "many small republics, weak yet independent, provided an ideal setting for penetration with a minimum of formal responsibilities," that is, without the burdens of formal colonialism (Weibe 1967, 239).

Latin America was the only area in which United States business could expect to compete effectively with European capital. But China, despite its distance, was simply too huge and disorganized to relinquish to the Europeans. The islands in the Caribbean and the Pacific would become stepping stones for U.S. firms to penetrate the fabled China market and from which to compete more effectively in Latin America against European business.

The United States had expressed territorial ambitions in the Caribbean decades before embarking on war in 1898 (See Martínez-Fernández 1994). In 1848 President Polk offered to purchase Cuba from Spain for $100 million. In 1866 Denmark agreed to sell its Caribbean possessions to the United States for $7.5 million; however, the Senate refused to ratify the treaty (Nearing and Freeman 1925, 239, 210). In the midst of the U.S. Civil War, the secretary of state wrote to his minister in Spain that the United States "have constantly indulged in the belief that they might hope at some day to acquire those islands [Cuba and Puerto Rico]" (Fitzgibbon 1964, 12). According to U.S. diplomatic historian Robert Beisner, in 1891 the Harrison administration "seriously considered" acquiring Cuba, Puerto Rico, and the Danish West Indies, and requested Senate ratification of a treaty for Hawaii's annexation (Beisner 1968, 188). Senator Henry Cabot Lodge, one of the more influential and relentless expansionists of the period, wrote in an 1895 issue of the *Forum*, "England has studded the West Indies with strong places which are a standing menace to our Atlantic Seaboard. We should have among those islands at least one strong naval station, and when the Nicaragua canal is built, the island of Cuba . . . will become to us a necessity" (Quoted in Van Alstyne 1960, 207).

For three decades expansionists were consumed by two policy objectives: to establish naval bases in the Caribbean and Pacific and to build a transisthmian canal (Campbell 1976, 67). The naval bases and coaling stations were necessary to protect maritime commerce and defend the entrances to the proposed canal.

President Garfield's secretary of state, James G. Blaine, negotiated treaties with strategic Caribbean islands that could be used as bases to protect the proposed Panama Canal (Challener 1973; LaFeber 1962). In 1889 he pressured the Senate to adopt reciprocity provisions to gave certain Cuban and Puerto Rican products preferential tariff treatment in the US (Taussig 1931, 278–279). Blaine wrote to Garfield that "Cuba, because of its relation to the future canal and the Gulf trade, must never be permitted to pass out of the American system" (Pratt 1939, 23). He was a proponent of Caribbean and Pacific naval bases and confided in the President in 1889, "I think there are only three places that are of value enough to be taken, that are not continental. One is Hawaii, the others are Cuba and Porto Rico. Cuba and Porto Rico are not imminent and will not be for a generation" (quoted in Grenville and Young 1966, 85). Exclusive U.S. control of the interoceanic canal was the key to strategic and commercial domination of the hemisphere (Seager 1953, 506). Naval bases and coaling and cable stations were needed in defensible Caribbean islands that had good harbors for the empire's navy.

Of Economic Depression and Expansionist Euphoria

The Progressive Era (1890s to 1916) marked the emergence of the United States as a global power. Of all the events of this heady period, the foremost must have been McKinley's decision to embark on war with Spain. This "splendid little war" announced the formal arrival of the United States as the latest empire. By 1898 the expansionist sectors of the state and capital felt confident the country was ready to acquire by war what it had failed to attain by diplomacy—territorial possessions that could serve as gateways to Asia and Latin America. Scholars of the Progressive Era seem to agree that the decision to embark on war was driven by domestic economic factors and international competition. Among the most important were growing excess capacity of the nation's industries and declining domestic consumption, combined with anxiety over possible European encroachment in the Caribbean and fear of being locked out of China.

At the turn of the century the United States faced a situation that seemed to mandate that it adopt a more aggressive posture in international relations. During the 1890s the economy was undergoing a disruptive transition characterized by the growing importance of manufacturing capital and the emergence of monopolistic firms. Important sectors of the business community and key policymakers were certain that without foreign markets industrial growth was threatened. However, U.S. aspirations for global economic expansion were tempered by the reality that powerful European rivals stood ready to protect their markets from U.S. incursions.

The global depression of the 1890s propelled a new round of European imperialism. As is the case with all complex economic events, no one factor can explain the economic collapse of 1893. However, economic historian Eric Hobsbawm demonstrates that the depression was precipitated by a persistent deterioration in the profitability of investments (Hobsbawm 1989, 36). Europeans who had invested heavily in the highly speculative and booming U.S. economy began to withdraw their investments when the financial crisis hit in their home economies. The depression revealed major imbalances in the U.S. economy— growing surplus manufacturing capacity, saturation of domestic markets, declining corporate profitability. An adverse shift in the U.S. balance of payments in the early 1890s further aggravated the investment problem (Brands 1992, 8). Nervous foreign capitalists liquidated their U.S. investments and converted their dollar holdings into gold, which they repatriated. Between 1890 and 1894 European investors sold off about $300 million of their holdings in U.S. companies, The net outflow of gold from the United States outran domestic gold production (White 1982, 5). The financial retrenchment and ensuing credit panic precipitated an acute shock for the U.S. economy.

European capital had financed the expansion of U.S. heavy industries, primarily railroads, but also steel, iron, and coal. Once Europeans began to dispose of their equity in these firms, many companies were forced to curtail their production, causing widespread unemployment. The economic downturn, combined with the depletion of the gold reserves, triggered a stampede by U.S. depositors to withdraw their holdings from financial institutions, further intensifying the drain on U.S. reserves (Brands 1992, 8). In the ensuing panic the stock market plummeted, resulting in the greatest number of bank failures and suspensions in U.S. history to that date (see Hoffman 1970, 57; White 1982). As banks and speculators hoarded their capital during this period of financial instability, credit was severely reduced, leading to a contraction in production and further unemployment.

The crisis came in the wake of an unprecedented period of growth and economic restructuring. After the end of the Civil War the country's productive capacity increased dramatically. During the 1880s exports tripled, aided in large measure by tremendous European demand for wheat and cotton (Callcott 1942, 71; Campbell 1976, 141). Industrial output was also increasing at a staggering rate, resulting in a substantial rise in exports of manufactured goods. In 1890 the United States had only 3.9 percent of worldwide trade in manufactured goods, but by 1898 it controlled 9.8 percent, and by 1913 11 percent (Pletcher 1984, 177). Machinery exports, in particular, increased rapidly, from 15 percent of the value of manufactured exports in 1890 to 23.3 percent in 1899 (Becker 1973, 478).

During the Progressive Era, the economy was moving from a competitive to a corporate stage of capitalist development. The depression was an added stimulus to a reorganization of the corporations that controlled productive and financial resources (Becker 1982, 35–42, Vatter 1975, 238–263). Firms experimented with new organizational forms, trade associations, pools, and holding companies in an effort to counteract the business cycle downturn (Becker 1973, 469). Between 1898 and 1904 this process of corporate reconstructing grew into a merger mania (Sklar 1988, 4–5). The organization of giant holding companies and mergers was an attempt to restore the erosion in corporate profitability caused by overproduction and accumulated surpluses. The large corporations that dominated the economy became important instruments for "capital investment imperialism" (Sklar 1988, 81–85).

Export-oriented agricultural firms intensified their efforts to compel the U.S. government to develop overseas markets during this period of economic difficulties (Williams 1969, 36). Some of these corporations were monopolies that invested heavily in the colonial possessions. Most prominent among these giants was the American Tobacco Company, which started manufacturing cigarettes in Puerto Rico in 1899. In 1902 the American Cigar Company, another monopoly firm, incorporated the Porto Rican-American Tobacco Company as a tobacco-growing subsidiary (Wilkins 1970, 156). Investment banking houses and trust companies were formed in an attempt to overcome the problem of saturated domestic markets and to sop up surplus capital (Sklar 1988, 72). These great financial houses became the principal financial instruments for investment and were firm advocates for opening foreign markets (Weibe 1967, 231). Firms such as Morton Trust Company, House of Morgan, and Kuhn and Loeb were established in the wake of the corporate restructuring. Organized specially to find profitable investment outlets for this capital, these firms had direct and ready access to the investable stocks of accumulated capital (Parrini 1993, 44). These financial firms, however, could not rely on domestic markets to consume the "enormous congestion of capital in excess of legitimate demand" (Conant 1898, 337).

The Panacea:
Promoting Expansion to Avert Domestic Crisis

Policymakers and businesspeople alike believed that in the absence of foreign markets for surplus production not only would the United States be mired in stagnation, but the social fabric of the republic would be jeopardized. They feared that opportunities for domestic investments were disappearing and that employment had leveled off. The domestic market, which had been thought to be inexhaustible and infinitely elastic, was incapable of consuming the escalating output from the nation's industries. The following observation about the state of the U.S. economy was representative of much of the thinking at the time: "The Western land will not absorb farm hands at the same rate as in the past; while in the East industry has developed so fast that the home market is already fully stocked with most kinds of manufactured goods, profits have fallen, and there is little inducement for a large increase of factories"(Lowell 1899, 148).

The belief that external markets would absorb this surplus became an article of faith in late 1897. The State Department cautioned, "Every year we shall be confronted with an increasing surplus of manufactured goods for sale in foreign markets if American operatives and artisans are to be kept employed the year round"(quoted in Brands 1992, 9). W. W. Judson reported that the United States expected "the policy of expansion in the West Indies and elsewhere to yield a great increase of trade and new opportunities for the profitable use of American capital . . . [and to] increase our national prosperity and our influence for the world's good in the council of nations" (Judson 1902, 383). Fear that profit opportunities were rapidly disappearing reinforced long-standing desires to acquire overseas territories and external markets (Weibe 1967, 230). In 1895 leading U.S. industrialists established the National Association of Manufacturers (NAM), which became a leading force for commercial expansion. NAM's platform stated that "to the largest extent our home markets should be retained and supplied by our own producers, and our foreign trade relations should be extended in every direction and manner not inconsistent therewith" (quoted in White 1982, 83). NAM president Theodore C. Search declared in 1897 that "many of our manufacturers have outgrown or are outgrowing their home markets and the expansion of our foreign trade is their only promise of relief" (quoted in Sklar 1959, 59).

Columbia University professor Franklin H. Giddings was an active proponent of commercial expansion who contributed to an emerging imperialist logic. His writings, particularly his 1898 article "Imperialism?" reaffirmed the structural imperative for foreign markets: "We cannot continue indefinitely to sacrifice foreign trade to domestic industry. . . . That American manufactures were already, in many instances, outgrowing the home demands, and like our agricultural products must have a foreign market was becoming daily more obvious before the recent hostilities began" (Giddings 1898, 82).

Charles Conant was the most influential theorist for U.S. imperialism of the period. His research on the relationship between surplus capital, corporate restructuring, and imperialism influenced foreign economic policy making (see Parrini 1993; Sklar 1988, 72–85). Conant observed that all the industrialized nations were encountering severe limitations to their continued expansion. He attributed this to a glut of capital and limited domestic investment opportunities. In his highly influential article, "The Economic Basis of Imperialism," Conant argued that an outlet for surplus capital was critical "if the entire fabric of the present economic order is not to be shaken by social revolution" (1898, 326).

Conant wrote during a period of profound social ferment in the United States. Large-scale violent labor unrest often broke out into pitched battles between armed strikers and the private security forces of the corporations, as well as the national guard and federal troops. Increasingly strident socialist agitation and a spreading populist movement that decried the concentration of capital and organization of monopolies threatened to alter the country's political dynamics. Socialism, with its ringing critique of monopoly capital and the robber barons, was gaining adherents among growing contingents of workers, who were forming industrial unions (Zinn 1992, 247–289).

Conant warned that "under the present social order it is becoming impossible to find at home in the great capitalist countries employment for all the capital

saved which is at once safe and remunerative" (1898, 330). This problem was pro-
pelling an "irresistible tendency toward expansion" that demanded new opportunities for U.S. business and outlets for U.S. capital (326). According to Conant,
"The United States cannot afford to adhere to a policy of isolation while other
nations are reaching out for the command of these new markets. . . . New markets and new opportunities for investment must be found if surplus capital is to
be profitably employed" (338).The United States had to either establish external
markets for the accumulated capital "or continue the needless duplication of existing means of production and communication, with the glut of unconsumed
products, the convulsions followed by trade stagnation, and the steadily declining
return upon investments" (339). The United States had to assert its "right to free
markets in all the old countries which are being opened to the surplus resources
of the capitalistic countries" (339).

Conant's work had a profound impact on the thinking of the empire builders,
and he was rewarded handsomely for his contributions. He was Elihu Root's adviser on the Philippines monetary issue, was appointed to the Commission in International Exchange, and was an agent for the House of Morgan, as well as a
board member of Morton Trust. Politicians, naturally, echoed the concerns of ex-
port-reliant sectors of capital. Senator Albert J. Beveridge played a prominent
role in elaborating an ideology of territorial acquisition that was laced with racial
superiority and a martial spirit. Perhaps Beveridge did more than any other public figure to popularize the idea that foreign markets and territorial expansion
were fundamental for national economic health.

> American factories are making more than the American people can use: American
> soil is producing more than they can consume. Fate has written our policy for us; the
> trade of the world must and shall be ours, and we will get it as our mother [England]
> has told us how. We will establish trading posts throughout the world as distributing
> points for American products. We will cover the ocean with our merchant marine.
> We will build a navy to the measure of our greatness. Great colonies governing them-
> selves, flying our flag and trading with us, will grow about our posts of trade. Our in-
> stitutions will follow our flag on the wings of commerce. . . . And American law,
> American order, American civilization, and the American flag will plant themselves
> on shores hitherto bloody and benighted. (Quoted in Bowers 1932, 69)

Several years after the war of 1898, a Commerce Department official reaffirmed the importance of the war of 1898 to U.S. capital:

> The Spanish-American War was but an incident of a general movement of expan-
> sion which had its roots in the changed environment of an industrial capacity far be-
> yond our domestic powers of consumption. It was seen to be necessary for us not
> only to find foreign purchasers for our goods, but to provide the means of making
> access to foreign markets easy, economical and safe. (Quoted in Zinn 1992, 299)

The Clarion Call for Commercial Competition and Expansion

By the mid-1890s key political and corporate leaders felt the nation was developing the economic and military capacity to finally assert the inviolability of the Monroe Doctrine. Secretary of state Richard Olney reasserted the primacy of U.S. interests in Latin America and reinforced the international image of the nation as an emerging empire about to break with its isolationist past. In 1895 Olney issued his now famous declaration to British Lord Thomas Bayard:

> Today the United States is practically sovereign on this continent, and its fiat is law upon the subjects to which it confines its interposition. Why? . . . It is because, in addition to all other grounds, its infinite resources combined with its isolated position render it master of the situation and practically invulnerable as against any or all other powers. (Text in Link and Leary 1970)

Although England dismissed this churlish flexing of the imperial muscle, Olney's brash statement was a warning to Europeans that the United States was staking its claim in the Western Hemisphere. Europeans worried that the United States, with its rapidly expanding industrial plant, vast quantities of natural resources, and an abundant labor supply, would in the very near future pose a competitive threat (see Guerra y Sánchez 1961; Viallate 1923). Prominent British journalist William T. Stead prophesied the decline of England and warned his readers that the disintegration of the British empire and its "definite displacement from the position of commercial and financial primacy is a matter of time, and probably a very short time," unless England merged with the "English speaking United States" (Stead 1902, 6). The *Statist* of London alerted European industrialists: "The capacity of the United States to compete in foreign markets with the most advanced nations of Europe has been made superabundantly manifest" (quoted in Viallate 1923, 32).

All these developments—the depression of 1893, domestic economic restructuring, labor unrest, European expansionism, and the staggering growth of industrial output—constituted the ideal juncture for imperialist sectors of the state and capital to mount a campaign of military expansion and territorial acquisition. During the decade of the 1890s a militaristic cadre of political and corporate leaders who subscribed to the tenets of social Darwinism and its notions of racial superiority propelled the national debate on expansion and imperialism. They were instrumental in elaborating an aggressive policy of empire building and fostered the unprecedented peacetime militarization of the economy. This group of influential expansionists molded public opinion in favor of overseas expansion. Senators Henry Cabot Lodge and John T. Morgan and secretary of state John Hay were among the most influential advocates for territorial expansion. Beveridge urged the nation toward conquest with his ultranationalist ranting. Theodore Roosevelt, the assistant secretary of the navy during the first McKinley administration and vice president during McKinley's second term, used his considerable influence to prepare the United States for war, while he ridiculed the anti-imperialist forces.

The social Darwinism of the period preached the idea of Anglo-Saxon racial superiority. Key political leaders adhered to this ideology and its notion of an inevitable destiny of conquest and rule. These ideas were prominent in the thinking of Beveridge, Lodge, Hay, and Roosevelt (see Hofstadter 1992). Elihu Root, who was to emerge as the major architect of U.S. colonial policy, also subscribed to the tenet of the inherent superiority of the Anglo-Saxon. As I will discuss in the next chapter, Root's conviction that Puerto Rico's subject populations were incapable of self-rule was grounded in these notions of Anglo-Saxon racial superiority.[1]

The thinking of these politicians on the political and economic imperatives for expansion were influenced by the writings of naval officer Alfred T. Mahan and Brooks Adams. The political economist Charles Conant, Professor Franklin H. Giddings of Columbia, and professor of government Paul S. Reinsch of Wisconsin University were seminal thinkers who influenced the policy process. Major periodicals, including the *New York Tribune*, published by Whitelaw Reid, the *North American Review*, edited by Mayo Hazeltine, and the *Review of Reviews*, edited by Albert Shaw, were influential, widely read forums for the pronouncements of the expansionist voices of the state and capital.

These influential figures were also the proponents of a doctrine of sea power that articulated the interrelationship between domestic production, international trade, naval prowess, territorial possessions, and spheres of influence. This doctrine dominated the strategic thinking of the time, and the expansionists were relentless in seeking its realization. Throughout the 1890s they pursued a coherent and forceful campaign to break the country from its traditional isolation. Fully two years before the United States went to war with Spain, Roosevelt, Lodge, and their coterie had formulated an "imperialist philosophy for the United States, had mapped out a program and had marshaled their forces" (Beale 1962, 63). Historian Julius Pratt maintains that by 1898 Lodge and Roosevelt had developed these ideas into a "large policy" that aimed at no less than making the United States the indisputably dominant power in the Western Hemisphere, "having a great navy, owning and controlling the isthmian canal, and with naval bases in the Caribbean and Pacific" (Pratt 1932, 23).

The expansionists pressed the United States to acquire insular territories. On January 29, 1893, the *New York Tribune* editorialized, "It must be recognized at least, that we are close upon the time when the traditional hostility of the United States toward an extension of authority, if not also of territory, among the islands near our coasts must to some extent give way to the necessities of our increasing commerce" (quoted in Pratt 1932, 228). In the same year Senator Beveridge warned the Commercial Travelers Association that the European powers "seize islands and archipelagos, a new territory everywhere to make monopolies for their markets and fortresses for their flags, while the United States remains without a single naval rendezvous in any sea" (quoted in Braeman 1971, 23). Cabot Lodge repeated these concerns when he warned in 1895 that "it had become apparent that unless we were prepared to see South America share sooner or later the fate of Africa it was necessary for us to intervene" (quoted in Widenor 1980, 107). Theodore Roosevelt also worried that the European powers would establish a naval presence in the region; he wanted "the ultimate removal of all European powers from the colonies they hold in the Western hemisphere" (quoted in Collin 1990, 56). These men heavily influenced the foreign policy of their party. In 1896 the Republican Party adopted an explicit imperialist policy that called for the annexation of Hawaii, a government-built and owned canal through Nicaragua, the purchase of the Danish West Indies, and the removal of European powers from the Western Hemisphere (Pratt 1932, 230–231).

Puerto Rico did not figure in the national debate on the global commercial expansion. When the United States went to war with Spain, neither the Caribbean nor Latin America were prominent investment areas. In 1897 U.S. direct investments in the Caribbean were less than in Canada or Mexico, and far less than in Europe (Wilkins 1970, 153). U.S. investments in the Caribbean, including Central America, totaled only $70.2 million, and approximately $50 million of this amount was concentrated in the Cuban sugar estates (Wilkins 1970, 153). Puerto Rico was simply not perceived by the business community or the U.S. state as a crucial investment site that could contribute, in itself, to resolving the crisis of overproduction and overaccumulation. Although Cuba was more important economically, only specific sectors of the United States stood to gain significantly from bringing Cuba into the orbit of U.S. trade. On the other hand, Cuba and Puerto Rico, along with Hawaii and the Philippines, could materially reduce U.S. reliance on imported European beet sugar, and serve as minor, although not insignificant, markets for industrial goods. But overall, the dominant expansionist sectors of U.S. capital did not attach much economic significance to the islands.

Naval Power and Commercial Expansion

Alfred T. Mahan was one of the most influential thinker on the relationship between global navy strategies and commercial expansion. A distinguished lecturer at the Naval War College, Mahan had been in regular correspondence with Theodore Roosevelt since 1890 and was instrumental in shaping his thinking on the necessity of a modern navy to achieve regional hegemony. A British naval officer familiar with Mahan observed that his purpose "was to awaken public opinion in the United States to the importance of a strong navy, and to bid them to look 'outwards,' taking their rightful place among the nations" (Clarke 1898, 293).

Mahan explained the need to plan commercial competition in the context of potential military or naval conflict with the European powers. Throughout the decade Mahan was a persuasive advocate for naval buildup as a precondition for the United States to embark on territorial conquest. He pointed out that European "aspiration for commercial extension, for colonies and for influence in distant regions . . . have brought them into collisions with ourselves" (quoted in Livezey 1980). But the United States was "woefully unready, not only in fact but in purpose, to assert in the Caribbean and Central America a weight of influence proportionate to the extent of her interests." Mahan warned that "the piercing of the Isthmus is nothing but a disaster of the United States, in the present state of her military and naval preparation" (quoted in Livezey 1980, 104).

Similar caution had been echoed a decade earlier by Representative Harris of Massachusetts, who warned in 1880, "For a nation which proposes to dominate a hemisphere, and to dictate to the great naval powers of Europe non-interference in the affairs of the American republics, the United States is singularly neglectful of the means by which she may make her manifesto effectual" (quoted in Seager 1953, 505). And well before Mahan surfaced as the acknowledged advocate for naval expansion, secretary of the navy William Chandler had effectively lobbied Congress for an oceangoing navy and emphasized the need to acquire coaling stations. "The question of providing coaling stations abroad . . . becomes year by year more important and pressing." He warned that if the new navy were to rely on sailing power, "its offensive power will be reduced to the lowest unit" (quoted in Seager 1953, 508). In 1883 Chandler asked Congress to obtain fifteen coaling depots stretching from the Caribbean to Liberia, Madagascar, and Korea. Technological advances in steam propulsion convinced a navy board in 1884 to recommend abandoning the use of auxiliary sails on warships. This decision, according to the board, "forces the single conclusion that coaling stations must be provided"(quoted in Seager 1953, 508). Between 1885 and 1887 Chandler and his supporters convinced Congress to authorize the construction of four steel naval ships (Campbell 1976, 156).

Stepping Stones in the Caribbean and the Pacific

Alfred Mahan was an astute observer of the changing political economy. His major contribution to the emerging imperialist philosophy was to convincingly demonstrate the use of sea power to establish and protect lines of communication. Colonial possessions were not necessarily held for economic exploitation but would better serve as strategic stepping stones from which to penetrate foreign markets. Territories on which to build naval bases and coaling stations were essential not only to protect maritime commerce, but to gain access to the enormous markets and raw materials of Latin America and Asia. According to Mahan, "control of the seas, especially long and great lines drawn by national interest, is the chief among the material elements in the power and prosperity of nations" (quoted in Beard 1955, 24). He wrote that "it is from the potential effect upon these lines of communication that all positions in the Gulf or the Caribbean derive their military value or want of value" (Mahan 1897, 638).

Mahan felt that the insular colonies would "provide resting places" for warships "where they can coal and repair." Acquisition of these bases, according to Mahan, "would be one of the first duties of a government proposing to itself the development of the power of the nation at sea" (Mahan 1890, 83). Ideally, this type of colony "should be able to hold out, independent of the fleet, for a length of time dependent upon its importance, both to the general defense system and in its intrinsic value" (quoted in LaFeber 1962, 681). "From this necessarily follows the principle that, as subsidiary to such control, it is imperative to take possession, when it can righteously be done, of such maritime positions as contribute to secure command" (quoted in Beard 1955, 24). Although opposed to a large-scale policy of colonial acquisitions "with large populations whose loyalties might prove dangerous to a naval base," Mahan felt such possessions were at times necessary (quoted in Gannon 1978, 17).

However, he warned against too many bases in the Caribbean, and sought to influence the annexationists to confine their aspirations to those territories that were in the immediate neighborhood of the isthmus. Bases in Puerto Rico, Cuba, and St. Thomas were "deemed sufficient" by Mahan. He testified in Congress that "every naval station while affording facilities for naval operations, on the other hand imposes upon the fleet a burden of support and communication. The just balance between too few and too many should therefore be carefully struck"(quoted in Livezey 1980, 155). A year before the United States went to war with Spain, Mahan wrote an influential article that demonstrated that control of Cuba was indispensable to control of the Caribbean. Mahan observed, "Regarded, therefore, as a base of naval operations and as a source of supplies to a fleet, Cuba presents a condition wholly unique among the islands of the Caribbean and of the Gulf of Mexico." He argued that "Cuba has a position that can have no military rival among the islands of the world except Ireland" (Mahan 1897, 685, 690). For Mahan, Cuba, more than any other island, was ideal not only because of its strategic location, but because it was "susceptible, under proper development, of great resources—of self-sufficingness" (684).

Since the 1880s the proposed isthmian canal and the need for forward bases to protect it had figured prominently in the strategic thinking of the naval establishment. Naval strategists never planned to defend the canal only with fortifications "at its termini." The navy expected to control the Caribbean and provide security for the canal with naval positions on the perimeter. "The bases controlling the principal passages into an essentially landlocked sea, would enable the United States Navy to put the cork in the Caribbean bottle." One cork was Puerto Rico, which gained strategic value because it straddled the Anegada and Mona passages (Challener 1973, 88). Early in the 1880s the Naval College had devised strategic doctrines for the isthmian canal, and it emphasized the necessity of U.S. control of approach routes and outlying areas to protect the canal (Healy 1988, 79). Writing in 1902, well before the canal was built, W. W. Judson echoed Mahan: "No matter how strongly the isthmian canal may be fortified it would in war serve us no purpose—indeed, through war, we might lose it entirely—if our fleet could not control its approaches" (Judson 1902, 391). In Puerto Rico and Cuba the United States could build the bases the Naval War College thought were indispensable for protecting the canal.

By emphasizing the strategic, rather than the wealth-creating, role of colonial possessions, Mahan discarded the European notions of colonialism and advocated an "open door commercial empire secured by naval bases and a battleship fleet"(quoted in LaFeber 1962, 685). The possessions of such an empire had a limited economic role in generating national wealth, but were central elements of a global strategy of imperialism. U.S. officials propagated a view of almost "incidental" acquisition through war and conquest of foreign lands as corollary outcomes of commercial expansion. Frederic Emory, the chief of the State Department's Bureau of Commerce, stated as much in 1900. Territorial expansion, he wrote, had come "as an incident of the commercial expansion. The recent acquisitions are but outposts of our future trade, and their chief importance consists not in their resources and capabilities, but in their unquestionable value as gateways for the development of commercial intercourse" (quoted in McCormick 1963, 155). In his influential work, *World Politics: At the End of the Nineteenth Century*, Reinsch summarized the relationship between sea communications and imperialism:

> In this connection the growing importance of sea communications, protected trade routes and naval stations, claims our attention. Modern imperialism is more vitally interested in commercial expansion than in territorial acquisition; the great nations are becoming more and more dependent on transoceanic markets. To obtain these and to secure their future accessibility and development the trade routes leading to them must be protected; and to this end navies as well as coaling stations and trade entrepots, are indispensable. (Reinsch 1900, 31)

Although the possibility of naval confrontation with European powers in the Caribbean was genuine, only Great Britain was perceived as having the naval and military capability to thwart U.S. expansionist drives in the Caribbean. Spain, the only other European nation with a naval presence of note, was a minor military annoyance at best. Nevertheless, Spain, economically exhausted, diplomatically isolated, and militarily weak, was still the most immediate impediment to U.S. expansion. Roosevelt was convinced that Spain was easy prey and in 1896 informed Lodge that he did not "think a war with Spain would be serious enough to cause much strain on the country, or much interruption in the revival of prosperity; but I certainly wish the matter would be settled this winter" (quoted in Collin 1990, 56).

Immediately before the outbreak of war the British journal *Outlook* stressed the "unanimous sentiment" in England as to the "strength and justice of the North American position," and noted that "never in the history of the two countries had there been such an instance of public support for U.S. policy" (quoted in Guerra y Sánchez 1961, 361). Given its proximity to the region, U.S. resolve to locate markets for its surpluses, and British acquiescence in U.S. territorial ambitions, military expansion into the Caribbean region was a realistic and attainable goal. To the expansionists' glee Great Britain did not oppose the territorial aspirations of United States. U.S. expansion into the Caribbean would serve as a counterweight to Germany's ambitions in the region, and for this reason Great Britain did not oppose U.S. diplomatic and military efforts to establish hegemony in the region (Gould 1982, 82).

McKinley finally decided to move against Spain, in part from fear that the financially strapped Spanish would transfer sovereignty over the Pacific and Caribbean islands to Germany. In 1896 noted journalist Mayo Hazeltine warned in the influential *North American Review* of the need for alacrity in moving against a feeble Spain that was unlikely to retain its possessions. He argued that if the United States failed to act, "not only would Cuba be lost, but Spain has other possessions of which, were she beaten at sea, she might be deprived—Puerto Rico, the Canary Islands, the Philippine Archipelago and the Balearic Islands" (quoted in Latané 1907, 78).

Spain had proven incapable of suppressing insurrection in Cuba and was compelled to reluctantly grant Autonomic Charters to Puerto Rico and Cuba. It was a frail adversary that the U.S. military establishment was convinced could be readily defeated. Given the groundswell of public support for war with Spain after the sinking of the U.S.S. *Maine*, continued procrastination and indecision by McKinley could have unraveled his administration. On April 11, 1898, McKinley sent a special message to Congress requesting its authorization for "the forcible intervention of the United States as a neutral to stop the war" between the Cuban rebels and the Spanish authorities (Text of statement appears in Link and Leary 1970).

Puerto Rico's Place in the War of 1898

U. S. thinking on Puerto Rico's function in the calculus of imperial expansion evolved gradually. Except for some high-level naval planners, the foreign policy making apparatus knew little of Puerto Rico's strategic significance and potential economic value in the years immediately preceding the outbreak of hostilities with Spain. Puerto Rico was but one small piece of a complex puzzle of global expansion and hemispheric domination, albeit a piece that key empire builders increasingly felt was essential to complete the puzzle. Between 1896 and 1900 Puerto Rico's perceived value to U.S. objectives increased dramatically. Prior to embarking on war, U.S. attention centered almost exclusively on extracting Cuba from Spain. Although war planners did not develop a plan to annex Puerto Rico before the war, it is certain that "the small but influential group of public men who had absorbed the doctrines of Captain Mahan had not lost sight" of Puerto

Rico (Trask 1981, 339, 341). Puerto Rico and Cuba were both potential strategic assets of great importance that could be wrested from Spain. Eventually more specific roles in a global strategy of commercial penetration would be developed, but in 1898, expelling Spain from the hemisphere and imposing some type of protectorate over its colonies was the objective of the U.S. military and foreign policy establishment.

The Naval War Board reported in 1898 that as a strategic arena the Caribbean possessed only a few positions of "commanding commercial or naval import." Control of the Windward Passage, however, was of absolute necessity to control the Caribbean and protect the canal (Challener 1973, 87). Cuba was unquestionably the military target of crucial import, since it possessed well-protected harbors in Santiago and Guantánamo from which battleships could readily control the passage. In 1895, as the Cuban war for independence raged, the Naval War College prepared contingency plans for liberating the country from Spain. The naval officers argued that "the strategic location of Cuba to the Gulf of Mexico is so close and intimate that the value of that island to the United States in a military and naval way is invaluable" (quoted in Trask 1981, 74). Alfred Mahan reiterated this in an article he wrote two years later: "Regarded, therefore, as a base of naval operations, as a source of supplies to a fleet, Cuba presents a condition wholly unique among the islands of the Caribbean and of the Gulf of Mexico" (Mahan 1897, 685). The expulsion of Spain from the continent and the establishment of a heavily fortified naval base in Cuba were the central military objectives. Nonetheless, naval planners considered Puerto Rico of genuine strategic value as well, because it stood astride the Mona and Anegada passages—two of the three "navigable breaks in the northern barrier enclosing the Caribbean Sea" (Judson 1902, 390; Livezey 1980, 149).

Before embarking on war, the U.S. Naval War Board had decided that Cuba, St. Thomas, and Samaná Bay in the Dominican Republic were all superior to Puerto Rico as locations for military bases (Challener 1973, 100). In the event of war, however, Spain had to be deprived of the use of Puerto Rico. Puerto Rico's immediate strategic importance was that it would be used as base of operations from which Spain could erode a blockade of Cuba or frustrate a U.S. invasion. Alfred Mahan maintained that Puerto Rico "would be invaluable to the mother country [Spain] as an intermediate naval station and as a base of supplies and reinforcements for both her fleet and army" (quoted in Trask 1981, 339).

On December 17, 1896, the Naval War Board identified San Juan, Puerto Rico, as the only fortified port that would likely be used as a supply base by Spain in the event of a blockade of Cuba. The navy planned to cut submarine cables installed in Ponce and San Juan that afforded "telegraphic communications with Europe and with Cuba," in order to isolate Puerto Rico, from "which country all necessaries for the subjection of Cuba must be drawn" (quoted in Grenville 1968, 39). The Navy Department wanted to blockade the deepwater ports of Puerto Rico, and stressed that "the strangulation process outlined can be quickened in its operation greatly by the bombardment of San Juan, Porto Rico" (quoted in Grenville 1968, 39). In June 1897 the Navy revised its war plans and called for the invasion and capture of Puerto Rico, because it "offered certain advantages for the rendezvous of Spanish ships of war coming from Europe, for the purpose of breaking and annoying our blockade of Cuba and reinforcing their navy there. . . . As soon as circumstances will permit, a detachment should be made from the force operating in the neighborhood of Cuba, for the purpose of reducing the island of Porto Rico" (quoted in Grenville 1968, 44).

As war appeared imminent the Naval War Board continued to revise its plans. On March 8, 1898, it planned for a large expeditionary force to invade Puerto Rico once Spanish naval forces were defeated (Trask 1981, 89). On April 4, 1898, a joint navy-army board reiterated the earlier strategy (mapped out in June, 1897) of attack against Puerto Rico to deprive Spain of its use as a base of operations (Trask 1981, 339). Surprisingly, the Naval War Board appeared to have scant knowledge of the geographical attributes that rendered Puerto Rico a potentially significant military asset. The board reported in the fall of 1898 that it "had just" heard of a promising site for a coaling station on Culebra, which was part of the territory of Puerto Rico (Challener 1973, 100).

Puerto Rico Invaded

Within the military high command General Nelson Miles was a lonely advocate for launching an initial attack against Puerto Rico prior to invading Cuba. Miles, who commanded the invasion force that landed in Guánica on July 25, 1898, wrote, "I was from the first in favor of taking Porto Rico, in order that the Spanish forces could not use it as a base against us" (quoted in Trask 1981, 340). Miles wrote in his memoirs that "Porto Rico and the eastern half of the island of Cuba were the objective points . . . for the active operations" of the army (Miles 1911, 274). Influential public figures endorsed Miles's invasion plans. Writing from Spain, U.S. industrialist Andrew Carnegie warned Miles that the Spanish preferred an attack on Havana because it was well fortified; he "advised the taking of Porto Rico first, for its effect on Europe" (Miles 1911, 274). Senator Lodge also supported an initial attack on the island before invading Cuba, and wrote to Roosevelt, "We ought to take Porto Rico as we have taken the Philippines and then close in on Cuba. Let us get the outlying things first" (quoted in Widenor 1980, 111). Secretary of the Navy John D. Long rejected Miles's proposal. Long was convinced that the island was too distant to hold as a base of operations against Spain; he concluded that "the conquest of Porto Rico promised no results commensurate with the sacrifices such action would entail (quoted in Trask 1981, 339–340).

Unperturbed by his failure to convince Long, General Miles then attempted to persuade President McKinley to postpone the Cuba expedition in favor of an attack on Puerto Rico. Miles argued that the army lacked the ammunition and fresh water supplies necessary for the more ambitious amphibious operations against Cuba (Gould 1982, 74). But McKinley rejected Miles's request as well. An unprovoked attack on Puerto Rico would have been difficult to justify to the international community and would have provoked bitter domestic political discord. The insurrection in Cuba, and not Spanish possession of Puerto Rico, was the long-standing irritant that furnished the pretext for waging war against Spain. Congress extolled its noble goals for intervening in the Spanish-Cuban War, in order that the "people of the island of Cuba . . . be free and independent," and to compel Spain to "withdraw its land and naval forces from Cuba and Cuban waters" (quoted in Link and Leary 1970, 25).

Neither McKinley nor Congress had uttered any thoughts of acquiring Puerto Rico or of installing a permanent military base on the island. McKinley's decision not to order an initial attack on Puerto Rico was consistent with his disclaimers of any territorial ambitions in the Caribbean. In his proclamation of war McKinley demanded Cuba's independence from Spain, but did not mention other Spanish possessions. Alfred Mahan himself was forced to concede that the "professed motives" of the war (gaining independence for Cuba) "prevented preeminence" being assigned to Puerto Rico in the military campaign strategy (quoted in Livezey 1980, 149). The expansionists were outspoken advocates for launching an invasion of Puerto Rico, and once it was invaded they were relentless in their zeal to convince McKinley to annex the island. Annexation of Puerto Rico would give the United States what the expansionists had long clamored for—a permanent naval station in the Caribbean. Shortly after the hostilities broke out, the U.S. consul in San Juan, Philip C. Hanna, recommended an early invasion, since he was certain that "10,000 American soldiers landed in Puerto Rico can hold the island forever." He reported to his superiors in Washington that he was "convinced that a large number of Puerto Ricans will arise and shake off the Spanish yoke as soon as they are assured of help" (quoted in Trask 1981, 340).

After the capitulation of Santiago de Cuba, General Miles finally was ordered to prepare for his attack on Puerto Rico. After the Santiago campaign, U.S. forces were exhausted and large contingents of soldiers were afflicted by malaria and dysentery. Given the depletion of the army forces, Miles was able to convince McKinley that the attack on Havana should be aborted in favor of an expedition against Puerto Rico (Gould 1982, 74). On June 4, McKinley sent a telegram to Miles, who was still stationed in Tampa, asking how much time he would require to organize an expedition to "take and retain Puerto Rico" (quoted in Carr 1984, 27).

An overlooked but significant figure who influenced Miles's military plans for Puerto Rico was the spy Captain Henry T. Whitney. General Miles reported, "I found Captain Whitney's knowledge of the country and the information gained by him in his perilous journey through Puerto Rico to be in every respect thoroughly accurate and of great value to me in the conduct of the campaign" (quoted in Chadwick 1911, 291). Puerto Ricans also played a role in the preinvasion plans of the United States. José Julio Henna and Roberto Todd met with Theodore Roosevelt and navy commanders on a number of occasions, providing them with maps of Puerto Rico and information on military installations and troop strength. Henna assured U.S. officials that 25,000 Puerto Ricans would rise against the Spaniards as soon as the U.S. military landed in Puerto Rico (Todd 1939, 10). Puerto Rican exiles who were collaborating with the Cuban Revolutionary Party in New York appealed to the United States to invade Puerto Rico; they also provided translators. The U.S. military set up three military units of Puerto Ricans that provided intelligence, assistance, and support to the invading forces. The Puerto Rican Commission was charged with serving as an intermediary between the invading army and Puerto Ricans; it was to explain the purpose and goal of the invasion and prevent the formation of anti-U.S. guerrilla forces. Members of the commission accompanied General Brookes's expeditionary force when it landed in Ponce on July 31, 1898 (Negroni 1992, 367–368).

Miles received his marching orders on July 18, and set sail for Puerto Rico on July 21. His invasion force of 3,300 troops was expected to fight 8,233 Spanish regulars and 9,107 volunteers (Miles 1911, 296). Miles originally planned to land in Fajardo, but thinking that the Spanish knew of his plans and were waiting for him, landed instead in Guánica on July 25. Shortly after his troops disembarked, reinforcements were dispatched to Puerto Rico (see Chadwick 1911, esp. 291–292). Troops poured into Puerto Rico at a steady rate. On July 21, 2,800 regular infantry, cavalry, and artillery arrived from Tampa. Between August 3 and 5, General Brooke disembarked in Arroyo with 5,000 additional troops. During the next three weeks additional contingents of soldiers landed, and brought the total invasion force to 17,000 men (Cosmas 1994, 234).

Most studies of the Puerto Rican campaign describe it as a brilliant military exercise that was well planned and aggressively executed (Chadwick 1911; Cosmas 1994; Lodge 1899; Miles 1911; Trask 1981). Puerto Ricans took a direct role in the hostilities by furnishing guides for attack columns and providing animals and transportation for the invaders (Cosmas 1994, 232). The Spanish authorities apparently were shocked that their colonial subjects enthusiastically welcomed the invading force (Rosario Natal 1989, 228). Within nineteen days after landing in Guanica, U.S. troops had overrun nearly the entire western half of Puerto Rico. Once in Puerto Rico, General Miles ordered the formation of the Puerto Rican Scouts. The scouts were a contingent of 70 mounted Puerto Ricans and saw action against the Spanish (Negroni 1992, 368).

Annexation: Serendipity or Calculation?

Spain sued for peace on July 18, the very day that Miles received his marching orders to invade Puerto Rico. On July 30, Secretary of State William R. Day presented the formal peace protocol, which the Spanish considered to be almost in "the form of an ultimatum" (Tompkins 1970, 163). Spain's military position was untenable, and it was unable to marshal European support to halt the U.S. dread-nought. It capitulated, and reluctantly signed an armistice protocol on August 12. The armistice protocol imposed conditions the Spanish had not expected. The United States would cease hostilities if Spain relinquished its sovereignty over Cuba and immediately evacuated its troops. In lieu of monetary indemnity for the losses it sustained in prosecuting the war, the United States demanded the cession of Puerto Rico "and other islands . . . in the West Indies." The United States also obtained an island in the Ladrones (Guam) "to be selected by the United States" and was "entitled to hold the city, bay and harbor of Manila pend-ing the conclusion of a treaty of peace which shall determine the control disposi-tion and government of the Philippines" (text of protocol in Morgan 1965, 231).

Some histories of the war of 1898 suggest that U.S. territorial acquisition was serendipitous (see Bemis 1955). After acquiring overseas possessions the United States found itself, according to some observers, "unexpectedly the owner of a large estate. The acquisition of the Spanish colonies was an accident, in the sense that the war was not waged with any deliberate intention of expansion" (Lowell 1899, 145). A similar theme appears in contemporary scholarship that argues that McKinley had not planned Puerto Rico's annexation before the United States went to war with Spain. Historian David Trask writes that "prewar planning did not contemplate major territorial acquisitions. Attacks on Spanish territories such as the Philippines, Puerto Rico and the Canaries were intended only to sup-port operations against the prime objective—always assumed to be Spain's forces in and around Cuba" (Trask 1981, 78). Trask maintains that the "demand for an-nexation stemmed from the specific situation in May 1898, rather than prior de-sign," even though the strategic advantage that would flow from acquisition of the island was well known (343).This view was expressed at the time by British diplomat James Bryce : "How stupendous a change in the world these six months have brought. Six months ago you no more thought of annexing the Philippine Isles and Porto Rico than you think of annexing Spitsbergen today" (quoted in Collin 1990, 510).

The Navy Department may not have contemplated Puerto Rico's annexation before the United States embarked on war with Spain. Yet momentum for Spain's expulsion from the Caribbean and Pacific and for the acquisition of its colonies by the United States had been steadily building. Anti-annexationist leader Tennat Lomas was convinced that the Republican administration was embarking on an imperialist war. He warned on June 20, 1898, that "the imperialists demand that we shall hold the Philippines as a conquered province, convert the island of Puerto Rico to our use . . . ,[and] permanently occupy Cuba" (quoted in Latané 1907, 112). According to historian Julius Pratt there was no doubt that after the defeat of the Spanish in Manila, U.S. business was "building high hopes upon the supposed opportunities for trade and exploitation in a string of dependencies stretching from the Philippines to Puerto Rico. . . long before the conclusion of peace with Spain" (Pratt 1939, 278).

Once McKinley issued the proclamation of war on April 12, 1898, Puerto Rico's invasion was certain, and annexation inevitable. For fifty years the United States had sought a coaling station in the Caribbean. Even with an independent Cuba, the United States had no guarantee that it would acquire its cherished naval base in the Caribbean. Annexation of Puerto Rico would provide the United States with at least one permanent naval base in a strategic location. Indeed, according to Paul Reinsch, "The more complete control of the Isthmian Canal route has been the prime motive for the acquisition of Porto Rico" (Reinsch 1911, 76).

For the expansionists the possibility of obtaining a permanent U.S. naval installation in the Caribbean was just too good to ignore. Lodge and Roosevelt were the two most relentless and irrepressible exponents for annexing all of Spain's colonial possessions. The moment war was declared, the pugnacious Theodore Roosevelt could no longer contain his militaristic fervor. He resigned as assistant secretary of the navy to accept a lieutenant colonel's commission with Colonel Leonard Wood's volunteer regiment of Rough Riders (Collin 1990, 508). From his camp near San Antonio, Texas, Roosevelt wrote Lodge, "I earnestly hope that no truce will be granted and that peace will only be made on consideration of Cuba being independent, Porto Rico ours, and the Philippines taken away from Spain" (quoted in Beard 1955, 25). On May 24, 1898, Lodge encouraged Roosevelt: "Porto Rico is not forgotten and we mean to have it. Unless I am utterly and profoundly mistaken, the Administration is now fully committed to the large policy we both desire" (quoted in Livezey 1980, 148).

Confident of the impending victory, McKinley seemed determined to acquire Puerto Rico. On June 3, almost six weeks before Miles invaded Puerto Rico, McKinley secretly informed John Hay, the U.S. ambassador to Great Britain, that the United States would require the cession of Puerto Rico at the war's end rather than monetary indemnity (Trask 1981, 343). On June 22, 1898, a month before Puerto Rico's invasion, Roosevelt, who was on the U.S. transport *Yucatan* at Port Tampa, urged Lodge, "you must prevent any talk of peace until we get Porto Rico and the Philippines as well as secure the independence of Cuba" (quoted in Alfonso 1970, 25). Lodge confided in Roosevelt that Day had told him, "There is of course no question about Puerto Rico, everyone is agreed on that" (quoted in Healy 1988, 48). By July 23, 1898, Lodge was convinced that Puerto Rico would be annexed; he informed Roosevelt, "I had a long talk with the President before leaving Washington and he was very clear and strong about both Cuba and Porto Rico" (quoted in Callcott 1942, 103).

By retaining Puerto Rico the United States obtained the permanent Caribbean base it had long coveted. The Senate Naval Affairs Committee requested before the protocol of August 12, that the Naval War Board determine "what coaling stations should be acquired by the United States outside their own territorial limits" (quoted in Livezey 1980, 148). The Board postulated that the Nicaraguan canal would draw European naval powers to the region and recommended the acquisition of fortified bases, including Culebra in Puerto Rico, that commanded the points of entrance to the future canal (Grenville and Young 1966, 295). Before peace was declared between the United States and Spain, Mahan revised his early assessments of Puerto Rico's somewhat muted strategic significance: "Porto Rico considered militarily is to Cuba, and to the future Isthmian canal, and to our Pacific coast, what Malta is, or may be to Egypt and the beyond." He argued, "It would be very difficult for a trans-Atlantic state to maintain operations in the Western Caribbean with a United States fleet based upon Porto Rico and the adjacent islands" (Mahan 1899, 29). The military significance of Culebra, located about twenty miles east of the main island of Puerto Rico, to the Caribbean was not lost on foreign correspondents. As the war raged, the *Times* of London reported on August 1, 1898,

> Puertorico . . . occupies a commanding position between the Mona and Anegada passages and possesses far greater resources than the little island of St. Thomas. Its harbours are small but capable of improvement, and a squadron based upon them commands at short range the main sea routes from Europe to any future transisthmian canal. The strategic importance of Puertorico is so great and the drawbacks to its annexation so small that its cession was certain to be demanded. (Quoted in Rodríguez Beruff n.d., 9)

On September 17, 1898, the *Times Leader* reported, "For strategical reasons the conquest and occupation of Puertorico were seen to be indispensable at an early period in the campaign and no doubts could arise as to the expediency of retaining possession of that fertile island" (quoted in Rodríguez Beruff n.d., 9). With the passage of time Puerto Rico's strategic significance became more apparent and indispensable. In 1901, as negotiations with Denmark for the purchase of the Danish West Indies were taking place, the Navy General Board decided that Culebra was the preferred site for a northeastern naval base. A heavily fortified base would be constructed on Culebra, and San Juan would serve as the supply and reserve collier base for ships docked in Culebra (Challener 1973, 102; Grenville and Young 1966, 301). Culebra eventually assumed great military importance because of its deepwater harbor. Culebra was also highly coveted by Germany, which had drawn up plans for its invasion and the occupation of Puerto Rico (Herwig and Trask 1979, 54–56). In 1904, two years before France sold its Panama Isthmus holdings to the United States, W. W. Judson wrote,

> Porto Rico . . . has upon the main island no harbors that are especially fit for naval stations, although there are several that might be used at a pinch. . . . Culebra . . . possesses an excellent harbor, better prepared for war purposes than any in Porto Rico. . . . A naval station in Porto Rico might conceivably have great advantage over one at St. Thomas. Porto Rico might be made self-sustaining during blockade, which St. Thomas could never be. (Judson 1902, 389–390)

In 1906 the Naval War Board reported that "when properly strengthened" the bases in Guantánamo and Culebra, plus the fortifications of the proposed Panama Canal, would satisfy the navy's base requirements in the Caribbean (Turk 1978, 193). Historian Lloyd Chester Jones concluded in his 1916 study of the Caribbean that Guantánamo and Culebra "give the United States an unequaled position for the control of" the Windward and Mona Passages and "bases of operation not to be matched by any other power in this region" (Jones 1916, 319, 321). The United States was determined to obtain exclusive possession of a strategically situated coaling station in the Caribbean; it invaded Puerto Rico and made its transfer of sovereignty a prior condition in its negotiation of a peace treaty with Spain (Gannon 1978, 25). The record suggests that the expansionists were well aware before the commencement of hostilities that Puerto Rico could well serve as a permanent naval base.

The Logic of Annexation

McKinley insisted that "the plain teachings of history" made necessary the independence of Cuba and the annexation of Puerto Rico. McKinley claimed that the war had cost $400 million, and as the victorious belligerent the United States had every right to extract reparations from Spain. But since Spain was virtually bankrupt McKinley instructed his peace commissioners to make peace on the basis of territorial concessions (Neale 1966, 107ff.). McKinley demanded the cession of Puerto Rico in lieu of financial indemnity because he was "desirous of exhibiting signal generosity" (quoted in Pratt 1939, 330; also see Rosario Natal 1989, 260–264). He instructed his negotiators to tell the Spanish that "it was not compatible with the assurance of permanent peace on or near our own territory that the Spanish flag should remain on this side of the sea" (quoted in Trask 1981, 441).

Whitelaw Reid, a member of the peace delegation and former ambassador to France, informed the Spanish that "the judgment of the American people is so fixed" for retaining Puerto Rico "that the administration could not make peace on any other terms if it wanted to" (quoted in Healy 1988, 47). The peace protocol provided for "the cession to the United States of Porto Rico and other islands under Spanish sovereignty in the West Indies," and for "the immediate evacuation by Spain of Cuba, Porto Rico, and other Spanish islands in the West Indies" (text of protocol in Link and Leary 1970, 26–27). These islands were Culebra, Vieques, and tiny "islands off the east coast of Puerto Rico" (Pratt 1951, 397).

On December 10, 1898, the United States and Spain signed the Treaty of Paris, which brought to an end the period of Spanish colonialism in the Western Hemisphere. Within months of the declaration of war in April 22, 1898, the United States had acquired direct control over islands it needed to realize its imperialistic ambitions in the hemisphere. Once the Senate ratified the Treaty of Paris, the United States had a "blanque check to treat the Caribbean as its exclusive sphere of influence," which meant, according to U.S. historian Richard Van Alstyne, "that

whatever independence (or self-determination) was enjoyed by the local republics situated on the islands and along the littoral of the Caribbean Sea was
henceforth mortgaged to the foreign policy of the United States" (Van Alstyne
1960, 166).

Spain transferred sovereignty of the subject populations of the Philippines,
Puerto Rico, and Guam—over eight million inhabitants—to the jurisdiction of
the United States. No representatives of these colonized people were invited to
participate in the treaty conference in Paris. Even the Cubans, who had fought
the Spanish and depleted their forces—making a U.S. military victory a virtual
certainty—were excluded. Although granted independence, Cuba was subject to
U.S. military occupation and its leaders were shocked to learn that their country's
sovereignty lay with the United States. Cuba remained under military rule until
1902, when its political leadership adopted a political system and constitution
that was virtually dictated by the United States.

Despite the national euphoria at the overwhelming victory, the McKinley administration faced considerable Senate opposition to the treaty and initially
lacked the necessary votes for ratification. The forces arrayed against annexation
of the former Spanish territories were well organized and well financed. They
were represented by the Anti-Imperialist League, which drew support from different business sectors, including tobacco and beet sugar, who feared competition from the territories. Labor leader Samuel Gompers was also opposed to annexation, in part because of the "menace of cheap Oriental labor" (Faulkner,
1951, 18). Moorfield Storey, a leading anti-imperialist, attempted to persuade
Secretary of State Long that there was no legal basis for granting independence
to Cuba and denying it to Puerto Rico (Trask 1981, 432). The anti-annexation-
ists orchestrated a national debate challenging the constitutional authority of
Congress to acquire colonial possessions (see Beisner 1968). Roosevelt and
Lodge were genuinely concerned that their imperialist ambitions, particularly
the annexation of Puerto Rico, would be scuttled by anti-annexationist senators
(Coletta 1957, 132).

Expansionist Senator O. H. Platt pontificated, "The history of territorial expansion is the history of our nation's progress and glory. It is a matter to be
proud of not to lament. We should rejoice that Providence has given us the opportunity to extend our influence, our institutions, and our civilizations into regions hitherto closed to us rather than contrive how we can thwart its designs"
(quoted in Nearing and Freeman 1925, 256). Senator Beveridge joined the attack
against the anti-imperialists, telling them that "we do not need more capital—we
need more circulation, more employment. . . . Think of the thousands of Americans who will pour into Hawaii and Porto Rico when the republican laws cover
these islands with justice and safety" (quoted in Bowers 1932, 76). Admiral Royal
Bradford, a member of the General Board, reaffirmed the crucial relationship between the acquisitions and the proposed canal in an 1899 article: "In the future
our maritime interests cannot be greater in any part of the world away from our

own coasts than in the vicinity of the Caribbean Sea and the Isthmus of Panama. It is of paramount importance that we have coaling stations and depots for supplies located near all the great strategic points in the West Indies" (Bradford 1899, 738–739).

Andrew Carnegie opposed Philippine annexation because it could not be "accomplished without the direct use of force on the native population" (Beisner 1968, 176). But he endorsed Puerto Rico's annexation since, according to Carnegie, it had a large white population that was peaceable and predisposed to association with the United States. Senators argued that "the Puerto Rican case was different [from the Philippines]—that the people of that island were not opposed to American rule, that they could properly be incorporated in the American system, or that annexation of the island was justified by considerations of national safety" (Pratt 1939, 348). Carnegie was impressed that "the American forces were greeted as liberators" by the Puerto Ricans. He believed that Puerto Rico would eventually become "American in every sense," and was convinced that its people would become true Americans instead of "foreign races bound in time to be false to the Republic in order to be true to themselves" (quoted in Beisner 1968, 176). Carnegie, who was a leading anti-imperialist before the war, decided to support the annexation of Puerto Rico, since it would never be relinquished because it possessed an excellent naval base (Beisner 1968, 176).

As the senatorial debates on treaty ratification were coming to an end, Lodge wrote to Roosevelt, "The drift of public opinion in favor of an imperial policy seems to be absolutely overwhelming, and the Democrats here seem to be going to pieces over it" (quoted in Brands 1992, 31). The treaty was ratified by the Senate on February 6, 1900, by a vote of fifty-seven to twenty-seven, or one vote more than the necessary two-thirds majority. The treaty did not define the territorial status of Puerto Rico, and reserved for Congress the authority to determine "the civil rights and political conditions of the natural inhabitants of the territories ceded to the United States."

The Treaty of Paris was novel in the annals of U.S. diplomatic history. In contrast to other treaties of annexation the United States had negotiated, the Treaty of Paris left unresolved the territorial status of the acquired islands. It is clear that the U.S. had decided to retain Puerto Rico as a territorial possession for an indeterminate period. According to Charles E. Magoon, law officer of the War Department's Division of Insular Affairs, "Porto Rico is now a conquest, or property seized as a spoil of war, and held to reimburse this nation for the loss of blood and treasure occasioned by the war, and to deter other nations from engaging in war with the United States" (USDW 1902, 25). The constitutional basis for Congress to determine the disposition of conquered territories had long been established by the Supreme Court in *Fleming v. Page* (1850). Supreme Court Judge Taney (who participated in the Dred Scott decision) ruled that the president "may invade the hostile country, and subject it to the sovereignty and authority of the United States. But his conquests do not enlarge the boundaries of this

Union, nor extend the operations of our institutions and laws beyond the limits before assigned to them by the legislative power" (quoted Trías Monge 1980, 1:154).

Puerto Rico and the Caribbean

The specific commercial and strategic interests of the United States had clear political ramifications for Puerto Rico. In a seminal work on the economics of intervention, Jeffry Frieden writes that the "analysis of the economic motives in imperial expansion and contraction demands a differentiated approach to economic aims, for the political implications of economic activities vary." He observes that "it is the differences among various economic activities that make economic explanations of political affairs useful and that are the focus of modern political economy" (Frieden 1989, 55). The decision to retain Puerto Rico as a territorial possession was the product of the U.S. imperative to acquire a strategic stronghold in the Caribbean. Given its limited size and small population, Puerto Rico was not acquired for its direct economic contribution to increasing U.S. national wealth. Once the canal was built, Puerto Rico would gain in commercial importance, since it would be transformed into a major transshipment point for the distribution of commodities between North America, South America, Europe, and Asia (Reinsch 1911, 78). Although national security considerations figured heavily in the U.S. decision to permanently annex Puerto Rico, its specific function in the imperial calculus took some time to develop.

Note

1. Of course these expansionists were expressing thoughts similar to those of their British counterparts. The following quotation from a British diplomat, which appeared in 1898 in the *Annals of the American Academy of Political and Social Science,* would have resonated very favorably with Theodore Roosevelt: "I will not go so far as to say that the faculty of governing the tropics lies wholly with the Anglo-Saxon race but I am firmly of the opinion that without the strong hand of the man of the north to hold things together the tropics will never advance beyond the point which has been reached by the central American republics" (Ireland 1898, 64).

2

Military Occupation, 1898–1900: Building the Colonial State

We have not come to make war upon the people of a country that for centuries has been oppressed, but, on the contrary, to bring you protection, not only to yourselves but to your property, to promote your prosperity, and bestow upon you the immunities and blessings of the liberal institutions of our Government.

—Major General Nelson A. Miles, 1898

Citizens of the United States in adequate numbers cannot reasonably, consistently and rightly be denied ultimate participation in federal affairs, but to the citizens of Porto Rico, all of an alien race and foreign tongue, there could and should be such denial until it be shown by experience that they are fitted for such participation.

—Brigadier General George W. Davis, 1909

The War Department and Colonial Rule

With the signing of the peace protocol, the War Department was given responsibility for governing Puerto Rico, Cuba, and the other territorial acquisitions. Until February 1900, when the Treaty of Paris was ratified, the people of Puerto Rico lived under military government. According to Charles Magoon, now of the Bureau of Insular Affairs, a military government "is the authority by which a commander governs a conquered district when the local institutions have been overthrown and the local rulers displaced, and before Congress has had an opportunity to act under its powers to dispose of captures or to govern territories" (USDW BIA 1902, 19). Invading General Nelson Miles described the power of the occupying power as "absolute and supreme and immediately operating upon the political conditions of the inhabitants" (PRFAA 1988, 50). President McKinley, in his capacity as commander in chief of the army of occupation, exercised virtually unrestricted authority over the territories, and did so for almost two years.

In July 1899, McKinley appointed New York corporate attorney Elihu Root as secretary of war. Root was the principal architect of U.S. colonial policy, and under his direction Congress enacted a coherent body of legislation for each of the possessions. From August 14, 1898, through May 1, 1900, Puerto Rico was ruled by a string of military governor-generals who set about to dismantle the administration set up by the Spanish Autonomic Charter. According to Colonel Clarence Edwards, who served as chief of the Bureau of Insular Affairs (BIA) in 1902, "the War Department found itself without adequate machinery to handle this new work. Its bureaus were restricted to military requirements, while the new conditions extended to all classes of government affairs." The most immediate task the War Department faced after establishing order was collecting and disbursing customs revenues to sustain the operations of the newly installed military government (Edwards 1904, 239–240). The army appeared to be the most experienced and organized agency to administer the new territories. R. L. Rowe, a prominent colonial official and policymaker, observed, "In the army we have a police force thoroughly disciplined and able to command the respect of the population." Rowe argued that "every branch of the service seems especially adapted to some public purpose" (Rowe 1904, 121). Alfred Mahan, in a statement dripping with martial pride and infused with the dogma of Anglo-Saxon superiority, explained why the military was best prepared to administer the possessions: "The officers of the army and navy are better qualified to deal with these subject races than men engaged in the hard fight of ordinary existence" (quoted in Rodríguez Beruff n.d., 1). Since the War Department had a critical and enduring role in devising policy not only for Puerto Rico, but also for the Philippines, Cuba, and the other territorial possessions, I will briefly review the evolution of its colonial office.

The Bureau of Insular Affairs:
The De Facto Colonial Office

Three days after the Treaty of Paris was signed, on December 13, 1898, the acting secretary of war established the Division of Customs and Insular Affairs. The division was responsible for collecting, sorting, and filing the growing body of papers related to customs matters and civil affairs in Puerto Rico, Cuba, and the Philippines. Four clerks were assigned to keep the records of the division as best they could (Edwards 1904, 240; Pomeroy 1944, 525). As Congress debated the disposition of the territories, the War Department's responsibilities in administering the territories continued to increase in volume and complexity. Its officers were charged not only with collecting duties and taxes, but also with enforcing sanitary measures, establishing a school system, and reforming municipal administrations and the judicial system. On December 10, 1900, Elihu Root upgraded the unit to the Division of Insular Affairs and assigned it a larger staff, including a chief (who reported directly to the secretary of war), an assistant chief, a law officer, translators, accountants, stenographers, and clerks charged with recording, indexing, and copying documents (Edwards 1904, 243; Samonte 1925, 47). In his 1901 annual report, Root noted that the division was performing a "variety of duties which in other countries would be described as belonging to a colonial office" (quoted in Pomeroy 1944, 525).

On July 1, 1902, the Division of Insular Affairs was reorganized as the Bureau of Insular Affairs (BIA), and its duties expanded. The BIA's duties embraced "all matters pertaining to civil government in the island possessions of the United States subject to the jurisdiction of the War Department." In 1907 the bureau had a staff of seventy employees, three army staff officers, one law officer, a purchasing and disbursing agent, and a superintendent of "Filipino students" (Hunt 1913, 162). By the early 1900s the BIA was the federal agency responsible for devising colonial policy, and its chief advised the secretary of war on all federal matters concerning the possessions. Its staff was instrumental in drafting much of the colonial legislation that was submitted to Congress. The BIA's legal officer represented Puerto Rico and the other colonies in the courts of the United States (Clark 1930, 99). In addition, the bureau was the chief fiscal agent for the colonies and had exclusive authority for arranging the sale of Puerto Rican and Philippine insular bonds. Finally, the BIA was also the official repository of all information on "these dependent peoples" (Hunt 1913, 162).

The BIA was ordered by Elihu Root in 1901 "to determine and prescribe the framework of the insular government; to lay down the rules of policy to be followed upon the great questions of government as they are foreseen or arise." According to Root the task was complicated, since, "we have had no precedents . . . and it has been necessary to decide every question upon its own merits and to make our own precedents for the future" (quoted in Edwards 1904, 240, 244). Puerto Rico's last military governor, General George W. Davis, agreed there was "no American precedent to which we can refer as an aid to decide on the form of civil government that should be set up" (USDW United States Insular Commission 1900b, 73–74). However, the BIA drew heavily upon information the occupation armies acquired through their direct contact with the subject people and societies to develop specific policies for each possession.

The governor-generals continually experimented with different administrative structures to govern the colony. Each enacted measures he thought necessary to insinuate U.S. institutions into the country and effect stable colonial rule. In setting colonial policy the governor-generals were guided by the laws of war, their assessment as to the applicability of constitutional limitations, prior territorial practices, and international law as it applied to Puerto Rico's changing political status from occupied enemy territory (when the armistice was signed) to an unincorporated territorial possession of the United States (when the Foraker Act went into effect). When the Foraker Act went into effect the War Department's jurisdiction over Puerto Rico ended. (Its role in colonial affairs was henceforth confined to the Philippines and Guam.) Governor Beekman Winthrop, who complained about the difficulties of administering Puerto Rico, was among the first officials to recommend that Congress establish a colonial office. In his 1905 report he informed his superiors, "The insular government feels greatly the need of some bureau or division of the Central Government in Washington, which could act as a representative in its relations to the Federal Government and the outside public, and which could furnish information and data without delay to officials and others interested in Porto Rico and its resources" (U.S. Department of State 1905, 42).

President Roosevelt apparently heeded the advice, and on December 6, 1906, informed Congress, "The administration of the affairs of Porto Rico, together with those of the Philippines, Hawaii and our other insular possessions, should be directed under one executive department; by preference the Department of State or the Department of War" (quoted in McIntyre 1932, 298). After his visit to Puerto Rico, Roosevelt sent Congress a special message requesting that it authorize a bureau to oversee the administration of the territories. Roosevelt told Congress, "It is a mistake not so to arrange our handling of these islands at Washington as to be able to take advantage of the experience gained in one when dealing with the problems that from time to time arise in another" (quoted in Parsons 1907, 123).

A bill to set up a colonial office in the War Department generated intense debate. Congressman Parsons wanted to concentrate the expertise gained by the War Department in one special unit under its auspices. He rejected the critics' claim that the colonial office "involved a policy of centralization, would lead to a bureaucracy of colonialdom, and would tend to retain these possessions in a dependent and colonial position instead of relieving us of responsibility for them" (Parsons 1907, 127). President Taft wanted to transfer jurisdiction over Puerto Rico from the civilian executive departments to the War Department because the existing "arrangement, which followed the customary territorial procedure, was found to be wholly unsatisfactory" (McIntyre 1932, 296). A specialized unit for insular affairs was never set up, and the War Department's BIA continued to operate as a de facto colonial office.

Taking Stock of Puerto Rico and Its Economic Possibilities

The United States took an inventory of Puerto Rico's natural resources and assessed its potential for economic growth. The Insular Commission (report issued on June 9, 1898) and the Carroll Commission (report issued on October 6, 1899) were two of the more prominent fact-finding bodies sent to Puerto Rico. Henry K. Carroll had been commissioned by the Treasury Department to report on the country's industrial and commercial condition (U.S. Department of the Treasury 1898). In addition, in June 1900, a third commission to study Puerto Rico's agricultural conditions, with "special reference to the establishment of an agricultural experiment station," arrived in the country (House 1901).

In March 1899 General Davis was ordered to submit reports on "General Opportunities for Investment." One district officer reported, "The future of the island is bright. . . . But until Americans, with their ideas, energy and capital invade the island any decided change will come very slowly." Another observed, "The opportunities for investment are good if the laws and methods of taxation were such as to make an investment safe." All the officers reported the need for credit institutions, modernization of the infrastructure, and revision of the tax code as stimuli for investments. Another commander reported, "With a tax on his products sent to the United States and another on his imports from that country, the planter is ground, as it were between the two millstones of taxation." The Mayagüez commander recommended that "only Americans should be permitted to come here and enter into business. All other classes, kinds, and colors should be excluded from this time forward" (USDW 1899a, 82–84).

A Brief Moment of Autonomy

The Constitution of 1897 (commonly referred to as the Autonomous Charter) was issued on November 25. It established an insular parliament consisting of a Council of Administration and a Chamber of Representatives (*Cámara de Deputados*). The queen of Spain appointed a governor-general who was the supreme colonial authority. Despite his extensive powers, the governor-general could not intervene in civil and political matters unless authorized by the Council of Secretaries, or cabinet. This council consisted of secretaries of grace and justice and the interior, of finance, of public education, of public works and communications, and of agriculture, industry, and commerce. The Charter also established a popularly elected insular parliament. In a major concession to the *hacendados,* the Crown gave the insular parliament the authority to establish tariffs and set duties on imported products. The new charter took effect on February 11, 1898. Elections were held on March 27 of that year, in which all males over age twenty-five were granted the right to vote. The first and only meeting of the Chamber of Representatives was held on July 17.

On July 25, 1898 the U.S. Army landed in Puerto Rico, and by September the Autonomic Charter Puerto Rico's elites had negotiated from Spain was virtually dismantled. Some members of the professoriate of elite U.S. universities, certain the United States would embark on colonialism, volunteered their ideas on administration of overseas territories. Even before hostilities were concluded articles appeared in important scholarly journals. A. Lawrence Lowell wrote a number of articles that were to influence U.S. colonial policy. In May 1898, barely one month after the United States went to war, Lowell argued that the racial and behavioral differences between the people of Puerto Rico and the Philippines had implications for the type of colonial administration and political rights the United States should provide. According to Lowell, unlike the culture of the Philippines, "civilization in Porto Rico, as in the United States, is essentially European, and hence our aim must be to develop the people in the lines of our own life. In Porto Rico the political aspirations of the people cannot be disregarded" (46).

However, Lowell advised against admitting Puerto Rico as a state of the union until "it has been trained in self-government, and has acquired the political, social and industrial habits that prevail in the United States." This period of education would be so long "that statehood is too remote to be taken into consideration in determining the immediate administration of the island"(53). He recommended a highly centralized colonial administration headed by an appointed governor, in which legislative powers would be vested in a council to be partly elected and partly appointed. Finally, Lowell was convinced that "if the people of Porto Rico are to acquire our political ideas and traditions it must be chiefly by means of the courts of law. The important thing is that the organization and authority of the American courts should be planted in Porto Rico" (58).

Dismantling the Autonomous Government

After the departure of the Spanish, the U.S. military began to systematically dismantle Puerto Rico's political and legal institutions. The BIA wanted to retain the military government "until there is established in said islands a civil government which comports with the interests and inclinations of the dominant power" (USDW BIA 1902, 16). Although they lacked a blueprint for a system of colonial administration, the governor-generals issued scores of decrees and orders with the purpose of installing an "organized government in harmony with American methods," which would promote the Americanization of the colonial subjects (Edwards 1904, 239).

Before Root set up the Division of Insular Affairs, the governor-generals relied on past territorial practice and established military regulations to administer the subject people. In fact, neither the War Department nor the president knew to what extent the Constitution conditioned their legislative activities in the possessions. Nonetheless, within the brief span of less than two years the governor-generals installed a highly centralized administration that ruled by decree and that was profoundly insulated from local political forces. They dismantled Puerto Rico's autonomous government, established new court and police systems, implemented universal free public education, installed an internal revenue system, and began the process of modernizing the infrastructure of roads. Military decrees and executive orders were promulgated that dramatically altered the productive system and profoundly affected the material conditions of virtually every sector of society. The military governors initiated a process of economic change and institutional transformation that shattered the existing way of life.

During this unsettling period the military employed coercive, material, and ideological means to achieve the changes they sought. The military governors not only pacified the new colonial subjects, but they also formulated a policy of institutional transformation that served as the foundation upon which Congress modeled its colonial policy for Puerto Rico. William F. Willoughby, who served in different capacities in the colonial administration and wrote extensively on the subject, observed that although Puerto Rico "was in possession of a complete system of local government, the principles upon which this system was based, and especially the manner in which it was actually administered, were so completely at variance with American theory and practice that it was inevitable that radical changes would have to be made at the earliest possible moment" (Willoughby 1905, 119).

The governor-generals quickly began to reform the judiciary, the criminal procedure system, and the tax regime. They also scuttled the elitist educational system inherited from the Spanish and introduced mass public education. The governor-generals were determined to promote Americanization through educational restructuring. Indeed, according to Major General Guy V. Henry, who served as Puerto Rico's third governor-general, "The work of Americanizing a new colony inhabited by an alien people, of a race diametrically opposed to the Anglo-Saxon in very many respects," was one of his primary responsibilities. His duty was "to encourage native talent in adopting our ideas or morals, government and institutions," and to "educate those inhabitants of the island to our way of looking at things who were by nature and education best fitted for the work" (Henry 1899, 1475). Brigadier General George W. Davis, Puerto Rico's last governor-general, identified his mission comparably: "The problem now before us is not to give the people of Porto Rico an opportunity to show their capacity for self-government, but to train that capacity to its full development" (Davis 1900, 161). Willoughby saw the "problem of political education" in Puerto Rico as one of the principal tasks of colonial administration. The aim was to "educate and train the people governed to the end that . . . the management of their own affairs shall be placed in their own hands" (Willoughby 1909, 160).

The task of administering the new colonial possessions was not confined merely to reforming existing institutions and reasserting social stability. From the outset the military governors were engaged in a campaign to disseminate their conception of U.S. values and attitudes throughout the subject population in order to legitimize and facilitate colonial rule. Education Commissioner Roland P. Falkner echoed these objectives. "The primary object of our administration in Porto Rico," he informed his colleagues at the 1908 Lake Mohonk conference, "should be to infuse into the political, social and economic life of the Porto Rican people, the spirit rather than the form of American institutions" (Falkner 1910, 171).

General Davis identified three distinct legal periods of military rule: from the invasion on July 25, 1898, until the signing of the peace protocol on August 12; from the protocol until the ratification of the Treaty of Paris on April 11, 1899; and from that date until the signing of the Foraker Act on May 1, 1900 (PRFAA 1988, 42). During each period the governor-generals decreed institutional changes that intensified Puerto Rico's subordination to the metropolitan state.

The First Period: July 25–August 12, 1898

Three days after disembarking in Guánica Major General Nelson A. Miles issued his first proclamation to the people of Puerto Rico: "The chief objective of the American military forces will be to overthrow the armed authority of Spain and

to give to the people of your beautiful island the largest measure of liberty consistent with this military occupation" (PRFAA 1988, 49). On July 29, he instructed his subordinates that "the effect of the military occupation of the
enemy's territory is the severance of the former political relations of the inhabitants, and it becomes their duty to yield obedience to the authority of the United
States (PRFAA 1988, 50).

President McKinley issued executive orders to govern the military administration of Cuba, but he did not do so for Puerto Rico. The authority for the general
of the occupying army of Puerto Rico to issue "orders changing existing laws and
instituting reforms" was derived from General Order 101 (USDW 1900b, 15).
These orders were originally issued to guide the conduct of the commanding officer over those portions of Cuba that came under U.S. military control (PRFAA
1988, 49). The orders decreed that the commanding officer "possesses the power
to replace or expel the native officials in part or altogether, to substitute new
courts of his own constitution for those that now exist, or to create such new or
supplementary tribunals as may be necessary" (quoted in Trías Monge 1980,
1:160). Citing legal precedents, Charles Magoon affirmed that "the conquering
power has a right to displace the preexisting authority and to assume to such an
extent as it may deem proper the exercise by itself of all the powers and functions
of government." According to Magoon the purposes of the military government
in Puerto Rico were to "promote conditions which will justify the transfer of the
administration of civil affairs to the civil branch of the government" and to police
the territory and preserve peace and order until Congress approved legislation
"required by the conditions existing in the territory" (USDW BIA 1902, 15, 26).

During his brief command in Puerto Rico General Miles did not effect any
changes in the civilian government. Miles instructed his officers that the municipal laws should be continued in force "as far as they are compatible with the new
order of things" (quoted in PRFAA 1988, 50). The ordinary tribunals were expected to administer the laws under the supervision of the commander of the
military forces. The governor-general could replace or dismiss the officials and
establish new tribunals if it became "necessary to the maintenance of law and
order" (quoted in PRFAA 1988, 50). General Miles issued orders voiding the jurisdiction of Puerto Rican courts over offenses and crimes committed by U.S.
military forces. He established military commissions to try person accused of violent crimes and provost court to try all other crimes committed by and against
army personnel or employees of the occupying army.

After the defeat of the Spanish military forces, General Miles was obligated to
reestablish social order and public safety. This mission proved to one of the
army's greatest challenges. In the aftermath of the collapse of the ancient authority and the evacuation of Spanish troops, widespread violence (*partidas sediciosas*) broke out in the rural areas. The rural brigandage was concentrated in the
areas of coffee cultivation in the interior of the country, especially in San Sebastián, Lares, Arecibo, Moca, and Las Marías. The violence was perpetrated by

groups of rural workers and indebted small landowners against Spanish merchants and *hacendados*.

These *partidas sediciosas* were not rural insurrections against the new colonizers. The military authorities portrayed these disturbances as spontaneous outbursts of common criminality directed against the symbols and representatives of the old order. They constituted a repudiation of the Spanish social and economic regime and "a settling of accounts with the most visible representatives of that hated order" (Picó 1987, 201). General Davis observed that the "evil disposed classes rose against the Spaniards, and murders, robberies and arson were common." He admitted, "The difficulties encountered by the United States Army in stopping these outrages was very great. All was strange to the officers and men" (USDW 1900b, 19). The mayor of Quebradillas reported that "when the Spanish troops left after the occupation, vengeance entered," and he called on the U.S. army to "make the Spaniards clear out," as the "only hope for the peace of this country" (quoted in Carroll 1899, 601). The *partidas* proved particularly difficult for the U.S. army to extinguish, and the rural bandits continued to terrorize the rural elite through the last months of 1898. In the hope of suppressing the violence, Miles mobilized the Porto Rican Guards as an auxiliary military force. The Guards, comprised exclusively of Puerto Ricans, were stationed in towns formerly patrolled by the Spanish Civil Guard (Negroni 1992, 368–69).

The Second Period: August 12, 1898–April 11, 1899

Two days after the signing of the armistice protocol, which formally ended the hostilities, General Miles left Puerto Rico. During the second period of military occupation, "the United States had the status of belligerent nation, in legal possession and control through hostile occupation, of a colony of Spain" (PRFAA 1988, 52). On October 1, 1898, President McKinley established the Military Department of Puerto Rico, which divided the island into the geographical districts of San Juan and Ponce (USDW 1900b, 89). General John R. Brooke, who chaired the committee that arranged for the evacuation of the Spanish troops, was the governor-general from October 18 until he was recalled to Washington on December 9, 1898. Spain's governor-general left Puerto Rico on October 16, and two days later the remaining Spanish troops were evacuated. With the final lowering of the Spanish flag on October 18, 1898, sovereignty of Puerto Rico was transferred to the United States.

General Brooke's first general orders reaffirmed that the military government's authority was "absolute and supreme." As long as the "inhabitants yield obedience to the civil representatives of law and order," Brooke did not expect "that the military shall intervene." As long as they were "compatible with the military government" and did not violate the U.S. Constitution, Puerto Rico's laws would be enforced. But he warned that "the military will sustain the civil authority with armed force to secure the prompt arrest and punishment of malefactors" who failed to render obedience to the law. Brooke retained "the judges and all other officials connected with the administration of justice," including the local constabulary and police, "who accept the allegiance to the United States" (USDW 1900b, 89–90). General Brooke wrote to his superiors in the War Department that he intended "to leave undisturbed the existing conditions, believing it to be for the best interests of the Island that the former system of laws through unequal and oppressive in many respects [be retained] . . . rather than to run the chance of chaos and disorder by instituting changes with which the people were unfamiliar" (Trías Monge 1980, 165).

Nevertheless, Brooke's two-month tour of duty was marked by considerable activity, and he modified and adapted Puerto Rico's laws "to suit the change that must soon come, . . . complete territorial autonomy" (USDW 1900b, 84). Brooke retained the Insular Council (also known as the Council of Secretaries) that had been established under the Autonomous Charter. Luis Muñoz Rivera was the secretary and was appointed council president. Juan Hernández López served as secretary of justice, Julián E. Blanco was the secretary of finance, and Salvador Carbonell was in charge of public works.

On November 29, Brooke abolished the elected legislative body known as the *diputación provincial*, which he "considered as wholly unnecessary and incompatible with the present administration of public affairs." Its responsibilities were reassigned to the Council of Secretaries, all of whom were appointed by the governor-general. (USDW 1900b, 91). Barely three weeks before the *diputación* was dissolved, its vice president, Manuel Egozcue, had testified before Commissioner Carroll that "it would be a pity at present to do away with the only institution in the island whose officers were elected by popular vote" (Carroll 1899, 238). The *audiencia territorial*, the appellate court of the Supreme Court of the Crown of Spain, was dissolved and replaced by a seven-member supreme court of justice (USDW 1900b, 92).

General Brooke appointed military chaplain Reverend E. Sherman, S.J., to head a commission to study the country's social and economic conditions. Sherman urged Brooke to exercise "the strong hand of the military arm, aided and abetted by a system of civil police and rural guard [to be] composed where possible of some of the better class of Porto Ricans," to suppress the rural banditry. Sherman recommended that General Brooke hold "the civil authorities, beginning with the commissaries of the barrios personally responsible" for maintaining order in their districts (Berbusse 1966, 113). He was certain that the withdrawal of U.S. forces would have resulted in "disastrous consequences." According to Brig. General Davis, "During the period of hostile operations and following, bandits and outlaws raided the island. Great quantities of coffee were forcibly taken, houses and mills burned and the people terrified" (USDW Division of Insular Affairs, 1900, 28). Brooke claimed that only the Spaniards had been victimized by the rural bandits—the English, French, and German plantations were apparently spared during this period (Rosario Natal 1989, 310). Before being evacuated the Spanish governor-general Macías ordered his troops to cooperate with the U.S. army in suppressing the *partidas* (Rosario Natal 1989, 252).

On December 6, 1898, military command was transferred to Brigadier General Guy V. Henry, who served as governor-general until May 8, 1899. Henry reported that when he "assumed control of" Puerto Rico "I found confronting me all the difficulties and problems that are natural to such a chaotic condition of government as the Spaniards left"(Henry 1899, 1475). Henry continued to overhaul the colonial administration, and further centralized authority. He was a committed and resolute agent of Americanization and claimed that one of his key roles was to "educate the people to appreciate and understand our ways so they would be equal to the task" of self-government (Henry 1899, 1475). He reported that he was trying to educate Puerto Ricans, "giving them kindergarten instruction in controlling themselves without allowing them too much liberty" (Berbusse 1966, 88). Henry's tenure was notable for his undisguised efforts to limit the influence of the Federal Party in the conduct of government. The Federal Party had gained most of the elective posts, and its adherents were appointed to insular and municipal posts. The Federals, led by Muñoz Rivera, had the political acumen and determination, which they readily employed, to impede the institutional changes Henry decreed.

Government Reorganization. General Henry was energetic in his pursuit of institutional reform. Under his command an educational program was devised, an islandwide board of health was established, the constabulary was reorganized, and a new tax system imposed. On February 6, 1899, Henry decreed that "after a trial of two months, the organization created under the Spanish system, known as the Insular Council, and continued by the Military Governors, is not compatible with American methods and progress, and is therefore dissolved" (USDW 1900b, 98). Henry replaced the Insular Council with four departments, for each of which he appointed a secretary: State (Francisco de P. Acuña), Justice (Herminio Díaz Navarro), Finance (Cayetano Coll y Toste), and Interior (Federico Degataú y González). Two of the appointees were Republicans and two were Federals, but all received "the necessary directions from him". (USDS 1903, 10, USDW 1900b, 98). He warned his new secretaries that he would not tolerate resistance to his decrees: "Heads of departments or others objecting to the introduction of American methods of business and progress or to the investigation of the affairs of the departments when properly ordered will be relieved from office or their resignations accepted if tendered" (USDW 1900b, 98).

Henry assigned military officers to advise the secretaries of the Departments of Finance and Justice. The military adviser for the Justice Department was ordered to assist the secretary "in preparing laws or systems in accord with those in vogue in the United States." First Lieutenant Frank McIntyre, who was appointed chief of the Bureau of Insular Affairs in later years, was ordered to advise the finance secretary "with reference to American methods in the conduct of his department" (USDW 1900b, 99). The reconstituted cabinet was similar to that later set up by the Foraker Act in that each department was independent of the other and answerable to the governor. The secretaries were to receive "orders from and correspond" directly with the governor-general (USDW 1900b, 100). This decree abrogated the powers Spain had granted the council under the Autonomous Charter. Historian Edward Berbusse observes, "It was clear that these secretaries of the government were to be mere instruments of the governor-general. They had lost the autonomous powers that had been given the Insular Council by the Constitution of 1897, democracy had taken a step backward" (Berbusse 1966, 92).

Muñoz Rivera and the other Puerto Rican members of the council resigned on February 9, 1899, to protest the council's dissolution. With the abolition of the council Muñoz announced that the military regime had denied Puerto Rico the only avenue "for collective representation." The council had been progressively losing its decision-making powers to the military governor and found "itself more decorative than useful" (Barceló 1925, 512). General Henry had become impatient with the impertinence of his colonial subjects and chose to dissolve Insular Council because it was "contrary to that which should exist under the present form of government, in which there can be only one head, the Military Governor of the island" (USDW 1900b, 100). Muñoz announced to the press, "We fell from power because we refused to accept the wiping out of the shadow of *self-government* that still exists. . . . We seek to serve the United States; but in serving her, we will never abdicate our ideals" (quoted in Berbusse 1966, 92–93). Given his antipathy for the Federals, who he was convinced were an obstreperous clique subservient to Muñoz Rivera, General Henry may have chosen to provoke the resignation of the Federals in order to restructure the colonial administration without interference (Gannon 1978, 141).

A lengthy and often vitriolic period of wrangling between the Federal Party and the governor-generals began with this initial act of resistance. Henry turned to the Republican Party, which was more amenable to colonial dictates and "which became the administration party," to staff various government positions (Wilson 1905, 68). He dismissed the Federal Party's claims that it was the dominant representative force for Puerto Rican aspirations and had an electoral mandate to effect change. Indeed, Henry sought to counteract the power of the Federal Party by appointing Republicans to government posts even though they lacked the electoral support the Federals enjoyed. According to another governor-general, when making municipal appointments Henry "attempted to regulate the balance of political power by requiring vacancies to be filled in such a way that the councils would be half and half, Federals and Republicans" (USDW 1900b, 59).

General Henry appointed a military officer as president of the newly established board of health. The board developed and enforced regulations on sanitary conditions, and undertook an islandwide vaccination campaign to immunize the population against smallpox. The governor-general dissolved the Public

Works Board, since it was "not compatible with American methods," and assigned a military officer to reorganize these public works (USDW 1900b, 93). Henry, who was a Christian reformer, appears to have been disturbed by the behavior of San Juan's residents, and he sought to legislate against the "immoral conditions existing in this city" (Gannon 1978, 137). He imposed an evening curfew on unescorted children, regulated gambling, and called for efforts "by all good citizens and by the police to protect the young from evil and to bring to punishment those who defy the laws of decency, morality, and manhood" (USDW 1900b, 107).

Other Administrative Changes. General Henry did not hesitate to intervene in the affairs of municipal governments when they failed to measure up to his standards. On February 12, 1899, he suspended civil authority in Aguadilla and Moca, and decreed the dismissal of their mayors and councilmen. Henry complained that municipal affairs were mismanaged and "that the councilmen quarrel with one another, that they refuse to act in the interests of the people, and that money is corruptly used." The municipalities were placed under the authority of his officers (USDW 1900b, 101). On February 20 Henry warned the popularly elected *alcaldes* (mayors) and councilmen that his orders were "to be obeyed." Shortly after replacing the municipal governments in Moca, Henry warned, "If they [the councilmen] fail to preserve law and order or show an indifference and neglect of duty, towns in which said neglects occur will be put under a military officer and necessary troops and the functions of the alcalde, council, and courts suspended and the town governed by military law" (USDW 1900b, 102–103). However, the governor-general was ultimately forced to restore civilian government after a particularly vociferous campaign by the press accusing him of military despotism (Estades Font 1988, 93).

General Henry warned that he would use violence if necessary to control the troublesome colonial subjects. Henry told a leader from Adjuntas who threatened a popular uprising to protest his dictatorial rule that he would order his troops to shoot Puerto Ricans "the moment they resisted the authority of the proper officers" (Henry 1899, 1476). Henry imposed press censorship and arrested the editor of *La Metralla* in an effort to silence the mounting chorus of criticism to his rule. On April 14, Henry issued a decree placing all periodicals under the direct supervision of the military government (Berbusse 1966, 95). He also wrote a number of articles for influential stateside weeklies in which he justified his administrative changes and dismissed the reports that he was prone to arbitrary and dictatorial rule. On March 20, Henry warned that "it is not believed that any thought of determined opposition to law and order exists in Puerto Rico, but should such be the truth it would be crushed at once and would prove to be the suicide of the island." He cautioned that the "restless state of affairs," was "intimidating the work of capitalists desiring to invest here . . . to the injury of the well being and progress of the island (USDW 1900b, 106).

In early March 1899, a presidential Insular Commission comprised of two military officers and a justice official arrived in Puerto Rico. The Insular Commission was the first official delegation from the United States to study Puerto Rico's institutions. The commission was instructed to "report on all matters relating to currency, laws, taxation, judiciary, public improvements, education and civil affairs generally" (USDW 1899b, 3). The commissioners submitted their final report on June 9, 1899, which called for a complete overhaul of the civilian administration and concluded that "radical and immediate reforms are necessary for the protection of the people and the upbuilding of the island" (USDW 1899b, 8). The commissioners called for a system of mass public education to rapidly Americanize the country. Such a law, they claimed,

> will be more effectual in unifying the people, Americanizing the island, preparing them to become acquainted with our laws, customs and literature, and hastening the day when Spanish influence will be thrown off, illiteracy banished, and the people become fully qualified to exercise the full duties of American citizenship than all other recommendations proposed, with the children speaking the English Language and the young people reading American books and using the American tongue all will strive to obtain an education to become full Americans. (USDW 1899b, 63)

The Insular Commission called for wholesale dismissal of the teaching staff and the adoption of a curriculum closely patterned on those offered in the United States:

> The same system of education and the same character of books now regarded most favorably in this country [the United States] should be given to them. The teachers in these schools, should in a great part, be Americans, who are familiar with the methods, systems and books of the American schools, and they should instruct the children in the English language. It is idle to talk of teaching the present instructors the English language and American methods of teaching in order to fit them as instructors of the children of Porto Rico. (USDW 1899b, 53)

Early Attempts at Americanization Through Education.   Acting on the commission's recommendations General Henry set up a Bureau of Education in February 1899. He appointed Major John Eaton, a former U.S. commissioner of education and an ordained minister, in charge of all educational affairs in Puerto Rico (USDW 1900b, 165). Eaton inherited a school system that in October 1898 consisted of 528 public schools (380 for boy and 148 for girls), which provided instruction to 18,243 children (Puerto Rico, Office of the Secretary 1911, 71). Eaton endorsed the Insular Commission's proposal for mass English language training, which he included as a cornerstone of his program for universal public instruction.

On May 1, 1899, General Henry promulgated the Code of Educational Laws, which was designed by Eaton. School boards were set up in all townships, and the law mandated municipal financing of public instruction. English language instruction was the primary goal of public education. Accordingly General Henry appointed sixteen English language supervisors, all of whom were "of American or English parentage, and [were] familiar with the American school system" to undertake this task (USDW 1900b, 165, 166). He ordered that all of Puerto Rico's teachers learn to speak English and instructed the municipal authorities to hire only teachers fluent in English. English language competence became a condition for employment, to the extent that "all teachers not at present holding positions in Puerto Rico schools, who shall hereafter be granted certificates to teach in any public institutions of Puerto Rico shall present evidence of sufficient knowledge of Spanish and English to be able to teach in either of those languages" (quoted in Gannon 1978, 243). Henry, who wanted the municipalities to absorb the expenses for the public education mission, set about "to ascertain how many teachers the municipalities can pay to teach the American or English language commencing with the younger children" (USDS 1908, 221).

The Insular Commission had also recommended the abrogation of all Spanish laws and codes and their replacement with the federal and common law of the United States: "[In] our judgment the best way to Americanize Porto Rico is to give them the benefit of our complete system, and not to try and engraft partial reforms upon the Spanish system. The code to be presented will be based on the fact that Porto Rico belongs to the United States and its people are Porto Rican-Americans; and that it is from henceforth to be American" (USDW 1899b, 61).

However, Elihu Root did not accept the Insular Commission's recommendation to substitute English common law for Spanish civil law, and observed that the latter was "an excellent body of laws, adequate in the main, and adapted to the customs and conditions of the people," and that it was suited to the Puerto Ricans since "it was an outgrowth of Spanish character and life" (quoted in Jessup 1:1938, 376). Although Root advocated a comprehensive Americanization of Puerto Rico's institutions, he also gauged where possible opposition could emerge and moderated the pace and scope of the changes he wanted implemented.

Like his predecessors, General Henry was unable to suppress the rural banditry. It was evident to the military and the indigenous elite that the structure of property relations and social order was threatened by the widespread acts of violence. According to one chronicler of the period,

A matter of grave concern to both Military Governors [Brooke and Henry] was the state of brigandage that prevailed on the island. The lawlessness manifested itself principally in deeds of violence against the Spaniards who had incurred the ill will of Porto Ricans during the years of their oppression. Murder, arson and robbery were of frequent occurrence in the country regions. Millions of dollars worth of property was destroyed and scores of heartless murders were committed. Military tribunals were established to deal with these offenders. (Wilson 1905, 55)

Major Francis Mansfield reported to General Davis that between October and November 1898 he was "continually called on for protection to various plantations and other property," particularly in the vicinity of Moca and San Sebastián. He estimated property damage in San Sebastián at $800,000, and reported "it was only by ignoring to some extent the orders against leaving detachments at plantations that much property was saved" (USDW 1900b, 302). Delegations of businesspeople alerted the colonial authorities that the "banks and merchants have practically closed business with the interior," and warned that "if the present condition continues, there will soon be a complete paralysis of business" (Carroll 1899, 602). U.S. consul Philip Hanna investigated rural violence and reported:

> Almost every case of burning of a plantation is traced to the hired men on the plantation. Old grudges, the memories of persecution and low wages and of a condition worse than slavery have caused these people, at this time of change of governments, to give vent to their wrath and resentment and to try to even with their masters. . . . Nearly every case of crime which has been committed by persons of this unfortunate labor class has been committed out of revenge. (Carroll 1899, 795)

The Insular Commission dismissed the significance of the *partidas*, claiming that "the reports of lawlessness and contemplated insurrection upon the island of Porto Rico are without foundation. There is absolutely no tendency to insurrection at this time, nor has there been at any time at any point upon the island" (USDW 1899b, 59). On December 8, 1898, General Henry established military commissions to try cases of individuals accused of arson and murder. The commissions had jurisdiction in the areas surrounding San Juan, Ponce, Mayagüez, and Arecibo, where the violence attributable to the *partidas* had created a virtual state of war (Picó 1987, 149). Prosecution for acts of arson and murder were transferred from the civilian magistrates to the commissions, since General Henry believed the former "cannot act with sufficient promptness against the bandits that are still committing crimes of arson and murder on the island, there not having been a single conviction in such cases" (USDW 1900b, 93). Moreover, some Puerto Rican judges reasoned that in the absence of a treaty of peace a state of war between Spain and the United States existed, and jurisdiction over these case resided with the military government (Picó 1987, 148). Despite Henry's efforts, the *partidas sediciosas* reached their zenith in September and October 1898 (Rosario Natal 1989, 252). By the end of 1898 violence was no longer confined to the Spanish and foreign merchants and landowners, as the *partidas sediciosas* directed their wrath against the Creole landed elite (Picó 1987, 134–35).

During this period four companies of the U.S. Army Eleventh Infantry and two batteries of the Fifth Artillery, as well as the eight companies of the Porto Rico regiment, the municipal police, and the newly established insular police force, were responsible for preserving public order and protecting private property (USDS 1901, 83). However, the U.S. regular army units proved "unable to apprehend the marauders," which prompted the governor-general to create a local constabulary whose "continued maintenance for some time to come" was seen as indispensable for suppressing the rural banditry (USDW 1900b, 19, 99).

In January 1899, Henry established a "special department of police . . . the head of which will be subject to the direct orders of the governor-general." He transferred jurisdiction from the State Department to his office, and appointed a U.S. army officer who reported directly to him as commander of the Insular Police of Porto Rico (USDW 1900b, 19, 99). This force was specifically established "for the protection of lives and properties in the rural sections of the island" (USDS 1901, 401). Police forces were deployed in the rural districts and in towns of less than six thousand inhabitants, but the mayors of the larger cities had authority over the existing municipal police forces that had been established by the Spanish. Initially the insular police force consisted of 6 officers and 100 guardsmen, but within the year it was augmented to 16 officers and 350 men (Fernández García 1923, 273).

General Henry offered a reward of $100 "for the apprehension and delivery to military authorities and conviction of anyone guilty of arson, murder, robbery or violent assault . . . on the part of anyone forming a combination known as the banditti" (USDW 1900b, 102). The measures may have proven effective, given that on May 2, 1899, Henry announced that "the insular police have succeeded in quieting the bandits and arresting violators of the law and securing criminals. This could not have been done by the United States troops, owing to their unfamiliarity with the people, the country and the language" (USDW 1900b, 109). The reward for the "banditti," however, was not revoked until August 29, 1899 (USDW 1900b, 146). General Henry's last general orders were an expression of gratitude to the insular police for suppressing the bandits (USDW 1900b, 109).

In 1899, President McKinley asked Congress to authorize an increase in the strength of the army and to permit enlisting inhabitants of the occupied territories into the U.S. army. By establishing insular army units made up of Puerto Ricans, the army could redeploy regular army detachments from Puerto Rico to the Philippines, where an insurrection raged (Estades Font 1988, 95). Pursuant to an act of Congress, Henry issued Circular No. 6 on March 24, 1899, which ordered the formation of a 400-man Volunteer Battalion of Puerto Ricans. On June 5, the enlisted strength of the battalion was increased to 448 men and placed under the command of a U.S. army major. The militarization continued under Henry's successor, General Davis, who ordered the organization of a second, mounted battalion on February 20, 1900 (Fernández García 1923, 107). The battalion was recruited from "the poorer classes of the island" (Rowe 1901c, 334). According to

Davis, "the battalion of native Puerto Ricans" was "especially useful," as the soldiers were "acquainted with the country and the people and speak the local language." They "proved to be good soldiers and a success for the purpose for which they were organized" (USDW 1900b, 18, 291).

The political consequences of establishing the battalion and insular police were significant. These units were established to crush the *partidas* and to protect the holdings of the propertied classes. Puerto Ricans in the employ of the colonizers were charged with preserving the very structure of property relations and social authority that had oppressed the laboring poor during the long period of Spanish rule. The governor-general established a coercive force made up of colonial subjects who owed primary allegiance to the U.S. army. Moreover, the Puerto Rican regiment developed attitudes in young men that were important for their future employment. One official observed:

> Whatever may be our opinion as to the evils of militarism, we must recognize that there are certain stages of a people's development at which it becomes absolutely necessary to enforce new standards of conduct through some form of discipline. . . . The educational problem in Porto Rico is not exclusively one of reading and writing, but rather the mental and moral discipline which comes from unremitting enforcement of those rules of conduct without which industrial and moral progress are impossible. (Rowe 1901c, 335)

U.S. policymakers embraced the British practice of recruiting colonial subjects into the police and armed forces, and knew that the army was a potent ideological device. Even before the United States had invaded Puerto Rico, Harvard professor Lowell recommended that "natives of the island be recruited into the ranks" of the army and the navy because it was "a potent force in fostering the affection of the people of Porto Rico for the United States. There is certainly nothing that stimulates loyalty to a flag so much as serving under it" (Lowell 1898, 59). Governor William Hunt was "certain that the organization of the Porto Rican provisional regiment has been of material aid in the general work of education. "Its existence," he wrote, "has stimulated patriotism and aroused a pride in the honor of the flag" (USDS 1903, 15).

The Third Period: April 12, 1899–May 1, 1900

The proclamation of the Treaty of Paris, on April 11, 1899, ushered in the third period of military rule, and preceded by less than a month the appointment of General George Davis as Puerto Rico's fourth governor-general (May 9, 1899, to May 1, 1990). According to the War Department, "the sovereignty and jurisdiction of the United States permanently attached to Porto Rico, and the island became territory appertaining to the United States." With the formal termination of hostilities, the military no longer had the right "to exercise the undeniable, illimitable power of belligerency; the laws of peace were again operative" (USDW 1902, 19, 18). The purpose of continued military occupation "should be to create conditions which would enable the civil branch to assume the ascendancy in the affairs of civil government" (USDW 1902, 16, 23).

Although Puerto Rico had entered the final stage of military rule, General Davis complained that he "was without instructions to regulate his administration of civil affairs according to any theory of the extension or denial to Porto Rico of the constitutional guarantees" (quoted in Thompson 1989, 161). Nonetheless, Davis, like his predecessors, continued to administer and legislate subject only to his understanding of constitutional limitations and the orders issued by his superiors. He imposed sweeping administrative changes and created entirely new institutions that he argued "have been in the direction of ultimate self-government for Puerto Rico" (Davis 1900, 161). Davis wanted to retain the rule of military government, since Puerto Ricans "were poor beyond possibility of our understanding," and "the people have no knowledge of any duty or obligation but to obey the orders of the governing classes." He argued that if a "government of repression should be suddenly relaxed and for it another substituted . . . the tendency of lawlessness should . . . greatly increase" (USDW 1900b, 20).

Advising the General, or Telling Him What He Wants to Hear.   In an August 15, 1899, circular to his subordinates Davis set forth his objectives. He explained that under the U.S. constitution "it is impossible to supply any other form of government control than the military . . . until Congress shall . . . fix a form of civil government" (USDW 1900b, 83). But Davis expected that Congress would establish a territorial form of government in Puerto Rico in anticipation of the island's eventual incorporation into the union. In the interim he proposed to set up a civilian administration that would have the legal and corporate powers to attract investments and promote economic growth. According to Davis,

> Such a government should be competent to contract and fulfill all the usual obligations. If a loan is desired, it should be able to place it, to grant franchises to corporations for the development of the country, to provide for the building of roads and for the erection of public buildings. . . . To re-establish industries it will be necessary to obtain capital from outside the island, with proper security for loans made. (Davis 1900, 161)

However, Elihu Root warned Davis that his plans for a colonial administration might be construed as encroaching on the legislative responsibilities of Congress. Root noted that "the President is of course through his Secretary and his Generals wielding an enormous and very arbitrary power over Spanish islands, and in the nature of things the exercise of that power will be attacked on the floors of

Congress," where the president will be accused of endeavoring "to extend his power into the field properly belonging to Congress" (quoted in Jessup 1938, 374–375). Despite this caution, Davis decreed more sweeping change during his year of service than any of his predecessors. Davis issued scores of decrees and circulars that accelerated Puerto Rico's institutional transformation and Americanization under the direction of a highly centralized administration subject to military rule. But unlike his predecessors, he established advisory boards comprised of influential Puerto Rican professionals and politicians.

The oppositional tactics of the Federal Party and their bitter struggles with Republicans were anathema to Davis. He described the internecine political battles as "one of the inherited vices here." Davis wanted to diminish the "predominant influence of persons having only political ambitions to serve." He warned his superiors that to "hastily abandon the island to local control unrestrained by superior power would, or might, result in the greatest disaster" (USDW 1900b, 10). Davis countered criticisms that he was favoring one party over another by claiming that "he has in no case been actuated by a thought of promoting the ambitions of any party" (USDW 1900b, 135).

Muñoz Rivera, who had chosen to live in New York after resigning from the Council of Secretaries, continued to campaign for the end of military rule. Muñoz wrote in the *Independent* that his party was "working earnestly for the abolishment of the military government and the establishment of a territorial form of government, in which home rule is recognized." Reminding his readers that Puerto Ricans had not waged a bloody civil war against the Spanish, Muñoz Rivera argued that "this law abiding spirit deserves some substantial recognition in the shape of a civil government in which Porto Ricans are given the widest possible field in which to show their ability for self-government" (Muñoz Rivera 1899, 1284). He warned, "There is such a growing feeling against the present military powers that it will develop into a spirit of dissatisfaction that cannot be so easily quenched if some better form of self-government is not soon established on the island" (1285).

Davis proceeded to restructure the administration with the aim of diminishing the influence of the Federal Party on colonial policy. To challenge the political dominance of the Federals Davis set up advisory boards on judicial and governmental reform that included equal representation of Federals, Republicans, and men unaffiliated to either of the parties. On August 17, Davis issued General Order 121, which established an insular affairs advisory board made up of ten Puerto Rican men. Initially the judge advocate of the military had proposed establishing a commission on insular policy made up of an "an equal number of representatives of the two political parties (Republicans and Federals) and a like number of persons independent of party affiliations." However, this plan was abandoned, since the Federals refused to cooperate, claiming they had "greater partisan strength than the other [party] and demand[ing] majority representation" (USDW 1900b, 112).

According to Davis it was "very difficult to administer many important matters without the assistance of men who were familiar with local economic and social conditions." He also acknowledged that a purpose of the boards was to establish "a predecessor of a legislature such as a territorial government would require." Although the proceedings of the board were "not without friction," on balance the board provided Davis with the opportunity to work closely with the "eminent residents of the island, all natives"(USDW 1900b, 55). No doubt the participation of prominent Puerto Rican men also served to legitimize the policies of the military regime. According to Davis the changes he decreed were consistent with the advice rendered by these consultative units (USDW 1900b, 83).

On August 12, Davis dissolved the Departments of State, Treasury, and the Interior. The departments were ostensibly abolished because severe internal dissension threatened to destroy their usefulness (Rowe 1902, 28). From these Departments the Federal Party had mounted its campaign to influence the contours of colonial policy. The departments were replaced by the Bureaus of State and Municipal Affairs, Internal Revenue, and Agriculture. These bureaus were placed under the supervision of the newly created office of the civil secretary, who responded directly to the governor-general. Despite the appointment of Puerto Ricans to these bureaus and boards, Davis assigned administrative powers to his military. One student of the period reported that Davis had "reduced the government to a military basis, by placing various administrative departments in charge of army officers, assisted by advisory boards" appointed by him (Wilson 1905, 69). The bureau of education was put under the authority of a "board of education, similar to like boards in States of the Union," with "the president of the board reporting directly to the military governor." Victor Clark was appointed president of this board. Another army major presided over the board of charities (USDW 1900b, 134–135, 119, 157). Davis appointed Puerto Ricans and U.S. military personnel to head these bureaus.

General Davis abolished the Bureau of Harbor Works of San Juan "as not being compatible with American methods," and this unit as well as the Bureau of Public Works was placed under the authority of a Board of Public Works, with an army captain as president (USDS 1901, 323). He also established a Superior Board of Health, headed by an army officer, which assumed exclusive responsibility for coordinating the improvement of sanitary conditions in the country. Its duties consisted of organizing local boards, drafting sanitary laws, enforcing compliance with the laws, and administering an islandwide inoculation program (USDW 1901, 8). Board chief Major Van R. Hoff reported that by June 30, 1899, "one stupendous undertaking" (Root 1916, 178) had been accomplished, the inoculation of 786,290 persons—"almost the entire population" (USDW 1901, 8).

By the late nineteenth century policymakers were well acquainted with studies that demonstrated that public health policies and mandatory universal education increased the productivity of U.S. workers (see Higgs 1971). These lessons were applied to Puerto Rico. Travel writer W. D. Boyce reported with disconcerting candor that the United States had improved sanitary "conditions so that nearly a million of dirty people crowded on the island at that time could live longer, and that our white American officials might escape death in doing their duty" (Boyce 1914, 431). Three decades later Governor Roosevelt acknowledged the important work of the Health Department, for "without it we can not have economic habitation, for an underfed diseased man can not do proper work" (USDW Annual Report 1930, 11).

General Davis authorized an aggressive road-building program, and he estimated that an investment of $8 million was necessary to build a suitable system of highways. According to Davis, "In no country in the temperate zone is this necessity half so imperative as here. Without them industrial development is impossible" (USDW 1900b, 44). The Department of War authorized the expenditure of $950,000 for the construction of military roads between October 1899 and May 1900, and $581,000 from insular funds for civilian roads and public works (Root 1916, 181). In the last year of military rule, the governor-general expended $390,000, or approximately 20 percent of the insular budget for repairing and building new roads (USDW 1900b, 51).

New Courts and Old Laws.   For General Davis the whole system of law in Puerto Rico was "un-American and strange" (USDW 1900b, 26); he decreed that those "local laws of Spanish origin . . . which are . . . repugnant to our political character and institutions, must not be executed" (Gould 1958, 58). He established an independent judiciary, discontinued the Department of Justice, and assigned some of its responsibilities to a judicial advisory board (USDW 1900b, 84). Davis thoroughly reformed Puerto Rico's judicial system. The *audencias* were replaced by a supreme court consisting of one chief justice and four associate justices. Puerto Rico was divided into five judicial districts, each with a three-judge court that had jurisdiction over civil and criminal matters. The Spanish system of lower courts, consisting of sixty-nine municipal courts of three judges each, and sixty-nine police courts with the *alcalde* as the judge, was retained. The system of new courts "and their jurisdiction" were "projected on the usually established system of State courts in the American Union" (USDW 1900b, 136–144, 26).

With the signing of the Treaty of Paris the state of belligerency ended, and with it the military commissions lost legal standing. However, Davis argued that the commissions were necessary to mete out justice in those districts still "in an unsettled condition, acts of violence being still committed by armed bands . . . of banditti in various parts of the country" (USDW 1900b, 210). Davis wrote, "The spirit of revenge showed itself in a most alarming form, and before it could be checked several Spanish families were put to torture"(quoted in Rowe 1904, 121). In April 1899 President McKinley replaced the military commissions with a United States provisional court, which had jurisdiction over the same kind of offenses the military commissions had formerly covered. The provisional court was patterned on the U.S. circuit and district court system and consisted of three judges, two of whom were army officers and the third a U.S. lawyer. The provisional courts were established in part to prosecute alleged perpetrators of the *partidas sediciosas*, since the ordinary courts continued to be ineffective in suppressing these bandits (Samonte 1925, 107).

Armed with the provisional courts, insular police, and regular army units, Davis redoubled his campaign against the *partidas sediciosas*, and, as I have explained above, was able to suppress them (Todd 1943, 10). He reported that the successful prosecution of the campaign "impressed upon the more turbulent element of the native population the lesson, not likely soon to be forgotten—that American sovereignty means, above all, respect for law and order, and that the slightest breach of this rule entails swift and certain punishment" (quoted in Rowe 1904, 121).

The provisional court system was the predecessor of the U.S. district court system and had jurisdiction in cases involving offenses against U.S. citizens and foreigners. It was empowered to consider the same kinds of cases over which the federal district and circuit courts had jurisdiction. These courts served to protect the interests of U.S. citizens and placed them beyond the reach of the local magistrates. But these courts also had jurisdiction over Puerto Ricans accused of violating decrees issued by the military government. The provisional court system and the entire concept of a dual system of administering justice were targets of fierce criticism by the Federal Party.

New Efforts at Educating the Colonial Subjects.   Public instruction was vital to prepare a trained labor force, and to create a cadre of Puerto Ricans who could promote U.S. corporate interests in Latin America. Commissioner Victor S. Clark emphasized that "technical and industrial education here will give us a corps of young Puerto Ricans, trained in both the English and Spanish language and in our industrial and commercial methods who will be valuable pioneers in extending our trade in Latin America" (quoted in Berbusse 1966, 214). However, education in itself would not, according to colonial officials, prepare Puerto Ricans to exercise self-government. Willoughby emphasized the necessity of imparting "civic virtues" to members of "the upper class, from which must be drawn the directors and administrators of public affairs." Also, the type of instruction that was required was "primarily and essentially one of training rather than of education, of character-building rather than scholastic instruction" (Willoughby 1909, 162–165).

General Davis did not accept the Insular Commission's call for radical and sweeping changes. He observed, "With all deference to the distinguished gentlemen who compose that commission, it is suggested that the arbitrary installation at this point of any system, no matter how perfect would be most unfortunate, as tending to defeat the very object sought to be accomplished" (USDW 1900b, 27). Similarly, he did not implement the educational code that his predecessor, General Henry, had promulgated. Davis felt that "the changes which result from the new code are very radical and have been subject to some complaint" (USDW 1900b, 23). The code was not adapted to Puerto Rico's economic or cultural conditions and "was largely based on the Massachusetts school law, and was doubtless somewhat too radical a change . . . to produce the most salutary effects" (USDS 1908, 221). In fact, the educational codes had generated intense opposition, and Davis made "a determined effort . . . to set aside" Eaton's recommendations (USDS 1908, 223).

General Davis appointed a new commission, composed of three Puerto Rican teachers and headed by Dr. Victor Clark, to study the problem of illiteracy. The problem was undoubtedly daunting. The census of 1899 reported that 77.3 percent of the population over ten years of age was illiterate. The report claimed that Puerto Rico was "in a more dense cloud of illiteracy than any other West Indian island or any other Spanish-American country for which statistics are obtainable, except Guatemala" (quoted in Mixer 1926, 66). The commission recommended sweeping changes of the existing education laws, and in particular emphasized a program for the rapid and universal teaching of English. It called for the "introduction of sixty or seventy normal trained American teachers . . . to assist in familiarizing the Puerto Rican teachers with the methods of school organization and teaching and discipline followed in the states," and proposed "that in rural schools attended by both sexes preference be given lady teachers in making appointments" (USDS 1908, 223; USDW 1900b, 172).

On July 8, 1899, the governor-general established a Board of Education, patterned on school boards in the United States. This board was also chaired by Victor Clark, who became the island's highest educational authority and reported directly to Davis (USDS 1908, 224). Clark took on his mission with evangelical fervor and clearly saw his role as a social engineer responsible for creating a new class of citizenry:

> If the schools are made American, and teachers and pupils are inspired with the American spirit, . . . the island will become in its sympathies, views and attitude toward life and toward government essentially American. The great mass of Puerto Ricans are as yet passive and plastic. . . . Their ideals are in our hands to create and mold. We shall be responsible for the work when it is done, and it is our solemn duty to consider carefully and thoughtfully today the character we wish to give the finished product of our influence and effort. (USDW 1900b, 180)

Many influential Puerto Ricans openly rejected this campaign to mold them into pliable colonial subjects. Clark reported that "there is opposition to the American school," but he insisted that "if left to itself Puerto Rico would not establish them until that time comes when a controlling majority of its intelligent classes had received their education in the institutions of the United States" (USDW 1900b, 179). Given the urgency of socializing the colonial subjects, the military government dismissed attempts by Puerto Ricans to exercise more influence over the content of the instructional programs of the school system. When municipalities failed to hire North American teachers or others fluent in English, the power to appoint teachers was taken over by the board of education.

According to Elihu Root another goal of the educational system was to prepare a literate electorate. "I think the basis of suffrage should be that all who can read and write, or who hold property up to a specific small amount, may vote, and no others. With a sufficient system of free education the entire people should acquire the suffrage on this basis as soon as they are capable of using it understandingly" (Root 1916, 167). In an article in the *Independent* General Davis wrote, "Since only ten percent of the people can read and write, it will not seem surprising that they are not prepared for self-government. A further educational system must be the foundation of civil government" (Davis 1900, 161). This would be expensive. According to Davis the costs of simply building the schoolhouses and buying equipment, excluding the salaries of teachers, would not be less than $1.5 million. Clark had cautioned Davis that "it will be impossible for local taxation to support a public school system in Puerto Rico" (USDW 1900b, 25, 178).

In 1899, President McKinley sent a second commission to investigate the civil, industrial, financial, and social conditions of Puerto Rico. This commission was chaired by Henry K. Carroll, who also recommended obligatory public education in which the study of English was required and recommended financing public education with customs receipts (Carroll 1899, 64–65). He thought that Puerto Ricans could "learn under the pressure of responsibility" if they were given a traditional territorial form of government, but called for the right of the United States to intervene in local affairs if necessary (Perkins 1962, 116). The commission also analyzed the impact of the Spanish tariff on Puerto Rico's economic growth, recommended changes to the tariff, and described in considerable detail the characteristics and investment potential of diverse manufacturing and agricultural sectors. The commission wanted to extend the constitution and laws of the United States to Puerto Rico, and it recommended the establishment of a territorial form of government, the election of a delegate to Congress, and universal male suffrage. These recommendations were supported by Puerto Rico's political leadership but opposed by Elihu Root, the secretary of war.

The First Test: Local Elections. Davis would permit elections only "when the municipalities or towns have demonstrated their capacity and ability to govern themselves." Since only the military would assure "carefully and honestly regulated elections," they would be held "under the general direction and control of an army officer" (USDW 1900b, 150). Municipal elections took place between October 26, 1899, and February 5, 1900, the period known as One Hundred Days of Elections, "under orders of the military commander prescribing the qualifications of electors and the method of election" (Root 1916, 181). Army officers and a representative each from the Federal and Republican Parties supervised the elections. Claiming that the heated electoral campaigns would incite violence, Davis invoked an antisedition statute of U.S. law to control the content of local newspaper reporting. Employing a logic that was ironic, if not cruelly cynical, Davis decreed as seditious any publication that was "calculated to alienate the affection of the people by bringing the Government into disesteem" (USDW 1900b, 127).

General Davis rescinded the universal male suffrage provisions of the Autonomous Charter in accordance with Elihu Root's preference. The municipal elections were conducted under a very restricted franchise limited exclusively to taxpaying and literate males. Permitted to vote were those males who were recorded as having made tax payments of at least one dollar during the preceding eighteen months, or who "at the moment of voting . . . paid a predetermined amount of money." Davis chose to restrict the male franchise because he was convinced that if the more liberal Spanish electoral franchise was preserved, "the control [of the government] will be given to the masses who are uneducated." The more restrictive franchise would transfer control to "the hands of the minority," which presumably posed less of a of a threat to colonial rule (quoted in Mixer 1926, 65). Out of a population of 953,000, a total of 51,650 males voted, or slightly less than 5.5 percent of Puerto Rico's people (Samonte 1925, 114). The Federal Party obtained 28,880 votes, while the Republicans garnered 22,769 votes. The Federals also gained control of 44 of the 66 municipalities (Pagán 1972, 1:61).

Davis had ignored the Carroll Commission recommendation to lower the voting age for males to twenty-one years. The commissioners had warned that "any propositions for restrictions, however, will be in the nature of a curtailment of popular rights conceded by the Spanish law." They reminded the president that "no such restrictions were proposed in any of the acts granting Territorial government" (Carroll 1899, 62). In language imbued with the arrogance of a colonial master who had callously mutated Puerto Ricans into foreigners in their own country, Davis explained the logic for having denied males the vote.

> The inhabitants, all of a foreign race and tongue, largely illiterate and without experience in conducting a government in accordance with Anglo-Saxon practice, or indeed to carry on any government, were not deemed to be fitted and qualified, unaided and without effective supervision, to fully appreciate the responsibilities and exercise the power of complete self-government. (Davis 1909, 152)

The military regimes initiated a sweeping and systematic transformation of Puerto Rico's key institutions in a remarkably brief period. Difficult as it is to accept, General Davis did caution zealots "who wished to see the island Americanized . . . in a day" of the need "to respect the existing prejudices" of Puerto Ricans. Davis observed that in contrast to Puerto Rico, "it was easy to Americanize the sparsely settled regions of the West for there was no civilized population to be amalgamated" (USDW 1900b, 27). Nevertheless, the Bureau of Insular Affairs and governor-generals had effected so complete a transformation of Puerto Rico's key institutions that General Davis could confidently report, on the eve of the Foraker Act taking effect:

> On April 30 the machinery of civil government was in the charge of experienced public officers, and the organization, with departments, bureaus, and other branches, both insular and municipal, was such that the new government ordered by Congress to be instituted could the following day be launched and carried forward in an efficient and economical manner. (Quoted in Root 1916, 183)

The Early Economics of Colonialism

The new colonizers encountered an agrarian economy that was dominated by a small group of *hacendados* and merchants, a sizable number of whom were Europeans—French, Spanish, and British capital had established a significant presence in coffee production and commerce. The *hacendados*' political power was virtually unchallenged, and under the Spanish grant of autonomy they had hoped to employ this power to fortify their economic wealth. With its control of land and labor resources the landowning class was an impediment to U.S. firms interested in investing in Puerto Rico. Undoubtedly the entry costs for U.S. business would increase as long as the *hacendados* maintained their control over key resources.

The United States devised an economic and a political strategy to incorporate Puerto Rico into the metropolitan economy and to remove the obstacles to the entrance of foreign firms. Presidential proclamations and military decrees altered Puerto Rico's fiscal, monetary, and tariff systems, reconfigured the country's export role in the global economy, and led to profound disruptions in investment and production. Colonial economic policy transformed the insular labor market and land tenure systems, and led to the reallocation of tangible and financial assets. For a wage-based economy to quickly take hold both land and labor have to be released for use by capitalist firms. Consequently, colonial economic policy was aimed at decomposing the existing social relations of production that blocked the rapid development of capitalism. By accelerating the transition to a wage-earning labor force, U.S. colonial economic policy promoted the move toward generalized commodity production. This transition accelerated the development of Puerto Rican markets for U.S. manufacturers and farmers and led to the integration of the insular economy into the U.S. national economy.

Within two decades important sectors of the property-owning class were virtually eradicated as productive forces. They similarly lost their capacity to effectively resist the drive by U.S. firms to dominate the economy. According to Angel Quintero Rivera, it is erroneous to argue that merely technical superiority permitted U.S. companies to establish their "hegemony." "Of greater importance

[was] a series of economic measures taken by the first North American governors, or directly by the metropolis, aimed at displacing insular producers and assuming control of the means of production" (Quintero Rivera 1980, 116). Drawing partly on the work of J. H. Herrero, Quintero maintains that the economic measures were intended to displace the domestic producers in order to allow U.S. sugar corporations to establish their hegemony over the economy.

Economic policy not only undermined the material base of the dominant economic actors, but led to an erosion of their political and social power. Puerto Rico's landowners were not merely victims of invisible market forces; they were undoubtedly harmed by fiscal and monetary policies designed to integrate Puerto Rico's economic system into the metropolitan structure of production and trade. But this intervention by the state was not a necessary condition for U.S. capital to establish its hegemony over Puerto Rico's economy. Eventually sugar and tobacco corporations would have dominated Puerto Rico's productive resources. But by eroding local control over productive resources, the United States was able to lower the economic rent for U.S. firms to extract profits from Puerto Rico. This reduction in turn made Puerto Rico a highly lucrative investment site and accelerated direct investments by U.S. firms. The consequences of this insertion was a wholesale reconfiguration of the economic basis of politics in Puerto Rico.

Agriculture: From Diversity to Dependence

In 1898 Puerto Rico had a relatively diversified export economy based on sugar, coffee, and tobacco. Puerto Rico also had a thriving cattle industry, which virtually disappeared after pasture lands were converted for sugarcane cultivation. (Cuesta [1929] 1975, 58). The commissioner of agriculture reported in 1925 that "sugar 'fever' brought about a diminution and even complete conversion of whole regions previously devoted to cattle raising to sugar cultivation." He attributed the marked decline in the livestock industry to the rapid development of sugar (USDW Annual Report 1925, 520).

Before the hurricane of 1899 the coffee industry was the backbone of Puerto Rico's agrarian economy. In fact, Puerto Rico was excessively reliant on coffee as the principal export crop, which accounted for approximately 70 percent of export earnings during the three years preceding the change of sovereignty (U.S. House 1901, 18). As late as 1899 the export value of coffee was $5,164,210, compared to $2,670,288 for sugar (USDW 1901). Coffee growing proliferated in the municipalities of Puerto Rico's *cordillera central* and as capital flowed into the region small farms were increasingly supplanted by larger holdings. According to historian Laird Bergad, the initial phase of the creation of a rural labor force dependent upon daily wages was well under way in the principal coffee regions before 1898. By the late 1880s the most significant feature in the development of the coffee industry in this region was the growth of landless workers in relation to a landed population. (Bergad 1983, 134, 105, 197). Yet despite the increase in a wage-earning landless labor force, in the early 1900s the vast majority of Puerto Rico's coffee lands continued to be owned by small farmers. In 1902, 21,693 plantations which averaged 27.5 acres each were in operation (Wood, Taft, and Allen, 1902, 296). As late as 1925 an official study reported that still "the average farm in the six representative coffee municipalities of Adjuntas, Barrios, Las Marías, Maricao, Utuado and Lares consists of 41.5 acres." This pattern of land holding in coffee contrasts markedly with the sugar industry. In the sugar-producing municipalities of Arroyo, Dorado, Guánica, Luquillo, Salinas, Santa Isabel, Toa Baja, and Vieques the average farm was 223.6 acres (USDW Annual Report 1925, 511).

By the early 1900s the composition of Puerto Rico's export trade and the utilization of land had undergone noticeable change. In 1899 sugar was planted in 72,146 acres; by 1903 the acreage planted in sugar had increased to 112,416. In contrast the amount of land planted in coffee had declined from 197,031 acres to 177,754 acres during the same period (USDCL 1907, 117). The value of sugar exports increased from 21 percent of total exports in 1897 to 54.9 percent by 1901 (History Task Force 1979, 94). Coffee underwent a relative decline in its export value, dropping from 65.8 percent in 1897 to 19.6 percent in 1901 (Bergad 1978, 74). Two crops cultivated during 1898 and 1900 yielded over 64 million pounds of coffee, which represented slightly more than half the total coffee exports for the preceding two years (1896–1897) (USDCL 1907, 55). During the twenty months of military occupation, coffee exports totaled $7.4 million, sugarcane exports were valued at $3.9 million, and tobacco exports were less than $732,000 (USDS 1901, 39).

Before 1898 Puerto Rico had a number of trading partners, including France, Spain, Germany, and Cuba, and was not dependent on any one market for its economic survival. Between 1887 and 1889 the United States was Puerto Rico's leading trading partner. However, between 1893 and 1896 Spain regained its prominence, accounting for 28.8 percent of Puerto Rico's foreign trade; the United States was second, with 19.4 percent, and Cuba was third, accounting for 13.4 percent (Hitchcook 1898, 9). Because Puerto Rico specialized in cash crop production it depended heavily upon imported food products to supply the domestic market. In 1895 food accounted for 47.6 percent of total imports. The principal import items were rice, wheat flour, and pork products; the British East Indies and Germany supplied over three-quarters of the rice consumed in Puerto Rico (Hitchcook 1898, 23). Almost immediately after the change in sovereignty the United States practically became Puerto Rico's sole supplier of basic food commodities.

Given its diversified export profile in 1898, Puerto Rico's economy seemed less vulnerable to cyclical market conditions than traditional monocrop economies. Puerto Rico was, however, as potentially vulnerable as other small export-oriented economies because the level of production and exchange value of individual crops varied according to the changing demands of metropolitan markets. Each export commodity was subject to unanticipated periods of growth and contraction. Speculation in cash crop production characterized the investment pattern of capitalists, many of whom were foreigners who tended to repatriate their profits. This theme was emphasized by a congressional committee that studied Puerto Rico's agricultural possibilities: "Evidence conclusively establishes the fact,"the committee reported, "that, while the income of the coffee farms was considerable, the profits did not go into the hands of the tillers of the soil, but went to enrich the capitalist, who in many cases returned to Spain in a few years to enjoy his wealth" (U.S. House 1901, 26).

Agricultural production in Puerto Rico, as in other Latin American countries, tended toward a high degree of market variability, with the resulting abrupt shifts in capital and labor from the declining to the emerging export sectors. Indeed, this kind of shift was occurring in the coffee industry on the eve of the U.S. invasion, as the price for this commodity in the international markets declined (Bergad 1983, 205). Coffee was Puerto Rico's dominant export crop during much of the eighteenth century, particularly from 1885 to 1897, when global coffee prices soared (Bergad 1983, 145). However, after 1898 coffee went into a decline from which it never fully recovered, although coffee remained an important export crop until 1929. In 1898 the price of coffee plummeted. Brazilian coffee sold at five cents a pound in Europe and the United States, and the best grade of Puerto Rican coffee could command no more than ten cents. Previous to this global drop in coffee prices, the lowest price for Puerto Rican coffee was fifteen cents a pound (Forbes-Lindsay 1906, 142). Puerto Rico's other export crops had undergone similar periods of expansion and contraction.

After the change in sovereignty Puerto Rico was transformed from a diversifed agricultural export economy that was responsive to shifting market demands to a monoculture economy that was almost exclusively dependent on sugar production for the U.S. market. On the eve of the invasion Puerto Rican commercial relations with the United States were growing, but the level of trade with European and other countries easily surpassed commercial activity with the United States. Between October 1898 and February 1901 Puerto Rican trade with its traditional partners plummeted. Exports to Europe and other countries totaled $9.8 million and imports were $9.4 million between 1898 and April 1900. However, by February 1901, exports to these markets dropped to $2.4 million, while the value of imports was $1.6 million (History Task Force 1979, 93). In contrast, the total value of trade with the United States was $3.9 million in 1897, but increased to $12.7 million by 1901 (USDS 1901, 23). In 1897, 19 percent of Puerto Rico's commercial trade was with the United States; by 1900 Puerto Rican trade with the United States counted for 62 percent of its global trade (USDCL 1907, 47).

Puerto Rico's trade with the United States, prior to its acquisition, was almost exclusively in sugar and sugar-based products. In 1896 the United States purchased almost 60 percent of Puerto Rico's sugar exports, valued at over $2.1 million (Hitchcook 1898, 25). After the change in sovereignty Puerto Rico's role as a supplier of sugar to the U.S. market was radically intensified, and by 1901 its exports to the United States doubled over the previous two years to $4.9 million (Smith 1900, 8). By the beginning of the century, Puerto Rico was inexorably, and irreversibly, absorbed into the network of U.S. commodity trade and investments. What follows is a discussion of the impact of the various fiscal, monetary, and tariff measures on Puerto Rico's political economy.

The Tariff and Dashed Dreams

Spain enforced a colonial policy that impeded the development of productive forces and failed to promote social progress in Puerto Rico. Strict mercantilism maximized the gains for Spanish producers, and discouraged private investment in competitive product areas. Stiff tariffs on imported technology, high duties on Puerto Rican exports that competed with those of Spanish producers, failure to promote credit facilities, a refusal to invest in the country's infrastructure, and other restrictions limited capital accumulation and inhibited the widespread application of modern production technologies. In addition, patterns of resource ownership and the investment practices of landowners affected the prospects for modernization. Immigrant merchants who controlled credit and marketing facilities in the coffee zones were more prone to repatriate profits to Europe rather than to reinvest them in Puerto Rico (see Bergad 1983; House 1901, 26). Cyclical fluctuations in commodity prices and shifts in market demand also tended to discourage exporters from making significant investments in modernizing their operations. The prospects for promoting the modernization of the country's productive resources were brighter after Spain enacted the Autonomous Charter. However, because of the change in sovereignty the liberal trade provisions of the Charter were abrogated.

With the change in sovereignty Puerto Rico's landed elite expected the United States to set in motion a regenerative process of economic modernization. Commissioner Carroll reported that the "Golden Dream of Porto Ricans" was unrestricted access to U.S. markets (Carroll 1899, 768). According to Carroll, "Porto Ricans of all classes are united in urging that the markets of the United States and Porto Rico shall be as free, reciprocally, as those of New York and Jersey. . . . They look to the markets of the United States as the natural markets in which they shall sell their exports and buy their imports" (390). Puerto Rico's landowning class anticipated unrestricted access to metropolitan markets, capital, and technology, and were certain the new relationship would lend stability to commercial export relations. Free trade with the United States held out lucrative prospects for energizing the dormant sugar industry.

Pending the ratification of a peace protocol, Puerto Rico was under the sovereignty of Spain, and was considered a foreign nation subject to the various U.S. tariff laws in effect. On August 19, 1898, after Spanish forces had been defeated, President McKinley issued an executive order to impose a "tariff of duties and taxes, to be levied and collected as a military contribution" (USDCL 1907, 42).

McKinley also ordered that all trade between Puerto Rico and the United States be conducted exclusively in U.S. registered vessels. On January 20, 1899, the War Department promulgated the Amended Customs Tariff and Regulations for Ports in Porto Rico, which rescinded the more favorable tariff rates that had been in place since 1894 (USDCL 1907, 42).

With the ratification of the Treaty of Paris Puerto Rico became a foreign territory to Spain, and its favorable tariff arrangements and commercial treaties with Cuba, Spain, and other European countries were terminated (USDCL 1907, 42). As a consequence the more liberal reciprocal commercial agreements Puerto Rico had with these foreign nations were abrogated and the country was thrown behind a highly restrictive trade wall that virtually eradicated overnight long-standing markets for its most important cash crops. Commissioner Carroll reported that "since American occupation, it [Puerto Rico] finds itself without a single free market either of sale or purchase. Customs duties bar it from Spanish ports and from the ports of the United States with equal rigor. The sister island of Cuba, which used to buy coffee and cattle of it, and manufactured its tobacco, is now foreign territory" (Carroll 1899, 60). Elihu Root urged President McKinley to abolish the tariffs. "I think we are bound, without further delay, to stop the exaction of duties upon the importation of Porto Rican products to this country, either by Executive order, or by calling Congress together in an extra session. I see no other recourse, except to see the people starve" (quoted in Jessup 1938, 1:372–373). Despite these recommendations, McKinley did not prevail on Congress to alter the tariff policy, although he did reduce the tariff on Puerto Rican sugar imports and lowered the duties on some food products exported to the island. However, a more comprehensive approach on tariff policy toward the territories was a vexing political and constitutional issue that was only addressed by Congress when it passed the Foraker Act in 1900.

The Tariff and Trade

The inclusion of Puerto Rico within the U.S. tariff system had a devastating effect on the coffee industry and contributed to an economic depression on the island. In 1896 Cuba, Spain, and France consumed 71 percent of the 58 million pounds of coffee Puerto Rico exported (USDCL 1907, 18). Once Puerto Rico entered the U.S. customs area its coffee, which accounted for over two-thirds of the country's exports, was subjected to retaliatory customs duties by Spain. Cuba imposed substantial duties on Puerto Rican coffee and tobacco exports, which severely reduced exports of these critical cash crops. Puerto Rico's annexation to the United States did not open any new markets for its coffee, since the commodity had been admitted duty-free into the United States since 1872 (USDCL 1907, 18). Although Puerto Rican coffee was subjected to European and Cuban tariffs, it was not protected from foreign competition by a U.S. tariff, and it entered the U.S. market under the same conditions as South American coffees. U.S. coffee drinkers preferred the weaker Brazilian blends over Puerto Rico's strong varieties. Puerto Rican coffee growers, moreover, employed the expensive wet process method and could not compete with the cheaper and inferior Brazilian grades consumed in the United States (Carroll 1899, 443; Gannon 1978, 4). The superior Puerto Rican coffee was highly favored in Europe, but the imposition of tariffs dramatically increased the price of the coffee, making it a valued luxury crop affordable only to a very limited sector of the population. Puerto Rico's coffee industry had been promoted by Spanish commercial policy, which provided bounties and preferential tariffs. These production props were eliminated after 1898 (Puerto Rico, Office of the Secretary, 1911, 154).

Even though much of the drop in coffee production was attributable to the effects of the San Ciriaco hurricane, the change in sovereignty, according to Puerto Rico's resident commissioner, Tulio Larrinaga, was the more significant factor. In 1905 Larrinaga strongly criticized U.S. tariff policy. He reported that "the island is suffering from a great commercial depression caused by the loss of our markets for coffee, which is our main staple." Larrinaga observed that since Puerto Rico was victimized by the retaliatory tariffs the Europeans had imposed on U.S. commodity trade, "we cannot send our coffee there, where it commands a very high price, but we have to send it here, to the states, and sell it at a low rate" (Larrinaga 1905, 55–56). The change in sovereignty was a serious blow to the coffee industry and dashed any hopes it had of sustaining its prominent position in the insular economy.

Puerto Rican sugar also initially faced trade impediments. It not only encountered competition in the United States from imported European beet sugar, but was subjected to discriminatory tariffs imposed by the Dingley Tariff Act of 1897. According to Ricardo Nadal, a sugar producer from Mayagüez, "the only remedy" was the duty-free entry of sugar and tobacco to the United States: if it was "not granted we are all lost. There is no possible salvation" (quoted in Carroll 1899, 68). Despite protests from U.S. sugar beet producers, McKinley authorized an 85 percent reduction in the tariff on imported Puerto Rican sugar in 1899 (Crist 1948, 189). The favorable tariff treatment made sugar an extremely profitable export crop.

Prohibited from negotiating reciprocal trade relations with other nations, Puerto Rico was a virtual captive of the United States for industrial inputs, manufactured products, and basic commodities. Yet lacking income because of severely reduced export earnings, the country found its capacity to supply domestic needs restricted. Prices on basic commodities and food escalated rapidly and imposed debilitating financial burdens on the poor and working class. The tariff barriers accelerated the dissolution of small-scale cash-crop farming. The virtual collapse of economic activity was a direct cause of landlessness, unemployment, and growing poverty (Diffie and Diffie 1931; Luque de Sánchez 1980; Ramos Mattei 1974; Sloan 1929). The threat of starvation and pauperization was genuine, given the dramatic increases in the price of imported food staples.

Obviously concerned with mounting warnings of an imminent human catastrophe on island, McKinley ordered some temporary corrective measures to arrest the social deterioration. On January 1899, after an investigation by special commissioner Robert P. Porter, President McKinley ordered a reduction on duties on basic commodities (Carroll 1899, 447). Although this reduction was done to better "the condition of the poorer classes," Carroll reported that the resulting "cheapening [of merchandise] augments consumption, thus increasing the volume of business" (Carroll 1899, 448). The commission had proposed the elimination of tariffs on basic farm tools and implements, but had not singled out expensive agricultural machinery for favorable tax treatment (Carroll 1899, 393). This the governor-general did on August 12, 1899, by placing all imported agricultural and sugar-making machinery on the duty-free list (USDW 1900b, 100). The Central Aguirre Syndicate, an absentee sugar corporation which had established operations in 1899, requested and was granted a license to import sugar-making machinery duty free (García-Muñiz 1996, 18). This decision to impose tariffs on some Puerto Rican products imported to the U.S., pending the outcome of legislative action, constituted one of the most significant measures adopted by the federal government and was to fundamentally alter the functioning of the local economy.

Fiscal and Monetary Policies

On February 12, 1899, General Henry suspended foreclosures and judicial proceedings on agricultural properties and machinery for one year "in the interest of equity and to save the agricultural industry from loss and ruin" (USDW 1900b, 101). This decree was ostensibly issued to protect small farmers from arbitrary foreclosures by Spanish merchants anxious to terminate their operations and repatriate their profits to their country. In defense of the law, Commissioner Carroll argued that merchants and bankers were foreclosing on properties and liquidating their business "in order to withdraw and enjoy the proceeds in foreign lands" (Carroll 1899, 334). Since indebtedness was widespread, colonial officials claimed the foreclosures would precipitate widespread bankruptcy. Private indebtedness, as indicated by recorded mortgages on real estate, exceeded $26 million, about one quarter of the assessed valuation for tax purposes of all property in Puerto Rico (Foraker 1900, 465). In 1898 about 70 to 75 percent of the coffee plantations were heavily mortgaged; almost a third were mortgaged to the full value of the property (House 1901, 17).

The impact of the decree was palpable and had a perverse effect on both landowners and commercial credit lenders. Lending almost ceased, since banks and commercial credit houses were effectively prohibited from holding land as collateral. A further damaging effect of the foreclosure act was the rapid inflation it promoted and the subsequent increase in the price of basic commodities (Herrero 1971, 16). Particularly affected were those *hacendados* and cash crop farmers who financed their operations with short-term credit arrangements by putting up their land as collateral (Bergad 1978, 74; Picó 1988, 228). Landowner Guzman Benítez testified that "the order impedes contracts of every description. The right of property holders is blocked by the order and nobody cares to buy" (Carroll 1899, 333).

Coffee growers were more seriously damaged than sugar growers. The former were unable to meet overdue payments or secure additional credits, while the sugarcane plantations did not encounter the same difficulties in obtaining loans (USDW 1900b, 58). By the 1880s and 1890s immigrant capitalists, primarily Spanish, had established their domination over commercial coffee cultivation by virtue of their control of credit and marketing facilities (Bergad 1983, 152). Puerto Rico had built its commercial export economy on the credit supplied by resident Spanish merchants. For this reason Spanish business interests railed against the foreclosure law, claiming that by paralyzing "the credit system on the whole island," General Henry was attempting to ruin them (Berbusse 1966, 93).

On January 20, 1899, President McKinley ordered the devaluation of the Spanish currency at the rate of sixty cents to the Spanish silver peso and decreed the use of American currency. Prior to the executive order the exchange rate had been set up arbitrarily, according to General Davis, at the rate of fifty cents to the peso (USDW 1900b, 31; Di Venuti 1950, 19). The governor-general issued a directive on July 1, 1899, ordering the use of U.S. currency for all monetary transactions, including payment of municipal taxes (USDW 1900b, 104). Commissioner Carroll reported that "bankers, merchants and agriculturists of Ponce and Mayaguez" who "unquestionably represent extensive money and business interests . . . propose that the peso" should be retired at 66.6 cents in U.S. currency. The Spanish Bank of Porto Rico recommended that the exchange rate be fixed at 75 cents to the U.S. dollar (Carroll 1899, 451, 474). The rate finally adopted by McKinley was recommended by Robert Porter, special U.S. commissioner (USDCL 1907, 45).

The forced devaluation further aggravated a situation of capital scarcity by reducing the value of savings and assets held in Spanish currency by approximately 33 percent. The Insular Commission calculated that the $5.5 million estimated in circulation at the time would have a value of $3.3 million after the devaluation (USDW United States Insular Commission 1899b, 16). The devaluation undermined the commercial and banking sectors, which saw their outstanding loans and reserves depreciate in value. On the other hand, devaluation tended to improve the financial conditions of those sectors of the local landowning class that had dollars or gold and silver (Carroll 1899, 471; Herrero 1971). The currency change adversely affected coffee plantation owners. Coffee sales in Europe earned foreign exchange in gold bullion for the exporters, who paid the producers in depreciated silver (USDS 1904, 20). The value of the silver was approximately 40 percent less than the value of the gold, which translated into an additional margin of profit on the product (Lyle 1906, 791). Those *hacendados* lacking independent sources of financing were adversely affected, since the devaluation further reduced the existing stock of domestic capital, making credit, when available, even more costly. According to Cayetano Coll Cuchi, an official in the colonial administration, the devaluation was a bonanza for investors, primarily U.S. capitalists, who had access to dollars. He noted, "The silver from which our money was coined equaled that from which the United States currency was coined. Nevertheless, each of the native dollars was taken over at the rate of sixty cents, immediately recoined and placed on the market in the United States for circulation with a palpable gain to the latter of 40 percent of its intrinsic worth" (Coll Cuchi 1909, 177).

Like all colonial powers, the United States wanted to make its colonial possessions self-supporting. On January 19, 1899, General Henry decreed a territorial tax on agricultural lands "in accordance with the various types of cultivations existing in the island and the quality of the land" (USDW 1900b, 96). The territorial tax replaced the former method of assessment based on property income. The new tax assessed valleys at one dollar per acre, midlands at fifty cents, and highlands at twenty-five cents; these rates were applied whether the land was cultivated or not (USDW 1899b, 29). Since land had direct as well as indirect economic functions, the tax tended to benefit those landowners who were able to extract the maximum financial gain from their holdings. Pasturelands, land held fallow for brief periods, and other acreage that did not generate earnings, were heavily taxed relative to cultivated land. Money-losing coffee plantations on prime land paid the same tax as the more profitable sugar plantations.

According to Commissioner R. L. Rowe, the tax "aroused great dissatisfaction," since the rates imposed failed to correspond to the real productivity of the land and fell most heavily on farmers not engaged in intensive cash crop production (Rowe 1904, 191). J. H. Hollander, who served on the tax code commission, complained that "the principle adopted with respect to agricultural land was a crude, primitive device—namely, a classification of lands according to use and quality and the imposition of specific taxes thereon" (Hollander 1901, 557). The Insular Commission roundly criticized the tax, noting that the improved sugarcane lands, which were "worth from $100 to $300 per acre . . . are assessed . . . without question as to value or improvements . . . the same as other lands on the mountains which are entirely unimproved and produce nothing" (USDW 1899b, 31). Despite their preferential treatment sugar planters criticized the territorial tax. Spokespeople for the industry testified that "sugar . . . can not possibly support further imposts until the markets of the United States are opened to us" (Carroll 1899, 382). Not surprisingly cattle raisers and inefficient landowners intensely opposed the tax measure because it increased their liabilities (Gannon 1978, 325–327).

The territorial tax further eroded the capacity of many landowners, particularly indebted coffee growers already struggling under the capital shortage, to sustain their operations. It undoubtedly forced the most debt-ridden landowners to sell off their land to pay off the obligations. When combined with the increased costs for imported capital goods, dramatic declines in earnings due to the loss of traditional markets, and devaluation, the taxes imposed a ruinous financial burden on landowners (Herrero 1971; Quintero Rivera 1980). In 1900, the territorial tax generated $410,000 for the insular treasury, or approximately one quarter of estimated receipts (Carroll 1899, 20; USDW 1900b, 51). Custom duties, a temporary fee on the import duties, and special taxes on loading and unloading freight were the largest source of receipts for Puerto Rico's insular treasury (Carroll 1899, 20). However, the department could not secure through the existing tax system the $3 million it estimated would be required to finance the operations of the insular government, public school system, and public works projects (Gould 1958, 148). In view of the revenue shortfalls, the War Department requested that duties and excise taxes collected by the federal government on imported Puerto Rican merchandise be returned to Puerto Rico.

The Hurricane, Charity, and Workfare

The severity of the policy-induced economic disruptions was aggravated by the devastation wrought by San Ciriaco on August 8, 1899. The War Department reported that the hurricane killed 2,280 persons; probably another 500 were killed of whom there was no record (USDW 1901, 139). The hurricane "rendered homeless and destitute a large number of human beings," and the "incidental effect is to curtail importations, therefore revenue. It is now a serious problem, the raising of revenues adequate to the maintenance of orderly government" (USDW United States Insular Commission 1899a, 6). The impact on the country's leading export sector was devastating. The hurricane damaged 70 to 75 percent of the coffee plantations. The director of the Board of Charities reported that coffee, "a promising crop, valued at $7,500,000, was rapidly reaching maturity, giving work to thousands and sustenance to hundreds of thousands of the laboring classes, when suddenly in a night this crop was destroyed" (USDW 1901, 200). He estimated that over 200,000 laborers were dependent on the coffee industry.

Agriculture specialist S. A. Knapp, who headed a commission to report on Puerto Rico's agricultural conditions, warned that "abandonment of the coffee plantations would mean death to many laborers who could find no other immediate employment" (*Cong. Rec.* 1901, 18). Four years later Governor Hunt reported:

> It is hard to exaggerate the condition in which coffee growers and those dependent upon the coffee industry, a majority of the people of the island found themselves as a result of the storm. Planters' houses were destroyed or greatly damaged, their coffee trees were blown almost to death, their lands were washed, their machinery was destroyed and their crops utterly ruined for a year. (USDS 1904, 9)

Within a week of the hurricane, General Davis charged the Board of Charities "with the supervision of the distribution of food to the needy" and instructed all military departments to provide "such assistance as it may call upon them for in the prosecution of the relief work" (USDW 1900b, 134). Since the fruit and food crop was destroyed as well, the task that confronted the military regime "was a question of saving human lives, not for a day or a week, but for months" (USDW 1900b, 274).

The War Department solicited funds from private sources, and appropriated about $400,000 from its budget to provide food to the victims of the hurricane of San Ciriaco (Gannon 1978, 150).[1] Elihu Root telegraphed the mayors of the fourteen largest cities in the United States, as well as the governors of all the states, appealing for assistance. Root established a Central Porto Rico Relief Committee, which sent one thousand tons of food each week until mid-October 1899 (Jessup 1:1938, 373). In contrast to the urgency with which the War Department treated the disaster that befell Puerto Rico, Congress, which was ideologically opposed to providing welfare to its colonial wards, reluctantly appropriated the paltry amount of $200,000 to feed the majority of the 950,000 inhabitants of Puerto Rico (Diffie and Diffie 1931, 35). The War Department arranged for the military government in Cuba to lower the duty on Puerto Rican coffee to offer some relief to the devastated industry (Gannon 1978, 150). President McKinley also authorized the distribution of food supplies held in military depots.

In a seminal article, Stuart Schwartz demonstrates how San Ciriaco presented the military government "with opportunities for using its response to forward a particular political program," which included demonstrating to the colonial subjects the benefits of U.S. sovereignty (Schwartz 1992, 319). While this ideological goal was undoubtedly a key motive behind the relief effort, the military regime also wanted to impart a uniquely U.S. notion of the appropriate "work ethic" to Puerto Ricans. General Davis was convinced that unless compelled Puerto Ricans would eschew gainful employment. He wrote that "work not being a necessity, therefore, the present incentive to labor is so small that it seems to matter little to the average peon whether or not he is employed at all" (USDW 1900b, 36). Davis feared the relief efforts would promote idleness among rural workers and peons. After learning of reports that able-bodied men were refusing to work, he decreed "a policy of no work no ration" and ordered "that no such man who refuses will be permitted to draw food for himself or his family" (Allen 1902, 169; USDW 1901, 144). Food was to be "issued to prevent starvation" and channeled to "the worthy poor" who "gives a full day's work in return" (USDW 1900b, 280).

By restoring the destroyed plantations through a planter relief program administered by the Board of Charities, General Davis hoped to avert widespread starvation (Schwartz 1992, 326).

He justified his intervention in the market by the fear that "idleness among the laboring classes" threatened "disaster to the island." General Davis reported that the "greatest difficulty is found in making the able bodied men work for food." He was convinced that the army had to act to prevent a human disaster because the "Puerto Rican authorities have no organizing power to utilize the enormous working force" to rebuild the country (USDW 1900b, 281). On September 16, 1899, the Board of Charities announced an agreement with the planters "whose lands have been devastated and who are in financial stress" to provide them with food to be distributed as daily rations to laborers employed by the landowners. The agreement stipulated that the planters would help the laborers restore their dwellings and lend each a small plot on which to grow food (USDW 1900b, 281). While the relief program seemed to favor the coffee economy, Davis and the growers feared that free food and clothing and access to land would discourage workers from accepting the low wages the planters thought necessary to sustain Puerto Rico's coffee prices in a highly competitive world market (Schwartz 1992, 330).

Although the Puerto Rican coffee industry never recovered from the effects of the change in sovereignty and the hurricane, during the initial stage of colonial rule the War Department supported the industry. The coffee growers, devastated not only by the hurricane but also by the loss of traditional markets and the effects of fiscal and monetary policies, were able to employ a labor force at the expense of the colonial regime. Given the centrality of the coffee economy to employment, the military government may have had little option but to attempt to partially restore the industry in order to inject a measure of political stability.

The Economic Aftermath of the Military Regimes

The turbulent changes Puerto Rico experienced at the end of the century transformed that country's economy and society forever. Fiscal, monetary, and tariff measures eroded the ability of landowners to resist the sweeping changes to their country's productive structure. These measures facilitated the accumulation of land and other productive resources by metropolitan capital and compelled Puerto Rican capitalists to redirect their activities to the new market opportunities. Although it was inevitable that U.S. capital would eventually overwhelm the Puerto Rican economy, it is also undeniable that the military regimes created the basis for this process to unfold quickly.

By virtue of their control over financial, commercial, and agrarian capital and labor resources, the Puerto Rican capitalists did pose a potential impediment to the rapid expansion of U.S. business firms. As long as they controlled resources, whose market value would undoubtedly escalate as commerce and trade increased, they could extract a high price from potential U.S. investors. However, because of higher taxes, increased cost of credit, depreciation of the national currency, a new tax regime, and evaporation of long-standing markets, many local capitalists were forced to sell their land and increasingly lost control over resources that came to be in great demand. Landowners were compelled to relinquish resources in order to sustain an increasingly precarious existence. The escalating market price for prime land that could be cultivated in sugarcane encouraged many small independent farmers to sell their holdings to corporate speculators. These resources, once ceded by Puerto Rican landowners, became available for purchase by the highest bidders, invariably capital-rich U.S. corporations. The economic changes of the era resulted in financial ruination for many landowners and heightened vulnerability for those who survived the shakeup. The effect of these measures was to create the foundations for a substantial denationalization of the Puerto Rican economy.

Moreover, many self-sufficient, small-scale producers lost their land and were converted into a propertyless class of people available for wage labor. A similar fate befell independent artisans, as their crafts were displaced by mechanization and cheap imported manufactured products. Rising levels of unemployment related to the changed market conditions further increased the legions of workers available for hire. The pool of labor increased at the moment U.S. sugar and tobacco corporations began their operations in Puerto Rico. General Davis noted the "superabundance of labor" in Puerto Rico: "No other West Indian island except Barbados is so densely populated. Labor is increasing much more rapidly that the capacity of the island to employ it, and the natural consequence is low wages" (USDW 1900b, 36). The military regimes advanced the process of primitive accumulation by helping create the conditions that led to the growth of a labor force that was compelled to sell its energies and talent for a wage.

Although policy was important in accelerating the advance of capitalism, the capacity of local capital to resist the onslaught of the sugar and tobacco corporations was limited at best. These corporate giants, which were also aggressive advocates of free trade with Puerto Rico and Cuba, were technologically advanced, highly capitalized monopolies that could easily have overwhelmed Puerto Rico's landowning class under any circumstances. Domestically owned sugar *centrales* and medium-sized landowners engaged in sugar production did have a significant economic presence into the 1920s. Nonetheless, the net effect of the colonial economic policy was to reduce the entry costs for U.S. enterprises to invest in Puerto Rico, and to provide incentives for the wealthiest and most enterprising Puerto Rican capitalists to invest their resources in sugar production.

The impact of the trade restrictions on material conditions and productive capacity should not be underestimated. Puerto Rican society and economy underwent a profound and wrenching process of dislocation. Rather than leading to greater opportunities for agricultural producers, the change in sovereignty led to the collapse of the coffee industry and the expansion of sugar production, which by the late 1920s was overwhelmingly under the control of absentee corporations.

The Legacy of the Military Period

Although inexperienced as an overseas colonial power, the United States proved adept at imposing colonial administration under military rule. The War Department not only implanted a new structure of governance, but devised an ideological framework intended to transform the country into a loyal ward of the United States. The War Department set about to define the scope of Puerto Rican participation in their own governance and laid the foundations for the smooth transition to the civilian colonial administration. Members of the divided elite were selectively incorporated into the colonial administration, often in titular positions and never as policymakers. Through their participation in advisory boards Puerto Ricans were exposed to a mentality that stressed subservience to and acceptance of colonial authority. The incorporation of Puerto Ricans into the colonial regime as advisers, justices, minor functionaries, soldiers, and police officers was, according to U.S. officials, a measure of the colonized people's consent to their own subordination. Although there was little direct opposition to military rule, the governor-generals did expend a substantial portion of the budget on internal security. Expenditures for police, prison, and judicial functions in 1899 amounted to $580,000, or about 30 percent of total insular expenditures. Insular police and prison expenditures accounted for $378,700 of this total (calculated from USDW 1900b, 50–51).

Dismantling the civilian administration and judiciary was but an element of a broader process of change that was designed to effect a transformation of Puerto Rico's economy and society and to insert the country fully into the U.S. network of trade and investments. The transformation of Puerto Rico's political economy, however, cannot be solely attributed to the machinations of a military regime in collusion with metropolitan capital. Changing market conditions and consumer preferences, the reaction of sectors of metropolitan capital that feared competition, and the actions of expatriate merchants and capitalists were additional factors that cannot be dismissed.

Confronted with a divided leadership and a huge subject population immersed in poverty and on the threshold of starvation, the colonizers were able to achieve the requisite social control to effect the required economic and political changes. The new colonizers assumed a role in the lives of the displaced workers and forgotten rural families that was previously unknown in Puerto Rico. The relief programs to aid victims of the hurricane of 1899, public works that provided needed jobs in road-building, advancements in health and sanitary conditions, and the establishment of state-run charities, all served to build popular support for the United States. These measures not only provided employment to selected sectors of society, but further undermined the moral and political authority of Puerto Rico's elites. Modest as they were, these programs were in marked contrast to the policy of neglect of the Spanish colonial period. Nonetheless, it was the very process of colonialism that had engendered such profound economic hardship and human immiseration.

Racialist constructions of Anglo-Saxon superiority were central ideological rationalizations for denying Puerto Ricans a decisive role in their own society. Reverend A. F. Beard, secretary of the American Missionary Association, expressed a commonly held view that linked tropical climate to lethargy. Beard observed "you will not . . . expect to find a sturdy or pushing race, nor will you expect to see marked changes among such a people within a short time; no, nor changes even in a long time." Moreover, he intoned, "Indeed a people who live in tropical countries are not likely to be a book people. Therefore, we may not expect very soon a literary or reading habit among the people of Porto Rico." Beard claimed that because of these characteristics of the Puerto Rican people and climate, "Our hope for Porto Rico is not to be in the present generation. It is in the coming generations and in their education" (Beard 1901, 103–104). Needless to say, Beard, who did not read Spanish, made these denunciations with only the most superficial knowledge of the cultural and intellectual achievements of the former Spanish colonies.

It is important to recall that colonial policy toward Puerto Rico was not designed solely to promote the interests of capital; it was intended to realize hemispheric strategic goals of the United States. Minimally these included establishing a permanent and stable base from which U.S. naval and military forces could operate freely in the region and which could contribute to U.S. business penetration of the Latin American markets. It is in this context that the establishment of a loyal and stable colonial outpost in the Caribbean was a primary goal of the War Department. The cold logic of the period—grounded as it was in racist conceptions of moral and intellectual superiority and technical prowess—dictated that U.S. men of business and colonial managers would carry out the Americanizing mission to convert Puerto Ricans into loyal colonial subjects. Congress and the executive branch learned much during this brief period of military rule. The lessons learned provided the basis for U.S. colonial policy, not only in Puerto Rico, but in the other possessions and Cuba as well.

Note

1. This money from the War Department budget was not a grant. Under Section 38 of the Foraker Act the Puerto Rican people were required to "reimburse the United States for any moneys which have been or may be expended out of the emergency fund of the War Department for the relief of the industrial conditions of Porto Rico caused by the hurricane of August eight, eighteen hundred and ninety-nine."

3

The Foraker Act: The Politics and Economics of Colonial Legislation

I have found it necessary . . . to advert in strong terms to the general unfitness of the great mass of the people for self-government, and unfortunately the number of intelligent, learned, and responsible natives bears very small ratio to the illiterate and irresponsible.

—Brigadier General George W. Davis, 1899

Once admit that some people are capable of self-government and that others are not and that the capable people have a right to seize upon and govern the incapable and you make force—brute force—the only foundation of government and invite the reign of a despot.

—William Jennings Bryan, 1900

Manifest Destiny and Imperialism

In 1898 the United States went to war, confident in the divine morality of its venture and armed with a doctrine of Anglo-Saxon racial superiority. According to its most vocal ideologues, men such as Representative Charles F. Cochran, the United States had embarked on a civilizing mission; territorial expansion was incidental to the duty of establishing the "reign of the Aryan, with justice, enlightenment and the establishment of liberty" (quoted in Stephanson 1995, 89). Some of the islands the United States forced Spain to relinquish were densely populated by people with a common language, common customs and governmental institutions, and a shared sense of history. Puerto Rico in particular was a densely populated island whose population could not be easily relocated. Moreover, Congress was bound by treaty to determine the political conditions of Puerto Rico's inhabitants.

Primarily for these reasons U.S. officials treated the new colonial subjects differently from the Native Americans and Mexicans who lived in the Western territories. General Davis reported that the Americanization of Puerto Rico should be gradual because the island "was densely populated." In contrast he claimed that "it was easy to Americanize the sparsely settled regions of the West . . . for there society had no organization and there was no civilized population to be amalgamated" (USDW 1900b, 27). Through war and conquest many of the people living in these regions were either eliminated or forced to move. Once these areas were depopulated, the territories were incorporated into the United States with the aim of eventual statehood. A half century after the United States acquired Puerto Rico George F. Kennan repeated the myth that "our territorial acquisitions had been relatively empty land" that would be held as territories "until they were filled with our own sort of people and were prepared to come into the Union." But the territories acquired in 1898 "were not expected to gain statehood at all at any time, but rather, to remain indefinitely in a status of colonial subordination" (Kennan 1951, 14–15).

The possessions, on the other hand, could not be depopulated and thus were not incorporated into the Union. Justice Brown, in *Downes vs. Bidwell*, spelled out the racial logic of a legal doctrine for the colonial subjugation of the people of Puerto Rico and the Philippines:

> It is obvious that in the annexation of outlying and distant possessions grave questions arise from differences of race, habits, laws and customs of the people, and from differences of soil, climate and production, which may be quite unnecessary in the annexation of contiguous territory inhabited only by people of the same race, or by scattered bodies of Indians. (quoted in Leibowitz 1989, 22)

U.S. expansion westward, rationalized by the white supremacist doctrine of Manifest Destiny, was promoted with the aim of incorporating newly acquired territories into the Union. The seemingly unlimited natural resources of the western territories, combined with massive European immigration, virtually assured the United States a preeminent role in the international economy. According to historian Frederick Merk, Manifest Destiny was the antithesis of the imperialism of the 1890s. In contrast to the former, which "envisaged the elevation of neighboring peoples to equal statehood and to all the rights and privileges which that guaranteed," imperialism at the turn of the century was insular and "involved the reduction of distant peoples to a state of colonialism" (Merk 1963, 256–257). However, both the imperialism of the 1890s and Manifest Destiny were thoroughly imbued with racial constructions that extolled the superiority of the U.S. Anglo-Saxon people. They differed, however, in that Manifest Destiny was based on the idea of conquest and either displacement or destruction of peoples, and imperialism was based on conquest and subjugation of peoples and their eventual Americanization.

U.S. continental expansion went hand in hand with the virtual eradication of Native American populations, the forced relocation of the remaining nations and tribes to reservations, and their subsequent legal subjugation to the metropolitan state. The United States realized its ambition of controlling the unbroken landmass from the Atlantic to Pacific Oceans by violently appropriating almost half of Mexico's national territory and expelling Mexicans from their lands.

Through incentives, land grants, and propaganda, the U.S. state encouraged the rapid resettlement of the territories by recent European immigrants. Massive subsidies went to the railroad companies, which made the move west affordable and linked Northern capital with the growing markets and wheat belt of the West. Since the goal was eventual annexation of these territories as states of the Union, Congress and the Supreme Court created the constitutional basis to designate these contiguous areas incorporated territories that would eventually be granted statehood.

However, Congress harbored no similar intention of granting statehood to brown-skinned tropical peoples with a Spanish-based culture, who practiced Catholicism and did not speak English (See Schurz 1955, 78). Congress and the Supreme Court proved to be remarkably resourceful in devising the "legal" doctrine to deny the people of the former Spanish territories U.S. citizenship and the hope of statehood. Congress claimed the constitutional basis to exercise direct rule over these territories while denying the inhabitants any say in the conduct of government. Puerto Rico's First Organic Act of 1900, known as the Foraker Act, was the instrument through which the metropolitan state imposed colonialism. The Foraker Act was an act "temporarily to provide revenues and civil government for Puerto Rico, and for other purposes." It proved to be a more durable document, remaining in effect until March 2, 1917.

Why and how the United States devised a constitutionally valid doctrine permitting it to acquire and claim sovereignty over another people is an important, although often overlooked, episode in U.S. history. In this chapter I analyze four related themes: (1) the congressional and constitutional reasoning for colonialism; (2) the impact of U.S. sectional economic interests in shaping colonial policy; (3) the role of the War Department in promoting capitalist development in Puerto Rico; and (4) the structure of the colonial state and its function in achieving U.S. strategic and economic objectives in the region.

New Territories and Alien Peoples: The Great Debate

On December 5, 1899, after one and a half years of military rule in Puerto Rico, President McKinley announced to Congress that the time was "ripe for the adoption of a temporary form of government for this island," and called for Puerto Rico "to be brought within the tariff limits at once" (quoted in Latané 1907, 141). McKinley instructed Congress, "Our plain duty is to abolish all customs tariffs between the United States and Porto Rico and give her products free access to our markets" (*Cong. Rec.* 1900, 2423). On January 5, 1900, the Senate Committee on Pacific Islands and Porto Rico began deliberations on legislation for a temporary system of governance for Puerto Rico, to remain in effect until its laws could be revised and codified and a permanent form of territorial government installed. The House Ways and Means Committee considered legislation pertaining to customs duties and internal revenue. In keeping with McKinley's request, Senator

Foraker and Representative Payne dutifully introduced bills with provisions for U.S. citizenship, the complete application of U.S. constitutional protections to Puerto Rico, and free trade. After several weeks of committee hearings, Foraker and Payne reported back to their respective chambers. The bills underwent significant modification, and in the end neither resembled the relatively liberal measures that were originally considered (see Ringer 1983, 954–960).

Congressional treatment of the overseas possessions marked a definite break with a long-standing policy of territorial incorporation. Prior to the ratification of the Treaty of Paris, Congress adhered to the doctrine that all U.S. territories and their inhabitants were integral components of the United States, to which the protection of the constitution applied (Native Americans being the obvious exception). Eventually, after a suitable period of civilian administration, these territories would be admitted as states into the Union. When it came to the former Spanish colonies, Congress chose to reassess its policy of incorporation, and decided to deny the inhabitants of the territories constitutional guarantees. Congress also denied them the status of an incorporated territory—the legal basis for eventual statehood. This marked the first instance in which Congress refused to contemplate statehood for territories the United States had annexed (see Kennan 1951, 14–15).

The Foraker Act provoked an intense national debate on the principles that would guide the United States' conduct in its treatment of former Spanish colonies.[1] The Democrats and Republicans waged a highly visible and intensely partisan battle, often cloaked in the mantle of moral imperatives and standards of fairness, on the kind of treatment that should be accorded the peoples of the acquired territories. Ideological cleavages pitted Democrats, who supported free trade, citizenship, and territorial incorporation, against the majority Republicans, who advocated protectionism, denial of citizenship, and colonialism. Democrats claimed that if Congress denied the inhabitants of the territories the basic rights guaranteed in the constitution it would repudiate the fundamental democratic principles the United States was founded on (see Sumner 1899). Republicans, many of whom were ardent proponents of colonialism, feared the effect on the social fabric of the Union if the inhabitants of the possessions, "all of an alien race and foreign tongue," were to be incorporated into the body politic (For a discussion of these debates see Beisner 1968).

Despite these political and philosophical differences, Republicans and Democrats forged a foreign-policy consensus that called for retaining the Philippines and Puerto Rico. However, they disagreed on the relationship between the federal government and the territories. Should the territories be incorporated into the Union or held as colonial dependencies? This dilemma precipitated fierce debate on whether the United States had chosen to embark on a morally objectionable campaign of conquest and domination. The Congressional battles also exposed divisions within the state, as well as within U.S. business, as to Puerto Rico's role in the metropolitan economy. The issue of Puerto Rico's territorial status provoked debates between the Democrats and Republicans over national tariff policy. The key foreign economic issue that Congress wrestled with was whether it should adhere to a long standing policy of tariff protection or abandon it in favor of free trade with the possessions?

Although Republicans and Democrats wrestled over the constitutional basis of Congress legislating over subject peoples, both parties were determined to retain the territories. Representative Schurz dramatically summarized the imperialists' argument: "The Pacific Ocean will be the great commercial battlefield of the future, and we must quickly use the present opportunity to secure our position on it. The visible presence of great power is necessary for us to get our share of trade with China. Therefore, we must have the Philippines" (Schurz 1955, 81). Senator John T. Morgan, the influential Democratic member of the Senate Committee on Foreign Relations, saw as "repugnant to the principles of our national Constitution" a colonial policy that discriminated against the peoples of the territories. Yet Morgan would not permit an independent Puerto Rico, since "the ability to sustain an independent government is more questionable because her population cannot increase in so limited an area to the strength that is essential to independent statehood. Her geographical position is too important to distant nations, to admit of her independence" (Morgan 1898, 63). In the final analysis, the U.S. state abandoned constitutional doctrine on territorial incorporation to the imperative of adopting an explicit colonial policy for Puerto Rico and the Philippines in the interest of national economic security.

The Constitution, Puerto Rico, and the Philippines

After the ratification of the Treaty of Paris Congress had to decide on the type of territorial government to set up in the possessions and how to finance its activities. On the surface these issues would appear to be relatively routine matters for Congress to resolve. Yet the process through which these issues were finally settled, culminating in the passage of the Foraker Act and subsequent Supreme Court review of this act, was an important episode in the annals of U.S. imperialism and constitutional history. Congress had to redefine the legal and political status of long-established societies in relation to the Constitution. Congress also had to decide whether it had the constitutional authority to impose a tariff on merchandise trade between the new territories and the United States. Colonial legislation for Puerto Rico would "naturally be looked upon as a model" for other territories that might be acquired by the emerging empire of the North (Callcott 1942, 166).

Two considerations heavily influenced Congressional thinking on the territorial status of the possessions. For one thing, U.S. firms feared commercial competition with the possessions. According to proponents of tariff protection, the unregulated importation of tropical products from the Caribbean and the Philippines posed a threat to domestic producers. Second, Congress was alarmed that unrestricted immigration from the possessions would jeopardize the jobs and well-being of U.S. workers. Some racist Congressmen pleaded for restrictions against immigration from the tropics because Puerto Ricans and Filipinos would dilute the racial composition and tarnish the cultural homogeneity of U.S. society. Given these perceived threats to economy and society, Congress moved with alacrity to discover a constitutionally valid doctrine to justify the exercise of unrestricted legislative power over the possessions. The United States wanted to regulate the flow of peoples and commodities across its continental borders. Senator George Gilbert, southern Democrat, explicated his racially based motivations:

> I am opposed to increasing the opportunities for the millions of Negroes in Puerto Rico and the 10,000,000 Asiatics in the Philippines of becoming American citizens and swarming into this country and coming in competition with our farmers and mechanics and laborers. We are trying to keep out the Chinese with one hand, and now you are proposing to make Territories of the United States out of Porto Rico and the Philippines Islands. (Quoted in Raffucci de García 1981, 86)

But it was the Philippines, with its population of ten million, much more than Puerto Rico, with its population of one-tenth that number, that perturbed the empire builders. Congress was loath to establish a constitutional precedent in its treatment of Puerto Rico that would apply to the Philippines. It was resolved to devise different colonial policies for Puerto Rico and the Philippines. Representative Newlands justified this difference on the basis of presumed cultural differences between the two subject populations. He expected Puerto Ricans, unlike the Filipinos, to make obedient colonial subjects. He told Congress that the island "was easily governed, its people friendly and peaceful." Moreover, "we all agree that no great danger to the industrial system of this country can come from the acquisition of Puerto Rico" (quoted in Cabranes 1979, 29).

Representative Sibley expounded on the importance of racial purity and commercial competition:

> The debate upon Puerto Rico is the mere incident in the broader proposition. The issue being determined is whether or not the United States possess the right and have the will to so legislate that the products of the Orient shall not be permitted as a disturbing factor to American production, and that the yellow man of the Orient shall not come here, clothed with the full power of citizenship, to compete upon terms of equality with American labor in our own markets. (Quoted in Gould 1958, 154)

Congress, intensely committed to a policy of tariff protection, and populated by contingents of social Darwinists, was virtually unanimous in its opposition to the territorial incorporation of the Philippines. Its society and its people were considered particularly objectionable to the race-conscious nation. Representative William E. William concisely expressed this view. "I understand full well that the Administration does not care a fig for Puerto Rico"; the Foraker Act is "not for the mere sake of deriving revenue from that island, but as a precedent for our future guidance in the control of the Philippines" (quoted in Torruella 1985, 35–36). Congress decided to use Puerto Rico to test the constitutional issues involved in colonial legislation. Puerto Rico was an experimental station for testing the constitutionality of unprecedented legislation (Capó Rodríguez 1916, 315). Representative Jacob Bromwell summarized the situation, explaining that "in order to show our assertion of authority we must make an example of Porto Rico; and that we are anxious to have a test case made before the Supreme Court to find out just what authority we have in legislating on our new possessions, and that we can use Porto Rico for the purpose" (quoted in Cabranes 1979, 32).

Congress was opposed to granting U.S. citizenship to the Filipinos. To preclude this possibility the U.S. Congress enacted an extraordinary resolution only a week after the signing of the Treaty of Paris. The Senate resolved, "It is not intended to incorporate the inhabitants of the Philippine Islands into citizenship of the United Sates, nor is it intended to permanently annex said islands as an integral part of the territory of the United States" (quoted in Capó Rodríguez 1921, 536). Although the House failed to act on the resolution, it was a clear expression of congressional attitude on the issue of race and annexation. Congress faced the tricky task of devising a constitutionally valid rationale for denying the people of Puerto Rico and the Philippines the rights and privileges accorded to U.S. citizens by the Constitution.

Another dilemma that faced Congress was how to incorporate Puerto Ricans into the Union while denying them representation and a voice in the formulation of policy. Characteristically, the ultranationalist Albert Beveridge addressed the fears of the xenophobes. He blustered that if the Constitution imposed territorial status on the conquered islands, and "they become parts of the United States, with ultimate statehood at the end of the syllogism," then "we had better abandon them at once. Porto Rican, Filipino and Hawaiian Senators and Congressmen are not a refreshing prospect" (quoted in Braeman 1971, 47).

Elihu Root and Charles E. Magoon greatly influenced the colonial legislation that Congress ultimately enacted. In his first annual report Root argued that the Constitution did not place constraints on the authority of Congress to legislate for the territorial possessions, but

> that as between the people of the ceded islands and the United States, the former are subject to the complete sovereignty of the latter, controlled by no legal limitations except those which may be found in the treaty of cession; that the people of the islands have no right to have them treated as States, or to have them treated as the territories previously held by the United States have been treated. (Quoted in Jessup 1938, 1:346–347)

The congressional leadership accepted this argument as the legal basis for excluding the possessions from the full guarantees of the Constitution. Senator Foraker confidently asserted that the Treaty of Paris is part of the supreme law of the land. It is therefore, binding on all concerned. Under this provision of the treaty, the Congress, was, therefore, invested with full power to legislate with respect to these islands and their inhabitants in any way it might see fit, on all subjects affecting their civil and political status, restrained only by the general spirit of our institutions. (Foraker 1900)

Root and others argued that Congress was not legally obligated to extend constitutional guarantees to territories. It thus followed that legislation for the possessions did not have to conform to the uniform taxation clause of the Constitution. ("All Duties, Imports and Excises shall be uniform throughout the United States." See Torruella 1985, 24–35.) Thus Congress could not only impose tariffs on the colonies, it was free to decide what constitutional guarantees it would extend to the colonies. According to Congress, since the Constitution did not follow the flag, Congress had complete plenary powers in dealing with the territories. Having asserted these powers, Congress could arbitrarily determine the type of government it would impose on the inhabitants of the possessions. Foraker argued that Congress could "govern a Territory that simply belongs to the United States as it may think best" (quoted Berbusse 1966, 162). According to Senator Foraker, Puerto Rico was to be a dependency of the United States, but not an integral part of it (Torruella 1985, 37 n. 156). Having disposed of Puerto Rico, Congress was free to legislate as it saw fit for the Philippines, where a full-scale insurrection was under way.

Colonialism Is Constitutional.

In 1901 the Supreme Court decided the constitutionality of the Foraker Act in a series of decisions known as the Insular Cases. The five-to-four vote marked the most extraordinary division of opinion in the history of the Supreme Court (Rowe 1901b, 226). The court was required to determine the extent of constitutional restraint on congressional treatment of the newly acquired territories. In *Downes vs. Bidwell*, one of the most significant Insular Cases, Justice Edward D. White introduced the doctrine of incorporation as a legal instrument to define the constitutional status of the possessions. According to legal scholar Frederic Coudert, the Supreme Court formulated "the theory of incorporation as a definite legal category in classifying territory under American sovereignty" (Coudert 1926, 824). Justice White reasoned that "in all cases of territorial acquisition, except those territories acquired with the ratification of the Treaty of Paris, the treaty of acquisition had specifically provided for incorporation of the territory into the Union for eventual statehood." Since the Treaty of Paris did not specifically provide for territorial incorporation, the Supreme Court ruled that Congress had a constitutional basis to claim its plenary powers over the territories.

Justice White ruled that Puerto Rico "was subject to the sovereignty of, and was owned by, the United States, in a domestic sense, because the island had not been incorporated into the United States, but was merely appurtenant thereto as a possession" (quoted in Snow 1902, 564). Puerto Rico was relegated to the residual category of an unincorporated territorial possession. The Supreme Court established mutually exclusive types of territories—incorporated and nonincorporated territories. The power of Congress to legislate is restricted in incorporated territories, where the Constitution applies in its entirety. In the unincorporated territories, which are possessions, only certain "national" or "fundamental" constitutional provisions applied (Dávila Colón 1979, 605).[2] The politics of colonial rule and the nature of the colonial state were heavily influenced by the Supreme Court decisions. The rulings reaffirmed the War Department's claim that Congress had unrestricted constitutional authority to determine the structure of governance of the new territories, the political and legal rights of colonial peoples, and the nature of their economic relationship to the metropolitan state. The Court asserted, in so many words, that the U.S. state possessed the constitutional authority to impose a system of colonial administration without the consent of the governed for an indeterminate period.

The significance of the rulings was clear: they empowered "the political organs of the government [Congress and the executive branch] to deal with the newly acquired territory in accordance with its requirements" (Rowe 1901b, 249). The Supreme Court upheld Elihu Root's argument on the constitutional issues relating to the territorial possessions. Elated with the rulings, Root interpreted the decision as meaning that "Ye—es as near as I can make out the Constitution follows the flag—but doesn't quite catch up with it" (quoted in Weibe 1967, 228). The decisions and doctrines established by the Insular Cases became central components of the wider U.S. colonial project (Rivera Ramos 1996, 228). In 1902, two years after the Foraker Act was signed into law, and approximately one year after the Supreme Court ruled on the constitutionality of the law, Congress enacted an Organic Law for the Philippines. The system of colonial administration for the Philippines closely resembled the system created for Puerto Rico (Thompson 1989, 167).

Congress had demonstrated the legal acuity to devise a colonial policy for Puerto Rico and the Philippines, which was subsequently declared constitutionally valid by the Supreme Court. A deeply divided Supreme Court gave Congress the constitutional authority to devise colonial policies whose economic and political provisions could be adjusted to respond to the changing requirements of the U.S. state and capital. Puerto Rico was the only territory in which Congress established civilian government without any indication as to its future, either as an independent republic or state of the Union (Trías Monge 1980, 1:232). Deprived of their Spanish citizenship and denied U.S. citizenship, the people of Puerto Rico were converted into an anomalous body politic lacking any identity in international law.

Tariff:
The Overriding Political Issue of the Moment

The Foraker Act represented a partial victory for the protectionists, since it restricted commodity trade between Puerto Rico and the United States. Since the

Civil War, U.S. foreign economic policy had been designed to serve domestic manufacturing and agricultural producers. Virtually all other foreign economic issues
were secondary to the need to protect U.S. farmers and manufacturers by imposing highly protective tariffs (see Frieden 1988). The Republicans argued that the
country's prodigious economic growth after the Civil War was in no small measure due to the highly protectionist policies they had enacted. Notwithstanding its
claims of fidelity to protectionism, Congress had gradually transformed the tariff
from simply an instrument of protection to a policy tool that could be manipulated to promote U.S. exports while continuing to protect the home market (Lake
1988a, 91). Between 1887 and 1897 the Democrats and Republicans pursued the
same trade strategy, aiming to expand exports by removing duties on selected imported Latin American raw materials, although they may have differed on how to
achieve this foreign economic policy objective (Lake 1988b, 117).

But the McKinley administration came under pressure to revise this long-
standing protectionist policy and enact trade concessions (free trade, reciprocity
treaties, duty-free entry of selected commodities, etc.) to stimulate the development of Puerto Rico's export potential. McKinley's decision to endorse immediate incorporation of Puerto Rico into the protected U.S. tariff system, without offering countervailing measures to protect the home industries, provoked the ire
of the sugar beet industry and caused a virtual rebellion by its advocates in the
Republican Party. Many Republicans considered that McKinley had betrayed the
principle of protectionism. Under strong pressure from his party, McKinley was
forced to abandon his free-trade position. The motivations for this reversal had
more to do with unresolved constitutional issues regarding the plenary powers of
Congress to rule the colonies in the interests of the metropolitan state than the
damage to U.S. industry that free trade could presumably inflict.

Why the War Department Wanted Free Trade

San Ciriaco devastated Puerto Rico; its economy was in a shambles and international commerce had collapsed. The coffee industry suffered massive damage.
The Advisory Board of Insular Policy reported to General Davis on August 28,
1898, that the hurricane struck

> just at the moment when the producing classes were undergoing so severe a crisis as
> the consequence to the war, the withdrawal of capital in circulation, and the lack of
> markets wherein to place their principal fruits. It is therefore evident that such dis-
> asters must have reduced the island to the saddest and most pressing circumstances
> to which the life of a country can be subjected. (USDW 1900a, 11)

George Finlay, of the Puerto Rican Chamber of Commerce, testified during the
Foraker Act hearings that, due to the hurricane, "laborers are out of employment,
while families are in misery, and hunger threatens everywhere, the poor farm la-

borers being in such a state of destitution as they never have been before in the history of the island" (quoted in Berbusse 1966, 157).

Puerto Rico's people faced starvation and widespread disease. On August 18, 1899, Elihu Root wrote to McKinley urging immediate free trade: "I see no other recourse, except to see the people starve, for we cannot continue to support them indefinitely." Root warned,

> There is a limit to the extent to which we can feed them with rations ostensibly purchased for the use of the army. The great burst of public beneficence will not last long, and we will find a starving people on our hands very soon—starving because this great, rich country, after inviting the Porto Ricans to place themselves in our hands, refuses to permit them to send their products on our markets without the payment of a practically prohibitory duty. (quoted in Jessup 1938, 1:373)

The War Department needed quick infusions of funds to alleviate the deplorable social and material conditions. General Davis warned, "I can only give food for the hungry. Should the supply fail, there would be a famine such as in the past has swept over and depopulated large districts in India and China." He urgently requested the federal government to authorize a $10 million bridge loan "for aiding the prostrate land" (USDW 1900a, 7–8). Davis reported that "if the trade conditions between this island and the United States remain as at present only industrial paralysis can be expected. . . . American sovereignty for Puerto Rico has so far been disastrous for its commerce . . . for it has deprived the island of markets where were sent nearly one-half of its total output" (USDW 1900b, 32, 34). Davis's own commanders emphasized the urgency of free trade. First Lieutenant Alonzo Gray, commander of the San Germán post, informed Davis, "I can not see that American occupation has as yet done anything to improve these people. Improvement will come only when this island is treated as any of our western territories are and given absolutely free interstate commerce" (USDW 1900b, 324).

Root tried to marshal congressional support for the bridge loan. He asked the Treasury Department to return all the duties collected on goods imported from Puerto Rico after October 18, 1898, the date on which Spanish troops were evacuated. Accordingly, McKinley obtained congressional approval for these duties to "be placed at the disposal of the President to be used for the government now existing." On March 24, 1900, Congress enacted legislation "Refunding Customs Revenue Collected from Porto Rico for the Relief of its Government and People" which released to McKinley the $2,095,455 in duties that had been collected (Berbusse 1966, 150; Gould 1958, 104–105).

This was a temporary device to finance the needs of the colony; a more durable and reliable revenue base was necessary. Root's annual reports and those of General Davis, as well as the findings of the Carroll Commission, document in telling detail the extent of poverty, pauperization, and hunger that afflicted the population. Each recommended free trade as indispensable for alleviating Puerto Rico's dire economic situation (see Richardson 1900). Although he knew that his own party was firmly opposed to free trade, Root argued that the crisis of the Puerto Rican economy and the urgency of financing the colonial administration were extraordinary reasons for eliminating tariffs on merchandise trade.

In his 1899 annual report Root pressed the administration to remove customs duties on Puerto Rican products. He complained that "transfer of the island from Spain to the United States has not resulted in an increase of prosperity, but in the reverse." Under U.S. occupation Puerto Rico had "suffered a recession," and the island was "facing starvation," after having become encircled by the Spanish, Cuban and U.S. tariff barriers (Root 1916, 170). Testimony at the committee hearings reinforced the image of a society on the verge of collapse. From his self-imposed exile in New York, Muñoz Rivera wrote, "We need legislation of this kind to bring prosperity to Porto Rico. Present depressed commercial conditions cannot continue indefinitely without ruining the fairest prospects of this fertile place" (Muñoz Rivera 1899, 1285).

Under these conditions it was virtually impossible to generate revenue to finance the operations of the military government. Senator Foraker informed his colleagues "that many people who have heretofore been wealthy are unable to pay, have no money, and have no credit with which to command money. In other words, direct taxation upon the property in Puerto Rico, about which we have heard so much, is an impossible thing" (quoted in Raffucci de García 1981, 66). The House Ways and Means Committee chair Serano Payne echoed the same concerns: "Taxation would simply have destroyed these [island] industries and would have not have given us any appreciable revenue, no money for schools, no money for highways, no money for anything except the hard, stern realities of governing those people" (quoted in Ringer 1983, 970).

The War Department's barrage of reports on the implications of Puerto Rico's deplorable economic and social conditions for colonial rule gave McKinley a compelling reason to endorse the controversial free trade provision. However, just before Congress began to consider the Foraker Act, McKinley changed his mind and endorsed trade restrictions on Puerto Rico.

Business Reaction to the Free Trade Proposal

The tariff debates focused on the competing interests of the isolationist and expansionist sectors of agricultural capital. The Puerto Rican tariff issue was a foreign economic policy battleground on which the beet-sugar interests and tobacco growers confronted the sugar-refining and tobacco-processing trusts, as the latter pursued an aggressive campaign to achieve oligopolistic control of their industries. Those industries that had been shielded from international economic competition adamantly opposed free trade for Puerto Rico. Agricultural producers for the domestic market decried the free trade provision as a negation of the government's commitment to protect home industry. Sugar beet producers, who had benefited greatly from protectionism, waged a vociferous campaign against free trade. Sugar beet production had increased from 2,203 tons in 1890 to 76,859 tons in 1900–1901, and between 1899 and 1901 alone the industry increased its output by 50 percent (Foner 1972, 637). The industry was rapidly expanding its sales and had absorbed the Louisiana cane sugar industry. The industry's increased share of the domestic market was directly attributable to the highly protectionist Dingley Tariff of 1897 (Eichner 1969).

The tariff, which was enacted by the Republican-controlled Congress in 1897, imposed duties on imported raw sugar and provided countervailing duties against imported sugar subsidized by European governments. It also provided a manufacturing bounty of two cents per pound, and free importation of beet seeds and machinery used in sugar beet refining (Mullins 1964, 188). The Agriculture Department had vigorously encouraged the cultivation of sugar beets and actively promoted domestic consumption of the product, in the hope of diminishing the drain of foreign exchange for imported sugar (Crampton 1899, 276). State legislatures in the Rocky Mountain and Pacific regions also supported the industry by providing bounties and subsidies. The extraordinary protection accorded beet sugar was an indication of the industry's economic vulnerability as well as its political strength.

Despite this support, beet sugar production simply could not keep up with escalating domestic demand. In 1897 the United States still imported about a fourth of the sugar it consumed. U.S. demand for sugar at this time was estimated at two million tons, while domestic production in 1896 amounted to no more than 383,000 tons (Carroll 1899, 60). By 1899 the U.S. consumed two million tons of sugar of the total world production of seven million tons (Crampton 1899, 276). Puerto Rico, Hawaii, Cuba, and the Philippines could make the U.S. totally self-sufficient in sugar. But for this to happen the powerful protectionist lobby had to be appeased.

The Republicans were opposed to the duty-free entry of foreign merchandise and feared that the possessions would pose competitive threats to domestic agriculture. It was widely known, however, that Puerto Rico posed no danger to domestic sugar and tobacco producers, nor did it have the capacity to threaten job loss in the metropolitan economy. Puerto Rican sugar production was estimated at 61,000 tons, of which 35,512 was exported to the United States. Commissioner Carroll observed that "the comparative production of the two countries is at 6 to 1 in favor of the Union." Similarly, Puerto Rican tobacco imports to the United States were valued at only $255,000, while the total value of U.S. tobacco leaf imports amounted to $14.7 million (Carroll 1899, 60). In 1898 the U.S. Treasury Department had reported, "This island being small, its products which may be shipped to the United States will not be of sufficient amount to materially affect the rich producers of our great country" (U.S. Department of the Treasury 1898, 75).

U.S. sugarcane producers agreed that Puerto Rico did not pose a threat to the industry. John Dymond, spokesperson of Louisiana's sugar planters, wrote that, even though Puerto Rico "produces a considerable amount of sugar . . . as compared to the United States these quantities are but insignificant, and their competition with similar products within the limits of the old Union cannot have any very injurious effect" (quoted in García-Muñiz 1996, chap. 2, 3).

Nonetheless, domestic beet sugar growers opposed any preferential trade measures for fear of establishing a precedent for the importation of duty-free commodities from Cuba and the Philippines. Domestic producers and their allies in Congress were convinced that large-scale investments by the sugar and tobacco trusts would eventually convert the possessions into highly efficient export platforms and threaten their control over national markets. At the Congressional hearings Henry Oxnard, president of American Beet Sugar, testified: "What I claim is large investments will go into Puerto Rico in the sugar business as soon as it is found that this immense profit can be made" (quoted in Tugwell 1945, 299 n. 1). Oxnard spoke of "the great injustice to our competing home industries and perhaps to our labor," that free trade with Puerto Rico would cause. True, he agreed that Puerto Rico was not a threat, but he saw "the graver danger lying in Congress setting a precedent for other and far more destructive demands from Cuba and other tropical countries seeking to capture our markets and eventually destroying the production of products at home that we have long fostered" (quoted Luque de Sánchez 1980, 117).

The lobbyists were gaining support in Congress. Senator Foraker, for example, declared," We fear no competition from Puerto Rico . . . but . . . there may come a competition which would be prejudicial (quoted in Torruella 1985, 37). According to Foraker the importation of Puerto Rican duty-free sugar and tobacco "could not prejudicially affect our home industries because the amount is unimportant." But he warned that "it would be more serious with the Philippines" (Foraker 1900, 470). House committee chair Payne was explicit in his support for the domestic producers. Claiming that "the beet-sugar industry has been something of a pet of mine since I have been in Congress," he also admitted that "if they [beet-sugar factories] get incidental protection against the future out of this bill, I am glad of it. Also for cigar manufacturers" (quoted in Ringer 1983, 970).

The forces arrayed against free trade constituted a politically powerful lobbying force that was well entrenched in Congress, as well as in federal and state government agencies. Herbert Myrick, the chairperson of the League of Domestic Producers, demanded denial of duty-free Cuban and Puerto Rican sugar and tobacco, and cautioned the Senate committee against taking away "the farmer's protection while leaving it upon the manufacturer." The league's objective was "to put into the pockets of the farmers, capitalists and laborers of these United States the $100 million now exported annually to pay for imported sugar" (quoted in Berbusse 1966, 158). As Congress was considering the Foraker Act, the League of Domestic Producers spearheaded a drive to establish a national organization of domestic agricultural producers and labor organizations, including the American Cigar Workers Union and the American Federation of Labor that would oppose free trade with the possessions (Gould 1958, 94).

The American Beet Sugar Company and the Standard Beet Sugar Company were the most powerful advocates for tariff restrictions, particularly since they had benefited directly from the Republican-inspired protectionism. The much larger American Beet Sugar was established through mergers and incorporated in 1899, and for over a decade it had competed with the American Sugar Refining Company for control of various regional markets. The American Sugar Refining Company, also known as the Sugar Trust, was formed in 1881 when Henry O. Havemeyer, its aggressive president, successfully engineered a merger of all the major refiners of raw sugarcane.

By 1892 the American Sugar Refining had established a virtual monopoly over the sugar refining industry, and controlled almost 95 percent of the refining capacity in the country (Kirkland 1961, 320). The Sugar Trust was a well-capitalized firm with excessive refining capacity; consequently it was anxious to acquire new sources of raw sugar for processing and sale in the burgeoning U.S. market. Despite its political clout Havemeyer's drive for monopoly control of the domestic sugar market in 1900 was blocked by the beet growers and their supporters in Washington. The bitter competition between these major firms figured prominently in the congressional debates on tariff legislation for Puerto Rico.

For the export-oriented and import-dependent sectors of U.S. capital the possessions represented new markets and sources of cheap raw agricultural imports. These firms challenged the Republican farm bloc representatives in Congress and their steadfast adherence to protectionism. The American Tobacco Company, a giant trust formed in 1890 after the merger of a number of large processing firms, was eager to tap new foreign sources of cheap tobacco. It joined the American Sugar Refining Company in an alliance on behalf of free trade for the possessions. Republican Representative Watson reported that Havemeyer, "in discussing the whole situation was plain and outspoken regarding the position of Porto Rico and the Philippines, and declared that were was no reason in the world why sugars should not be admitted free of duty from these countries" (quoted in Tugwell 1945, 297). The Democrats supported the sugar trusts by offering an amendment to return collected duties "to the persons from whom they were collected," and introduced a resolution for duty-free "entrance of sugar, molasses, and everything entering into the manufacturers of sugars" (quoted in Tugwell 1945, 298).

Joining the sugar and tobacco trusts were the Chamber of Commerce of New York, the Merchants Association of New York, and the New Board of Trade and Transportation. In an effort to marshal industry support for Puerto Rican free trade, Elihu Root had written William Corwine of the Merchants Association to ask that his organization spearhead a letter writing campaign "urging the removal of duties between the United States and Porto Rico" (quoted in Jessup 1938, 375). The New York Chamber of Commerce also enacted a resolution condemning the proposed tariff and orchestrated a letter writing campaign to convince legislators to vote against the measure (Pettus 1900, 640). Rice producers from Louisiana supported free trade, noting the potential for significantly increased exports to Puerto Rico, which in 1895 had imported four million pounds of rice (Berbusse 1966, 155). The merchants endorsed free trade in anticipation that the trusts would undertake large-scale production in Puerto Rico, resulting in increased demand for industrial goods, food, and other commodities necessary to sustain the operations of the plantations and their work force.

At the time the political climate was unfavorable for the free trade cause advocated by the sugar and tobacco trusts. Foraker's comment that the Sugar Trust was "the most unpopular capitalistic combination in the United States," was probably accurate (quoted in Gould 1958, 96). Strong popular opposition to the growth of industrial trusts in the mid-1880s had persuaded Congress to enact the Sherman Anti-Trust Act. The protectionists portrayed the trusts as oligopolistic, relentless in their pursuit of profits, and willing to sacrifice domestic industry and workers' jobs. Lacking a sizable electoral constituency, and opposed by labor, the sugar refiners' base within the state appeared to be tenuous when contrasted with the domestic beet sugar producers. Moreover, McKinley had faced a virtual revolt by a group of ten Republican senators who tried to break ranks with their colleagues.

Among the dissidents was none other than the irascible Albert Beveridge, who had initially supported the tariff provisions. But after a deluge of letters from constituents and newspaper editorials attacking the tariff on Puerto Rico, he reversed himself and on March 19, 1900, introduced an amendment calling for the removal of all duties. Beveridge argued that tariff restrictions were unnecessary since the $2,000,000 in collected duties that were being returned to Puerto Rico could be used to finance the costs of the colonial administration until a system of insular taxation could be established (Braeman 1971, 48). The issue of the Constitution's applicability to the possessions could be suspended, he argued, with a declaratory provision "that his act shall not be construed as extending the Constitution of the United States, or any part thereof, over Porto Rico" (quoted in Bowers 1932, 127). Beveridge, however, was compelled by his colleagues to close ranks and supported the final version of the Foraker Act. It took intense administration pressure to get the bill through that chamber.

After highly charged debates Congress imposed a tariff on merchandise trade with Puerto Rico. In order to deny Puerto Rican products duty-free entry to the United States, Congress was required to exclude Puerto Rico from the uniformity clause of the Constitution, which mandates that all "duties shall be uniform throughout the United States." Given the United States' determination to deny Puerto Rico either independence or incorporation as a state, the country's exclusion from the uniformity clause—thus, denial of free trade status—was used as the basis to limit the extension of constitutional guarantees to Puerto Rico, and eventually to the Philippines. The tariff issue was the wedge to "legally" impose colonialism. According to Senate minority leader Bacon of Georgia, "Every feature of a free territorial government has been sacrificed in order that a tariff may be enforced against Porto Rico" (quoted in Gould 1958, 77).

In the end, by approving trade restrictions against Puerto Rico McKinley chose to publicly reaffirm the protectionist foreign economic policy the Republicans had pursed since the end of the Civil War. The U.S. Tariff Commission characterized the tariff policy that Congress ultimately adopted at the time as "framed primarily for the purpose of protecting the domestic manufacturer in the home market" and "colonies for the purpose of holding the colonial market for the producers of the mother country" (quoted in Foreign Policy Association 1929, 453 n. 96).

The Tariff and Restructuring of Corporate Capital

By the late 1890s, as foreign markets became increasingly important to manufacturers, the post-Civil War national consensus on protectionism began to gradually erode. The United States was determined to increase its level of trade with Latin America and arranged reciprocity treaties that reduced or eliminated tariffs on a variety of raw material imports in order to gain commercial access to the region.

The conflict between the import-dependent sugar trusts and the agricultural producers for the domestic market was surfacing precisely at the time the U.S. state was under growing pressure to reconsider its commitment to protectionism. The Foraker Act was an important early legislative battle in which the state's nascent foreign economic concerns were challenged by the protectionist demands of domestic producers and their congressional allies. Although only a limited number of industries would be directly and immediately affected by the decision on the Puerto Rican tariff issue, for U.S. capital in general the outcome was important. The relationship between changing protectionist tariff policy and shrinking the industrial surplus was underscored in Theodore Roosevelt's special message to Congress:

> The phenomenal growth of our export trade emphasizes the urgency of the need for wider markets and for a liberal policy in dealing with foreign nations. The customers to whom we dispose of our surplus products in the long run, directly or indirectly, purchase those surplus products by giving us something in return. Their ability to purchase our products should as far as possible be secured by so arranging our tariff as to enable us to take from them those products which we can use without harm to our own industries and labor. (*Cong. Rec.* 1901, 84)

At the turn of the century U.S. industry was developing at a rate that would soon make it a global economic force. Rising labor productivity, broad application of new productive technologies, excess capacity in a range of agricultural products, and the growing international competitiveness of U.S. manufacturing firms created possibilities for new export markets. But the tariff was an impediment to increased trade. According to manufacturers, U.S. tariff policy amounted to a tax on imported raw materials that were required for U.S. manufactured products (Campbell 1976, 144). During the congressional debates Senator Foraker had resurrected the old expansionist argument to support his tariff position: "We have reached that point in the development of our resources, in the aggregation of capital and in the command of skilled labor where we are producing many millions in value beyond what we are able to consume. For this surplus we must find markets abroad" (Foraker 1900, 470).

The idea that the country's economic growth was contingent on opening up foreign markets, tapping new sources of raw materials, and international lending had become the expansionists' credo. However, expansion into the international economy posed risks for those sectors of domestic capital that were not competitive, and the resulting conflict required a state that could effectively negotiate the competing interests of the U.S. capitalist class. Congress's decision on the Puerto Rican tariff issue not only evinced the political influence of both of the competing sectors, but demonstrated the state's ability to accommodate the antipodal requirements of U.S. business.

Financing Their Own Subordination

Congress, faced with the need to finance the operation of the colony, decided to impose tariffs on Puerto Rican merchandise trade as a temporary revenue-generating measure. Congress heeded Chester Long's advice and refused to authorize the use of federal funds for this purpose. Senator Long of Kansas emphasized the responsibility of the colonial subjects to finance the activities of the colonial regime:

> Revenues must be obtained from some source to pay the expenses of government and provide schools for a people nine-tenths of whom cannot read or write. . . . We should not pay the expenses of government out of the United States Treasury. Porto Rico should be self-supporting . . . and all the gross revenues collected here on her products are to be expended for the benefit of the people of the island. (Long 1900, 1)

The imposition of the tariff between Puerto Rico and the United States threatened to further intensify the island's economic difficulties. General Davis opposed the tariff and was convinced that free trade would promote economic growth. In his 1899 report on industrial conditions, he argued:

> If this island could have free trade with the United States, not much more in the way of financial help would be needed. It would set all the wheels of industry in motion, for the margin of profit on sugar and tobacco would then be large enough to justify foreign capital to come here, and it would come in large sums. This would give employment to labor, and the future of the island being assured. (USDW 1900a, 9)

However, Senator Foraker strongly opposed free trade. Since Puerto Rico was destitute, he argued that "a direct tax on property, which is the usual way of raising revenue to defray the expenses of local government, would be a great and impossible burden for these people" (Foraker 1900, 465).

Charles Allen, Puerto Rico's first governor, reported that all government expenses "must be compassed within the sources of revenue provided for in the organic act without the American treasury to rely upon to make up any deficiency (Wood, Taft, and Allen 1902, 340). The salaries for all colonial officials appointed by the metropolitan state were also to be paid from taxes and collected import duties.

The Organic Act of 1900, also known as the Foraker Act, was passed in the Senate on April 3, 1900, by a vote of 40 to 31, and in the House on April 11 by a vote of 161 to 153. President McKinley signed the bill into law on April 12. Section 3 of the Foraker Act imposed a duty of 15 percent of the prevailing rates set by the Dingley Tariff Act on all merchandise trade between the United States and Puerto Rico. The 15 percent duty was actually a compromise recommended by General Davis to his superiors in the War Department (Root 1916, 182). The House Ways and Means Committee had proposed a higher duty of 25 percent, but the public outcry convinced McKinley to pressure the committee into accepting the lower duty.

In addition, the Foraker Act imposed a tax on "articles of merchandise of Puerto Rican manufacture . . . equal to the internal revenue tax imposed in the United States upon like articles of merchandise of domestic manufacture." The House committee argued that this "provision is necessary in order that our manufacturing of cigars and spirits may be at no disadvantage on account of the low tariff between Puerto Rico and the United States, on account of our internal revenue laws" (quoted in Ringer 1983, 962). The duties collected on these imported products were transferred to the treasury of Puerto Rico. Once a revenue system was put into effect, the 15 percent tariff would be eliminated and free trade established, but no later than March 1, 1902.

In another concession to domestic industries, the Foraker Act mandated that all merchandise trade between the two countries be conveyed in U.S.-built and -registered ships. This mandate was for the benefit of the U.S. merchant marine, which had experienced a dramatic decline in its share of foreign trade tonnage. In 1897 U.S.-registered ships carried only 15 percent of the value of imports and 8.1 percent of the value of exports (Kirkland 1961, 296). This provision was included even though the administration was aware that because of higher wages and costs U.S. maritime shippers could not "compete on equal terms with foreign ships" (Root 1917, 260) The tariff on Puerto Rico was widely reported as an unqualified victory for the protectionist forces and the farm bloc. The *Independent* reported, "The interests represented by the sugar and tobacco spokesmen are power interests, and we are told that the force of the pressure of these interests in Washington was irresistible" (*Independent* 1900, 560). Representative Richardson wrote in the *Independent*: "The bill breaks our faith with Porto Rico and oppresses the people of that island for the purpose of enriching some citizens of the

United States. I earnestly protest against the adoption of a robber policy which makes this Republic take the place of the ruthless monarchy, Spain, in despoiling Porto Rico, now a portion of the United States" (Richardson 1900, 469).

McKinley was accused of buckling under the pressure of ultraprotectionists led by sugar beet and tobacco growers. He was ridiculed in the press, and suspicions were rife that the trusts had applied improper influence (Braeman 1971, 47–48). Presidential aspirant William Jennings Bryan warned, "To impose upon the people of Puerto Rico such taxes as Congress may determine when the people of Puerto Rico have no representative in Congress is to assert either that taxation without representation is right, or that it is wise for us to do wrong" (Bryan 1900, 62). On his nomination to the presidency, Bryan told the assembled delegates, "The Porto Rico tariff law asserts the doctrine that the operation of the Constitution is confined to the forty-five states." He "denounced it as repugnant" to the spirit of the U.S. Constitution (Bryan 1900, 79). Puerto Ricans were bitterly disappointed, and their reaction was equally as ardent. Azel Ames, an army major and medical doctor who was hired by the Federal Party as a lobbyist, passionately argued that given the country's economic distress, the tariff "was a refinement of cruelty. . . . There are no words in the English language sufficiently virile and comprehensive to adequately characterize such cold-blooded and perfidious indifference" (Ames 1900, 639).

The McKinley administration warned a wary Congress that in the absence of free trade, U.S. business would not invest in Puerto Rico and conditions would continue to deteriorate. Philip C. Hanna, the U.S. consul to Puerto Rico, wrote his superiors, "Hundreds of Americans representing millions of capital are waiting for the duty to be taken off American products." He was certain that once free trade was permitted, investments would flow, giving "employment to tens of thousands of the working class in Puerto Rico" (quoted in Ramos Mattei 1974, 20). The imposition of customs duties on commodity trade discouraged investments. Hanna testified at the Carroll Commission hearings:

> During the past two months I have received several thousand letters from all classes of business men in all parts of the United States concerning this island, very many of them asking me when the proper time will arrive for them to invest capital in Porto Rico. . . . But with the present high rates of duty upon all building material, machinery and all kinds of goods coming from the United States to Porto Rico, it would be impossible for these men to establish their factories here for the benefit of and the uplifting of the Porto Rican laborer. (U.S. Department of the Treasury 1898, 76)

Despite accusations that McKinley had capitulated to the ultraprotectionists, the American Sugar Refining Company and other import-dependent firms obtained significant benefits from the Foraker Act. The tariff was only moderately protectionist, and it was temporary. All import duties, except for those products subject to U.S. internal revenue, were to be eliminated within two years. The 15 percent duty actually made Puerto Rican sugar imports much more profitable than foreign imports and stimulated investments by U.S. sugar corporations. Notwithstanding accusations that McKinley gave in to the protectionists, the tariff provision was in fact a concession to the import-dependent sectors of capital—primarily the sugar and tobacco trusts.

The Foraker Act was also a victory for domestic producers, because it established the principle of politics over law. By asserting its plenary powers Congress could decide on a case-by-case basis the trading policy it would enact for the possessions. Congress had given the protectionist forces, who at the time were an immensely powerful lobbying force, an arena in which they could influence the policy process. This kind of arena is, after all, what they had wanted.

Puerto Rico and U.S.
Commercial Policy in Latin America

The War Department advocated free trade for Puerto Rico for a number of reasons that went beyond the urgency of the moment. The fiscal, monetary, and tariff measures put into effect constituted an integrated program to generate long-term revenues with the goal of making the colony self-financing. Unrestricted commercial relations —free trade—between the possessions and the metropolis was a pivotal component of this program. But colonial economic policy embodied a complex of ideas, some particular to the specific conditions of Puerto Rico and others emanating from the state's emerging role in promoting U.S. global investments and trade.

During this period the foreign policy machinery of the state was led by President McKinley, Secretary of War Root, and Secretary of State John Hay, individuals whom historian Thomas McCormick called "nondoctrinaire sorts . . . pragmatic expansionists . . . [who] followed the commonsense, businessman's approach to expansion—what would work best with the least cost" (McCormick 1962, 150). All three wanted to significantly expand U.S. commercial influence in the hemisphere; they promoted liberal trade relations, reciprocity, and receptivity to U.S. investors. As a key foreign policy adviser to Presidents McKinley and Roosevelt, Root played an especially influential role in advancing U.S. regional and global interests. In 1905, Root, who had by then been appointed secretary of state after Hay's death, articulated the need for commercial penetration of Latin American and Caribbean markets, backed by the ready use of military and naval force to protect the interests of U.S. investors and to compel governments in the region to honor their commercial obligations. He sought to impose stability and peace in the Caribbean through the application of the norms of international law and U.S. military power (Healy 1970, 70). He wrote, "The inevitable effect of our building the Canal must be to require us to police the surrounding premises. In the nature of things, trade and control, and the obligations to keep order which go with them, must come our way" (quoted in Jessup 1938, 1:371). Paul Reinsch summarized the doctrine that Root used to steer U.S. policy in the region: "The world must be policed, so that in every part of it investments of capital may be made securely, and so that industrial works may be carried on without annoyance or molestation from natives" (Reinsch 1900, 11).

Building and protecting an integrated system of coaling, cable, and naval bases was an essential corollary in U.S. designs to achieve commercial penetration and military dominance of the hemisphere. Puerto Rico and Cuba, because of their potential significance to the proposed Panama canal, were the two most important strategic outposts in the system of regional communications the United States was building. It fell on the War Department to create a model of colonial governance and economic relations that would firmly establish U.S. control over the newly acquired territories and impose the requisite social and political order.

Colonial economic policy is best understood in the context of a new metropolitan state role in responding to the demands of capitalist restructuring and commercial expansion. In *Corporate Reconstruction of American Capitalism*, Martin Sklar establishes that "capitalist investment imperialism" was a key feature of the reorganization of the U.S. economy at the turn of the century (1988). This phase of capitalist development required new financial institutions and international treaties and agreements. In 1898 the State Department reported that the "enlargement of foreign consumption of the products of our mills and workshops has, therefore, become a serious problem of statesmanship as well as commerce" (quoted in Rosenberg 1993, 40). The United States negotiated agreements or imposed requirements that tied "the host societies' monetary and banking system into the international monetary, banking and investment system." This was necessary in order to facilitate and protect the circulation of financial capital (Sklar 1988, 81). The imperatives of investment capitalism redefined the role of the U.S. state in international economic affairs and compelled the metropolitan state to intervene directly and/or diplomatically in the internal affairs of countries that loomed as potentially profitable investment sites for U.S. business.

The logic of state-promoted capitalist development shaped the formation of U.S. colonial and territorial policy as well. According to Sklar, investment imperialism

> required modernizing the host government's fiscal, budgetary and taxation systems, the host society's laws of property and contract along with its judicial administration, the host society's class structure in the direction of commoditization of land and the creation of a wage earning working class. It required the introduction and spread of secular and instrumental modes of consciousness at the expense of religious and traditionalist modes, through the institutions of education, media of communication, and otherwise. (81)

Sklar enumerates precisely those institutional changes specified in the Foraker Act. Robert Weibe, in his study of changing U.S. political and social values, makes a similar point. He maintains that U.S. investors demanded political stability, which invariably drew the metropolitan state deeply into the affairs of other countries and required its uninterrupted support (Weibe 1967, 235, 232). The political, financial, and diplomatic characteristics of the U.S. state's colonial and neocolonial policy, as well as its project for commercial and financial expansion into Latin America, were mediated by the requirements of this new phase of U.S. capitalism—investment imperialism.

The War Department was the agency responsible for developing political and economic institutions that would impose stability and convert Puerto Rico into a hospitable investment site. Elihu Root was unequivocal about the country's ability to undertake this task: "We of America, have discovered that we, too, possess the supreme governing capacity, capacity not merely to govern ourselves at home, but that great power that in all ages has made the difference between the great and the small nations, the capacity to govern men wherever they were found" (quoted in Healy 1970, 148). Root, who bore ultimate responsibility for colonial affairs, envisioned U.S. firms, especially large-scale enterprises, being agents for economic development. Opportunities for U.S. investors abounded in Puerto Rico, given the dearth of domestic sources of capital and the destruction of its agricultural resources and infrastructure caused by the hurricane. Free trade, the War Department reasoned, would be the catalyst for major investments. U.S. firms would create employment, generate revenues, and improve social conditions, which in turn would contribute to stable management of the colony. Under the rhetoric of the free-trade ideology, the War Department fostered U.S. corporate dominance of the colonial economy, which resulted in Puerto Rico's inextricable incorporation into the metropolitan economy. This logic prevailed for the other colonies as well (for example see Healy 1963, 189–206; May 1980, 129–178).

Regional Hegemony and
Puerto Rico's Colonial Status

Puerto Rico's economic importance to the metropolitan economy as a whole, as opposed to particular sectors, was marginal. Of greater significance was the effect that a successful model of colonial governance and economic growth would have on U.S. hemispheric designs. Commissioner Rowe succinctly identified the significance of the colonial experiment in Puerto Rico: "In the solution of the Porto Rican problem we are being subjected to a supreme test as an expanding nation. If we fail, our influence in the Western Hemisphere cannot long continue; if we succeed, our position of primacy will receive the sanction of every American country, and the Monroe Doctrine will acquire a new significance" (Rowe 1901a, 39).

A few years later Rowe reaffirmed the importance of Puerto Rico to U.S. imperial designs. "The real significance of the extension of the American dominion in the West Indies," he wrote, "lies not so much in the fact of territorial aggrandizement as in the adaptation of our political ideas and standards which this expansion involves" (Rowe 1904, 18). Another official appreciated the regional ramifications of a successful colonial policy: "If our efforts to regenerate Cuba and Porto Rico . . . are found to be fairly successful . . . its results will become an object lesson to other Spanish-American countries Our sphere of influence will become more potent in Spanish America" (Fisher 1899, 24).

The reform of Puerto Rico's fiscal, monetary, and budgetary systems was well under way before the Foraker Act became law. The Act made these measures permanent and expanded the investment prospect accorded foreign capital. At the inauguration of Puerto Rico's first appointed civilian governor General Davis extolled the economic benefits the Foraker Act would bestow on the country, "The Organic Act under which this island will be governed provides a basis for industry, trade and commerce which warrants the belief that the dark clouds of misery and want which have shadowed the past and the present will soon roll away" (USDS 1901, 414). The goal of the economic changes was Puerto Rico's incorporation into the metropolitan network of investment, trade and finance. William Willoughby, who served as secretary of state and the treasury in Puerto Rico, asserted with almost religious fervor the importance of monetary conversion to achieve this integration. "Were no other effect obtained than the moral one of identifying more closely the economic systems of the island and the mother country, the step could be considered as fully justified" (Willoughby 1905, 115). Such a fusion of financial, monetary, and commercial institutions would not only result in more efficient economic relations, but would also facilitate the task of "Americanizing" the colony.

Colonial planners were convinced that U.S. men of business would promote economic development, Americanization, and social stability. Commissioner Carroll observed that Puerto Rico "will furnish a field for American capital and American enterprise, if not for overflow of population. It is American and must and will be Americanized" (Carroll 1899, 61). Indeed, stability was essential for sustaining investment. According to Senator Morgan the possessions were a "new and inviting field for conquest and dominion, but no compulsion will be needed to hold it, beyond the temporary necessity of preserving peace in these islands, until the rightful government of their people can be established on safe foundations" (Morgan 1898, 649). By absorbing Puerto Rico into the metropolitan economy and investing it with the norms and values of the U.S. business culture, colonial officials hoped to transform Puerto Ricans into "Americans." Philip Hanna wrote to his superiors, that "I believe in making Porto Rico as thoroughly American as possible from the very start" (U.S. Department of the Treasury 1898, 75).

Profit-generating fiscal and monetary measures alone would not materially stimulate U.S. investments. Only free trade between the United States and Puerto Rico, in combination with the other measures, would yield the permanent subordination of the colony's human and natural resources to the necessities of the metropolitan state and capital. With Puerto Rico behind the U.S. tariff walls and serving as a market for U.S. manufactures and supplier of cheap food exports, it would be utterly reliant on U.S. markets and capital. Political independence became less likely under these circumstances.

Promoting the Sugar Industry

Immediately after the signing of the armistice Puerto Rico's commercial possibilities became a subject of increasing interest. The Bureau of Statistics reported a high volume of inquiries from the major manufacturing centers about Puerto Rican and Cuban imports, and the Department of State reported that many business firms had written urging the annexation of Puerto Rico, "for it was a garden, capable of contributing greatly to U.S. commerce" (quoted in Pratt 1939, 277, 275 n. 111). Travel writers, such as William Dinwiddie, Frederick Ober, and others, did much to popularize the new Caribbean possessions. "Puerto Rico," Ober informed his readers, "is not only a valuable property for us as a national entity, but a potentially lucrative investment." According to Ober, Cuba and Puerto Rico could satisfy U.S. demand for tropical produce. He told his readers that "the people of these islands manufacture next to nothing . . . and will look to us . . . for everything necessary for civilized communities" (Dinwiddie 1899; Halstead 1899; Ober 1899, 7, 2; see also Solomon 1898).

The McKinley administration promoted Puerto Rico as an important site for sugar production. In 1899 the War Department reported that sugar yield per acre was greater in Puerto Rico "than in any country except Hawaii and Java, but the costs in Puerto Rico" were the cheapest in the world (USDS 1901, 39). General Davis advised Root that with preferential tariff treatment sugar growers could be "as rich and prosperous as are now the Hawaiian planters" (USDW 1900a, 33). He added, "So long as the market of the United State is free to Porto Rican products and is heavily taxed for foreign products, cane-growing and sugar making will prosper and continue to increase in magnitude until all the land suited to cane is farmed" (quoted in Forbes-Lindsay 1906, 137). Charles Crampton, writing in the widely read *North American Review*, also instructed his readers about the importance of the tropical sugar industry:

> The commodity of which we stand most in need is produced in the greatest abundance in the new possessions; it is only necessary to stimulate the production of sugar in the colonies to the point of supplying our needs, and the entire amount of our expenditure for this food product, instead of going to Germany, Austria and France, as at present, will flow into Cuba, Porto Rico, and the Philippines, bringing back the equivalent in trade for our exports. (Crampton 1899, 277)

According to Crampton, "The solution of the problem of successful colonial expansion by the United States will be found in the rehabilitation and development of the tropical sugar industry" (275). Six years later Forbes-Lindsay, a well-known author who specialized in the study of U.S. and British colonial possessions, predicted that Hawaii, Puerto Rico, and the Philippines "should in time be able to supply American with all the sugar she needs to import" (Forbes-Lindsay 1906, 140). While Puerto Rico had "a superabundance of labor" and ample natural resources "so great . . . that the inhabitants can . . . exist without any remuneration," the country lacked the capital to develop industrially (USDW 1900b, 36). The islands were portrayed as well stocked with labor and untapped natural resources waiting to be utilized by the sober entrepreneurs from the North. Franklin Giddings, Columbia University professor and adviser to the U.S. government, observed,

> The product of the tropics is insignificant in comparison with what it may become under the more intelligent direction of the white races. Either the tropics must be held by the northern nations as plantations . . . or they must be held as territorial possessions, to be governed firmly, in the interest of both the world at large and of their own native inhabitants. (Giddings 1898, 600)

The campaign to develop the tropics was imbued with a moralism and social Darwinism that resonated with the military's understanding of the empire's colonizing mission. According to Captain Macomb, one of General Davis's district commanding officers, "The future of the island is bright, with its rich soil and salubrious climate. But until Americans, with their ideas, energy and capital invade the island, any decided change will come very slowly" (USDW 1899a, 82). Major Crampton wrote of the technical superiority of "the energetic race" from temperate zones: "When the ingenuity and push of the American nation are added to the natural advantages possessed by the tropical plant [over beet sugar], there will be formed a combination which will indeed be hard to beat" (1899, 280).

The theme of exploiting the possessions in order to bestow on them the benefits of civilization permeated much of the popular and academic literature in the period leading up to the war. Benjamin Kidd, in a highly influential work, made the case against a U.S. policy of colonial settlement. The United States could not colonize the possessions, since "the white races can never be acclimatized in the tropics . . . they must be permanently peopled by their natural inhabitants." Their economic potential could nonetheless be realized, if governed "from a base in the temperate zone," that is, the United States. According to Kidd, "under the proper conditions of administration," the production would be far greater in the tropics than in the temperate regions. Colonial administration to extract surplus was perceived by Kidd and his ilk as a duty of the United States. He intoned, "The highest duty of the civilized power that undertakes this responsibility . . . is to see that they [the natural inhabitants] shall be governed as a trust for civilization" (Kidd 1898, 725–726). E. L. Godkin, editor of the *Nation*, wrote effusively on the civilizing mission of the United States: "We are bursting today with good intentions, but what calls for our whole thought is not the means of holding our colonies, but the means of governing them for their own benefit" (Godkin 1899, 190).

According to War Department officials, the lack of investments was the most acute problem afflicting Puerto Rico's economy. Davis felt that "the only available remedy for the industrial condition [in Puerto Rico] . . . is the opening of markets for the accumulated surplus of production [of the United States]" (quoted in Gould 1958, 103). Similarly, Leo S. Rowe emphasized that "the progress of the island depends upon the influx of American capital," noting the need for large investments of capital by corporations (Rowe 1904, 163). Another policy adviser, Paul Reinsch, argued for a colonial economic policy specifically for the possessions: "A tropical country has no use for protective policy, it needs untrammeled trade. It needs a liberal labor supply, large territorial grants for plantation purposes, and before all, systems of communication with the interior" (Reinsch 1908, 951)

While Root fought hard for free trade for Puerto Rico, he was much more concerned with developing the revenue base necessary to put the colony on a firm financial footing. This he was able to achieve. Congress's major concession to the War Department and the Sugar Trust was to exclude raw sugar imports from customs duties. The effect of this decision was to convert Puerto Rico into an immensely profitable investment site for sugar corporations. Given that the market price for all sugar imports from foreign countries was set at the duty price, Puerto Rican sugar producers were in effect given a significant bounty, "for what was revenue to the American Government in the case of duty-paid sugar was an added price to the Porto Rican product with its duty free privilege" (Sloan 1929, 995). The immediate effect of the tariff provisions was to dramatically increase the profit potential of sugar production and convert the commodity into Puerto Rico's most valuable export. According to General Davis, the Foraker Act included provisions so that "every pound of sugar produced here will find a purchaser at a price more than 50% greater than was possible under former conditions" (414).

Given the tariff on Cuban sugar imports to the United States in effect at the time, Puerto Rico became a far more attractive investment site than its erstwhile competitor. Moreover, in 1900 Congress was undecided on how to proceed with McKinley's recommendation for trade reciprocity for Cuba, and the militantly protectionist domestic sugar beet industry promised to wage a bitter campaign to defeat the recommendations (Jessup 1938, 1:327). Elihu Root actively campaigned for reciprocity for Cuban sugar, as he had for free trade for Puerto Rico, and ultimately prevailed over the protectionist forces in Congress. But by the time the Cuban reciprocity treaty went into effect on March 31, 1903, some U.S. companies had been exporting duty-free Puerto Rican sugar to the United States for almost three years and were firmly implanted in the local economy.

The War Department played a critical role in promoting U.S. investments in Puerto Rico; in particular it was eager to assist in developing the sugar industry. A vibrant, functioning insular sugar industry under U.S. corporate ownership and management made commercial sense given the prevailing market conditions. The U.S. economy, highly reliant as it was on foreign sugar suppliers, not only expended foreign exchange to purchase sugar, but was susceptible to the vagaries of international trade and tariff politics. U.S. corporate dependence on European finance capital for much of the post-Civil War industrialization only increased the desire to dampen the economy's reliance on Britain, France, and Germany. It did not require an economist to appreciate that expenditures of over $100 million annually for sugar and $250 million for "purely tropical products" represented a substantial drain of U.S. resources (Ober 1899, 1–2). Sugar constituted the largest single import item, on which the United States expended over $80 million annually (Crampton 1899, 276). Permanent sources of sugar controlled by U.S. corporations would clearly make the country a stronger hemispheric economic and political actor. By annexing Puerto Rico, the Philippines, and Hawaii, and by establishing neocolonial control of Cuba, the United States acquired a diversified group of suppliers, which reduced the risk that natural disasters, plant disease, labor militancy, or political instability would halt the supply of sugar.

From the perspective of the U.S. sugar-refining industry, particularly the American Sugar Refining Company, the extracontinental sources of raw sugar were vital for its continued expansion. The American Sugar Refining Country relied heavily on European beet sugar imports. The sugar-producing possessions could be potentially limitless suppliers of raw cane sugar. With access to cheap Caribbean raw sugar, the American Sugar Refining Company could overwhelm the beet-sugar industry and eradicate this pesky competitor. With its dominant control of the local market, ample financial assets, access to credit markets, and international network of commercial relations, the Trust was ideally situated to maximally benefit from free trade with the insular territorial possessions. Moreover, to the extent that it could supply rapidly escalating domestic demand for refined sugar, Havemeyer's conglomerate served the foreign economic policy goals of reducing U.S. reliance on foreign, and potentially unpredictable, raw sugar supplies.

Although Havemeyer was much more interested in preferential trading arrangements with Cuba, his company was well poised to benefit quickly from duty-free Puerto Rican sugar. The country offered cheap and abundant sources of labor, accessible and affordable land, and an established sugarcane culture that could be easily adapted to more advanced methods of capitalist production and organization. The United States offered a massive market, excess refining capacity, and a well-developed distribution network. What was missing in this calculus was the institutional and profit-making context to encourage investors to develop Puerto Rico's sugar industry. It was in this arena that the War Department could make its contribution.

The War Department and American Sugar Refining confronted the organized political power of the sugar beet producers and their congressional representatives. Elihu Root was no stranger to the U.S. sugar industry. He was an influential corporate attorney, and much of his practice consisted of organizing and representing trusts and holding companies. On behalf of his clients Root fought reformist politicians and organizations that wanted to regulate and break up the trusts (May 1980, 5). In 1880 Root had been retained by the Havemeyers, who, according to Root's biographer, "as lords of the sugar trust, long continued to be his clients" (Jessup 1938, 1:132). The War Department saw its role as an agent for change, and it was willing to promote the interests of those sectors of national capital whose own profit aspirations were in harmony with the policy objectives of the state. The sugar beet industry, highly protectionist and reliant on direct state assistance for its growth, posed a threat to the colonial policy the department sought to devise. For this reason Root wrote that he fought the sugar beet industry "up and down the line . . . by every means at his disposal" (quoted in Jessup 1938, 1:327).

General Davis's early reports on economic conditions emphasized the country's potential for developing into a major sugar producer. Similarly, the Sherman and Carroll commissions noted Puerto Rico's enormous possibilities. Throughout the early years of U.S. rule, the colonial administration maintained that successful and efficient sugar production required massive investments that only large corporations were capable of making. "The manufacture of sugar can be undertaken profitably only by capitalists and on a large scale with modern machinery," according to Puerto Rico's secretary of state (Puerto Rico, Office of the Secretary 1905, 13). General Davis, special commissioners, and subsequent governors emphasized that modern sugar production required heavy investments (technologically sophisticated refining mills, railroads to link suppliers to refiners, extensive system of irrigation works, fertilizers, ports, and warehouses) well beyond the capacity of the Puerto Rican capitalist class to provide. General Davis exhibited considerable understanding of the requirements and impact of sugar corporate investments on Puerto Rico's economy and society. According to Davis, only through combines and trusts could sugar be produced at a profit. He was convinced that

> the cane lands will ultimately be owned or practically controlled by these huge "central" proprietors. There will be a few thousand owners, managers, overseers, clerks, etc., and many hundreds of thousands of peon laborers, whose social . . . conditions will be . . . without hope of improvement. The people will still remain in a state of serfdom, and generation after generation, living in fief to a merchant monopoly. (USDW 1900b, 38)

Three other provisions of the Foraker Act were designed to provide the colonial administration with the decisionmaking power to promote direct investments. These provisions pertained to corporate landholdings, the authority of the colonial administration to issue franchises for construction and exploitation of natural resources, and the application of U.S. internal revenue laws to Puerto Rico. The first two provisions were amendments to the original legislation and were enacted before the Foraker Act took effect.

Attempts to Control the Monopolies

Before the Foraker Act went into effect President McKinley requested a change in the law to permit military officers to retain their commissions while they continued to occupy administrative posts in the colonial administration. This request provided the Democrats with the opportunity to rescind two particularly obnoxious provisions in the Foraker Act. The Democrats wanted to impose limitations on the size of corporate landholdings and to rescind the governor's power to grant franchises for public works.

The Democrats claimed that "for months representatives of great railroads, telegraph, and other corporations have been besieging Congress to grant them the most valuable concessions of the island" (quoted in Raffucci de García 1981, 102). They warned that "organized capital would own everything of value" and would reduce the condition of the population "to absolute servitude" (quoted Ringer 1983, 148). Democrats decried the governor's power to grant franchises as the most obnoxious feature of the act because "it puts in the hands of a carpet-bag governor, the power to grant and dispose of all franchises and public privileges . . . and yet they are not responsible to the people of Puerto Rico. What a field of bribery and corruption" (quoted in Raffucci de García 1981, 100).

The national press, which also had overwhelmingly supported free trade for Puerto Rico, endorsed the limitations on corporate landholdings and restrictions on the granting of franchises. Under a vociferous Democratic attack the Foraker Act was amended to require the president's approval for franchises for railroads, street cars, and telegraph and telephone systems. The governor was given the authority to issue all other franchises. Congress also mandated that corporations engaged in agriculture revise their charters to include a clause restricting land ownership to five hundred acres. According to Rexford Tugwell, who served as governor of Puerto Rico in the 1940s, this provision was pushed by lobbyists and legislators from the sugar-producing states to impede "the development of a vigorous sugar industry which could compete with that of the continent" (quoted in Rosenn 1963, 336). The War Department opposed the 500-acre limitations on corporate landholdings. The limitations on corporate landholdings and restraints on franchises did not discourage sugar and tobacco corporations from investing in Puerto Rico. The 500-acre limit was so seriously flawed as to render it ineffective in preventing the sugar corporations from acquiring vast landholdings. The law did not prohibit other organizational arrangements, such as proprietorships and partnerships, which allowed corporations to acquire vast holdings under one management unit. Moreover, Congress had chosen not to establish a federal agency to enforce compliance with the law (see Rosenn 1963).

The Foraker Act exempted Puerto Rico from U.S. internal revenue laws, reserving for the colonial administration the power to levy and collect taxes. According to J. H. Hollander, the finance expert hired by Root to revise Puerto Rico's tax laws, General Davis was "instrumental in securing the insertion" in the Foraker Act exempting Puerto Rico from U.S. internal revenue laws, and "thus leaving the way clear for a system of insular excise taxes" (Hollander 1901, 559). This provision was required because Congress, having chosen to exclude Puerto Rico from the uniformity clause of the Constitution, could not extend federal revenue laws to the possessions. In the absence of specific legislation, the profits of U.S. corporations operating in Puerto Rico would be subject to the same tax laws in effect for U.S. corporations with operations in foreign countries. Excluding Puerto Rico from federal revenue laws gave the colonial administration the opportunity to devise beneficial corporate tax laws with the aim of creating a favorable investment climate for U.S. corporations.

The Foraker Act was designed to establish the institutional basis for U.S. corporate penetration of the insular economy and its conversion into an export platform for sugar and tobacco. The structural changes in Puerto Rico's economy would create a market for those U.S. sectors engaged in the production of industrial products and capital goods. A market for basic foodstuffs would also rapidly emerge, given the anticipated increases in land use for agricultural export production and the attendant expansion of a wage-earning proletariat. In general, the Foraker Act legalized the assault launched by the military regimes on local economic institutions and actors and accelerated the process of displacing indigenous actors from control of key productive structures. The apparent goal was the incorporation of a reconstituted insular economy, now dominated by these corporations, into the metropolitan network of production and consumption. C. H. Forbes-Lindsay observed that the Foraker Act "was designed to facilitate the introduction of American capital into Porto Rico. . . . Immediately after its passage preparations were made on a large scale for the investment capital and the development of the island upon the most promising lines" (Forbes-Lindsay 1906, 159–160).

However, it is important to recall that the goal was not merely to convert Puerto Rico into an investor's paradise. Colonial strategy was being formulated for Cuba and the Philippines at precisely the same time; the economic provisions of legislation for each were extremely similar, and at times virtually identical. Although each of these countries had a specific strategic function in the broader scheme of U.S. imperial expansion, the economic objective of colonial policy was consistently to create the institutional complex to promote rapid economic growth. Economic growth under U.S. corporate direction was justified in the interests of establishing "prosperity and stability," but in later decades it led to the emergence of systematic and partially effective challenges to colonial rule.

The Colonial State and the Transformation of Puerto Rico

Having rejected statehood for the indeterminate future, Congress set about to design a system of colonial rule for Puerto Rico. Muñoz Rivera pleaded in vain that "the greatest need of Puerto Rico to-day is more self-government and less intervention from outside authorities" (1899). However, the Bureau of Insular Affairs strenuously opposed self-government. In his 1899 report General Davis observed, "I can not find warrant or justification . . . to vest Puerto Rico with the faculties and power of self-government." He wanted Puerto Rico to be "styled a Dependency and placed under the executive control of the President." Puerto Ricans should have a legislative assembly, but "only when experience shall have shown that the people comprehend the gravity of the duties and obligations of self-government will be soon enough to establish the lower house." According to Davis Puerto Ricans should be denied self-government "until there shall have been a plain demonstration of their competence to exercise it." Davis claimed that "the knowledge which I possess of the inhabitants of this island . . . forces me to the conviction that" self-government "would be a disaster to them and to the best interest of their fair island." (USDW 1900b, 75). Senator Foraker disagreed and proposed an elected legislature "as the best and quickest way to qualify a people for self-government" (quoted in Gannon 1978, 295). Davis also wanted the governor to have the authority to order U.S. army troops stationed in Puerto Rico to quell "cases of riot or disturbance of the peace, and in cases of imminent danger to the peace of the community" (USDW 1900b, 76, 82, 78).

Elihu Root supported the general's ideas and called for "a form of government . . . which will assure the kind of administration to which we are accustomed" (quoted in Trías Monge 1980, 1:203). Root was convinced that a highly centralized structure of colonial rule was necessary. He reasoned,

> The Porto Ricans, as a people, have never learned the fundamental and essential lesson of obedience to the decision of the majority. . . . It would be of no use to present to the people of Porto Rico now a written constitution or frame of laws, however perfect, and tell them to live under it. They would inevitably fail without a course of tuition under a strong and guiding hand. With that tuition for a time their natural capacity will, it is hoped, make them a self-governing people. (Root 1916, 203)

The idea that Puerto Ricans and Filipinos lacked the capacity to exercise responsible self-government was a virtual article of faith among colonial officials. *The Principles of Colonial Government*, written by Horace Fisher, is an 1899 monograph, whose significance lies in the fact that the Foraker Act coincidentally, or otherwise incorporated many of its recommendations. According to Fisher's assessment of the Spanish colonies,

There is no instance on record of any one of them having emancipated itself, within the first generation of freedom, from the evil influence of vice, lethargy and misrule. . . . A different system of government must be devised to correct the evils of a system which has reduced the original self-governing and energetic Spaniard to such a condition of political incapacity as described above. (Fisher 1899, 20–21)

Puerto Rico had to be protected from "foreign encroachment and internal misrule during its apprenticeship in the art of self-government." During this period the colonial power should provide assistance in order for the colony "to attain the utmost practical measure of modern civilization" (22). McKinley also wanted to restrict Puerto Rican involvement in their country's administration: "I have not thought it wise, to commit the entire government of the island to officers selected by the people because I doubt whether in habits, training and experiences they are such as to fit them to exercise at once so large a degree of self-government" (quoted in Gould 1958, 75). Ultimately Congress enacted a model of colonial government for Puerto Rico based almost entirely on Root's recommendations (Jessup 1938, 1:375).

The passage of the Foraker Act was a humiliating defeat for the Federal Party. Muñoz Rivera criticized the excessive concentration of political power in the hands of an appointed governor, complaining that "the governor is invested with all the executive power." He admonished that "with such resources at his command, the governor is made a supreme and mighty arbiter, irresponsible to the people, who lack the means to prevent his errors or to stop his abuses." Muñoz observed that "The governor is highly enthroned, as the Olympian Jupiter, centralizing, controlling the executive, legislative and judicial power. He is . . . a sort of semi-god with only his absolute will and omnipotent caprice as a limit to his official attributions" (Muñoz Rivera 1911, 188).

Indeed, the Foraker Act established a highly centralized administrative system whose most powerful officials were appointed by the president and accountable to him. The president appointed the governor with the advice and consent of the Senate. An appointed eleven-person Executive Council served as both a cabinet and upper house. Six council members headed executive departments: the state secretary, the attorney general, the treasurer, the auditor, and the commissioners of interior and education. The heads of the three most important departments—the attorney general, the commissioner of education, and the auditor—were appointed by the president with the advice and consent of the Senate, and were directly accountable to him. The auditor served as fiscal agent for the U.S. Congress, and controlled all the expenditures and assured that they conformed to the budget. This office had extraordinary powers to influence the allocation of funds approved by the legislative assembly (the House of Delegates and the Executive Council). The three other department heads were appointed by the governor with the advice and consent of the Senate. The five remaining council members, none of whom headed departments, were appointed directly by the governor, and functioned as legislators. The act required that at least five council members be "native inhabitants of Porto Rico."

The Foraker Act set up a lower House of Delegates composed of thirty-five popularly elected representatives, five from each of the seven electoral districts the Executive Council was to set up. Only a male resident of Puerto Rico literate in either Spanish or English and "possessed in his own right of taxable property, real or personal, situated in Puerto Rico" was eligible for election to the House of Delegates. All bills required the approval of the majority of both houses. A gubernatorial veto could be overridden by a two-thirds majority of both houses; a veto was unlikely, however, given that all the secretaries of departments in the Executive Council were appointed by the president and responsible to him.

Nonetheless, the president had the authority to veto any act the legislature passed over the veto of the governor. Since Congress had plenary power over the possessions, it could also annul, veto, or amend all local legislation. Puerto Rico was given a symbolic presence in the chambers of power through an elected resident commissioner to the United Sates, who would be entitled to official recognition as such by all departments. Since Puerto Rico was not an incorporated territory, Congress decided not to permit its people to elect a delegate to the House of Representatives (Capó Rodríguez 1921, 535). The Foraker Act gave Puerto Ricans only symbolic representation in the machinery of colonial government. Eventually a cadre of Puerto Rican political and business leaders would be trained in U.S. methods of administration and socialized into the norms and values of the colonizing society. When the period of "tutelage" had achieved its desired aims, Puerto Ricans would be allowed to assume some role in the governance of their own country. The House of Delegates and Executive Council was an important training center for Puerto Rican political leaders.

Section 33 of the Foraker Act vested judicial power in the "courts and tribunals of Puerto Rico as already established and now in operation." Congress preserved the laws in effect during the military period and enacted a court system that was essentially a reproduction of the structure set up by the BIA (Thompson 1989, 168). The municipal and police court systems established by General Davis were retained intact, as well as the Supreme Court, with its seven district courts. The president appointed the chief justice, associate justices, and the marshal. The Foraker Act also established a district court of the United States in Puerto Rico. With the advice and consent of the Senate the president appointed the district judge, attorney, and marshal. The district court had "jurisdiction in all cases cognizant in the circuit courts of the United States," and the use of English was mandatory in all cases pleaded before the court. From 1900 to 1909 no one federal agency had direct operational responsibility over this complex structure of administration. However, the Bureau of Insular Affairs, although deeply involved in colonial policy in the Philippines and Cuba, continued to influence policy formulation in Puerto Rico.

The Beginnings of a Colonial State

The Foraker Act retained much of the structure of colonial administration implanted by the War Department. Key features of military institutions—hierarchy, centralization of authority, accountability only to superiors, and supervision and monitoring of the colonial subjects—were properties of the newly designed colonial state. Decisionmaking, policy formulation, program implementation, resource allocation, and other key functions were in control of legal aliens appointed by and responsible to the chief executive of a metropolitan state. The policy formulation process continued to be highly centralized and insulated from popular review and approval.

Congress had legislated the establishment of a colonial administration that had the attributes of a modern state. With its judicial, legislative, and administrative units, the colonial state was a microcosm of the metropolitan state. It possessed a judicial system to prosecute, convict, and punish violators, as well as a constabulary to enforce the laws and apprehend those who broke them. The governor could authorize the deployment of U.S. military forces to suppress the populace. The Executive Council had the power to tax and collect revenues and finance the modernization of the infrastructure. It established and operated an islandwide system of free public education and had a specific role as an ideological agent.

This colonial administration ultimately functioned as an extension of the metropolitan state. The centralization of the colonial regime worked to insulate colonial officials from popular scrutiny and accountability, while permitting them the autonomy to pursue the Americanization of Puerto Rico as they thought most effective. Yet the newly created state was burdened with a contradiction particular to colonialism: It was ultimately subordinate to the dictates of the metropolitan state, but not accountable to the subjects over which it ruled. Moreover, since ultimate authority rested in the metropolitan state, corporate capital could, and did, use its power to influence policymaking at that level.

These properties of the colonial state demonstrate that Congress had no intention of enacting a system of governance by the people and for the people, at least not the Puerto Rican people. The Brookings Institute Report of 1930 commented that "the government of Porto Rico has been set up by Congress as an agency of that body for the conduct of local affairs of the Island of Porto Rico. The relationship between Congress and the government of Porto Rico is that of principal to agent" (Clark 1930, 111). Puerto Ricans were effectively shut out from the decisive structures of power within their own society and had only symbolic representation in the federal government.

With the exception of the elected House of Delegates, which was powerless to decide policy and which was comprised of literate tax-paying males, Puerto Rican participation in deciding the content, direction, and timing of transformation was nonexistent. For the United States the task of transforming Puerto Rican society so that it could assume its delegated role in promoting U.S. hemispheric hegemony was too momentous to be trusted to Puerto Ricans whose loyalties to the new sovereign were second to their national and class interests.

The Executive Council

The Executive Council was a singular institution in the history of U.S. territorial government, since it had both legislative as well as executive functions. William Willoughby, who served as the Executive Council's first president, explained,

> The work to be done was essentially one of administrative and governmental reorganization, in order that the island might have political institutions and a system of public law conforming, as nearly as local conditions would justify, to American principles and practices. It is difficult to see how this work of reconstruction could possibly have been performed with any thing like the success that has been achieved had the American representatives in charge of the administration of the island not been able to take an active part in securing the legislation necessary to effect the required changes in the law. (Willoughby 1907, 565)

Governor Charles Allen commented that the council had "legislative powers analogous to those usually exercised by a State senate or upper legislative body, together with certain other powers that were exclusive" (USDS 1901, 107). The Executive Council acted as a check against the lower house and regularly vetoed legislation that it thought impeded its transformative mission. William Willoughby observed that, with this arrangement Congress eliminated the danger "that a people inexperienced in self-government and legislative methods might enact injurious legislation" (Willoughby 1907, 568). A long period of "tutelage," consisting of supervised management of their conduct in the political process, socialization into U.S. modes of thinking and behavior, and indeed, acceptance of the legitimacy of their colonial subordination, was required before Puerto Ricans were permitted to actually manage their internal affairs.

According to Governor Allen the council "was able easily to take the lead in all important measures. . . . It proved also as has always been intended for similar chambers, to be a valuable conservative force in the onward rush for progressive legislation" (USDS 1901, 76). Given that the economic and political power of Puerto Rico's capitalist class was under assault by the new colonizers, the logic of denying this class a substantive role in the Executive Council becomes apparent. The principle of the separation of powers was readily abandoned in the interest of accelerating the Americanization campaign. In the process those sectors most adversely affected by the change in sovereignty were denied a forum to protect their interests.

Since it functioned as the governor's cabinet, the Executive Council was in permanent session. In contrast, the sessions of the House of Delegates were limited to sixty days annually. This gave the council a significant advantage over the lower house. Council members had direct contact with the governor, the executive departments in the federal government, and the Bureau of Insular Affairs. The Executive Council not only wrote the vast majority of legislation that was approved, but it was responsible for implementing these laws. The men who were appointed to the executive departments during the first decade of U.S. rule generally were recognized experts in their respective fields (education, finance and tax law, civil and common law). They were social engineers responsible for transforming Puerto Rico. Council President Willoughby observed that when the United States "adopted, as the most essential feature of its policy, the transformation of existing institutions, so as to bring them into conformity with those of its own, it is evident that the difficulties of the task are multiple and many fold." He went on to report that "the authority of the insular government is thus one of control and supervision" (Willoughby 1905, 80).

According to Rowe, "It has been necessary to retain in the central government sufficient power to guard the local authorities from the result of their own inexperience. This necessity has given the insular administration a far more centralized character than is to be found in any of the States of the Union" (Rowe 1904, 158). In effect the Executive Council acted as " an imperial office protecting the metropolitan interests against the local legislature" (Lewis 1963, 108).

Removing Obstacles to Capitalist Development

The Foraker Act established a colonial state, which continued the campaign of economic and institutional transformation that had been initiated by the military governments. Its actions proved decisive in setting conditions for generalized commodity production to flourish and accelerated Puerto Rico's transition into a primary product export platform. The colonial state functioned as an agent for capitalist development, and it was aggressive and resourceful in its efforts to promote the rapid conversion of Puerto Rico into a commodity-based market economy under the dominance of U.S. capital. The eventual concentration of resources by U.S. firms, particularly by absentee sugar corporations, altered the prevailing social relations of production and set the context for the development of modern capitalism. Moreover, through its power to grant franchises, to tax, to enforce labor discipline, to regulate land sales, and in general through its control of the instruments that bore directly on society's productive capabilities, the colonial state facilitated the development of a labor regime dedicated to export-commodity production. By the beginning of the century, Puerto Rico was inexorably and irreversibly absorbed into the network of U.S. commodity trade and investments. The relationship between these transformative processes and the structure and properties of the state was not merely coincidental.

The Foraker Act was not just an economic document. Although Congress did respond to the interests of particular sectors of capital, the Foraker Act did not represent the capitulation of the McKinley administration to these sectors. The overriding interest of the U.S. state and ascending sectors of international business was to maximize investments, trade, and lending in Latin America and the Far East. This interest required a strategic capability, including foreign military bases, necessary to advance these economic objectives. The U.S. goal was to convert Puerto Rico into a stable and loyal outpost from which it could more readily dispense gunboat diplomacy and guard the crucial shipping lanes to the southern United States, Mexico, and South America.

An active presence by U.S. firms in Puerto Rico would not only deepen the country's incorporation into the national economy, but would further the process of Americanization and promote stability. Policymakers argued that U.S. investments would increase employment and that the deplorable material conditions of the inhabitants of Puerto Rico would be ameliorated. This improvement would not only contribute to stability, but also promote wider acceptance of U.S. institutions and methods. Moreover, the supremacy of U.S. corporations would irrevocably undermine the colony's landowning and commercial elite, the sector that was most organizationally and materially capable of complicating U.S. objectives in Puerto Rico. But the economic changes initiated by the Foraker Act failed to mitigate the intensity of immiseration in Puerto Rico. An influential Brookings Institute report was explicit: "If American political institutions are to succeed in Porto Rico, the material conditions of life must be greatly improved" (Clark 1930, xvii). The persistence of poverty, hunger, and disease provided fertile ground for the political turbulence of the 1930s.

The Nature of the Colonial State

The colonial state devised policy and implemented programs that were supposed to convert Puerto Rico into a manageable and loyal ward of the United States. It was the institutional embodiment of the interests of the metropolitan state and capital. This institution of colonial rule was, however, a foreign, alien system of governance that was grafted onto a society that had its own legal and political traditions. The colonial state was not the product of a historical process particular to that society and did not evolve as the product of class struggle. Puerto Rico did not undergo an acute confrontation between a domestic bourgeoisie and the nobility—as had been the case in much of Europe. Nor was the colonial state a historical product resulting from the struggles by Creole landed elites for liberation from the Spanish-dominated political order—as was the pattern in Latin America. In both instances state institutions evolved historically and were transformed through class conflict.

The United States created and imposed an alien structure of governance on a nation whose leaders, only months before the transfer of sovereignty, had deftly negotiated significant autonomy from a declining empire. With the transfer of sovereignty these elites expected that the new metropolitan power would grant

Puerto Rico a high degree of self-government. But the political leadership was denied a voice in the system of rule that would govern the lives of Puerto Ricans. For this reason, the colonial state was imbued with the potential for generating disaffection and resistance to metropolitan rule.

U.S. colonial authorities had the tasks of directing Puerto Rico's institutional transformation according to the requirements of the metropolitan state and of maintaining political stability and the legitimacy of colonial rule. Congress designed an administrative structure that intentionally circumscribed Puerto Rican involvement. However, U.S. officials recognized that they would eventually have to accede to Puerto Rican demands to participate in the governing process. Only when the colonial authorities felt confident that they had suppressed viable challenges to their rule would Puerto Ricans be given the opportunity to participate in governing their own country.

Notes

1. The Democratic Party platform decried the imperialism of the Republicans: "We denounce the Porto Rican law enacted by a Republican Congress against the protest and opposition of the Democratic minority, as a bold and open violation of the nation's organic law and a flagrant breach of the national good faith. It imposes upon the people of Porto Rico a government without their consent and taxation without representation. It dishonors the American people by repudiating a solemn pledge made in their behalf by the Commanding General of our Army, which the Porto Ricans welcomed to a peaceful and unresisted occupation of their land."

The Republican platform emphasized the responsibilities and benefits of expansionism: "No other course was possible than to destroy Spain's sovereignty throughout the West Indies and in the Philippine Islands. That course created our responsibility before the world, and with the unorganized population whom our intervention had freed from Spain, to provide for the maintenance of law and order, and for the establishment of good government and for the performance of international obligations. Our authority could not be less than our responsibility. . . . The largest measure of self government consistent with their welfare and our duties shall be secured to them by law." Both party platforms are reproduced in LaFeber 1971, 1919–1928.

2. Luis R. Dávila Colón observed that "the Insular Cases set the tone for future Congressional discriminatory treatment by establishing the criterion of locality or political status as determinative of the degree of constitutional protection afforded to the citizens of the unincorporated possessions" (Dávila Colón 1979, 605).

4

The Colonial State at Work:
The Executive Council
and the Transformation
of Puerto Rico, 1900–1917

In order to make the laws and language of the mainland and the island uniform, which in due course of time will be necessary, every effort must be made not only to teach new doctrines and ideas, but at the same time to destroy the prejudices, ignorance and the false teachings of the past. In this way permanent, not transient, success will be had and the ends achieved will redound to the glory of our country and humanity at large.

—*Governor William H. Hunt, 1904*

These inhabitants, all of a foreign race and tongue, largely illiterate and without experience in conducting a government in accordance with Anglo Saxon practice, or indeed to carry on any government, were not deemed to be fitted and qualified, unaided and without effective supervision, to fully appreciate the responsibilities and exercise the power of complete self-government.

—*Brigadier General George W. Davis, 1909*

It is a grave error to affirm that Puerto Rico cannot govern itself until its present idiosyncrasies be a thing of the past and until for them can be substituted the customs, habits and language prevailing in the United States. . . . The destiny of Puerto Rico must be entrusted to Puerto Ricans, who . . . are alone capable of making laws to govern them.

Cayetano Coll y Cuchi, 1909

The Executive Council: Agency for "Americanization"

The Executive Council had the task of orchestrating the complete overhaul of Puerto Rico's political and judicial institutions and implanting a new ideological construct—a process U.S. officials called "Americanization." Puerto Rican scholarship has generally ignored the Executive Council and its role in institution building and capitalist expansion. With the exception of the Department of Education, little work has been done on individual agencies of the colonial state. I make no pretense here of providing a detailed analysis. Instead, in the following pages I will briefly examine three Executive Council agencies that had the most visible roles in advancing the colonizing mission of the metropolitan state: the Departments of Education and the Interior and the office of the attorney general, including the judiciary.

Concretely, the Executive Council was responsible for developing public policy, drafting legislation, implementing programs, raising revenue, and regulating administrative and political matters. William Willoughby reported, "The greatest freedom was given to the newly constituted government to work out the great problems of revenue, of education, of public works, of local government, and in fact, of practically every question requiring the exercise of governmental authority" (Willoughby 1902, 35). According to Willoughby, the council "may be said in a way to constitute the center or keystone to the whole system" (Willoughby 1905, 98). It had the legal authority and financial resources to convert vague notions of Americanizing Puerto Rico into concrete policies and programs. Much of its legislative work "had to rectify errors committed during the period of military rule, it had to completely harmonize and perfect certain legislation, and it had to adjust the principles of old legislation to the principles and ideals of the American system" (Rodríguez-Serra 1908, 165).

A callous dismissal of Puerto Rico's institutions and the capabilities and achievements of its people typified the imperial attitude of U.S. colonial officials. After dismantling the country's political institutions, U.S. officials further demeaned Puerto Ricans by charging that they lacked the rudimentary skills to govern their own country. Having expounded this self-serving rationale for prohibiting Puerto Rican participation in the policy-making process, U.S. officials placed all key agencies of the colonial state in the hands of Euro-American male U.S. citizens. In fact, during the life of the Executive Council (1900–1917) virtually all the commissioners were white males from the United States who did not speak Spanish, and who had no direct experience or understanding of the Puerto Rican reality. The Bureau of Insular Affairs and the newly established Executive Council were the primary agencies for converting Puerto Rico into what it was hoped would be a pocket edition of an idealized United States. Puerto Rico's transformation into a modern colony consisted of three broadly related components: ideological, economic, and coercive. These were the concrete elements of a comprehensive program of Americanization devised and guided by the Executive Council and the BIA.

The Executive Council devised and directed the campaign of Americanization in Puerto Rico. Some U.S. council members seemed to have been driven by a missionary zeal to Americanize Puerto Rico by radically transforming its institutions and values. Roland Falkner, the commissioner of education, informed the participants in the 1905 Mohonk Conference that "the problem which confronts us in Porto Rico is that of the Americanization of the island." He identified a number of values, including equality before the law, honesty, integrity, and a fair chance for all as "the fundamental principles upon which the American body politic rests." Falkner posited that "when these principles pervade the public and private life" of Puerto Rico, "the labor of Americanization will have been completed" (Falkner 1905, 159–160). Three years later Falkner emphasized that "the primary object of our administration in Porto Rico should be to infuse into the political, social and economic life of the Porto Rican people the spirit, rather the form of American institutions" (Falkner 1908, 171). Education Commissioner McCune Lindsay was certain of Puerto Rico's significance to the realization of hemispheric objectives:

> The army and the navy will tell you that we have a strategic position in Porto Rico for military affairs. We have a strategic position also in Porto Rico in regard to the development of the people in the North and South American continent which is vastly more important than is the strategic position of Porto Rico with regard to our naval affairs. Here is our national social laboratory in which, if we pursue a generous policy, we will win the hearts of the people of South America and we will weld together the civilization of the North Central and South American continents. (Lindsay 1906, 134)

Americanization also entailed the implantation of governmental and judicial institutions in the colonies. Governor Beekman Winthrop wrote that "the work of the officials sent to Puerto Rico is twofold: First, to install American institutions and American governmental principles, and second, to educate the Porto Rican on these lines. For this reason it is desirable that Porto Ricans be employed whenever possible in the different departments" (USDS 1905, 41). The Executive Council was entrusted with the task of actualizing the colonizing mission of the metropolitan state. U.S. officials had given the Executive Council an explicit mandate: "Public education had to be extended, road construction had to be continued, public order had to be maintained and insular obligations had to be met" (Hollander 1901, 562).

Each Executive Council department was directly or indirectly engaged in the Americanization process and in building the foundations for the advance of U.S. capital into the colony. The process of Americanization, or what I have referred to as the colonizing mission, can be divided into three broad policy areas: ideological, developmental, and coercive. While these policy areas were distinct, they are closely interrelated and mutually reinforcing. The War Department, specifically the Bureau of Insular Affairs, was engaged in a similar process of inculcating these "ideals" and political institutions in Cuban and Filipino society. Americanization was the leitmotif under which the executive departments implemented concrete and precise programs.

The Department of Education was the most visible agency involved in the Americanization process. It was crucial in constructing and implanting an alien worldview that was divorced from the historical context of the Puerto Rican people's lived experiences. One of its most important tasks—often its exclusive priority—was to teach the colonial subjects the language of the colonizer. The education commissioners set about to build popular understanding and acceptance of U.S. norms, customs, and historical myths. They were keen to implant a patriotic spirit for Uncle Sam and socialize Puerto Ricans into accepting the superiority of U.S. institutions and the "Anglo-Saxon race." In addition to language instruction and socialization of the colonial subjects, the Education Department had a comprehensive manual training and industrial arts curriculum that was designed to furnish the economy with skilled craftspeople, workers, and managerial personnel.

The secretaries of the interior and the treasury, the director of health, and the director of charities were responsible for promoting the physical and human infrastructure. The Executive Council installed legal systems to enforce contracts and protect property, and it enacted commercial codes familiar to metropolitan businesses. These changes were deemed essential for U.S. firms to migrate to Puerto Rico. U.S. firms were routinely provided free of charge or at minimal costs first-rate roads, subsidized irrigation projects, and cheap electric power. In addition, the colonial state provided essential prerequisites for capitalist development: monetary stability, well-capitalized financial institutions, and most important, protection of property rights backed by the judicial supremacy of the metropolitan power. Other agencies were responsible for promoting a healthy, literate, and disciplined labor force.

The Interior Department modernized the country's infrastructure through ambitious public works projects: irrigation systems, hydroelectric plants, roads, warehouses, and piers, and a telegraph system. The Executive Council also issued franchises for railroads and street cars, for telephone service, and for hydroelectric plants. These construction activities, financed either directly by the state or by private investors, created the foundations for the development of Puerto Rico's sugar-based export economy. The Council was also responsible for imposing a new internal revenue system to finance the operations of the colony. A large bureaucracy was rapidly established to assess property, collect taxes, grant exemptions, and prevent tax evasion. The director of public charities and the director of health were in charge of staving off mass starvation and destitution, and eradicating diseases and epidemics that depleted Puerto Rico's workforce and endangered the lives of U.S. colonial officials.

The coercive apparatus of the state included the supreme court, the district and municipal court system, the bureau of prisons, and the insular constabulary, as well as the military. Its function in Puerto Rico was no different from that in the United States. These agencies were responsible for protecting private property and enforcing compliance with the laws and ordinances of the state: they apprehended, prosecuted, and punished violators of these laws, and enforced commercial transactions and contracts. The courts, and the body of jurisprudence that guided their conduct, were among the most important institutions for advancing the Americanization of Puerto Rican society. These coercive agencies were sup-posed to contain the anticipated anomie and resistance the change in sovereignty would provoke.

Each department of the Executive Council was an important employer, and collectively this bureaucracy was the primary employer of the country's educated and professional strata. As Puerto Ricans were hired to work in the colonial ad-ministration, they became purveyors of the standards and values of the metro-politan power. The attorney general's office and the courts, as well as the insular police force and the Puerto Rico Regiment, were important agents for socializa-tion and legitimated the new institutional order. Hundreds of Puerto Rican lawyers and judges acquired knowledge of a new body of jurisprudence and quickly developed an understanding of different legal codes and traditions. The police, marshals, and soldiers had to declare their absolute fidelity to the United States and be trained to unhesitatingly enforce new principles and protect the property recently usurped by foreigners.

Collectively the various departments trained Puerto Ricans in those skills that were necessary for the emerging corporate economy. Thousands were trained for service as government lawyers, judges, clerks, managers, tax assessors, police offi-cers, laborers, teachers, and so forth. In the process they were socialized into modes of thinking and conduct that were rewarded by the colonial authorities. Dependent on the colonial state for their jobs, in the midst of increasing unem-ployment and widespread poverty, these contingents of workers were important agents for Americanization. Their service in the bureaucracy also served to legit-imize the colonial regime. The hoped-for outcome of all these activities was not simply to conduct the business of colonial administration, but to create a perma-nent body of loyal colonial subjects.

New Schools and Alien Ideas

General Henry initiated the transformation of Puerto Rico's education system. But his efforts, as well as those of his predecessor, General Davis, were considered experimental and judged deficient by Martin G. Brumbaugh, Puerto Rico's first commissioner of education (see Lord 1908). Brumbaugh, who was a University of Pennsylvania professor and governor of the state, reported that in 1900, "there were scarcely six hundred effective schools in operation, and not a single build-ing in the island had been erected for public school purposes" (Brumbaugh 1904, 87). Moreover, the school system established by the military reached only about a tenth of the population (Brumbaugh 1911, 175).

According to Commissioner Rowe, systematic "plans were laid for a thor-oughly organized policy of popular education" after the Foraker Act went into ef-fect (Rowe 1904, 115). Brumbaugh's task was daunting. Governor Allen wrote in his first annual report that the "work of initiating a system of education here which will supply primary instruction to the 400,000 ignorant boys and girls by whom we are surrounded is a Herculean task" (USDS 1901, 93). Only 15 percent of the population could read or write, although the level of illiteracy was much greater in the rural than urban areas (Rowe 1904, 114). In 1900 only 15,440 boys and 8,952 girls were enrolled in the public schools, and 96 percent of these were in the lowest three grades (Osuna 1949, 135).

The commissioner of education had great latitude to design Puerto Rico's system of public education, and he operated without any accountability to the subject population or its representatives. He had control over sufficient resources to have a measurable impact on Puerto Rican society. As a member of the Executive Council, the commissioner was well positioned to have education-related legislation approved. Brumbaugh believed it was necessary for the commissioner to have this discretionary power, and "sufficient authority to continue the schools in spite of local indifference, should such indifference arise" (USDS 1901, 350). The aborted school system designed by General Eaton "gave municipalities full authority to elect properly qualified teachers for the local schools" (USDS 1908, 222). But this local control was soon changed by the School Law of 1900, which removed municipal government control over the educational process. The municipal school boards were totally independent of the municipal government, and were closely supervised by the commissioner. School boards composed of three elected males were established in the *municipios*. The law was to "make it obligatory upon the municipalities to devote a reasonable portion of their income" to maintaining the infrastructure of the school system (Willoughby 1905, 147). Each municipal government was required every year to turn over to the school board 25 percent of its revenue. The boards were also authorized to borrow from the insular government and were financially responsible for building, maintaining, and leasing school buildings. The responsibility of the *municipios* with respect to education was confined exclusively to this activity.

The School Law of 1901, prepared by Brumbaugh, further centralized the school system, and gave the commissioner the authority to deny the *municipios* any role in educational policymaking. The 1915 annual report of the governor described the commissioner's substantial powers.

> The commissioner has full power of appointment over all subordinates, except certain classes of teachers. He is empowered to determine the course of study, the length of the school year within limitations prescribed by law, and the length of the school day. He is in charge of the examination and certification of teachers, and no expenditure of public moneys for school purposes, on part of either the school boards or any of his subordinates in the department, can be made without his approval. (USDW Annual Report 1915, 314)

A number of reasons were given to explain this high degree of centralization. According to Commissioner Rowe, "Exclusive control of the entire education was

given to the Commissioner, in part because of the absence of local traditions"
(Rowe 1904, 157). The assistant commissioner of education, Everett Lord,
stressed Americanization.

> But as we desired to make public education a factor in the Americanization of the is-
> land, it was manifestly impossible to establish a school system in Porto Rico which
> would reflect Porto Rican public opinion. And so it was of necessity left to one man,
> the Commissioner of Education, appointed by the President of the United States, to
> determine the form to be given to the school system of the island, and to sustain it
> with a degree of authority unknown in any state school department. (Lord 1908,
> 166)

The plan was to give a single Euro-American male, who was unacquainted
with the needs and customs of the Puerto Rican people and who did not speak
Spanish, unrestricted power and independence to design and administer a highly
centralized and hierarchically organized system of public instruction. The objective of this system was unprecedented in that it sought not merely to socialize immigrant European populations, as was the case in the United States, but to transform a captured people and imbue them with values that the colonizing power
thought were essential. The start-up costs for mass public education came from
the "trust fund" made up of customs receipts and excise taxes collected on goods
Puerto Rico exported to the United States during the period of military rule.
Congress authorized the president to use the $2.7 million thus collected to fi-
nance the costs of Puerto Rico's colonial administration. By 1902 over $350,000
had been spent for school construction (USDS 1901, 355; 1909, 226). After the
initial support from the federal government, the funds for running the educational system, as well as for the salaries of the commissioner and his staff, were
generated exclusively from internal sources.

Given his extensive patronage powers and control over school building construction, the commissioner could generate political support for the colonial
regime. He directed an agency with the largest budget and staff in Puerto Rico,
which was also the single most important employer. In 1903 it spent $817,815 to
run the public school system, or approximately one-third of the state's budget
(USDS 1903, 101; 1909, 227). During the first ten years of U.S. occupation, end-
ing on June 30, 1908, the department had spent over $7.4 million to run the
school system (USDS 1909, 279). In 1917 total expenditure for education was
$2.1 million, which represented about 30 percent of government expenditures.
School boards provided $588,067 of this total (USDW Annual Report 1917, 17,
256). Between 1925 and 1929, expenditures for public schools averaged 29 percent of the total disbursements of the colonial state, and accounted for 15 percent
of the municipal budgets (calculated from USDW Annual Report 1929, 132;
Clark 1930, 149). According to Brumbaugh, the commissioner needed the sweep-

ing appointive powers in order to assure that competent teachers would be appointed and "to prevent partisan politics from entering into the selection of teachers" (USDS 1901, 351). The teaching staff grew quickly in the initial years. In 1902 the department employed 1,116 teachers (725 men and 391 women) (USDS 1903, 141). In 1910 the department employed 1,743 teachers (815 men and 928 women), and seven years later it hired 2,676 teachers, of whom 1,675 were women, and of these 193 were from the United States (USDW Annual Report 1910, 72; 1917, 461). By 1931 the department employed 4,523 teachers (1,246 men and 3,277 women) (USDW Annual Report 1931, 73).

The commissioner was directly responsible for a mini-building boom in public school buildings and playgrounds. By 1902 41 school buildings were built (USDS 1903, 153), and by 1911, the figures had increased to 323 buildings (USDW Annual Report 1912, 48). By 1930, the department had constructed 1,035 schoolhouses and buildings (Clark 1930, 73). The value of the acquired real estate and holdings of the department was not inconsequential. The assessed valuation of school property was $182.6 million, which almost equaled the gross assessed valuation of privately owned property, assessed at $187.9 million (5, 338).

Educational and Ideological Work of the Department

The education commissioners had a number of objectives whose significance tended to vary over time and depended on the changing requirements of the political economy. These goals ranged from teaching English to young Puerto Ricans to more amorphous objectives of converting the country into "a liaison point between English speaking and Spanish speaking America" (Clark 1930, 90). U.S. colonial officials dreamed that Puerto Rico's people could be molded into a bilingual community and serve as a bridge between the United States and Latin America. Juan B. Huyke, the first Puerto Rican education commissioner, reported that bilingual education was emphasized since "Porto Rico is about halfway between North and South America," and it was a "proper location . . . for training of students for the important work of uniting the Americas" (USDW Annual Report 1929, 375). Two decades earlier Brumbaugh recommended establishing in Puerto Rico "a great insular school," which would have a faculty from the United States and South America. According to Brumbaugh, "In no other specific way could these higher institutions of American thought extend their usefulness" to Latin America (Brumbaugh 1907, 68). By the early 1920s the University of Puerto Rico had de-emphasized its original purpose, which was to train teachers for the public school system, and had begun to redefine itself as a pan-American university with specific diplomatic and economic responsibilities. According to University of Puerto Rico officials, the university was "to lend to the leaders in extra-governmental activities in North, Central and South America the bilingual, bicultural, and intercontinental re-

sources of PuertoRico as a meeting ground for the discussion of practical problems of an inter-American nature in the fields of agriculture, industry, transportation, communications, law, finance and extra-political public relations"
(quoted in Rodríguez Fraticelli 1991, 155).

From a review of the various reports and articles by the commissioners of education, five objectives stand out: (1) imparting English language skills; (2)
Americanizing the population, including instilling civic values and patriotism for
the United States; (3) training Puerto Ricans for managerial, supervisory, and
technical positions in government and industry; (4) installing a gender-based educational program in which women were socialized and trained into performing
those roles necessary for the preservation of a male-centered family unit, specifically in home sanitation/health and hygiene procedures, cooking, sewing, and
gardening; (5) specific training in job-related skills in manual and industrial
trades for the boys and needleworks and domestic service for the girls.

The thousands of teachers needed to institute this new political culture received training in the newly established normal schools. In addition hundreds of
teachers were brought in from the United States to provide English language instruction to Puerto Rican teachers. Over the years thousands of Puerto Rican
men and women were sent to the United States for specialized courses on pedagogy and for English language training. This public education system was designed to transform a Spanish-speaking people with a four-hundred-year history
and distinct cultural outlook into patriotic colonial subjects. They would be con-
versant in the language of the colonizer and trained in labor skills that would
soon be in demand by foreign firms.

A U.S. Senate report emphasized that "industrial education is what is needed.
The three Rs, training of the hands, and training in thrift and other phases of self
control should be the end toward which Federal aid should look" (quoted in
Quintero Rivera 1977, 44). Education officials experimented with different cur-
ricula, language policies, and pedagogy to achieve these various objectives. In the
beginning, they attempted to implant practices and approaches that were particular to U.S. schools. The early educational administrators were pressured to develop a program of industrial education. But according to University of Puerto
Rico president Thomas E. Benner, the first educational model was "discourag-
ingly like that enjoyed by industrial Massachusetts. The best device for rating
school systems . . . placed the schools of Massachusetts first among the nation in
1900. They were poor schools for an agricultural state and especially poor schools
for Puerto Rico" (Benner 1929, 614). Education policy also focused on the work
ethic and political behavior of Puerto Ricans. The Education Department observed, "The purpose for which the public school system is organized is the training for good citizenship, and one of the first essentials is that the individual shall
be so trained as to support himself and those dependent upon him" (USDS 1903,
265, 273). The 1930 Brookings Institute report recommended that "the school
system should afford training relating to civic and social problems and provide

for the development of industrial intelligence and some degree of manual skill"
(Clark 1930, 82).

English Language Instruction. The foremost objective of the school authorities was to impart English language proficiency throughout the country. According to the secretary of war, "The people of Porto Rico are American citizens. Perhaps the most important factor in their complete americanization is the spreading
of the English language. Diligent efforts along this line are being made and with
very satisfactory progress" (USDW Annual Report 1920, 54). Education Commissioner Brumbaugh wrote, "The first business of the American republic, in its attempt to universalize its educational ideals in America, is to give these Spanish-
speaking races the symbols of the English language in which to express the
knowledge and the culture which they already possess" (Brumbaugh 1907, 65).

Colonial officials asserted that the "purpose of the education department has
been to establish and to develop a bilingual system of education which would insure the conservation of Spanish and the acquisition of English." Superintendent
Landrón of Arecibo wrote that the "aim in the future must be to graduate from
the graded schools every year a larger proportion of children with a good ability
to use the English in both the written and spoken language, without neglecting
the Spanish" (USDW Annual Report 1915, 340, 341). As late as 1921 Governor E.
Montgomery Reilly reaffirmed the centrality of English language instruction to
the colonial mission: "I hope to see the language of Washington, Lincoln and
Harding taught equally with that of Spanish in our Public Schools. . . . Therefore
English must be taught more and more. This I shall insist upon, and the Commissioner of education and all his subordinates shall be instructed accordingly"
(quoted in Clark 1973, 227).

Teachers were brought from the United States to provide English language instruction to Puerto Rico's teachers, as well as its students. In 1904 the Education
Department hired 120 teachers from the United States to provide English language instruction (USDS 1904, 16). In 1917 the government brought in 193
teachers from the United States, and by 1925 the number had been increased to
244 (USDW Annual Report 1917, 461; 1925, 297). It was of no importance if
these teachers did not know Spanish; according to the commissioner, since the
best results in language training were obtained "when no Spanish whatever is
used in the classroom . . . there is no disadvantage in employing American teachers who are quite ignorant of Spanish" (USDS 1905, 128–129).

In 1903 a normal school was set up as one of the major departments in the
newly established university to prepare English-speaking teachers. Education
commissioner Roland Falkner reported in 1905 that "the utmost effort has been
made from the start to advance the study of English among Porto Rican teachers"
(USDS 1905, 128). In the same year 540 Puerto Rican teachers paid part of the
expenses to attend a government-sponsored summer study program at Harvard
and Cornell Universities to study English (USDS 1905, 16). It was the policy of

the department to provide "every possible opportunity and inducement" to Puerto Rican teachers to learn English and "to prepare themselves to give instruction in this language" (USDW Annual Report 1915, 340). In fact, Puerto Rican teachers were required by law to study English and pass annual examinations in order to retain their certification.

Some Puerto Ricans became wary of the aggressive English language campaign and fought to preserve the primacy of Spanish as the national language. On January 11, 1915, the House of Delegates passed a measure declaring that Spanish was the official language "of the People of Puerto Rico, and its lexicon shall conform to the texts of the Spanish Royal Academy, augmented by the idioms and local terms of Puerto Rico." The English language was the official language for transaction of business between the colony and the metropolitan state (Domínguez 1915, 161). The measure was defeated by the Executive Council. Union Party leader Antonio Barceló criticized the educational system before a Senate committee in 1916 and noted "that our schools are practically operated for the sole purpose of teaching the English language rather than to prepare men and generations along practical lines" (U.S. Senate Committee on Pacific Islands and Porto Rico 1916, 47). Yet, despite the great effort and expense, colonial officials were disappointed with the results of the English instruction program. Puerto Ricans proved resistant to accepting the primacy of English; they rejected it as the vernacular. The preservation of Spanish as the principal language of instruction and daily interaction, even today, attests to the refusal of Puerto Ricans to relinquish one of the most important elements of their national identity.

English language policy shifted over time. English was initially the language of instruction (1903–1914). For six years, only English was taught in the first grade, which proved to be the least successful and most unpopular of all the language instruction approaches (USDW Annual Report 1925, 302). The policy was evaluated, and it "became evident that teaching of English as a special subject was not producing . . . tangible results." A new approach was tried in 1917 in which Spanish became the medium of instruction for the first four grades, a transition from Spanish to English took place in the fifth grade, and finally, grades six through eight were taught entirely in English, with Spanish as a special subject (USDW Annual Report 1915, 340; Osuna 1949, 344–350).

The effectiveness of English language instruction appears to have been of secondary importance to colonial officials compared to its role in Americanizing the population. English instruction was zealously promoted because it was seen as an instrument for building patriotism for the metropolitan power. The Educational Survey Commission reported in 1926 on the poor level of English language instruction and the limited success of the program, and noted that 84 percent of the children stay in school only until the end of the third grade. It recommended elimination of English from the first three years of education, and complained that "the curriculum of the elementary school is now so completely a language curriculum that content subjects are almost altogether crowded out" (quoted in Osuna 1949, 359).

However, Victor Clark rejected the recommendation and emphasized, as had his predecessors, the ideological function of language training:

> English is the chief source, practically the only source, of democratic ideas in Porto Rico. There may be little that they learn to remember, but the English school reader itself provides a body of ideas and concepts which are not to be had in any other way. It is also the only means which these people have of communication with and understanding of the country of which they are now a part. (Clark 1930, 81)

Education and Patriotism. Education officials understood the ideological function of the school system as an agent for Americanization. They promoted activities and educational programs to foster patriotism for the United States. In 1901 Brumbaugh observed proudly, "Almost every school on the island has an American flag. In almost every city of the island and at many rural schools, the children meet and salute the flag as it is flung to the breeze." Educational programming included organizing "patriotic exercises." One of the most ambitious was the celebration of Washington's birthday, attended by 75,000 people according to Brumbaugh, which did "much to Americanize the island." He noted that "young minds are being molded to follow the example of Washington" (USDS 1901, 361). He could not help beaming with pride when he reported that "above 30,000 children were singing our American National Hymn in the English language, and fully 25,000 were reading and speaking the English language" (Brumbaugh 1904, 89).

In 1904 R. L. Rowe confidently declared, "In the common schools of Porto Rico the process of Americanization is being carried on with so much vigor and with such assurance of success that there need be little misgiving as to the attitude of the native population toward American institutions" (Rowe 1904, 116). Rev. James H. Van Buren, who from 1902 to 1912 served as the Protestant Episcopal bishop of Puerto Rico, informed his colleagues at the 1913 Mohonk Conference that "loyalty to American principles and standards is a leading feature of the public school curriculum in Porto Rico." He called directly for using the public schools to instill patriotism "as we know it" (Van Buren 1913, 151–152). Education commissioner Dexter reported with pride that every one of the 1,064 schools "has the stars and stripes floating over it, the raising of which at the opening of each morning's sessions is made a ceremony." He claimed that the children were "learning to love" saluting the flag (Dexter 1911, 180). "The patriotic aim was emphasized" in public education, according to Puerto Rican education commissioner Juan B. Huyke. He noted that "The lives of noted men in American life and history are used to emphasize the social-civic objectives of education in Porto Rico" (USDW Annual Report 1929, 402).

Educating "Native" Colonial Managers and Training Legions of Young Workers. The education of selected Puerto Ricans in the United States was also a component of the Americanization campaign. The commissioner of education reported in 1923 that 432 Puerto Ricans students were in the continental United States. "Most of these students will return to Porto Rico at the completion of their courses and will, to a certain extent, aid in the further Americanization of the island by introducing many of the customs of the United States"(USDW Annual Report 1923, 190). In 1929 approximately 439 Puerto Ricans were enrolled in U.S. colleges and universities (USDW Annual Report 1929, 402).

Scholarships for young Puerto Rican men and women began to be provided in 1900 "as part of the plan for instituting American culture and American educational ideas into Porto Rico." Thirty-five boys and ten girls were sent to study in the United States, primarily in the Northeast, and ten boys and ten girls attended the all-black Tuskegee Industrial Institute in Alabama. A number of students were also sent to the Carlisle Industrial School, but the program was terminated when the commissioner of Indian affairs in Washington decided against admitting more Puerto Rican students (USDS 1903, 157, 311). In 1903 Governor Hunt observed, "The boys complete their studies and return to Porto Rico thoroughly imbued with American ideas, it is expected that they will exert a strong influence throughout the island" (USDS 1903, 22). In 1904 Governor Winthrop proclaimed: "The signs for the future of Porto Rico are encouraging. A greater number of young men are being educated every year on the continent of the United States, and these young men bring back with them a clearer insight into the ideas of American administrations and the ideals of American manhood" (USDS 1905, 40).

In 1908 the legislature established a scholarship program for fourteen women to study in the United States on condition that they return to "the island and devote four years to the service of the public schools" (USDS 1908, 201). In the same year the federal land-grant program was extended to Puerto Rico, and the fledging college of agriculture and mechanical arts was substantially strengthened. In 1913, as war was breaking out in Europe, male students were organized into a military battalion of four companies under the direction of a U.S. military officer and required to take military drill for three hours each week (USDW Annual Report 1914, 406). By 1917 the university had expanded to a College of Liberal Arts, a law school, and the College of Agriculture and Mechanical Arts in Mayagüez.

The educational system was a centerpiece of the colonizing mission of the United States. Initially, educators pointed with pride to the aggregate enrollment figures, which proved an unreliable indicator, to measure their success in educating the Puerto Rican population. Underlying much of their thinking was the belief that education would raise the living standards of rural populations mired in poverty and disease. Governor Colton emphasized this goal in his 1912 report:

To give them the necessary mental discipline through the study of practical subjects; and to make their school work better qualify them, both mentally and physically, to take their places as useful members of society, with respect for labor, capable of sustaining themselves and their dependents in accordance with modern standards of civilization—of being potential and good citizens of the Republic. (USDW Annual Report 1912, 46)

The department also provided mass public instruction and training in skills that were in demand in the rapidly changing labor market. In retrospect, the commissioners appeared to be naive in believing that this kind of training could be achieved primarily by increasing literacy and mechanical and domestic skills. It is apparent that from the outset the Education Department encountered difficulty in realizing the task of training young people for work in the emerging industries of the colonial economy. This was the message in a 1912 report of a special commission chaired by educator Meyer Bloomfield: "Although the Island schools are unquestionably helping to make good citizens, it is a grave question whether the present arrangements contribute materially to the making of homemakers, producers, skilled workers, self-reliant and efficient breadwinners" (quoted in Clark 1930, 83). After the governor's warning, colonial officials intensified vocational instruction.

In 1913 Edward Bainter, who was an acknowledged vocational education specialist, was appointed commissioner. Bainter included manual training, home economics, and agriculture courses as part of the curriculum. But his plans were overly ambitious; they could not be funded and ultimately failed (Fernández García 1923, 401, 403). Nonetheless, his idea of more systematically using the education system to train workers for the emerging corporate economy was incorporated into subsequent curriculum initiatives. Vocational training was combined with instruction in civics and citizenship. One of the missions of the rural schools was to develop "better trained citizens in the social and civic sense" (Fleagle 1917, 118). Social betterment clubs, primarily for girls and mothers under the direction of home economics teachers, were organized in practically all the towns of Puerto Rico.

An important task for the Education Department was to impart to a predominantly rural labor force the skills required by a modern agricultural export economy. Commissioner Paul G. Miller reported, "There is a demand for skilled labor—and unless industrial education is emphasized for the express purpose of training artisans skilled in various trades, serious labor troubles will probably ensue" (USDW Annual Report 1916, 357). In 1913 courses in manual arts and home economics were placed in the curriculum. The vocational curriculum in the rural schools was based primarily on cooking and sewing for girls and manual training for boys. Home economics courses were given in the grammar schools, where thousands of "girls are learning something about cooking and making their own clothes" (Clark 1930, 76–77). The course of study in the rural schools extended over six years and included basic knowledge of practical agriculture. Officials expected other industries to develop as quickly as had the embroidery and needlework industries. In 1917 Miller reported that "Employment for the thousands of unemployed persons, especially unemployed women, should be given every possible encouragement" (USDW Annual Report 1917, 467).

Responding to these anticipated labor market needs, the education department offered courses to prepare women for employment not only in the needleworks and apparel industries, but in hat- and basket-making as well; the latter two industries were quickly abandoned for lack of a market. Other courses on cooking, home economics, and sanitation were geared to preparing young girls for work in domestic service. Boys in the ninth and tenth grades enrolled in the urban high schools were required to enroll in manual training classes, including woodworking.

In the process of providing training, the education department obtained some free labor from the students. During the short-lived experiment in industrial education, schoolchildren constructed a two-room schoolhouse, built furniture for the school, repaired school property, and constructed manual training shops. The school board paid only for the material that the students used (Osuna 1949, 226).

Students regularly made salable clothing and handiwork merchandise, and the "teacher found a market for the goods" (Fleagle 1917, 117). Sewing instruction was provided for girls after regular school hours in sixty-three of the seventy municipalities. The clothing was turned over to the teacher if students were unable to pay for the cost of the materials (Verrill 1914, 181). Girls also prepared and served meals for the school lunchrooms (USDW Annual Report 1929, 10). The boys provided unpaid child labor: Part of their "education" included repairing and maintaining the school buildings and making furniture (Verrill 1914, 181).

An unstated objective of these educational programs was to socialize youngsters into understanding and accepting the legitimacy of a gender-based division of labor within the system of generalized commodity production that was rapidly unfolding. A gendered educational program was instituted in which women were trained in activities related to the economic reproduction of the family unit. Women were trained to perform household tasks that were not necessarily required in the formal labor sector. All girls, whether attending rural or urban schools, took courses in household economics from grades six through ten (USDW Annual Report 1913, 361, 363). Through their uncompensated labor, women reduced the economic costs of sustaining and reproducing the family unit. The economic compulsion for male workers in the formal sector to extract higher wages was diminished if female workers at home provided necessities that would ordinarily have to be acquired in the marketplace.

By 1912 unemployment levels were increasing. The superfluity of labor for capitalist production was precisely one of the more serious potential challenges to social stability. Programs in the common schools were expanded to train young people in carpentry, cooking, sewing, cultivation, and other skills that could provide a source of livelihood. Participation in this petty commodity production could supplement meager earnings from salaried work, or could provide sustenance income for those workers and their families who populated the growing contingents of surplus labor.

The Educational System Is of Limited Success

Although the Education Department swallowed up to a third of the colonial state's budget, the commissioners claimed that the funds were insufficient to realize their goals. As early as 1903 the commissioner complained that the federal government had not provided aid, except the initial funding from the trust fund, and called for substantial assistance to sustain the public education system (USDS 1903, 150). In 1909 Governor Post informed the insular legislature that although 100,000 children were receiving education, "it was impossible to sustain this rapid increase" (quoted in Rigual 1967, 80). According to Fred Fleagle, Dean of the University of Puerto Rico, income from insular sources was not sufficient to allow the colonial administration to sustain the continued expansion of the school system (Fleagle 1917, 53).

From 1913 to 1917 enrollments declined significantly, but most dramatically in 1914 (see Table 4.1). The commissioner of education attributed the decline to a $594,000 reduction in appropriations and an executive order that placed a limit on the number of students who could be enrolled with any one teacher (USDW Annual Report 1915, 346). Although the student-teacher ratio improved dramatically during this period, total enrollments declined as the school-age population continued to increase. Education commissioner Miller reported in 1917 that only 35.1 per cent of the total school age population was enrolled (USDW Annual Report 1917, 461), a significant decline from the 50 per cent enrollment rate in 1914 (USDW Annual Report 1914, 368).

In 1914 Governor Yager informed his superiors in Washington that 79 percent of Puerto Rico's 1.2 million people lived in rural areas, and of these, 70 percent were illiterate (USDW Annual Report 1914, 5). Yager reported that the problem of illiteracy was the "darkest and most stubborn of all social and political problems" (5). In his 1915 report the commissioner of education observed with alarm, "The enormous mass of illiterates, in its primitive, uncured condition, is not safe timber to build the good ship of state. We realize that there are serious social and economic problems that have to be solved before the people of Puerto Rico reach the desired goal" (USDW Annual Report 1915, 316). The following year, Governor Yager called for "more schools, more buildings, more teachers . . . before any serious impression can be made upon the tremendous illiteracy which prevails among the masses of the people" (USDW Annual Report 1916, 5). Yager lamented that only 27 percent of children in the rural districts were enrolled in school; he said of the goal of eradicating illiteracy, "How little apparent progress

TABLE 4.1   Statistics on Public Education System

Year	Total Enrollments	Average Attendance	Insular Expenditures	Municipal Expenditures	Number of Schools	Number of Teachers	Average Number Students per Teacher
1913–1914	207,010	155,830	$1,770419	$728,165	1,473	2,535	81
1914–1915	168,319	128,376	$1,312,040	$592,679	1,494	2,461	68
1915–1916	157,394	120,099	$1,848,306	$491,710	1,506	2,468	63.70
1916–1917	155,657	116,779	$1,848,306	$588,067	1,666	2,676	58
1917–1918	142,731	106,441	$1,634,314	$730,947	1,712	2,715	53

SOURCE: Nestor Rigual, *Reseña de los Mensajes de los Gobernadores de Puerto Rico*, 163.

has been made toward its accomplishment in spite of all our efforts. It does not seem possible that the island can possibly ever achieve the education of its masses without outside help. The enormous population relative to area and wealth is too great" (USDW Annual Report 1915, 4–5).

In 1917, Commissioner Miller conceded that as early as 1912 the massive literacy campaign had "reached the point where no further rapid extension was possible or advisable," and the department became more "devoted to the introduction of industrial arts" (USDW Annual Report 1917, 461). José González Ginorio, former general superintendent of schools, criticized the commissioners for failing to develop a long-term comprehensive program of instruction. He complained that "so far there is no definite policy adopted, or conception reached, as to the basic principles of the best system of education, and the best creative agent for the formation of citizens" (quoted in Fernández García 1923, 402–403).

Colonial officials were forced to conclude that after decades of steady investment in the educational system high rates of illiteracy continued to plague the population. The Brookings Institute reported in 1920 that 61 percent of Puerto Ricans over ten years of age were illiterate, and 74 percent of the adult rural population could not read or write (Clark 1930, 77). A decade later the situation had not materially improved. The 1930 United States census reported literacy rates of 37 percent for men and 45.7 percent for women (U.S. Bureau of the Census 1932, 141). In 1931 the commissioner of education, after reporting that fewer than half of the 483,348 school-age children were enrolled in school, adopted a new policy of "intensive rather than of extensive efforts." He admitted that the massive literacy campaigns amounted "only to a smattering of the rudiments of an education which will probably wear off very soon after the children leave school" (USDW Annual Report 1931, 69).

Building the Foundations for Economic Expansion

Although Puerto Rico was a small country, it was endowed with significant economic potential. But when the United States acquired Puerto Rico it encountered a country whose road and irrigation system, communications network, ports and warehouses, and hydroelectric plants were rudimentary and incapable of supporting a modern export economy. For the newly established colonial state, modernizing Puerto Rico's primitive infrastructure was an urgent undertaking. It was a task the Executive Council pursued with single-minded determination, supported by the House of Delegates. By the end of 1917 the Interior and Treasury Departments had left their imprint as dynamic agents in planning, financing, and constructing the development of Puerto Rico's physical infrastructure.

Early U.S. colonial policy in Puerto Rico followed a pattern that was typical of European colonizers. Territories were acquired for economic and strategic reasons, but colonizers needed to develop the territories to efficiently exploit their potential as markets for surplus commodities from the metropolitan economy, as sources of raw materials to satisfy demand in the home market, and as investment sites for financial capital. A colonial state was imposed and empowered to promote capitalist expansion with minimal oversight by the metropolitan state. The colonial subjects were then trained to implement policy and enforce the dictates of the colonial state. Puerto Rico's colonial development followed this trajectory.

The Department of the Interior was the point agency that directed an ambitious program of road, irrigation, and port construction. Development of these facilities was essential if U.S. firms were to be attracted to Puerto Rico. Various sources of revenues were used to finance this sweeping modernization. Returned customs receipts collected by the U.S. Treasury were initially the primary source of financing for road construction. Subsequently new sources of internal revenue and the bond markets provided additional infusions of investment capital. Some infrastructure projects were directly financed by the state, and others were undertaken by private investors who had been granted exclusive contracts.

The Executive Council granted franchises to private foreign firms that undertook much of the infrastructure modernization. It also granted exclusive rights to private firms to provide a range of infrastructure services, many of which were of direct benefit to sugar corporations. Public and private sector activity was mutually supportive. This cooperation between the Executive Council and foreign corporations had converted Puerto Rico by the 1930s into a small, but nonetheless important, market for the industrial goods and technology that were used to build and maintain over a thousand kilometers of roads, irrigation systems, dams and hydroelectric projects, railways and tramways, telegraph and telephone systems, and ports. According to economist Harvey Perloff, "About $45,000,000 of loan funds, in addition to tax revenues amounting to perhaps one-tenth this sum, were spent by the government on roads, schoolhouses, municipal utilities, and combined irrigation and power plants—helping to lay the foundations for economic expansion"(Perloff 1950, 27).

Through the 1920s road construction and irrigation systems were by far the most important development projects undertaken by the colonial state. The politics of public works illustrates the high degree of collaboration between the Executive Council and key foreign and domestic capitalists, and demonstrates how the colonial state set about to accommodate the needs of ascendant sectors of capital.

Creating a Healthy Working Environment

The colonial authorities also developed programs to maintain a healthy labor force and invested heavily in research on tropical diseases. Investment in sanitation systems, disease control, and public health programs were other important components of the colonial state's development project. According to the U.S.

Department of Commerce and Labor, Puerto Rico had a "decided superiority" over "its natural competitors," Cuba, Mexico, and Central America, "in the most essential element of industrial prosperity—an abundant labor force" (U.S. Department of Commerce and Labor 1907, 10). However, 90 percent of the country's population suffered from a debilitating form of anemia. Medical surgeon Baily K. Ashford discovered that hookworms were the source of this disease, which he identified as uncinariasis. He demonstrated that changes in hygiene and sanitation would eradicate the disease (see Puerto Rico. Commission for the study and treatment of "Anemia" in Puerto Rico 1904). The severe impact of the debilitating disease on the productivity of the already undernourished worker was well known. According to travel writer W. D. Boyce, "A person afflicted with hookworm cannot do hard work. Since the average anemic peon could do only half of his normal amount of work, you can see how great an annual loss there was both to the laborer and to the island itself" (Boyce 1914, 432).

The study and prevention of communicable diseases was a priority for the colonial state. Governor William Hunt called on the government to "stamp out the disease" in order to succeed in the "rehabilitation of the physique of the Porto Rico laboring people" (USDS 1904, 28). The legislature was disposed "to be generous," since it meant "nothing less than the physical regeneration of a million people" (U.S. Department of Commerce and Labor 1907, 10). Improvement of sanitary conditions was also a priority, although Congress had failed to authorize funds for this area. The Bureau of Insular Affairs reported: "The United States has much more than a humanitarian interest in this. The constantly increasing commercial intercourse and the increasing travel between the island and the mainland give it a very practical interest in the establishment of healthful conditions in the island that will avoid as far as possible the likelihood of serious epidemics" (USDW Annual Report 1911, 18). A sanitation service under the control of an independent health board was established in 1912. By 1916, on the eve of U.S. entrance into the European war, disease control was "regarded as unusually urgent because of the approaching encampment of solders in the island" (USDW Annual Report 1918, 8).

Roads for the Market

Colonial officials were determined to make the fertile interior of the country accessible to commerce and expand the opportunities for the agricultural exploitation of these regions. Road construction and maintenance became the single most important—and costly—component of the ambitious program to rebuild Puerto Rico's infrastructure. In 1899, Commissioner Carroll emphasized that building roads was the "subject of the greatest importance. It is fundamental to the well-being and progress of Porto Rico" (Carroll 1899, 40). General Davis also stressed the importance of modern roads. He reported that "without them industrial development is impossible. . . . In the sugar districts good metalled roads are indispensable (USDW 1900b, 44). The military regimes spent approximately $1 million for road construction and maintenance (USDW 1901, 73; USDCL 1907, 30). Tulio Larrinaga, Puerto Rico's first resident commissioner, testified before the Carroll Commission in 1899 that "the greatest drawback in the development and progress of the island of Puerto Rico has been the absence of good roads and of any other means of transportation" (Carroll 1899, 158). According to Governor Allen, "The crying need of the island is above all things roads. It is an imperative necessity to devote every dollar which can be spared from the surplus revenue to the construction of permanent roads" (USDW 1901, 73).

In 1900 half of the government revenues were used for building and maintaining roads and for education. In addition, the Department of the Interior received an allocation of $250,000 for "extraordinary expenses" to fulfill the contractual obligations incurred by the military (Hollander 1901, 579, 562). When the trust fund was exhausted in 1907, the council authorized the sale of $1,000,000 worth of bonds to finance the road campaign (USDCL 1907, 31). In 1916 an additional $2 million for road construction and maintenance was raised from sale of government bonds (USDW Annual Report 1917, 31).

At the end of the first eight years of U.S. rule about $5.1 million had been spent to build 788 kilometers of roads, three times as much as the Spanish had built (Clark 1930, 344). Transportation costs dropped dramatically; by 1906 savings in this area were estimated at 50 to 70 percent (U.S. Department of Commerce and Labor 1907, 30). By 1910 Governor Colton reported to the legislature that a thousand kilometers of roads had been built at a total cost of $7 million (Rigual 1967, 90). By 1912 road construction consumed over half of the Interior Department's budget (calculated from USDW Annual Report 1912, 323–324). A severe financial crisis in 1915 forced the suspension of all public works, and during the war years road construction activity was significantly reduced (USDW Annual Report 1915, 28). In 1917 the road building program was reactivated with the funds obtained from the sale of insular bonds, and by the end of the year Puerto Rico was covered by over 1,178 kilometers of macadamized roads, an annual average of 50.2 kilometers (USDW Annual Report 1917, 31, 395). Transportation costs dramatically declined with the improved road system.

The municipal governments were stripped of their control over road construction, and this function was centralized in the council. In 1902 Puerto Rico was divided into seven road districts, each supervised by an elected three-man commission. These commissions were wholly independent of the municipalities, and had "very extensive powers in respect to opening, laying out and maintaining local highways." However, as was the case with the district school boards and the authority of the commissioner of education, the commissions were "subject to the rigid control and supervision of the commissioner of the interior" (Willoughby 1905, 144). The municipalities were required to turn over to the commission 8 percent of all revenues generated from the property tax and authorized to issue road construction bonds. Although the municipal governments were the legal entities that incurred debt and collected taxes to finance the extensive road construction and education construction, they had no voice in how these programs were run. William Willoughby observed,

> The municipalities have practically no voice in respect to either education or public works. Their influence ceases when the perfunctory action has been taken of including each year in their budgets the sums which the law requires shall be handed over to the school boards. Although deriving their income from them they are independent in every way of the municipalities. (Willoughby 1905, 148)

The road construction and maintenance program helped alleviate an acute unemployment problem. Auditor Cabot Ward felt that the road-building program was motivated in part by this reason: "The large sums provided by the United States did much to give employment in road building, which was conducted with a view towards relieving the most needy district by building small pieces of road in various sections" (Ward 1908, 150). Under this program in 1900, according to the next year's annual report, "male heads of households were hired to break stones for road maintenance." But in 1901, the report continued, demand among Puerto Rico's unemployed for work on road construction "was so great many have to be refused." Those fortunate enough to get hired received "30 cents per day—a small amount, but doing a great deal of good" (USDS 1901, 328). Revenues, however, failed to keep up with the expenses associated with the ambitious road-building project. Judge H. G. Curtis, a member of the Insular Commission, warned of the need for continued public works employment: "Laborers stand idle, the road funds being exhausted, aimlessly and hopelessly seeking work. . . . If these men are held out of work trouble will follow and disorder ensue" (quoted in Luque de Sánchez 1983, 149).

Although lacking the funds to hire workers, colonial authorities remained firmly committed to sustaining the road projects and resorted to cost-cutting measures in order to so. By 1903, the program to hire day laborers in order to temporarily alleviate unemployment was terminated. The state resorted to the use of unpaid convict labor as a cost-cutting measure. On March 1, 1903 the Insular Police was ordered "to guard 300 convicts employed in building roads." According to police chief Colonel Hamill, "this work was never done heretofore by prisoners" (USDS 1903, 306). The commissioner of the interior reported that "scarcity of laborers along certain sections of the island made necessary the use of convict labor during the year." The prisoner camps were set up along the construction site, but "convict labor was also used on those sections of road lying within distances of about 6 kilometers from towns where there are district jails, from which the gang of prisoners" was taken out every day (USDW Annual Report 1917, 391).

Convict labor was used despite the high rates of unemployment, which had increased to about 18 percent in 1910.[1] The government reported that in 1914 "in all work of maintenance prison labor has been used as far as possible. Prisoners have been quartered in portable camps or in rented quarters and are paid a wage of 5 cents per day," which amounted to "less than one fourth the wage paid free labor" (USDW Annual Report 1914, 307). In 1915 the prison laborers "furnished 176,767 days labor" in road construction, and through this labor "much of the expense for maintaining penal institutions [was] returned to the government" (USDW Annual Report 1915, 47, 49).

Considerable savings were realized by relying on this captive labor force. The BIA reported that during 1910 and 1911 roads constructed by convict labor "averaged in costs $5,500 per kilometer, or some $500 less than when the work was done entirely under contract or by free labor" (USDW BIA 1912, 40). In 1915 the savings were estimated at $76,193, which represented approximately 10 percent of the insular government's expenses for salaries (calculated from USDW Annual Report 1915, 38, 262). The following year, in 1916, prisoners performed 69,161 days of work on state roads, but in 1917 this figure jumped to 112,159 days of labor, which according to the attorney general amounted "to a large saving in the expense of road making on the island" (USDW Annual Report 1917, 516–517). Governor Colton was so satisfied with the work of the conscript labor force "as to remove any doubt as to the advantage of permanently continuing its use in public works" (40). Governor Colton noted in the report that much of the cost of maintaining the insular penal institutions was reimbursed "in labor performed by convicts under legislative authority in the construction of roads," labor that he estimated was worth $86,475 (USDW Annual Report 1912, 49).

Despite its preference for unpaid convict labor, the Interior Department had to occasionally resort to wage labor for much of the construction. But the government did not want to compete with the growers and enacted a measure limiting the pay of common laborers to a maximum of 45 cents per day, "the legislation being intended to equalize wages and protect the coffee and sugar districts from the loss of labor consequent on the payment of greatly increased wages by the government" (USDS 1904, 23). Reliance on coerced labor and starvation wages failed to relieve the drain on the treasury as it continued to resurface Puerto Rico's terrain with stone-covered roads. Until 1907 road construction was financed from internal sources, but thereafter insular bonds were sold to generate capital for continued road expansion. From about 1910 to 1930, $20 million was raised for road construction and maintenance (Clark 1930, 344).

Commissioner Elliot's program to reduce the excessive high unemployment rates by hiring cheap labor for road construction was abandoned because of limited state revenues. But the objective of the road-building program—gaining access to the interior of the country in order to bring agricultural areas into productive use and increase the level of commercial activity—was indeed realized. The colonial authorities proved adept at using indigenous labor, talent, and resources to build a network of first-class roads throughout the island.

Water for Sugar

After touring the sugar districts shortly after his arrival in January 1900, Governor Allen informed Secretary of War Root: "There is at least $40 per ton gold profit on every ton of sugar and with that margin there's not a business in the U.S. can hold a candle to it; the great profits will be further increased by a [illegible] reduction in two years of the present easy duties. This of course means the immediate development of thousands of acres of sugar lands now unworked" (quoted in Gannon 1978, 328).

Large-scale commercial sugarcane cultivation could not be undertaken in the southern coastal plains because the area lacked sufficient water and rainfall. An extensive irrigation system had to be established before U.S. sugar corporations would invest in the area of the coastal plains. The Interior Department was given the task of constructing an irrigation system for 33,000 acres on the southern coast. The region included virtually the entire sugarcane growing district of Guayama (see Guayama sugar growers testimony in Carroll 1899, 88–89, 102–104). Guayama was an important economic district in which sugarcane was grown to the exclusion of all other export crops. But crop losses were usually substantial. The drought of 1907–1908 resulted in losses estimated at $4.3 million, and additional losses for 1909 were estimated at $2 million (USDS 1908, 188).

In 1908 the legislature authorized $25,000 for a feasibility study for the irrigation project. According to the BIA chief, the project would "reclaim in part and immensely benefit the whole of one of the largest and most important cane-producing sections of the island, heretofore suffering from more or less continuous or regular droughts" (USDW BIA 1909, 23). The chief engineer of the project reported,

> Indeed it would be directly for the benefit of the United States, owing to the fact that this country draws heavily on Porto Rico for its supplies of raw sugar. As the Porto Rican commodity is admitted duty free, whereas Cuban and Dutch East Indian sugar is subjected to duty, there is a manifest advantage to the American people in facilitating the extension of the industry in our West Indian colony. The irrigation project will be of inestimable benefit to the planters on the south side, and to the island in general. There are at present thousands of acres of arid lands that could be converted into rich soil if only water could be brought to the ground. (USDS 1908, 184)

The irrigation project was one phase of an ambitious program to develop the physical infrastructure of the southern region, and in the process to encourage intensive sugarcane cultivation in the area. In 1908 Puerto Rico issued a $4 million bond offering to finance the construction of the irrigation system (USDS 1908, 23). The following year Governor Colton asked the legislature to approve an additional $500,000 bond issue to complete the project (Rigual 1967, 100).

Cost overruns continued, and in 1915 the treasurer reported that an additional $400,000 had been raised through bonds for the irrigation project (USDW Annual Report 1915, 239). Altogether the BIA sold bonds totaling $5 million to build the irrigation system (Clark 1930, 360). Work on the project was completed in 1914 and provided water to some 24,000 acres lying in a 50-mile strip in the southern coastal plain (USDW Annual Report 1914, 42).

Three dams were completed in 1914, which according to Governor Yager constituted "the most important feature of the great irrigation system . . . and one by one as each was finished and filled its gates were opened and its canals filled with water for the hungry sugar lands" (USDW Annual Report 1914, 42). The intended beneficiaries of the new irrigation system were the large sugar corporations, which by 1910 already controlled or owned a substantial portion of the land in the southern coastal plain.

The Central Aguirre dominated the district; by 1920 its output of sugar accounted for 10.4 percent of Puerto Rico's total production (Quintero Rivera 1988, 161). Central Aguirre was one of the four largest sugar corporations in Puerto Rico; it had extensive landholdings and processing plants and operated railroads in the Guayama region. Guayama became one of the districts most characterized by the concentration of productive assets by absentee corporations. In their classic *Porto Rico: A Broken Pledge*, the Diffies observe, "The Porto Rican Government has constructed an irrigation system which protects the crops of this company from drought" (Diffie and Diffie 1931, 49).

According to the Puerto Rico Irrigation Service, the project was extremely successful: "The production of sugar from lands in the irrigation district was greater this season than ever before. . . . It would have been impossible to produce this increase, or even maintain the former output, during these dry years, without the water furnished by the irrigation system" (USDW Annual Report 1916, 338). Governor Yager also reported that the irrigation system "has been the salvation of the sugar planters in the district which it serves." After two of the driest years in the country's history, "most of the planters on the south side of the island would have been financially ruined" if not for the reservoirs (USDW Annual Report 1919, 41).

The prices of sugarcane acreage soared because of the increased yields and reduced risk attributable to the irrigation system. The market value of cane land increased from $30 per acre in 1898 to $200 per acre in 1910 (Puerto Rico, Office of the Secretary 1911, 156). Prices for sugarcane acreage were the highest in the fertile plains that were irrigated and that were situated near roads, railroads, and ports. In Guayama the value of cane land increased from $99 to $135 per acre between 1907 and 1913, and by 1917 had soared to between $350 and $400 an acre (USDS 1908, 76; USDW Annual Report 1914, 245; 1917, 336). Clearly the motivation for small sugar producers to sell their land to the absentee corporations was indeed great. The pressures to sell increased as the smaller farms expended their earnings to pay for crop-related expenses and monopoly prices for railroad transit, and to meet their tax obligations (Clark 1930, 625; Diffie and Diffie 1931, 210). Harold Sloan described the process: "The sugar centrals constantly reached out for more and more acreage in order to assure themselves an adequate supply of cane. Land values advanced, and small farmers by the thousands, tempted by the high prices, sold out their farms, only to find themselves permanently disenfranchised from the soil" (Sloan 1929).

The chief engineer of the Guayama Irrigation Service reported that "four large plantations included nearly 80 per cent of the land irrigated (Clark 1930, 362). The irrigation project also included canals that diverted water to the hydroelectric plants of the U.S.-owned Porto Rico Railway, Light and Power Company (Clark 1930, 359). While the irrigation project was under construction, the Executive Council approved a franchise for the municipality of Ponce to build a $300,000 pier to be financed by the sale of municipal bonds (USDW Annual Report 1912, 35). Ponce is adjacent to Guayama and the site of one of Puerto Rico's three most important ports. In 1915, a year after the irrigation system was completed, the Executive Council enacted an ordinance granting the municipality of Guayama a franchise to operate an electrical distribution system (USDW Annual Report 1915, 40). These plants provided electrical energy to the district, including the *centrales* that processed the cane.

Modern roads linked Guayama to other key centers. According to government officials, by 1910 Guayama could be "reached by excellent highways from San Juan, Ponce and the eastern end of the Island" (Puerto Rico, Office of the Secretary 1911, 97). Arroyo, the Guayama district's port, was rapidly developed and had access to worldwide cable communication. The largest commercial firms and consular offices were located in Arroyo. By 1914 an infrastructure was built that included modern roads, irrigation systems, hydroelectric plants, port facilities, and telegraph services—all financed and built by the colonial state. These utilities were made readily available to absentee sugar corporations. This early pattern of direct colonial state financing of infrastructure development, which was directly related to significant denationalization of productive assets, is one of the permanent features of capitalist development under colonial management.

Private Gain and Public Debt

The infrastructure development was a lucrative endeavor for U.S. corporations. Road construction was an important source of earnings and income for U.S. manufacturers of transportation vehicles, agricultural machinery, and construction materials. Table 4.2 demonstrates the increasing importance of capital goods imports in Puerto Rico's merchandise trade with the United States. Manufactured iron and steel products accounted for over $2.6 million, or over 7 percent of the total value of imports in 1916 (USDW Annual Report 1916, 9).

By arranging for the sale of tax-exempt, interest-bearing bonds to finance road and irrigation projects, the BIA and the colonial state were directly involved in

TABLE 4.2 Composition of Selected Merchandise Imports to Puerto Rico, 1901–1920

Class of Imports	1901		1914		1920		1901–1920	
	In Thousands of Dollars	*Percentage Distribution of Total Imports*	*In Thousands of Dollars*	*Percentage Distribution of Total Imports*	*In Thousands of Dollars*	*Percentage Distribution of Total Imports*	*Difference in Thousands of Dollars*	*Percentage Increase of Value of Imports*
Motor, Railway cars, Other Vehicles and Other Transportation Equipment	71	0.8	538	1.5	2,372	2.5	2,301	3,340
Machinery and Supplies used in Manufacturing	519	5.8	2,302	6.3	6,828	7.1	6,309	1,215
Machinery and Supplies for Agriculture	—	—	762	2.1	3,577	3.7	2,815	469
Building Materials	992	11.1	4,868	13.4	9,443	9.8	3,876	950

SOURCE: Adapted from Victor S. Clark, *Porto Rico and Its Problems*, 407.

transferring capital from Puerto Rico to investors in the United States. Customs receipts and internal revenue sources financed the purchase of machinery and technology necessary for road and irrigation construction, as well as to repay the bond-holders. These improvements disproportionately benefited the large sugar corporations that relied on the irrigation systems to increase their crop yields and on the roads to transport their product to port. In turn, the increase in productivity and reduction in delivery time to the market increased their profits, the overwhelming majority of which were repatriated to the United States.

By 1917 the sale of bonds was routinely arranged in order to obtain quick and large infusions of capital to finance public works projects. As early as 1911 the total insular and municipal bond indebtedness for road construction and irrigation projects was $5.3 million—an unusual level of debt considering that the total receipts in that year were $6.8 million (USDW Annual Report 1911, 41, 304). Three years later, in 1914, the bonded indebtedness had increased to $5.9 million, of which fully 65 percent was attributable to irrigation bonds (calculated from USDW Annual Report 1914, 15). The colonial state's debt continued to increase and by 1918 had doubled to $10.8 million (Clark 1930, 326). The purchasers of insular government and municipal bonds realized lucrative earnings on these bonds, which were marketed by the BIA and backed by the U.S. Treasury Department (McIntyre 1932, 299–300). The Brookings Institute reported that the borrowing policy had "been definitely harmful. The chief result of the borrowing has been a great waste of public revenue by diverting it to the payment of interest, while the piling up of debt charges is almost certain to cause hardships for the country during future periods of reduced prosperity" (Clark 1930, 304).

Years later Governor Theodore Roosevelt Jr. also criticized the colonial state's deficit financing schemes. "Not only this, but large bond issues had been sold for projects that were entirely out of keeping with a community as poor as Puerto Rico" (Roosevelt 1970, 109). The colonial state had shackled the Puerto Rican people with a substantial debt to finance an ambitious program of infrastructure modernization. This public works program was essential to lure investors and to create profitable investment climate for export oriented corporations. Yet, as I will discuss below, the very corporations that benefited handsomely from the infrastructure related public works strenuously fought any changes in the tax regime that increased their liability.

Although Puerto Rican taxpayers were shackled with ever growing public debt, the colonial administrators were convinced that borrowing afforded the only means by which to effect the transition to modern export agriculture. Treasury Secretary Charles Hill reported, "The providing of additional revenue was imperatively necessary to enable the government to continue its present activities" (USDW Annual Report 1916, 261). The interior department used the borrowed capital to finance the modernization of the country's archaic infrastructure with the aim of more effectively exploiting Puerto Rico's natural resources. Presumably both employment and commercial activity would increase and generate sufficient tax revenues which would be used to liquidate the public indebtedness. But, by 1916, expenditures by the colonial administration had seriously outstripped revenues.

Governor Yager announced that "the only solution" to the revenue problem was "to increase the tax on the property of the island which receives most of the benefits of government, and whose owners are the most able to pay for this support." Yager informed the legislature that "an unusually large percentage of the property of the island is owned by nonresidents." In an indirect reference to the absentee corporations, he criticized "these absent owners," because "they contribute practically nothing to the insular government which has done so much for them. The increase in the value of their property is almost wholly due to the improvements furnished by, and the fostering care of, the insular government" (USDW Annual Report 1917, 261). Yager went on to report that the "present taxes upon property in Porto Rico are very light compared with those of any other progressive country," especially the United States. In fact the tax burdens on the small domestic sugar producers were disproportionately greater than those paid by the large corporations. Almost a decade later Governor Towner reminded capitalists that "taxes are exceedingly small as compared with taxes in the United States" (USDW Annual Report 1924, 5). The Brookings Institute report documented the inequity of Puerto Rico's tax regime: "Puerto Rico's property tax . . . favors the rich farmer. The small farmer earns less upon his investment than the large, and his property taxes are a higher percentage of his income" (Clark 1930, 190).

Public Franchises: Regulating Competition and Allocating Resources

Even though the financing and construction of roads, ports, and irrigation systems were arranged by the colonial state and the BIA, the communications and rail transportation systems were owned and operated by private investors who had been granted franchises by the Executive Council. Few domestic firms had the capital, technological know-how, or management experience to compete with U.S. corporations in these areas. Before concluding his tour of duty General Davis emphasized that the state must become actively involved in infrastructure development.

> It is of the utmost importance for industrial development of the island that some way should be quickly found by means of which public improvements can be undertaken by foreign capital. Capitalists can not now invest under any satisfactory conditions, for there is no authority in Puerto Rico that can confer corporate rights and authority upon associated capital applied to the building of roads and the installation of manufactures. (USDW 1900b, 43)

Once the Foraker Act went into effect U.S. corporations immediately submitted applications for franchises. Between 1900 and 1905, sixty-three Puerto Rican firms and ninety-two U.S. firms applied for franchises. During this early period the single most frequent franchise request was for railroad construction permits; twenty-four U.S. firms and twelve Puerto Rican companies applied for these (Luque de Sánchez 1983, 157). The Executive Council approved hundreds of applications for franchises: Water rights for irrigation, and electric power were the most numerous. In 1917 the council enacted twenty-eight ordinances, seven of which were for irrigation of sugar plantations and eight for water rights to generate electric power (USDW Annual Report 1917, 459). Scores of U.S. firms were granted franchises to build and operate railways and street cars, telephone and telegraph systems, piers and docks, gas and hydroelectric plants.

The American Railroad Company was one of the earliest and most important companies to obtain a franchise. In 1902 the company obtained rights to build and operate a rail line between Ponce and Mayagüez (USDS 1903, 57). In 1903 it constructed a line connecting Aguadilla with Ponce, and in the process "giving great impulse to the sugar-cane industry" (Puerto Rico, Office of the Secretary 1911, 32). By 1905 the company had constructed additional rail lines that connected the large sugar *centrales* operating on the northern and southern coasts (USDS 1905, 26). American Railroad soon dominated the railroad system, after it took over the Porto Rico Railroad Company (Diffie and Diffie 1931, 114). American Railroad maintained extremely close relations with the U.S. absentee sugar corporations, which determined where the railroad company would install some of its lines (Luque de Sánchez 1983, 162). Many railroad companies were actually subsidiaries of the sugar corporations, and by the 1920s these furnished 86 percent of the railroad's freight (Clark 1930, 371). In 1913 the Fajardo Development Company, one of the largest absentee sugar corporations, was granted a franchise "to construct, maintain, and operate a railway" connecting the major towns in northeast Puerto Rico (USDW Annual Report 1913, 77).

U.S. and Canadian firms dominated the electric utilities. The Porto Rico Light and Power Company, a subsidiary of a Canadian firm, owned and operated the electric power and distribution system and the only tramway in San Juan (Diffie and Diffie 1931, 110). This firm also owned and operated the hydroelectric power plants that supplied energy to the sugarcane-growing section of Guayama (Clark 1930, 359). The communications system was overwhelmingly owned and operated by U.S. firms, some of them subsidiaries of large corporations. In 1913 a franchise was granted to Porto Rico General Telephone, a subsidiary of the International Telephone and Telegraph Corporation, to replace San Juan's antiquated system and to install a local and long-distance telephone system (USDW Annual Report 1913, 38). According to Governor Colton, this project was "one of the most important franchises approved that year" (USDW Annual Report 1912, 35). In 1913 Porto Rico General Telephone was granted a new franchise that allowed the company to connect all the towns on the eastern part of the island, which reduced receipts of the state telegraph service by 42 percent (USDW Annual Report 1913, 266).

Much of the communications, transportation, and energy infrastructure was built primarily to service the needs of the rapidly expanding export industries in tobacco, sugar, and fruits. In many instances the public service corporations operated as appendages of the sugar corporations, which tended to use the bulk of their services and generated the most fees. The BIA complained that no agency was established with "the purpose of keeping track of operations under franchises or of seeing that the obligation on the part of the grantees were rigidly complied with" (USDS 1908, 36). Unregulated, these firms often provided unreliable and inefficient service to the general public, and some failed to comply with the conditions of the franchises they were granted. In response to growing dissatisfaction with the poor service and excessive rates charged by public service corporations, and concerned with possible tax evasion and noncompliance with the franchise terms, the legislative assembly enacted a measure in 1908 to regulate these corporations. The attorney general was authorized to institute proceedings to enforce compliance with the orders of the Executive Council (USDW Annual Report 1911, 17). Two years later the council received an appropriation to investigate the public service corporations.

Laws, Cops, and Jails

Although often overlooked, the subject of the coercive agencies of the colonial state and their role in the process of Americanization is an important aspect of Puerto Rico's colonial formation. The colonial state was managed by a group of officials who believed in the moral superiority of their enterprise. They expected the colonial subjects to understand the wisdom of their evangelical crusade of Americanization. The colonizers expected Puerto Ricans to embrace the full panoply of institutional and economic change they proposed. But if Puerto Ricans resisted the colonizing mission, the colonial state was prepared to unleash its monopoly of coercive force to impose compliance. Puerto Rico was undergoing dramatic and unprecedented changes, which led to profound social disruptions and political opposition. Independent loci of political power and influence that could impede the colonial enterprise had to be eliminated. As we saw, the *municipios*, traditional seats of power for the political parties, were virtually stripped of effective political power and control over resources, and rendered impotent to challenge the dictates of the colonial state. Practically all positions of influence in the judiciary, constabulary, and penal systems were delegated to U.S. citizens from the metropole.

The coercive agencies of the colonial state were responsible for enforcing compliance with many of the laws that comprised the Americanization process. The insular police force apprehended violators of the law, protected private property, broke up strikes, and stood ready to suppress insurrection. The office of attorney general enforced local and federal laws, and prosecuted violators. An independent judiciary consisting of the supreme court and district and municipal courts interpreted the law and issued sentences. The U.S. district court provided protection to U.S. and foreign nationals in Puerto Rico. The Puerto Rican regiment of the U.S. army stood ready to suppress threats to the metropolitan power. This was an impressive judicial and repressive arsenal patterned on the systems in place in the United States. Naturally, all these agencies were extremely effective means of socializing Puerto Ricans into accepting the legitimacy of the new colonial power.

Americanizing Puerto Rico's Laws

Shortly after Puerto Rico's acquisition, Philip C. Hanna observed, "This island not only needs American officials to administer law, but it sadly needs American law to be administered." He lamented that "our American officers here are called upon to administer a set of laws which made Spain a failure for four hundred years " (quoted in Trías Monge 1980, 1:201). Harvard professor L. A. Lowell believed that Puerto Rico could not function under U.S. "political systems unless she first becomes thoroughly familiar with our judicial conceptions" (Lowell, 1898). According to some analysts Puerto Rico's legal system "seriously obstructed the introduction of American ideas and methods" (Wilson 1905, 105). According to William Willoughby, many of Puerto Rico's laws "were framed on principles so contrary to American practice that the substitution of other laws for them was extremely desirable" (Willoughby 1902, 38). Congress wanted to transform Puerto Rico's legal system quickly, and included in the Foraker Act a provision for a three-person commission to compile and revise the laws of Puerto Rico. The committee operated independently of the colonial administration and was instructed to present its findings directly to Congress. For R. L. Rowe, a member of the commission, "The question presented itself of how far the American system could safely be introduced without undermining social order and without introducing uncertainty and instability into public affairs" (Rowe 1904, 153, 155). Within nine months the commission rendered its report but Congress, possibly heeding Rowe's advice, took no action (Trías Monge 1991, 95).

Governor Henry, however, signed a measure in 1901 that established an insular code commission that "shall report appropriate codes to the next legislature." The recommendations of this second code commission set into motion the transformation of Puerto Rico's legal system (USDS 1901, 77–78). Secretary Willoughby was certain that with the new codes the legislature had enacted, Puerto Rico "will now be able to continue her advancement under a system of law closely in accord with American practice and principle" (Willoughby 1902, 38).

The Spanish penal code and laws of civil and criminal procedures "were replaced with exact copies of the California and Montana codes," which brought the Puerto Rican "system into complete harmony with the criminal law of most of the States of the Union" (Wilson 1905, 84; Graffam 1986, 115). The civil and commercial codes were amended according to the Louisiana Civil Code (Graffam 1986, 115). Governor Allen went on to inspire potential investors: "Capitalists can be assured of protection to their property and investments, guaranteed in the form of government, in the tax laws, and in the reorganization of the courts, and capital is pretty sure to take care of itself" (Wood, Taft, and Allen 1902, 366).

Spanish commercial law was revised to reflect U.S. concepts of corporate rights and protection. In order to establish a favorable investment climate, the colonial state passed generous corporate tax laws. According to Rowe, it was "a matter of importance to the industrial future of the island that this branch of the civil law [Spanish code of commerce] be made to harmonize with our American system" and to bring "the existing law into harmony with modern industrial needs"(Rowe 1904 163).

Americanization via the Courts: Two Judicial Worlds

By 1905 Puerto Rico had "a complete system of practice in the courts, similar in its main features to that existing in the code states of the United States" (USDS 1905, 32). In his 1905 review of Puerto Rico's institutional transformation Willoughby observed,

> In no other regard have institutions of Porto Rico existing under Spanish rule un-
> dergone so complete a change at the hands of the Americans as in respect to judicial
> organization and procedure. The entire system of courts, the civil and criminal law
> and judicial procedures have been wholly altered. Nothing remains of the system of
> courts that was found when the American forces landed. The Spanish codes, politi-
> cal, civil and criminal, have been abolished and in their place have been substituted
> others following in all essential particulars the system of law and procedure found in
> the American States. (Willoughby 1905, 107)

Two court systems operated in Puerto Rico: a U.S. district and an insular court system. The U. S. court had jurisdiction over cases that typically fell under the ju-risdiction of the district and circuit courts in the United States. It thus operated to protect the property and civil rights of U.S. citizens. The U.S. district court was an important institution for socializing the population in the norms of the U.S. legal system as well. Rowe observed that "as a distinctly American tribunal it has done much to acquaint the native population, especially lawyers, with the proce-dure of American courts" (Rowe 1904, 212). Governor Hunt similarly acknowl-edged the centrality of the judicial system in the colonizing mission: "There is no more ready or more practical method of Americanizing our new possessions than by the enactment and enforcement of American laws, and the introduction and practice of American jurisprudence" (USDS 1904, 26). The U.S. district court system was bitterly opposed by Puerto Rico's political leaders, who saw it as an instrument of the metropolitan state to protect the interests of its citizens against claims brought by the colonial subjects. Proceedings before the court had to be conducted in English.

The insular court system consisted of a supreme court, five district courts, and twenty-four municipal courts with jurisdiction over the colonial subjects. The chief justice and four associate judges of the supreme court were appointed by the president. The rulings of this court could be appealed to the U.S. Supreme Court. Each of Puerto Rico's district courts was composed of three judges, who were appointed by the governor. The judges of the municipal court system were elected by popular vote to serve for four years, but the governor retained the right to dismiss the judges for just cause (Delgado Cintrón 1988, 186).

Policing the Colony

Laws have meaning for the state only if they achieve the intended effect, and they are likely to be obeyed only if the authorities prescribe sanctions for noncompliance and have the coercive capability to identify, apprehend, and punish those who violate the edicts of the state. The attorney general was the principal officer responsible for enforcing the new and old laws of Puerto Rico. In 1901 Governor Allen observed, "On the whole this little island has been reasonably orderly and law abiding under the control of the civil government" (USDW 1901, 83). Although armed opposition to U.S. rule was virtually nonexistent, the colonial regime nonetheless under took a "very strict and far reaching crusade" to disarm the population (Verrill 1914, 147). As we have seen, the *partidas sediciosas* (1898–1900) were the most sustained and violent challenges to public order but were not directed against the military regime. Similarly, the Republican *turbas* were urban mob outbursts aimed at the Federal Party and the Federación Libre de Trabajadores, not the new colonizers.

During the first years of civilian colonial rule the insular and municipal police forces maintained public order. Governor Hunt confidently proclaimed in 1904, "Order prevails throughout the island. This is due principally to the efficiency of the insular constabulary force" (USDS 1904, 27). His successor, Beekman Winthrop, observed that "the success is still more remarkable, when it is considered that an island of 3,600 square miles with more than 1 million inhabitants, which during Spanish times was guarded by over a thousand men in addition to the regular force of municipal police, is now policed by this small body of 550 officers and men" (USDS 1905, 33). The municipal police had been under the control of the mayors, who acted as police magistrates. However, U.S. officials claimed that this system was inefficient and highly politicized; they viewed the municipal police as instruments of "political oppression by mayors against persons of opposite political faith" (USDW 1901, 104). In 1901 the municipal police were disbanded, the magistrate duties of the mayor were rescinded, and control over all police matters was centralized in the governor's office. The strength of the insular police force was increased from 420 to 739 men (USDW 1901, 83). The force was distributed among six military districts, and a school was established to provide semimilitary training to sixty men, ten from each of the districts (USDS 1903, 38). According to Governor Post, the insular police force was "semi military in both organization and appearance. The discipline, drill and regulations of the force are in many respects similar to those of the Army" (USDS 1908, 39).

The police force had the authority to enforce laws and regulations at the municipal and insular levels. According to the attorney general, the governor requested and obtained sole authority to appoint the sixty-six municipal police magistrates, "in order to absolutely remove these police magistrates from connection with local politics" (USDW 1901, 140). Commissioner Rowe reported, "Probably no other measure contributed as much toward allaying the feeling of uneasiness of the propertied classes, who showed great fear lest American rule might mean the dominance of the negro or the peon" (Rowe 1904, 157). It is important to recall that the Republican Party, which controlled all the seats in the House of Delegates, approved this legislation, which further undermined the municipalities that were an important source of local patronage and political power for the Federal Party—the Republican Party's archenemy.

In 1903, the newly appointed insular police chief and former captain of the Porto Rico Regiment, Terence Hamill, called for increasing the strength of the office by 250 men, including a 150-man mounted unit (USDS 1903, 309). The following year, after the constabulary was strengthened, the last remaining municipal police force was disbanded. In taking this action Governor Winthrop wrote, "Now the police regulations and administration are uniform throughout the island and the entire police force is the responsibility of the governor. We have relied upon the Porto Rican insular police, which is well able to meet any situation that may arise." (USDS 1904, 27)

In March 1908 the Insular Police Service was established and placed under the general supervision of a three-person Police Commission appointed by the governor. The commission set regulations and examined applicants for the force. It also reorganized the command structure and assigned the police force to patrol the municipalities. The chief of police continued to be appointed by the governor and was required to report directly to him (USDS 1908, 25; Puerto Rico, Office of the Secretary 1911, 78). Until the mid–1920s the insular police force numbered about 700 officers and men, although the force was strengthened during the electoral period from October to November.

The U.S. army had a garrison of twelve infantry companies and two batteries of artillery stationed in Puerto Rico, which could be mobilized for this purpose. In 1906 the Porto Rico Regiment had a strength of 548 enlisted Puerto Ricans, and 31 officers, 5 of whom were "citizens of Porto Rico" (U.S. Department of Commerce and Labor 1907, 37). One reason for the reduced military presence was Puerto Rico's proximity to the new metropolitan power. The United States could deploy troops in Puerto Rico much more quickly than Spain could have.

The Police and Workers on Strike

It is instructive to briefly review the role of the insular police in suppressing labor agitation and protecting the property of large landowners. As early as 1905 the insular police were ordered to handle "a strike situation in the sugar districts." William Lutz, acting chief of the insular police, reported,

> The services rendered by the members of the force can only be estimated by the enormous loss that would have been the consequence had the police not interfered with the twenty or thirty discontent agitators, who preaching incendiarism, were ready to sacrifice the sugar crop of the island. This again caused the appointing of 75 men for temporary duty, police protection withdrawn from other parts of the island to send them to the sugarcane districts.(USDS 1905, 144)

The Union Party supported legislation in 1910 that authorized the governor to provide police assistance to the sugar plantations. Under the law landowners were required to reimburse the insular treasury for the wages of police stationed on their property (Quintero Rivera 1976, 52). Landowners had a particular interest in supporting the insular police force and contributed money in 1913 to maintain the mounted constabulary when the legislature failed to appropriate funds for the unit (USDW Annual Report 1914, 25). Governor Yager observed that when the legislature abolished the unit it "proved to be a mistake, and this mistake became evident during the strike and disorders among the workers in the cane fields" (USDW Annual Report 1915, 17).

The insular police were engaged in suppressing a number of major strikes. In 1915–1916 eighteen thousand workers brought twenty-four of the thirty-nine largest plantations to a halt for three months (Fleagle 1917, 114). The director of labor observed that "the strike of agricultural workers from January to March 15, 1915 has been considered the most important in Puerto Rico since the American occupation" (USDW Annual Report 1915, 424). These strikes were among the most violent of the first two decades of colonial rule. "Fires occurred and other kinds of damage were done all over the island during that period," and the "work of the force was considerably increased during the past year by the strike of agricultural workers which began in January" (USDW 1915 Annual Report, 425; 1916, 18).

Governor Yager attributed the labor unrest to the "intervention of the labor agitators, who were interested in having the strike spread and continued for a longer period" (USDW Annual Report 1915, 36). According to the FLT, sugar corporation officials, "with the full knowledge of the government of Puerto Rico," sent dozens of armed men with the purpose of breaking the strike. The police were ruthless in suppressing the strikes. In the ensuing battles police and strike breakers killed five workers in Vieques and another in Ponce; dozens were wounded, and over three hundred workers were arrested (Iglesias Pantín 1958, 188–189). Yager wrote extensively about this event in his annual report:

> As soon as the outside agitators began to take part in the strike and to preach vio-
> lence and lawlessness as a means for securing high wages and shorter hours of work,
> fires were started in the cane fields at different parts of the island and great damage
> was done to the properties of employers. . . . The government could not ignore the
> appeals for protection against such acts of lawlessness and disorder, and in the at-
> tempts made by the insular police to restore order and to prevent the wanton de-
> struction of property clashes between the police and the strikers occurred, which un-
> fortunately resulted in the killing of five or six strikers and the serious wounding of
> two policemen. (USDW Annual Report 1915, 36)

The American Federation of Labor, on the other hand, could not ignore the police attacks on its Puerto Rican members. According to the FLT, Yager did not resort to mediation nor arbitration to prevent the strike (Iglesias Pantín 1958, 200). The open hostility of the colonial administration left the FLT little option but to seek the AFL's intervention on its behalf. Acting through its congressional supporters, the AFL was successful in having Congress appoint an Industrial Re-lations Commission to investigate the violence against the workers. The commis-sion reported that the series of strikes "which began in January, 1915, was not only justified but was in the interests of the progress of the island. The long hours, low wages, and exploitation of laborers could not have been relieved ex-cept by organized action" (quoted in Marcus 1919, 19).

According to the commission, "Whatever the actions of the strikers may have been, there cannot be any justifiable cause for the actions of the police and of the municipal authorities," who "violated the individual rights of the strikers, often times treating them with unforgivable brutality" (quoted in Santiago-Valles 1994). The commission also concluded that the insular police were primarily re-sponsible for the violence and criticized the actions of the local police magistrates (Mejías 1946, 87). According to Santiago Iglesias Pantín the workers' legal right to strike was effectively denied the moment the armed forces were placed at the ser-vice of the sugar corporations (Iglesias Pantín 1958, 189). Police brutality and re-pression did not dissuade workers from further militant strikes. In February 1916, forty thousand agricultural workers went on strike in San Juan and all the other major cities, and paralyzed the sugar industry (USDW Annual Report 1916, 416). The governor reported that the purpose of the strikes "was to try to secure for the workers in the fields higher wages and shorter hours as their fair share of the extraordinary prosperity of the sugar industry." He went on to report that "there were two or three regrettable clashes between the strikers and the po-lice" (USDW Annual Report 1916, 31). According to the director of the Bureau of Labor, some wage increases were granted, "yet the increase granted was not in proportion to the unprecedented price the employers were receiving for sugar," and since sugar "was selling at a price never dreamed of by the employers, the workers were fully justified in asking for an increase" (USDW Annual Report 1916, 442).

The attorney general investigated the conflicts between the police and strikers (USDW Annual Report 1916, 416). Representative Keating placed in the Congressional Record an FLT report, including affidavits, which documented the police brutality and provided evidence of collusion between the colonial authorities and the sugar corporations. The FLT reported that "the governor turned over to the police the whole rural region" and disbanded public gatherings of ten or more people, and that the Bureau of Labor "was helping the employers in breaking labor agreements" (*Cong. Rec.* 1916, 8410–8412). The AFL failed to get Congress to establish a commission to study the state of industrial relations in Puerto Rico. An amendment to the proposed Jones Act to respect the rights of Puerto Rican workers to form unions was introduced by Keating, but no action was taken by Congress.

In 1917 the insular police were again called to action. Governor Yager reported, "The work of the force was considerably increased by strikes among the longshoremen, agricultural and other laborers which were widely scattered throughout the island. . . . Public order was maintained" (USDW Annual Report 1917, 19). However, of the seventy-eight strikes tabulated by the Bureau of Labor in 1917, none matched in size and intensity those of the previous year (USDW Annual Report 1917, 552). After the United States entered World War I, and with the redeployment of the Porto Rican Regiment for overseas service, colonial authorities had to rely almost exclusively on the insular police force to maintain public order. According to Governor Yager, "the removal of the Porto Rican regiment from the island increases somewhat the responsibilities of the police." He recommended augmenting the insular police force above its authorized strength (USDW Annual Report 1917, 20). The police were repeatedly used to protect the property of U.S. firms. In 1922 Governor Reilly reported, "The only important strikes during the year were among the employees of the American Tobacco Co., and the American Railroad Co. and the police rendered valuable services in the protection of the property of these two companies, as well as of the lives of the passengers who traveled upon the trains of the latter" (USDW Annual Report 1922, 29).

Within three decades of U.S. colonial rule, expenditures by the coercive agencies of the colonial state—the attorney general, the U.S. district court, the insular courts, the insular police force, and the penal system—increased almost fivefold, although as a percentage of total colonial state expenditures, the amount expended on these agencies declined steadily from 25.8 percent in 1900 to 12.7 percent by 1929 (see table 4.3). During the period 1899–1930, Puerto Rico's population grew from 953,243 to 1,543,913, an increase of 61.9 percent (calculated from U.S. Bureau of the Census 1932, 123). The per capita expenditure on the coercive agencies of the colonial state increased dramatically.

TABLE 4.3   Expenditures and Disbursements: Coercive Appartatus of the State

Year	Attorney General	Insular Police	Insular Courts and U.S. District Court	Penal Institutions	Total for Coercive	Percentage Total Disbursements
1900	11,614	183,728	165,032	92,845	453,219	25.8%
1905	30,829	314,443	304,596	142,430	792,298	23.9%
1913	68,460	481,380	416,927	197,063	1,163,830	27.4%
1917	36,800	432,775	401,876	199,711	1,034,362	18.8%
1921	71,248	794,691	529,716	250,741	1,646,396	14.3%
1925	94,483	877,263	689,489	329,931	1,991,166	13.8%
1929	86,240	880,095	687,984	347,236	2,001,555	12.7%

SOURCE: United States Department of State, *First Annual Report of Porto Rico, 1900*, 281–285. United States Department of State, *Fifth Annual Report of Porto Rico, 1905*, 104–105. United States Department of War, *Annual Reports of the Governor of Puerto Rico, 1913, 1917, 1921, 1925, 1929, Report of the Auditor*, Tables for disbursements.

The Executive Council and Americanization

In any society, the arrival of a new colonizer fosters much anxiety and uncertainty, as traditional relations of production and legal and political institutions disintegrate. The arrival of an alien power that claims sovereignty is always traumatic, and historically has proven to be a wrenching and violent process. Puerto Rico's change in sovereignty did not precipitate massive social uprising and bloody confrontation between the colonizers and the indigenous peoples. But the change in sovereignty was, nonetheless, traumatic. No doubt the economic and political changes of the first two decades caused social instability, elite resistance, and profound worker militancy. We can speculate that resistance might indeed have been more strenuous and effective had the United States followed a less energetic campaign of Americanization

The magnitude of Puerto Rico's economic conversion threatened and ultimately destroyed a people's way of life. It undermined and eventually eradicated the sources of power and privilege of Puerto Rico's elites, but also elevated to prominence political actors who subscribed to the colonial enterprise. Throughout the first three decades of colonialism U.S. officials gained the support of the colonized to effect the new institutional order. Domestic capitalist and professional sectors who stood to gain under the new economic order worked closely with the colonial authorities. These sectors envisioned a new social order in which they would assume the perquisites of titular authority, as well as newfound social standing and material well-being. In a society wracked by unemployment, hunger, and disease, those fortunate enough to be employed by the colonial regime had a privileged status. Their presence in the colonial bureaucracy further served to legitimize metropolitan rule. Because of their involvement in the colonial bureaucracy, Puerto Ricans were portrayed by the colonial authorities as having consented to their own subordination.

Note

1. Unemployment rates reached approximately 30 percent in 1926, but the colonial government continued to rely on convict labor. In a manifesto appearing in the March 15, 1929, issue of *La Prensa*, the FLT condemned this practice, calling for the "absolute suppression of convict labor in all public works" (quoted in Cuesta [1929] 1975, 170).

5

Resistance and Accommodation

We swear loyalty to the flag of the United States and to American ideals, looking toward the prestige of Porto Rico as a member of the Federal Union, as this will reflect the greatness of the nation of which we desire to be a part.

—Puerto Rican Republican Party Constitution, *1898*

Few, very few, are the Americans living in Puerto Rico who sympathize with the people of our country, believing themselves superior to us.

—La Democracia, *1899*

Political Realignments and the New Colonizers

U. S. colonial officials demonstrated an unwavering resolve to impose their political values and cultural standards on Puerto Rico. But these officials were strangers to Puerto Rico and generally chose not to develop an understanding of the country whose people they ruled. Their task was to devise and implement colonial policies while minimizing opposition to Americanization. Colonial officials revealed their imperial attitude by derogating Puerto Ricans as incapable of conducting the business of government. These same officials extolled the capabilities of the Euro-American males they appointed, depicted them as rational, unbiased, selfless civil servants who wanted to elevate the material and spiritual well-being of their colonial wards. Not surprisingly, colonial rule was based on minimal consultation with the subject population. For these officials, Puerto Rico's political leaders were a necessary annoyance whose influence in the business of governing the colony had to be minimized.

Puerto Rican reaction to colonial rule was an intricate interplay of accommodation and resistance. Some Puerto Ricans cooperated willingly with the new colonizers, whereas others challenged them. By 1917 three organizations represented the country's diverse economic and political interests: the Unión Puertorriqueña, the Republican Party, and the Socialist Party. These political parties represented distinct material and social forces, and were at times openly hostile to each other. Colonial rule and capitalist development resulted in differential rewards for Puerto Rico's competing elites. Given the political fragmentation, broad-based opposition to colonial rule did not emerge, and effective resistance to Americanizing Puerto Rico's institutions was minimal.

Profound divisions among Puerto Rico's political parties notwithstanding, the Federal Party (1899 to 1904) and its successor, the Unión Puertorriqueña, were the dominant electoral forces and indefatigable champions of autonomy. Their intransigence and resourcefulness in pursuit of their goals complicated the task of the colonial governors. As a consequence officials were compelled to continually devise measures to derail the political influence of the Federal Party.

Local Alliances and the Americanizing Mission

Governor Allen reported in 1900, "There is no great difference between them [the Republicans and Federals] as far as appears in their platforms." But Allen also reported, "There can be no denying the fact that while the Republican party accepts the American control of the island in good faith, and gives a hearty support to the Administrations, the same can not be candidly said of their political opponents" (USDS 1901, 45). On the eve of Puerto Rico's acquisition by the United States the coffee *hacendados* and commercial elite were the dominant political and economic force. During the early period of U.S. rule this sector was the principal force in the Federal Party. In general, the Federals represented sectors that were apprehensive of the political and economic changes wrought by the new colonizer. However, the *hacendados*, who claimed to represent national aspirations for autonomous economic and political development, exercised a tenuous leadership. Urban artisans and laborers, the emerging rural and industrial proletariat, professionals, and many tobacco and sugar growers, refused to accept the Federal American Party as their representative.

The Republicans represented those sectors that stood to gain from permanent annexation. After 1899 the Republicans attracted disenfranchised workers who saw in the Federal Party a continuation of the paternalism and elitism of the period of Spanish rule. The Republican Party declared its fidelity to the new colonizers and patiently and effectively worked under colonial tutelage in the hope of eroding the influence of the Federal Party. In 1899 it announced its "sincere loyalty to the American flag and American ideals," and pledged "to strive to become worthy of the great nation of which we now are a part" (Bothwell González 1979, 1: 260). Party leader José Celso Barbosa was an aggressive proponent of the colonizing mission. Barbosa declared that the Republican Party "defended the Americanization of the island because we wish that our future government be grounded in the same democratic institutions in which the great Republic was founded and that our country assimilate all that has made the American people great and powerful" (quoted in Meléndez 1988, 41). He was convinced that "Americanization is not incompatible with Puerto Rican patriotism" (Barbosa 1939, 33, 37).

In contrast, the Federal Party fought strenuously for self-rule and autonomy in the hope of retaining its predominant political position and of protecting the economic base of the *hacendados*. The party leadership waged an aggressive campaign to discredit the governor-generals. U.S. officials and the BIA considered the Federals an impediment to Americanization, and they endeavored to relegate the party to an inconsequential role. For two decades colonial authorities tried, but they were unable to do so-until the death of Muñoz Rivera. The leadership of the Federal Party had cultivated a combative and independent political culture during their years of resistance against Spanish colonial rule. Given this history of dogged pursuit of autonomy, the Federal Party was convinced that it would persevere against the new colonizer. They wanted to resurrect the political autonomy and economic self-determination they had wrested from the Spanish. The Federal Party believed that under an autonomous regime it could once again exercise control over the trajectory of economic growth. The open hostility the Federals confronted, when combined with their lack of experience in navigating the intricate corridors of power in Washington, made the party's task of achieving self-rule daunting. But the party persisted in its campaign to impede the process of Americanization and fought to define and control this process of colonial transformation.

Uncertainty as to the impact of the change in sovereignty on their economic fortunes deepened the existing cleavages in Puerto Rico's political leadership. For their part, the colonizers fomented divisions among the leaders and sought to dampen the influence of the Federals by appointing Republicans to key government posts. The Republicans were given a role in colonial administration that was not commensurate with their electoral strength. Colonial officials were determined to promote local political leaders who would assist them in carrying out the Americanization process. The governors repeatedly sought to discredit the Federal Party by accusing it of sacrificing Puerto Rico's economic and social development in the pursuit of the narrow self-interest of the *hacendados*. Invariably, the party was portrayed as Muñoz Rivera's personal clique.

The period from 1900 to 1917 was marked by confrontations and bitter clashes between the colonial authorities and members of Puerto Rico's political leadership who wanted to reform the colonial regime, between these members and others who ardently supported colonial tutelage, and between capital and workers who, with increasing militancy and organizational skill, struck major centers of production. Temporary alliances among the parties, ideological clashes within party organizations, defections, and the establishment of new political forces, all came into play during the volatile period before the passage of the Jones Act.

The Federal Party: Resisting the Colonial Imprint

The first two years of colonial administration under the Foraker Act were arguably among the most significant in Puerto Rico's history as a U.S. possession. Governors William Hunt and Charles Allen enacted key institutional changes that were designed to accelerate Puerto Rico's economic and political absorption into the United States. At the first legislative session the governor signed into law a new tax regime and system of mass public education. In the second session the system of municipal government was reorganized and a new code of law was enacted (Willoughby 1902, 37). U.S. officials, who saw Puerto Rican society as Byzantine and imbued with a culture that was antithetical to modernity, justified their experiments in social and political engineering as necessary to elevate Puerto Ricans to the efficient and dispassionate standards of Anglo-Saxon rationality. William Willoughby saw this period as "the beginning of the real work of endowing Porto Rico with institutions and laws conforming to Anglo-Saxon ideals" (Willoughby 1902, 42).

As far as the colonizers were concerned, uncritical acceptance of their dictates and ready acquiescence were indicators of responsible "native" leadership. Submissive colonial subjects were portrayed as patriotic and reasonable, whereas Puerto Ricans who resisted absorption were practically labeled dyspeptic iconoclasts, self-absorbed, caught up in a socially dysfunctional pursuit of personal ambition. In these paternalistic and self-serving categories Puerto Rico's dominant political forces, the Federal and Republican Parties, were situated by the colonial governors. During its brief existence, from 1899 to 1904, the Federal Party emerged as unquestionably the most obdurate political impediment the colonizers confronted. Yet the Federal Party failed to understand the depth of U.S. resolve not to amend the Foraker Act.

The Federal Party was the dominant political party. In the only elections held under the Autonomous Charter, the Liberal Party—the Federal Party's predecessor—obtained 85,627 votes, while the Orthodox Party mustered only 18,068 (Todd 1953, 135). The Federals also vanquished the opposition Republican Party in the 1899 municipal elections, gaining control of forty-four of the sixty-six *municipios* (Silvestrini and Luque de Sánchez 1990, 405). In various forums Muñoz Rivera claimed that he "spoke with authority and according to instructions" from those who sent him, as the "representative of a larger part of the people" of Puerto Rico (Muñoz Rivera 1899, 1285). The Federal Party aspired for a novel form of colonialism. It called on the United States to grant the country territorial status with all the rights of a state of the Union, "except that of sending Senators and Representatives to Congress, where we will have, as other Territories do, a delegate with voice but no voting power." The Federals believed that racism was the motivating factor for U.S. refusal to grant Puerto Rico a territorial form of government, which was a condition for statehood. In their newspaper the Federals quipped, "The American people are resistant to the idea that the newly acquired countries, which they judge not only as being of different racial composition, but as inferior to them, might influence with their votes national issues" (*La Democracia*, quoted in Vélez Aquino 1968, 61–62). Resident Commissioner Larrinaga complained that "Congress has been very unjust to us, while on the other hand we have been charged with every indignity that a people is capable of."

Larrinaga wondered why there was "such persistent desire to represent the natives before the American people as unworthy of any rights or of any help." He asked what justified "depicting our people as morally inferior, and unworthy of any rights or any support" (Larrinaga 1907, 161).

The centralization of powers in the executive departments posed a real threat to the Federal Party's aspirations. Under the Foraker Act the Federal Party could be assured only of representation in the elected House of Delegates, a legislative body lacking any policymaking powers. By design Congress had marginalized the House, the only forum for popular representation, effectively excluding it from the policy process. According to William Willoughby, "It was the intention of Congress to take . . . conduct of the administrative departments from under the control of the legislative assembly and vest it in the hands of the departmental heads acting either individually or collectively through the executive council" (Willoughby 1905, 103).

The metropolitan state was convinced of "the necessity for exercising a considerable degree of control for some years to come" (Willoughby 1902, 35). All key administrative positions were appointive, and officials were accountable to either the central government or the colonial governor. Indeed, the decision to "concentrate power and responsibility, where ever possible, in single officials rather than in boards" was "one of the most important features of the administrative organization" recommended by the Porto Rico Code Commission (American Academy 1902, 162).

The meaning of this approach was obvious: In the new colonial regime Puerto Ricans would serve only at the pleasure of the colonizers and be accountable only to them. At this stage of the colonial enterprise Puerto Rican input was confined almost exclusively to serving as assistants to key administrators, as advisers, and as delegates to the lower house. In addition to being trained in the ways of colonial administration, these appointees sensitized the U.S. officials to the customs and characteristics of the society they were transforming. Governor William Hunt had cited this way of using Puerto Ricans as one of his achievements: "In the several government departments the President's appointees are assisted by experienced natives, it being a policy that great regard be had for Porto Rican institutions, native religious ideas and native freedom" (Hunt 1901, 1171). Puerto Ricans were relegated to a residual and supportive role.

Governor Hunt took office fully expecting that the Federal Party would challenge his authority. He was not disappointed. Once the civilian regime was installed the Federal Party immediately moved to have Congress rescind the most obnoxious provisions of the Foraker Act. The Federals orchestrated a campaign of noncooperation, public criticism, and protest designed to complicate the task of colonial management and undermine the Americanization process. According to R. L. Rowe, "they showed an unwillingness to cooperate with the American officials unless assured of a large share of the available offices" (Rowe 1902, 28). In their reports Governor Charles Allen and his successor, William Hunt, portrayed the Federal Party as a troublesome impediment. Hunt reported that "the Federal party has never been in accord with any American government, military or civil, since General Henry came to the island in 1898." He claimed that "the Federal press has always been vituperative in its attacks upon the policies, acts and the officials of the American administration" (USDS 1903, 9–10).

Governor Allen blamed Luis Muñoz Rivera and the machinations of the Spanish resident *hacendados*, who were determined to retain their privileges, for the problems that he encountered (Gannon 1978, 317; USDS 1904, 10–11). Allen reported that "the Federal party is so subservient to a leader who is malcontent that it has followed him to a large extent in his policy of obstruction, and . . . has persistently opposed the American policy toward the island" (USDS 1901, 48). Hunt believed that opposition to his rule demonstrated Puerto Ricans' political immaturity and intense partisanship: "Every native citizen of Porto Rico is an enthusiastic devotee of one or the other political party." The lack of "tolerance towards an opponent" was, according to Hunt, a feature of the Spanish cultural heritage that would be "dimmed" as Puerto Rico drew "closer to the United States proper" (Hunt 1901, 1171).

The colonizers were determined that the colonizing mission would proceed with or without the cooperation of the Federal Party. From the outset of his administration Allen sought to neutralize the Federals. He systematically displaced party adherents from administrative positions and assigned Republican Party officials to key positions (Negrón Portillo 1981b, 33). One of his first acts was to appoint two Republicans, two Federals, and an independent delegate to the Executive Council, in order to demonstrate "the purposes of the government to keep aloof from local party politics" (Hunt 1901, 1170).

The five Puerto Rican council members were instructed to draw up an electoral districting plan for the November 6, 1900, general elections. The Executive Council endorsed a plan designed by the independent Puerto Rican council member, but which was rejected by the Federal Party delegates because the plan gerrymandered the party out of the important district of Aguadilla, where they enjoyed an electoral majority (USDS 1901, 90; Wilson 1905, 90). Governor Allen, nonetheless, approved the plan (Berbusse 1966, 175–176; Rowe 1904, 252–253). In a move apparently calculated to create the colonial regime's first political crisis, the Federal Party instructed its delegates to resign from the Executive Council. Muñoz Rivera cabled President Roosevelt that the Federals were duty bound "to protest against the present administration in this island so long as we are unjustly treated" (quoted in Berbusse 1966, 176). The resignations were accepted and the Federals were replaced by Republicans. Rather than provoking a crisis, the resignations had, according to Allen, a salutary effect; he noted that "the vacancies thus created were not filled for two months, and matters moved on in the council with much more harmony" (Allen 1902, 165). Elihu Root congratulated Allen "on getting rid of your legislature without any explosion," and also allotted $10,000 for the militia of Puerto Rico (Jessup 1938, 1:377).

Nonetheless, the Federal Party's disruptive tactics were complicating Allen's task. Allen reported: "These obstructionists have also grown more virulent in their newspaper attacks on the members of the executive government, and have extended the field of their operations to New York and other cities of the United States" (USDS 1901, 49). He wrote Secretary Root that the Spanish planters were behind the activities of the Federal Party and accused Muñoz Rivera of being "intensely anti-American" (Quoted in Gannon 1978, 316) Apparently stung by the Federals' publicity campaign in the United States, Allen asked that the Republican National Committee finance a newspaper in Puerto Rico opposing the Federals (Gannon 1978, 317).

Just days before the November 1900 election, the Federal Party unexpectedly withdrew its candidates from the ballot. They did so claiming a "lack of protection for our right to vote and the manifest partiality of the council in favor of the Republican Party" (USDS 1901, 47). The elections were marked by a wave of politically motivated violence. Urban poor and landless peasants were prominently engaged in these sporadic outbreaks (Negrón Portillo 1990, 81; Santiago-Valles 1994, 99ff). These attacks, or *turbas*, were primarily aimed at the Federal Party leadership and resulted in the destruction of the party newspaper offices. The Federals were convinced that the mob violence had been tacitly endorsed by the government (Negrón Portillo 1981b, 36; Pagán 1972, 1:75–76). Hunt overlooked the attacks against the Federals and refused to order the insular police to protect them from attack (Berbusse 1966, 177; Iglesias Pantín 1958, 188). The refusal of the colonial authorities to provide adequate protection explains in part the Federal Party's decision to withdraw (Negrón Portillo 1990; Quintero Rivera 1977, 39). The Republicans campaigned for change in leadership and warned that a vote for the Federal Party was a vote in favor of preserving *el regímen antiguo*, "the perpetuation of Spanish traditions." The Republicans claimed that until they came to power "democratic rule could not prevail in Porto Rico" (Rowe 1904, 250)

As the dominant political force, the Federals hoped to discredit the electoral process and demonstrate that without their cooperation Puerto Rico was ungovernable. But the elections proceeded on schedule. In a remarkable display of Federal Party discipline only 58,515 of the 123,140 eligible voters went to the polls. Of these voters only 148 cast their ballots for the Federal Party candidates (Butler 1903, 186; Rowe 1902, 360). The decision to boycott the elections was disastrous for the Federal Party. The Republicans gained absolute control of the House of Delegates and elected their candidate for resident commissioner. The Federals had made a grievous political error, and Governor Allen decided that the party was "to be treated as politically non-existent." Rowe reported that this was further "indication of the inability of the native population to manage its own affairs" (Rowe 1902, 30).

The Federals wanted to extract concessions by adopting a strategy of noncooperation and obstruction. However, it was an anachronistic strategy. In 1900 the

Federals faced an industrialized and expansionist nation-state that was determined to consolidate its hegemony over the Caribbean. This was a radically different geopolitical situation from that of just three years earlier. The Federal Party's predecessors, the Liberals, had extracted concessions at the turn of the century from an economically backward nation that was being drained by the Cuban insurrection. Fearful of U.S. designs on its colonies, Spain sought to hang on to the last vestiges of its colonial empire by enacting measures to appease the autonomous forces in Puerto Rico, while it continued to battle the Cuban revolutionaries. Against the United States, the Federal Party waged a futile campaign to influence the course of capitalist development. In an ironic twist of history the Federals, who had fought Spanish reaction and promoted modernity, were now portrayed as advocates for the status quo of social hierarchy, and opposed to liberalism and economic development.

The Early Republicans:
Local Agents of Americanization

The promise of a new era of modern enterprise and progressive political and social institutions resonated with the educated professional sector that exercised leadership of the Republican Party (Quintero Rivera 1977, 57–58). Despite the partiality shown the Republicans by the colonial authorities, they were no match for the Federal Party. The Federals' decision to withdraw from government at the critical moment when fundamental legislation was to be drafted could not have been timed more perfectly for the Republicans and the colonial authorities. The Executive Council and House of Delegates had a very active legislative agenda, since the Foraker Act "made almost no provision regarding the fundamental laws that should regulate Porto Rican affairs" (Willoughby 1902, 35).

Although the Republicans realized that Congress would oppose Puerto Rico's entry into the Union for years to come, they were convinced that statehood was a historical certainty. They accepted the notion that Puerto Ricans were neither politically nor culturally prepared for statehood, and proclaimed that "Americanization" was necessary to prepare Puerto Rico for incorporation into the Union. With the support of the Republicans the Executive Council set up a new internal revenue system, reformed the municipal government, and revised the election laws. These measures were not only important components of the Americanization process, but diminished the economic base, patronage power, and electoral strength of the Federal Party. The Republican assisted the colonial authorities in disseminating a new ideological construct that legitimized the superiority of U.S. society and its institutions.

Between December 1900 and February 1902 the Executive Council introduced scores of measures that were approved by the Republican-controlled House. Collectively these laws radically reorganized the public administration, which had been the source of patronage and influence for the Federal Party. With key Republican leaders in the Executive Council, the party influenced the council to enact measures favorable to its electoral fortunes. Naturally, the Republicans had their adherents appointed to posts in the colonial bureaucracy and also blocked the hiring of Federal Party members. The task of transforming Puerto Rico's institutions was made considerably easier by the xenophile behavior of the Republican Party and the voluntary removal of the Federal Party from the legislature. Commissioner Rowe observed that the Federal Party's decision to withdraw from participation in the colonial regime was "a real advantage" to U.S. colonial officials who were assigned "the work of bringing the institutions of the island into closer harmony with the American system." According to Rowe these officials needed "the unqualified support of a party whose faith in American institutions was born of an unquestioned faith in the principles of our government" (Rowe 1904, 254–255).

Rowe observed that "The Republican leaders . . . brought to the new government a free and open acceptance of everything distinctly American, and a readiness to aid the American officials in the great work of civic organization" (Rowe 1902 358). He reported with obvious satisfaction that "the Republican party accepts the American control of the island in good faith, and gives a hearty support to the Administration." He went on to write, "The Republican party is firmly in favor of American methods, and renders an honest and intelligent support to the Administration and its policies" (USDS 1901, 45, 49). Governor Allen was demonstrably friendly toward the Republican Party and its leadership (Todd 1943, 17).

The party leadership publicly accepted the notion of Anglo-Saxon superiority inherent in the doctrine of Manifest Destiny. Its newspaper, *El País*, editorialized, "The American people, having arrived to the fullness of their development, fulfill the historic law of all great peoples, and carry to other peoples and other lands, the influence of their civilization and the authority of their genius" (quoted in Vélez Aquino 1968, 68). The Republicans expressed a fervent devotion to the colonizing mission of the United States. Party boss Barbosa described the Republicans as having become "auxiliary to the American government in Puerto Rico, and defended its actions insofar as it felt the intention was to transform the political and social conditions of the country" (Barbosa 1939, 59). In 1910 Barbosa testified before the House Committee on Insular Affairs, "Our party has stood by the side of the administration in order to Americanize the Island, and we mean by Americanizing to teach our people the spirit of the American people, so that the natives could understand the laws which have been enacted in the United States and to endorse the American policy in Puerto Rico" (quoted in Trías Monge 1980, 2:30).

The Republicans wanted to rescind laws that impeded foreign investments. In 1902 they proposed legislation to raise the limit on corporate landholdings to five thousand acres, to eliminate fees on franchises granted by the Executive Council, to set up a Bureau of Information in New York to promote investments and commerce, and to simplify existing legislation that "affected in a direct way the development of wealth"; at the same time they endorsed the continued development of "American civil institutions throughout the entire island" (quoted in Bothwell González 1979, 2:275, 281). According to Barbosa, "The process of Americanization marches on victoriously, and signifies democracy and liberty. The process of antiamericanization is a useless effort to revive that which has no future" (quoted in Bothwell González 1979, 2:221). The Republicans believed that U.S. men of business would spread democratic values and that the United States as a vital foreign economic presence was essential to the Americanization process.

Republicans devised legislation that eviscerated the Federal Party's monopoly of patronage positions and that eroded their political influence. Unwittingly the Federal Party had deprived itself of even a symbolic forum from which to challenge the dictates of the Executive Council. Once having chosen self-imposed political exile, the Federal Party could not halt the tide of legislation promoting Puerto Rico's economic and political absorption into the United States.

Fine-Tuning the Colonial Regime:
Financing Subordination

A new tax code was needed to generate revenues for public education, infrastructure development, sanitation, the insular police force, and salaries of government employees. For this task Elihu Root appointed J. D. Hollander, associate professor of finance at Johns Hopkins University. In his letter to university president Gilman requesting Hollander's services, Root wrote, "The system which was in force at the time of American occupation was so peculiar to the Spanish methods of administration, so inapplicable to the new conditions under which the people of the island are to live and to the ideas which we entertain for promoting their welfare, that a practically new system must be adopted" (Quoted in Jessup 1938, 1:378).

Hollander, who was appointed treasurer by Governor Allen, was the engineer of the tax code of 1901. The Foraker Act centralized financial administration exclusively in the office of the treasury and the auditor. The treasurer was also given responsibility for overseeing the financial affairs of the municipalities. Thus Hollander "was put in a position where he could exercise a direct influence in having the plans which he deemed desirable adopted" (Willoughby 1902, 36). Hollander's influence over financial affairs was further increased when he was appointed chairperson of the finance committee of the Executive Council (Adams 1901a, 447). Moreover, Hollander reorganized the Treasury Department and hired scores of former commissioned military officers and engineers to work as tax assessors (Gannon 1978, 330).

According to Secretary Willoughby, after the Hollander Bill was approved "the system of taxes in force under the Spanish regime was completely done away with" (Willoughby 1905, 115). Hollander's revenue act was based on those of states of the Union; it included a property tax, excise taxes, and inheritance tax and imposed a more effective tax collection and enforcement system (USDS 1901, 170). Land valued at less than $100, as well as the tools, crops, and products of farmers and planters, were exempted from taxation. This exemption applied to individuals "growing crops and products actually owned by the producer and still in his hands" (Rowe 1904, 192). Since landowners were not the direct producers but relied on hired labor, the holdings of *hacendados* and sugar and tobacco corporations, as well as all medium-sized farms and plantations, were subject to the new tax. The measure was passed unanimously by the Executive Council; only one House delegate cast a dissenting vote (Adams 1901a, 56).

Governor Allen reported that the measure "aroused great apprehension among the property owners" (Allen 1902, 173). Actually the "Hollander Bill" raised a storm of protest and met with intense hostility (see Adams 1901b). Hollander argued that the previous system had been skewed in favor of Spanish merchants. He claimed that Spaniards controlled virtually all the financial and commercial interests and had been assessed very low rates and did not pay a fair tax. In contrast, Puerto Rican-owned retail and manufacturing activities had been highly taxed (Hollander 1901, 556).

The Federals vehemently attacked the new tax code and were convinced the measure was another attempt by the Executive Council and the Republican legislators to further erode the economic base of the landowners. According to the Federal Party, "few are the farmers that can resist the Hollander Bill. The majority will have to turn over their properties to the American trusts now that they are organizing to buy up Puerto Rico" (quoted in Negrón Portillo 1981b, 40–41). The Federal Party newspaper, *La Democracia*, labeled the measure "The Death Warrant Bill, The New Hurricane," and called the House of Delegates the Chamber of Slaves, "in which a few Puerto Ricans . . . lent themselves to work . . . the chains that will suppress the unfortunate people" (quoted in Vélez Aquino 1968, 62). In an editorial, *La Democracia* warned that if the tax code devised by Hollander, "an ardent advocate of Americanization," was approved, "within a five year period most of the farms will have passed from the hands of Puerto Ricans to the hands of continentals. They will be the absolute owners of the country" (Quoted in Luque de Sánchez 1980, 148).

After the Hollander bill was passed Puerto Rico's largest property owners agreed to send a delegation to Washington to petition Congress to rescind the measure (Adams 1901a, 56). Governor Allen dismissed the opposition to the Hollander Bill as "inspired by characteristic and real apprehension of the people to any radical economic change" (Hunt 1901, 1172). In a personal communication to Root, Allen reported that the protest was "represented largely by Spaniards doing business in Porto Rico, against our beneficent and patriotic tax levy. This protest represents federals generally" (Gannon 1978, 332).

In fact the Federals were completely justified in their apprehensions. Since absentee sugar corporations had not made significant investments when the law was enacted, the burden of the property taxes fell on domestic landowners. While the property tax was presented as an equitable measure, its deleterious effects on domestic plantation owners and middle-sized farmers were pronounced. The timing and consequences of the law, which increased the indebtedness of lands already mortgaged, compelled many farmers to sell a portion of their holdings to meet the new tax liability. The effect of the law was to release agricultural land from local control and make it available for purchase by corporations waiting to invest in sugar production. The legislative assembly also drafted a general corporation law modeled after that of New Jersey, which was designed to stimulate the investment of capital under the corporate form of management (Willoughby 1902, 41). Under this legislation, corporate profits were not taxed, since the companies were "treated substantially as unincorporated concerns" and were "assessed by the treasurer upon the actual market value of their capital invested in Porto Rico" (Wood, Taft, and Allen 1902, 345).

Governor Allen's communications to the War Department left no doubt as to his administration's intention of promoting the sugar industry (Gannon 1978, 328). Allen, who felt that Puerto Ricans had failed to exploit this potential, threatened that he would "tax a little life into them. Every Portorican has a right to demand that every acre of rich sugar land should be developed, and I'd tax it until they had to put up or shut up" (quoted in Berbusse 1966, 174). Allen reported that what Puerto Rico needed were "men with capital, energy and enterprise to develop its latent industries and to reclaim its sugar estates" (USDS 1901, 75). He informed potential U.S. investors that agriculture provided "the best employment for American energy and American capital." But he cautioned:

> The peculiarities of the people and the distinct individuality of the island will for some time be a decided disadvantage, but with the introduction of American machinery and improvements, great changes will be effected, and with the thrift and industry which follows the Anglo-Saxon, in time this very individuality will disappear, and American capital, energy and intelligence will find a wide and favorable field for their successful exercise. (Wood, Taft, and Allen 1902, 309)

Usurping Local Political Control

Under the Autonomous Charter of 1897, the municipalities were granted substantial autonomy from the governor-general. The U.S. military governors had done little to reform the Spanish system of municipal government. The Executive Council set as one of its first tasks to radically alter the organization of local government and to restrict the powers of the elected mayors and municipal councils. Ironically, the council was opposed to the Spanish *municipio* system for "entrusting of both legislative and executive powers to the same set of individuals" (Willoughby 1902, 38). This is precisely the arrangement Congress had devised for the Executive Council and which Muñoz Rivera condemned, for it "unites or merges these two branches of government, the executive and the legislative, into a single power" (Muñoz Rivera 1911, 189). Under the Spanish system the mayors, or *alcaldes*, had substantial administrative powers. Major Glassford, an officer in the occupation army, reported to General Davis that the each *alcalde* was a "sort of captain general,"

> He was the commander of the town police and the fire department, its police judge, controlled the passport system within his district, and could call upon the civil guard in case of need; he was likewise responsible for the collection of municipal and state taxes, the disbursement of public funds. (USDW, Division of Customs and Insular Affairs 1899a, 86)

The Federal Party was entrenched in the *municipios,* which had been the ramparts of district political power of the old Liberal Party (now Federal). The *municipios* were the instruments through which the party hoped to challenge the colonial government. The Foraker Act had diminished the powers of municipal government by authorizing the secretary of Puerto Rico "peremptorily to veto any municipal ordinance or annul any act of a municipal officer that he believed improper" (Willoughby, 1909, 167–168). But Hunt and the BIA wanted to strip the *municipios* of virtually all their autonomy. Colonial officials discredited the *municipio* system and routinely accused its officials of corruption and fraud, intimidation of opponents, and the arbitrary exercise of authority. They alleged that the system was rife with venality, riddled with redundancies, and excessively costly. Secretary of State William Hunt claimed that the *municipios* "are subject to the influence of the party that predominates in them, and in many instances lend more attention to the private interests of the party which the majority of their members belong than to any benefit the public may derive from their acts" (USDS 1901, 103). Hunt added that the "system led to innumerable complaints of political oppression by mayors against persons of the opposite political faith" (USDS 1901, 104).

William Willoughby observed that Puerto Rico's system of local government was "so completely at variance with American theory and practice that it was inevitable that radical changes would have to be made at the earliest possible moment" (Willoughby 1905, 119). Lawrence Lowell recommended reforming the municipal system in order to prepare the population for a transition to U.S. notions of participatory democracy. He wrote that the "capacity for popular government . . . requires the gradual training of large numbers of men to the conduct of public affairs on a small scale." Colonial subjects would be educated to develop "a strong reverence for the authority of law, as distinguished from the commands of men." For this to happen, the local governments would be "administered under strict rules of law" (Lowell 1898, 56–57).

The Federal Party attempted to preserve the powers of the municipalities in order to counteract the excessive powers of the Executive Council. Willoughby reported that Puerto Ricans, "almost without exception, are demanding a greater voice in affairs" and that they want "governmental duties and functions as far as possible made municipal functions" (Willoughby 1902, 36–37). Lacking any role in the central colonial government, the Federal Party fought from the margins to defend the autonomy of the municipal districts and to preserve their resources.

The municipal reform law asserted central government control over the *municipios* and achieved the radical degradation of their powers. The *alcaldes* bitterly resented the law. They organized a meeting to affirm their autonomy and to denounce Hollander's order to the *alcaldes* to submit their budgets for his review. Hollander blamed the protest on malcontents and dismissed their demands for modifying the legislation (USDS 1901, 146). A similar plan for municipal reorganization in Cuba also elicited intense popular reaction (see Rowe 1905).

Twenty-one *municipios* were either eliminated or merged, leaving a total of forty-five *alcaldes* who were stripped of their legislative powers; the administration of the education system and authority over public works were taken away and centralized in the Executive Council; the judicial powers of the *alcalde* were dramatically reduced; the treasurer approved municipal budgets and taxes; municipal accounts were subject to examination by the auditor; and the municipal constabulary was replaced by an insular police force. The mayor's patronage powers were severely curtailed as well. Deprived of their patronage powers, the mayors lost their stature as local political leaders and were converted "into mere functionaries" of the central government (Quintero Rivera 1977, 35). Subjected to highly centralized regulation and supervision, the *municipios* could not serve as the Federal Party's base of resistance against the colonizing mission of the United States.

Willoughby reported that as a consequence of the law "the governor wields a very great influence," greater in fact than that of the governors of states in the Union (Willoughby 1905, 91). The governor had the authority to appoint replacements for vacancies in municipal elective offices, including district judges, council members, and mayors. In 1903 Governor William Hunt appointed 100 councilmen and mayors, and 55 municipal justices of the peace (calculated from USDS 1903, 61–64). Between 1910 and 1916 the governors made over 660 appointments to fill vacated offices in the *municipios* (compiled from USDW, Report of the Governor, 1910–1916). Governor Allen used his patronage powers to increase the minority Republican Party's representation in municipal government. He claimed that he did so "in order to secure minority representation and to check the abuse of political power in municipal administration," (Quoted in Clark 1969, 155). With these new appointive powers the governor now thought he could discipline the truculent Federal Party.

The Republicans stood to gain significantly by these changes, which eroded the Federal Party's virtual monopoly of local government. But loyal Republicans undoubtedly chafed at Willoughby's idea that paternalistic supervision by colonial officials would continue "until the upper class, from which must be drawn the directors and administrators of public affairs, have developed those civic virtues the existence of which is a *sine qua non* of good government" (Willoughby 1909, 165). This political humiliation was tolerable, however, if the consequence was hobbling the Federal Party. Ideologically in lockstep with the new colonizers, the Republicans conspired with them to unseat the Federal Party as the dominant local political force. With their adherents assured of employment in the expanding bureaucracy, municipalities, and judiciary, the Republicans functioned to consolidate United States power at the local level throughout the island (Quintero Rivera 1977, 69).

The Federal Party waged a withering attack against the Republicans and their metropolitan benefactors (Negrón Portillo 1981a). In turn, colonial officials derided the Federal Party leadership as lacking in democratic principles and devoid of any capacity for compromise. They criticized the party for inhibiting the modernization and democratization of Puerto Rico. Governor Allen called the Federal Party "carpers" who "refused to cooperate with their patriotic fellow citizens." He accused the party of aligning itself "with malcontent elements of every kind" in its campaign to annul the Hollander Bill (USDS 1901 77, 49).

In contrast, the Republicans were befriended because they embraced the task of remaking society in the image of the colonizers. Yet Governor Allen rejected any Republican proposals that diminished U.S. control over the pace and content of Puerto Rico's institutional transformation. Modest Republican proposals for a role in the decisionmaking process and for protection of small landholders were rebuffed by the Executive Council. Emblematic of this behavior was rejection by the U.S. members of the Executive Council of a measure (which may have been one of the earliest affirmative action programs) introduced by council member Roberto Todd to give preference to Puerto Ricans for civil service positions (Díaz Soler 1960, 1:216). During the first legislative session the Executive Council vetoed a bill approved by the lower house, "with the approval of practically the whole native population" and supported by the Puerto Rican members of the council, to establish a $3 million loan program for Puerto Rican farmers (Adams 1901a, 56; Allen 1902, 172). The loans would have aided the coffee growers, who had suffered huge financial losses because of the worldwide decline in coffee prices, the virtual elimination of their European markets, and the ruinous hurricane of 1899.

Despite the coffee industry's importance to the economy, the idea of providing direct financial support to the growers was anathema to the U.S. members of the Executive Council. Hollander reported that the loan proposal "smacks . . . hopelessly of economic fallacy" and "takes rank . . . with wild-cat panaceas and populist cure-alls." Hollander lectured the Puerto Ricans on the cold logic of the market, while absolving the Executive Council for instituting policies ruinous to the coffee industry: "Puerto Rico is undergoing the same economic revolution and industrial development which the Southern and Western sections of the

United States have experienced. In this transition scarcity of capital, stringency of currency, and necessity of liquidation are painful incidents" (USDS 1901, 198).

Although Barbosa believed that "governors Hunt and Allen were friends of the Republican Party," the Republicans were unable to pass any legislation beneficial to Puerto Rico's besieged farmers (Barbosa 1939, 192). Republicans regularly introduced legislation to establish an insular bank or loan fund to provide relief to indebted farmers, but they were repeatedly rebuffed by the Executive Council. In 1904 the Executive Council failed to act on a loan bill "solely for the purpose of providing funds to be loaned to the agriculturists of the island" (USDS 1904, 75). Republicans on the Executive Council were outvoted consistently by their U.S. counterparts. The Republicans introduced 105 bills during the first legislative session, but only 14 were signed into law. In contrast, 22 of the 28 Executive Council bills became law (Allen 1902, 170).

In an apparent policy reversal the Republicans tried in 1903 to curtail the ongoing centralization of municipal functions in the Executive Council. They voted for legislation to repeal sections of the law that conferred "supervisory control over the municipalities" to the office of the secretary and treasurer. Governor Hunt argued that the increase in municipal level investments "has been due to the knowledge on the part of investors that there has been and is a reasonable supervisory control" (USDS 1904, 36–37). The measure was rejected. As far as the colonial authorities were concerned the job of the Republicans was to support the Americanization process and to legitimize the subordination of Puerto Rican society under U.S. tutelage. Beyond these specific roles, the colonial authorities saw Republican involvement as troublesome at best, or obstructionist at worst.

Male Suffrage: Seeking Legitimacy and Manageability

Colonial officials experimented with different male electoral suffrage schemes after the municipal elections of 1899. From 1899 through 1916 Puerto Rico's election laws were regularly amended. These changes, which fluctuated between restrictive and liberal voting requirements, had much to do with the colonizers' need to generate political support for their programs. Election laws were evaluated in the context of their contribution to a realization of the country's institutional transformation. Initially it was deemed preferable to give only the privileged sectors the electoral franchise. Elihu Root advocated restricting the suffrage to males who were literate and who held property, and to "no others." But he linked the extension of the suffrage to education and argued that "with a sufficient system of free primary education, the entire people should acquire the suffrage on this basis fully as soon as they are capable of using it understandingly" (Root 1916, 167). Apparently General Davis accepted this logic and for the municipal elections of 1899 rescinded the more liberal provisions of the Autonomous Charter, which gave the vote to all males over twenty-five years of age.

Only twenty-one year old males who could either write and read or who were taxpayers of record were permitted to vote. These restrictions disenfranchised 75 percent of the adult male population. Davis reported that in the municipality of Adjuntas only 5 percent of the males were eligible to vote (USDW 1900, 17).

The War Department wanted to restrict the vote to the privileged sectors of society, whose conservative tendencies resonated, at least in theory, with the class identity and racial superiority of the colonizers. Yet Davis cautioned that a highly restrictive franchise would preserve the power base of the *hacendados,* who had resolutely challenged many of the military decrees. Davis warned that "those elected will probably be of the same class as those formerly in power" (USDW 1900, 59). He was certain the political leaders would manipulate "the illiterate masses" who had been "led and governed and controlled" and whose relation to the government was that of "obedient subject" (59). Despite these warnings the War Department imposed a restrictive franchise for the 1899 municipal elections; it did not think that responsible leadership would be elected under universal male suffrage. Actually, this decision appears to have favored the Federal Party, which tended to represent the higher socio-economic male sectors of the population. The Executive Council adopted less restrictive conditions for the November 1900 general election. Davis's contentious experience with the Federal Party from 1899 to 1900 may have emboldened the council to liberalize the franchise in the hope of expanding the electoral base of the Republican Party, whose constituency, as I noted above, included large contingents of uneducated and propertyless urban males.

Colonial officials and the political leadership regularly changed their positions on voting requirements. According to Rowe, "The Federal Party does not express itself clearly on the suffrage question, whereas the Republican Party does not hesitate to define its position" (1904, 249). In its 1899 program, the Federal Party stated that it "will advocate the most ample system of suffrage, without opposing, however, any limitations that may be thought prudent by the United States, but representing always their desire that all resident citizens of the island be permitted to vote" (program printed in USDW 1900, 287–288). But in his testimony at hearings called by Commissioner Carroll, Muñoz Rivera opposed universal male suffrage, and did so for class and racial reasons:

> The Anglo-Saxon race being a considering and debating and calm people, whereas the Latin race is excitable and undeliberative, and at the age of 21 years a man of the latter race has not formed character—I think it unwise to make the change suggested. . . . From the vote will proceed the government of the country, and experience has shown us already that it would be extremely dangerous to hand over our future to the masses, who are entirely without civic education and who might be wrongly directed by the audacity of agitators who would make them their tools. (Carroll 1899, 236)

Mr. Amadeo (presumably Luis Amadeo Antonmarchi of the conservative Orthodox Party) testified, "I have been adverse to universal suffrage. Restricted suffrage, moreover, acts as a stimulation. A man who desires to take part in the administration of the government must either save money or educate himself" (quoted in Carroll 1899, 355). Rowe was convinced that the Federal Party and landowning interests had "a fear of the results of a further extension of the suffrage to the poorer whites" (1902, 26). In contrast to this marked elitism, in 1900 the Republican Party openly endorsed universal male suffrage. The party platform announced a commitment to "the supreme and sovereign right of every lawful citizen, rich or poor, native or foreign born, to cast one free ballot in public elections" (USDW 1900, 288–289). Commissioner Carroll endorsed the Republican Party's position on universal male suffrage, but with the proviso that those who did not learn to read within ten years of the first general election held should be deprived of the vote (Carroll 1899, 63).

Which category of men should or should not be given the vote was a critical question that colonial officials could determine only on the basis of experimentation. While claiming to be committed democrats who believed in the right of all men to elect those who governed them, colonial officials were contemptuous of the idea of giving the vote to the rural workers—the *peones*, who General Davis described as "without ambition" and having "no incentive to labor beyond the least that will provide the barest sustenance" (USDW 1900, 17). By 1902 the problem of colonial administration had become the object of considerable academic interest, and the American Academy of Social and Political Science became a major forum for the analysis of colonial policy.

Henry B. Burch's work, *Conditions Affecting the Suffrage in Colonies*, was particularly noteworthy and appears to have guided suffrage policy in Puerto Rico. Burch made a compelling argument for restrictive male suffrage as necessary for effective colonial management. He reasoned that universal male suffrage was necessary only in the short term to remove political obstacles to the imposition of colonial government. Using a logic that was steeped in the racism of the time, Burch wanted to demonstrate the interrelationship between capitalism and civic responsibility.

> Suffrage is not a thing to be studied separately and apart by itself; it has a natural basis in the physical and industrial conditions of the environment on the one hand, and in the racial characteristics constituting heredity on the other. . . . Looked at from this point of view the idea that abstract or "American" principles *per se* can be imposed upon a newly acquired territory is seen to be fallacious. (Burch 1902, 99)

Capitalism was a bedrock for democracy, according to Burch: "With the development of commerce comes an influx of democratic ideas due to the intermingling of various types of men through business interests" (Burch 1902, 79). Conservatism was essential for efficient government administration, "which the ownership of property almost invariably nourishes, because of the additional interests and responsibilities which its ownership entails" (88). Burch warned that education in itself was not sufficient to create a responsible electorate, and he emphasized the role of culture in shaping political behavior and attitudes. Burch lectured that the "qualities which were taken for granted and upon which were built our whole political system are often lacking in the other races" (99).

Burch believed that it "was necessary to debar the most incapable from participation in political activity." These were the vast majority "of the agricultural laborers living on the margin of existence, with a generally low standards of life and the lack of development which that implies" (98). Burch thought that Puerto Rico's property qualifications were "practically worthless as a check to the industrially undesirable" because they were "placed at so low a figure" (98). Yet he was certain that the educated and property-owning colonial subjects would resist institutional and economic changes. According to Burch, "The reforms which must necessarily be introduced under the American regime would naturally be opposed by some of the large property-holders and advocated by the less favorably situated classes of the population" (100). For this reason, Burch felt that "At a given moment, the participation of large masses of the people may be a vital necessity to insure the adoption of essential laws"; he warned that restricting the vote to "ultra-conservative classes would be disastrous" (100).

According to Burch, "the more radical elements of the community may require considerable guidance, and may even present difficulties in the future management of the government, but the services which they have rendered in welcoming the introduction of important legislative measures of vital importance to Porto Rico cannot be forgotten" (101). In short, Burch argued that, while in principle the vast majority of Puerto Ricans should be barred from voting, for the sake of political expediency, that is, to permit the colonial officials to develop a political counterforce to the landed class, very liberal voting requirements should be adopted. After removing the elite which opposed the colonizing mission, universal male suffrage might have to be rescinded if "the radical elements" could not be controlled. In fact, this is precisely what occurred when the BIA in 1916 and again in 1917 tried to disenfranchise illiterate males who did not own property,

U.S. suffrage laws applied only to men (women were denied the right to vote) and shifted from restrictive (1899) to more liberal (1900) to virtually universal (1902) to universal (1904), and then became more restrictive (1906). After 1909 the BIA and the governors proposed very restrictive franchises. These changes were responses by the colonial managers to the growing electoral strength of the Unión Puertorriqueña.

Deciding Who Is Eligible.

Only a male twenty-one or older, who was literate, or who could demonstrate "ownership of personal property not less than twenty five dollars," or "owned real estate in his own right and name, or was a member of a firm or corporation or partnership which owned real-estate" was permitted to vote in the 1900 elections (USDS 1901, 112). The new franchise limited the vote to 123,140 males, about 58 percent of the male population aged twenty or older. The Council also established seven election district boards with three members each, one Federal, one Republican, and one U.S. citizen (113).

After gaining control of the house in 1900, the Republicans immediately moved to liberalize the suffrage requirements for the 1902 general elections. The new electoral law retained the literacy test and property qualifications of the previous law. However Benjamin F. Butler, who analyzed the elections for the American Academy of Social and Political Science, reported that the law had been amended to permit an elector who could produce "a tax receipt showing the payment of any kind of taxes for the last six months of the year in which the election was held" (Butler 1903, 188). The amount of the tax was immaterial, nor was the date of payment of the tax a consideration. The tax could be paid up to the date of voter registration, and some electors used tax receipts of as little as three cents to register (189). According to one observer of the period, "It practically made every peon a voter. Old registrations were continued without question. Political committees and candidates saw that their partisans were provided with the proper receipts. The registration was a definite defiance of the law" (Wilson 1905, 99).

During the second legislative session the Republican Party passed an election law that further increased its electoral advantages. Section 22 of the law restricted the nominations of candidates to any party that had cast 5 percent of the total vote in the last election, or to those candidates who had obtained petitions signed by five hundred qualified votes (Butler 1903, 187). Having chosen not to participate in the 1900 elections, the Federal Party was compelled to nominate all its candidates by petition (187). This was an arduous and time-consuming task. The Republicans imposed further limitations on the Federal Party: The election law stipulated the first day of registration as October 14 and the following day, October 15, as the deadline for filing the registration. Miraculously, the Federal Party complied with the registration requirements and mounted a credible campaign. For the 1902 elections 158,924 voting-age males registered, and 111,216 cast votes (Pagán 1972, 1:85). The Republicans obtained 73,823 votes, controlled 25 seats in the House of Delegates, and had their candidate elected resident commissioner in Washington. The Federal Party obtained 34,605 votes and 10 delegate seats (Bayron Toro 1989, 120).

The electoral fortunes of the Republicans changed dramatically in 1904 when they were defeated by a new organization, the Unión Puertorriqueña. The House of Delegates, now under control of the Unión, revised the suffrage requirements once again. The suffrage act of March 10, 1904, mandated an educational test effective on July 1, 1906, but gave the vote to all male residents of Puerto Rico or the United States who had resided in the country for at least one year (Rowe

1904, 206). According to the secretary of Puerto Rico, "this removed all previous restrictions . . . and in fact granted universal suffrage" for the 1904 elections (USDS 1905, 45). Voter registration for the 1904 elections increased dramatically to 225,262 (45).

Years later, Governor Yager recalled that extending the suffrage to all males over twenty-one was "the most important and fundamental mistake. . . . This has produced a body of electors in Porto Rico, about seventy-five per cent of whom are not only illiterate, but have had no sort of political experience or training that would fit them for the exercise of this important privilege." Yager concluded by warning, "No healthy political life is possible under the circumstances." He called for Congress to correct this situation "by establishing some fair and reasonable restriction upon the suffrage" (Yager 1915, 151–153).

The Unión Puertorriqueña: Struggle for Autonomy and Tradition

Until its electoral eclipse by the Unión Puertorriqueña the Republican Party had proven its utility as an agent for legitimizing the colonial regime. The Republicans approved virtually all the legislation proposed by the Executive Council; however, this collaboration with the colonial authorities cost the party dearly. It was subjected to a relentless attack by *La Democracia*, which accused the Republicans of betraying the country to foreign corporate interests and being indiscriminate proponents of Americanization. The Executive Council's refusal to approve legislation favorable to domestic producers or give Puerto Ricans a role in the policy process generated tensions within the Republican Party. Two major factions emerged: one continued to support the colonial order; the other advocated increased Puerto Rican input in the colonial administration. The factionalism came to a head in 1904, when key leaders abandoned the Republican Party and joined the leaders of the Federal Party to establish the Unión Puertorriqueña of Puerto Rico. The Unión Puertorriqueña was the first political alliance of the new colonial period (Díaz Soler 1960, 2:287).

The defections from the Republican Party were almost exclusively from the professional strata, and included six of its most prominent leaders (Quintero Rivera 1977, 95 n. 117, 60). A key proponent of the formation of the Unión Puertorriqueña was Republican Party leader Rosendo Matienzo Cintrón, who eventually became a forceful advocate for independence. Strains in the Republican Party were evident as early as 1901. Some of its leaders were critical of the direction and content of the Americanization process and the refusal to appoint Republicans to policymaking posts. The insolence of the Executive Council in its dealings with the elected legislature tried the patience of those Republicans. The dissident Republicans were disillusioned with the ongoing process of disenfranchisement from the administration of their country and with their inability to influence the conduct of government (Díaz Soler 1960, 2:217). Moreover, apprehension crystallized in certain quarters of the Republican Party as to the future of the Puerto Rican nationality. Matienzo Cintrón warned that "Puerto Rico senses the arrival of its apocalypse and senses with fear its disappearance" (quoted in Díaz Soler 1960, 2:220).

Serious cleavages were forming along economic lines as well. Those local capitalists who were incorporated into the emerging corporate economy dominated by U.S. capital became outspoken proponents of Americanization and "modernization." This sector rapidly ascended within the party and displaced the traditional professional sector that was the intellectual force of the Republican Party. Those in the professional sector—lawyers, doctors, merchants—were not necessarily reliant on the U.S.-dominated corporate economy for their survival. Those in this sector in particular chafed at a system of rule that deprived them of a voice in the governing process (Quintero Rivera 1977, 60; Silén 1980, 207).

The professionals were opposed by an array of new economic actors, including small and medium-sized domestic sugar producers who profited from the expansion of the absentee sugar corporations and suppliers of raw materials to the sugar and tobacco industries. As labor market conditions changed, new professions and occupations were formed,—corporate attorneys, administrators, managers, and technicians in the service of the U.S. corporations. This elite group derived most of its power and social status from its reliance on the U.S.-dominated sugar economy, and its fortune was tied directly to those of the absentee corporations (Curtis 1966, 17–18). According to Quintero Rivera these new economic actors constituted the "anti-national bourgeoisie," and opposed reforms leading to autonomy for Puerto Rico (Quintero Rivera 1977, 68) The professionals, on the other hand, their power eclipsed by local sugar barons, negotiated an alliance with the Federal Party.

The significance of the schisms in the Republican Party and the subsequent establishment of the Unión Puertorriqueña (UP) is difficult to interpret, but the developments are suggestive of important ideological shifts. The collapse of the Republican alliance points to an emerging Puerto Rican national consciousness among elites who finally realized that colonialism was incompatible with the goal of preserving their social and economic influence. These dissidents believed that Americanization was undermining Puerto Rico's national identity. The defectors from the Republican Party and the *hacendados* of the Federal Party sought to reconstitute the political ideal of *la gran familia puertorriqueña* through the new political organization, the Unión Puertorriqueña (Quintero Rivera 1977, 60–61).

The movement encompassed a nominal cross-class alliance of *hacendados* and small landowners, professional sectors (medicine, law, intellectuals), artisans threatened by proletarianization, and sectors of professional strata not dependent for their economic well-being on the metropolitan economy. The UP also incorporated those sectors of the property-owning classes and professional categories that had waged the battle for autonomy under the Spanish regime. The UP labeled itself a patriotic organization that embodied the spirit of autonomy. It declared it represented an authentic national interest against an alien colonial power—a power that despite its democratic and liberal traditions threatened to reconfigure Puerto Rican society and eradicate its culture.

The Unión demanded fundamental changes in the colonial regime, including the complete separation of legislative and executive functions, an elected legislative assembly, and gubernatorial (as opposed to presidential) appointment of department secretaries with the advice and consent of the U.S. Senate. It also proposed specific measures to protect the dying coffee industry. The UP opposed reform of the colonial administration that did not provide for full extension of the Constitution to Puerto Rico, "or that does not concede to the Porto Ricans a definite citizenship, satisfy the necessities of the country, and establish in Porto Rico self-government or autonomy, in which the people of Porto Rico may acquire full civil and political rights in governing themselves" (USDS 1904, 31–32).

In March 1904, the UP announced in *La Democracia* "we declare . . . that the island may be constituted into an independent nation under the protectorate of the United States, a means through which self-government may be achieved" (quoted in Vélez Aquino 1968, 80). If the United States would grant neither territorial status leading to statehood nor territorial autonomy, the UP declared it would champion independence (Bothwell González 1979, 1:286–89; Pagán 1972, 1:106–113). This declaration may have marked the first time in the history of Puerto Rico in which "a mass party" called for independence (Pagán 1972, 1:114). After learning of the UP platform, Governor Hunt angrily asserted that the United States would never approve independence and criticized the UP decision as "a most serious condemnation" of the people of the United States (quoted in Díaz Soler 1960, 1:289). Hunt warned those "men whose restlessness and ambitions lead them to attempt to stir feeling against American institutions and people" that "under present and future conditions quiet must be maintained" (USDS 1904, 32). Puerto Ricans who opposed colonial rule were ridiculed as antiquarians who were incapable of grasping the benefits to be gained under U.S. colonialism. Allen attributed the discontent to a "few older men," "who have little or no acquaintance with the new National power, and who can not realize that in the full development of the future every important consideration of political and material good for Porto Rico demands that the common interest of the people shall be best promoted by the encouragement of a patriotic spirit of national pride in the United States" (USDS 1904, 32).

The persistent agitation by the UP convinced President Theodore Roosevelt to propose U.S. citizenship for Puerto Ricans. In his 1905 message he told Congress, "I earnestly advocate the adoption of legislation which will explicitly confer American citizenship on all citizens of Puerto Rico." But he went on to reaffirm his conviction that the government established by the Foraker Act was appropriate: "The present form of government in Porto Rico . . . has proved satisfactory and has inspired confidence in property owners and investors. The problems of the island are industrial and commercial rather than political" (USDS 1904, 15). Roosevelt rejected amending the Foraker Act by asserting that the colonial situation was "far too grave and too delicate to admit of any other course being pursued" (quoted in Morales Carrión 1983, 163).

U.S. governors were often bedeviled by the recalcitrant and shrewd political leadership of the UP. The Unión dominated the electoral process, obtained overwhelming majorities in the lower house, and controlled most of the municipalities from 1904 through 1917. It continuously agitated for changes to the Foraker Act. Although the UP was virtually unrivaled, it was unsuccessful in enacting legislation that advanced the economic interests of its key sectors. In a study of the legislative activity between 1905 and 1914, Negrón Portillo discovered that the majority of bills approved by the House of Delegates were rejected by the Executive Council, and of those rejected the majority were measures to advance the interests of domestic agriculturists (Negrón Portillo 1978, 26). Other researchers have also documented the frequency with which the Executive Council blocked House of Delegates initiatives, whereas almost 80 percent of the council's own measures were approved (Silvestrini and Luque de Sánchez 1990, 395).

The UP was relentless in its pursuit of fundamental reforms leading to greater accountability by the colonial authorities, enhanced legislative powers, and protection for coffee growers and small producers. It called for agricultural credits to forestall the landowners' loss of their means of production. Having lost much of their influence after the reorganization of the municipal governments, the *hacendados* acted through the UP to reestablish the autonomy of the municipalities and reassert some control over the political process (Negrón Portillo 1978, 26; Quintero Rivera 1977, 49).

Beginning in 1903, *La Democracia* took up the cause of the coffee producers with particular urgency, claiming that they were the "victims most punished by American domination" (quoted in Negrón Portillo 1981a, 61–62). The refusal of the Executive Council to establish an agricultural credit bank resulted, according to UP resident commissioner Larrinaga, in "the greater part of the small coffee estates falling into the hands of the merchants and banks" (quoted in Negrón Portillo 1981a, 15). Larrinaga wrote in 1905 that Puerto Rico was "suffering from a great commercial depression caused by the loss of our markets for coffee, which is our main staple." Puerto Rico's traditional markets in Europe were drying up, since the Europeans retaliated against the Dingley Tariff by imposing high import duties on Puerto Rican coffee. Larrinaga reported, "The result is that we cannot send our coffee there, where it commands a very high price, but we have to send it here, to the states, and sell it at a low rate, in competition with the Rio coffee. That temporarily is a serious drawback in our financial condition" (Larrinaga 1905, 55–56). Two years later Larrinaga informed the Lake Mohonk Conference that coffee, "one of the best features of our industrial condition has disappeared. Coffee was the poor man's crop. Today all the small farms are in a few hands" (Larrinaga 1907, 163).

The UP blamed U.S. officials and policy for the virtual destruction of the coffee industry. This advocacy would suggest that coffee *hacendados* were a powerful sector within the party. Historian Negrón Portillo questions this view, and interprets the UP's advocacy on behalf of coffee as suggestive of an emerging national ideology that glorified the traditional socioeconomic order existing before the U.S. invasion (1981b, 61, 115). Stymied and frustrated by an obdurate governor and Executive Council, Muñoz Rivera waged a scathing attack in *La Democracia*. He lambasted Congress for creating a House of Delegates that was "inhibited, restrained and annulled by the preponderate actions of the governor and the council" (Quoted in Luque de Sánchez 1980, 143).

The Executive Council, which never overrode a gubernatorial veto, was considered a mere instrument of the governor (Capó Rodríguez 1919, 564). At the 1908 annual Mohonk Conference, Manuel Rodríguez-Serra blamed the council, with its dual legislative and executive functions, as the source of Puerto Rican discontent with U.S. rule. The council was "un-American, and anti-republican or anti-democratic." Popular will was subverted, since the "legislature is at the mercy of the six American members of the Executive Council" (Rodríguez-Serra 1908, 163).

The battle for reform of the colonial regime included the lobbying efforts of the resident commissioner, special committees and delegations that traveled to Washington, and use of the media to criticize U.S. policy. In addition, the UP established the Puerto Rican-American League in New York to influence public opinion on Puerto Rico (Díaz Soler 1960, 1:288). Colonial authorities continued to dismiss the UP demands as the pathetic plaintive calls of a decaying elite for restoration of a discredited social order and steadfastly endorsed the supremacy of its colonizing mission.

One of the ironies of this historical moment was the seeming ideological transformation of the autonomy-minded *hacendados*. During the last years of Spanish rule they were a progressive economic force who had fought to dismantle mercantilist policies that stifled international commerce. In 1897 the *hacendados'* struggle for Puerto Rico's autonomy was part of a broader national campaign to eradicate those colonial strictures that impeded the development of capitalism in Puerto Rico (History Task Force 1979, 77).

As we saw, these same *hacendados* welcomed the change in sovereignty because the United States held out the prospects of unlimited commercial expansion and institutional modernization. They were certain that the United States would move quickly to develop the island's productive capacity in agriculture, in contrast to Spain, which had proven to be an impediment to capitalist development. These *hacendados* mistakenly believed they would have a leading role in the economic boom they expected after the change in sovereignty. Although some *hacendados*, particularly those with ready access to capital, operated modern capitalist enterprises and had commercial relations with the United States, many did not. Many *hacendados* still had one foot in an antediluvian mode of production and articulated paternalist political values that were inconsistent with the evolving corporate-based economy driven by U.S. firms. The local capitalist sector belatedly discovered that Puerto Rico's economic transformation would be dominated by modern capital-intensive foreign firms, and that colonial policy would virtually guarantee their exclusion from the ensuing process of growth. Some *hacendados* had prominent positions in the UP, and they were determined to protect their class interest through the party. For almost two decades, from 1900 to 1917, the UP waged a campaign for political autonomy that entailed opposition to legislation that was designed to transform Puerto Rico's economy and displace its Spanish legal and political institutions.

Heavily influenced by the *hacendados*, the UP framed its campaign for political and economic autonomy in terms of promoting national unity in defense of Puerto Rican culture and identity. Fear of displacement by U.S. firms and their local partners led the *hacendados* to adopt a campaign of resistance that was at odds with the drive toward modernity that was a key element of the Americanization process.

The opposition portrayed the UP as dominated by elitist and paternalistic *hacendados* who were obsessed with reviving the old order in which they were the dominant economic and social actors. Although the UP dominated the electoral process until after World War I, the *hacendados'* quest to derail the colonial project of the United States and reclaim their former status was doomed.

The Empire Strikes Back, Almost

Despite years of government support for the Republican Party and an intensive campaign of Americanization, the colonial authorities were unable to squelch the decade-old Puerto Rican struggle for self-government. The elections of 1908, which resulted in a major electoral victory for the UP, served to confirm this inability. The Unión obtained 101,033 of the 155,995 votes cast (Pagán 1972, 1:126). It obtained majorities in all the electoral districts and had absolute control of the House of Delegates. In 1909 the UP orchestrated a legislative revolt, prompting Governor Régis Post to report, "The political situation during the past year has been most unsatisfactory." He observed that "more stress than ever has laid upon objections to the present system of government," and deemed the situation in the legislature "most ominous" (USDS 1909, 25). The budgetary authorization impasse of 1909 merits discussion because the clash between the Unión and the governor revealed a growing popular dissatisfaction with the colonial regime.

A young cadre of newly elected UP legislators pressured the old guard to adopt a more militant posture toward the colonial regime. According to one chronicler of the period, "A dangerous friction was developing between the youthful element" elected to the House "and the old fighters who tried to impose their will" (Díaz Soler 1960, 1:404). Governor Post expressed his concern with the new delegates, who openly challenged the colonial authorities as well as the established party leadership. Post reported that many of the "more conservative members" of the house were not renominated by the UP in its nominating convention, "and several extremists were nominated in their place" (USDS 1909, 25). He warned the UP that "the attitude of some of the gentlemen of the House might be noxious to the interests of the country" (Díaz Soler 1960, 1:411).

The overwhelming electoral victory gave the UP a mandate to seek changes to the Foraker Act. It convened a meeting of its central committee to debate and vote on a legislative boycott "in order to attract the attention of the United States to their opposition to the organic act" (USDS 1909, 25). Newly elected delegate Luis Lloréns Torres led the faction that was prepared to provoke a confrontation with the authorities. He argued that it would be possible to "destroy, overthrow, annihilate legislative power in Puerto Rico, if we resolve not to legislate, and refuse to approve all the laws of the Council. . . . We will then make it impossible for our Foraker government to exist, declaring ourselves on legislative strike" (quoted in Díaz Soler 1960, 1:407). The proclamation was too radical for Muñoz Rivera, who tried to influence the central committee to reject the resolution. But under pressure from the young legislators, the UP issued a resolution to rescind the Foraker Act, which was "destroying the Puerto Rican personality." It repeated the longstanding demand for the independence of the House of Delegates from the Executive Council (Bothwell González 1979, 1:300).

Drawing the Budgetary Battle Lines

The UP chose to make its stand against colonialism by refusing to accept the governor's budget authorization bill. The UP-dominated House introduced a measure to force the governor to appoint to vacant municipal offices only those individuals selected by the party. The UP's goal was to reclaim some of its patronage power and reassert some control over the *municipios*. The governor and the Executive Council rejected the measure, as well as other proposals, including the establishment of an agricultural bank to provide loans to debt-ridden landowners. The legislators reacted by authorizing a budget for the succeeding fiscal year that reduced the salaries of executive department officials. When the Executive Council refused to approve the bill, the House adjourned without passing an appropriations bill. Government operations technically ceased to operate at the end of the fiscal year.

Convinced the UP wanted to sabotage government operations, Governor Post decided to reject a compromise measure proposed by the House leadership and called for the president to intervene. After learning of this act of defiance, President Taft asked Congress to deprive the House of Delegates of the power of budgetary approval. Taft lamented that "In the thirst of certain Puerto Rican leaders to secure political power, the Puerto Ricans have forgotten the generosity of the United States in its relations with them" (quoted in Kidder 1965, 169). Taft explained his actions in the language of a benevolent patriarch who was profoundly disappointed with the conduct of his wards:

> When we, with the consent of the people of Porto Rico, assumed guardianship over them and the guidance of their destinies, we must have been conscious that a people

that had enjoyed so little opportunity for education could not be expected safely for themselves to exercise the full power of self-government; and the present development is only an indication that we have gone somewhat too fast in the extension of political power to them for their own good. (Quoted in Ringer 1983, 997)

As punishment Taft demanded "that the absolute power of appropriation is taken away from those who have shown themselves too irresponsible to enjoy it" (quoted in Clark 1969, 162). On July 15, 1909, the Olmstead Amendment was signed into law, which stipulated that the current year budget would be automatically carried over to the new fiscal year if the House of Delegates refused to approve the appropriations bill. In his report to Congress, President Taft accused the House of Delegates of subverting the government. According to Taft, "its members are not sufficiently alive to their oath-taken responsibility for the maintenance of government, to justify Congress in further reposing in them absolute power to withhold the appropriations necessary for the government's life" (Quoted in O'Leary 1936, 44–45)

During the Olmstead Bill debates New York Senator Depew accused the Unión of precipitating the crisis in order to monopolize the local political process. "The whole of this trouble grows out of an anxiety on the part of the few who are in control of the political parties, . . . [the leaders of] the Unionist Party, which has now gained all the offices and have every seat in the house of delegates" (quoted in O'Leary 1936, 48). A UP delegation explained to Congress that the purpose of the revolt was to "protest . . . against a regime that creates taxation without representation and government without the consent of the inhabitants" (quoted in Kidder 1965). In the midst of this political crisis *La Democracia* cautioned the colonial regime, "Either Washington grants justice to Puerto Rico and satisfies the clamor of its public opinion, or else it should give up its goal of Americanization of the country and achieving the bonds of affection and love. . . . Puerto Rico is grateful but not servile" (Quoted in Vélez Aquino 1968, 103).

In an additional display of presidential truculence, Taft reassigned jurisdiction of Puerto Rico to the Bureau of Insular Affairs (USDS 1909, 22). This executive order was significant for a number of reasons. Not least was the fact that the BIA was singularly insulated from congressional pressures and had demonstrated resistance to liberalizing the colonial regime. By assigning jurisdiction to the BIA, Taft made clear that the United States had no intention of rescinding Puerto Rico's colonial status.

Despite the clear indications of growing dissatisfaction with the colonial regime, U.S. officials were convinced that support for independence was inconsequential. The UP tactics were portrayed as a cynical ploy by its aging leadership to embarrass the United States. Nonetheless, the 1909 budget imbroglio was a catalyst that compelled Congress to rethink its colonial policy, including the citizenship status of the Puerto Rican people. The budgetary crisis demonstrated that for some sectors of Puerto Rico's elite, independence was to be preferred

above colonial tutelage. The Unionists demonstrated their political sophistica-
tion and willingness to employ their limited legislative capabilities to provoke a
crisis to force the federal government to intercede directly in colonial affairs.
Their goal was to convince the U.S. that without their cooperation, which could
be bought at the price of reform, Puerto Rico would become unmanageable. The
UP's defiance was sufficiently vexing for Taft to dispatch Secretary of War J. M.
Dickinson and BIA chief General Clarence Edwards on a fact-finding mission to
Puerto Rico in December 1909. The visit was designed to allay concerns capital-
ists might have had about investing in the politically contentious colony.

Dickinson reported that, although sentiment for citizenship was widespread,
to accept the UP demands for universal male suffrage and for the separation of
executive and legislative functions would be "disastrous for the health and economic and political welfare of the island, would jeopardize investments, retard
healthy development" (quoted in Ringer 1983, 998). According to Governor
Colton, "Men of means and energy had become discouraged over local conditions and the apparent uncertainty of the future and had determined to dispose
of their interests and leave the island." The governor reported of Secretary Dickinson's visit, "Of no less importance to the progress of the island . . . was the confidence inspired thereby in the future security to sound business enterprises"
(USDW Annual Report 1910, 4).

Dickinson was convinced that independence did not enjoy much support. He
drafted a bill for a new organic act, which was introduced by Representative Olmstead, the chairman of the Committee on Insular Affairs (*Cong. Rec.* 1916, 7470).
The Olmstead Bill was approved by the House, but was not taken up by the Senate. It was a conservative proposal for restrictive and centralized administration
that essentially subordinated Puerto Rico to the rule of the Bureau of Insular Affairs. The bill also called for a thirteen-member senate, which would replace the
Executive Council. Five of the senators were to be elected and eight appointed by
the president; after thirty-six years all the senators would be elected. The bill
called for an executive branch consisting of the governor and six department secretaries appointed by the president, a bill of rights, provision for biennial instead
of annual legislative sessions, increase of corporate landholdings to three thousand acres, and the appointment instead of election of certain judges (Parsons
1910, 134–140; USDW BIA 1910, 18). The original bill was amended to provide
for collective citizenship instead of the individual elective citizenship proposed
by the secretary of war (Cabranes 1979, 66; Clark 1975, 21).

The BIA proposed a highly restrictive franchise because it was convinced that
universal male suffrage would assure the UP's continued electoral dominance.
The Olmstead Bill aimed at undermining the political base of the UP and putting
in power what Governor George Colton called the "substantial and conservative
elements" (Morales Carrión 1983, 185). The measure would have limited the eligible electorate to literate males and imposed a minimum annual tax payment of
five dollars as an eligibility requirement. Colton endorsed the restrictions and

was convinced that if the UP was denied the peasantry's electoral support it would be defeated, resulting in "the removal of despotic political power from the hands of a few political bosses" (quoted in Morales Carrión 1983, 169). Walcott H. Pitkin, Puerto Rico's attorney general, intensely opposed any liberalization of the electoral franchise, because "the great majority of males were illiterate and propertyless." Pitkin was contemptuous of the UP leadership and adamantly opposed granting Puerto Rico self-government. He warned that under universal male suffrage self-government "will be nothing more than the control of a few despotic party leaders, since this element of the population, having nothing to lose and having only the crudest conceptions of political institutions, votes only as its immediate leaders dictate" (quoted in Trías Monge 1980, 2:49).

The BIA recommended that Puerto Ricans were to "be admitted to citizenship upon application to the courts and the taking of an oath of allegiance to the United States" (quoted in Cabranes 1979, 65). After a reasonable period only citizens of the United States should hold elective or appointive office. This proposal, when combined with the Olmstead Bill's literacy and contributory requirements, would have disenfranchised most of the electorate in Puerto Rico, where almost 80 percent of the population was illiterate, and where few were academically and financially prepared to comply with the legal requirements for U.S. citizenship (Cabranes 1979, 65).

The Olmstead Bill was severely criticized in the Senate, whose leadership saw it as a crude attempt by the BIA to exercise virtually absolute power over the colony (Clark 1975, 20). At the Lake Mohonk conference Judge Luis Muñoz Morales repudiated the bill and exposed its ludicrous provision for individual naturalization, which deprived Puerto Rican women of U.S. citizenship (Muñoz Morales 1910, 144). Even the faithful Republicans tired of the Congress's refusal to establish a territorial form of government. In September 1908 Barbosa called on Governor Post to substantially "liberalize the regime" (Barbosa 1939, 77).

The Senate failed to consider the measure because Senator Elihu Root, the former secretary of war, opposed the collective citizenship provisions. According to Root, U.S. citizenship for Puerto Rico would "dilute our electorate." He argued that U.S. citizenship would "inevitably" lead to "a demand for statehood," which he opposed (Jessup 1938, 1:378). The BIA continued to press for the adoption of the Olmstead Bill, and in order to bolster its case it advised Congress that "the subject of citizenship of Porto Rico is the underlying cause of whatever political and social unrest there is in the island" (USDW BIA 1912, 25).

Redefining the Terms of
Colonial Subordination: A First Attempt

After the fiasco of the Olmstead Bill, continued political agitation by the UP convinced Congress to propose a new organic act for Puerto Rico. Naturally, Congress received conflicting testimony from the key players. The BIA and the governor were insistent on the political expediency of conferring U.S. citizenship on Puerto Ricans. Colonial officials were certain that congressional refusal to grant citizenship was the primary source of discontent. However, the BIA wanted to move quickly on the citizenship issue without changing Puerto Rico's political status as an unincorporated territory or diminishing Congress's plenary powers over the colony. The UP rejected this argument and warned that growing opposition was due to repressive colonial rule; it opposed U.S. citizenship without a prior grant of self-government.

The conflicting views on the sources of colonial malaise were openly discussed at the February 25, 1914, hearings held by the Senate Committee on Pacific Islands and Porto Rico to consider a bill "to provide a civil government for Porto Rico." Governor Yager and BIA chief Frank McIntyre had been instrumental in drafting the measure that was introduced by Senator Shaforth. The BIA wanted to impose even more centralized control over the troublesome colony. Governor Yager testified that since Puerto Rico "is sure to remain a permanent possession of the United States, it is important that the government of the island should not only be safe and efficient, but should also satisfy, as far as possible, the aspirations of the people who live under it" (U.S. Senate, Committee on Pacific Islands and Porto Rico 1914, 3). He assured the committee that the bill "would go far toward allaying whatever discontent has arisen under the present law and under the changes in the tariff produced by the new tariff law" (4). Noting that Puerto Rico was the only Latin American nation, "over which the United States has had entire control," Yager testified that "if we can administer the government of Porto Rico in such a manner as to satisfy its peoples and at the same time secure the ends of good government, the effect will be that we shall greatly improve the relations of the United States to the whole of Latin America" (6).

Secretary of War Garrison acknowledged that "the people of Porto Rico are dissatisfied with certain phases of their government" and cautioned "there has been some expression of a view looking to a separation of the island from the United States." The source of the discontent was, according to Garrison, "the withholding of American citizenship, which so long requested has been resented in the island and out of this resentment has grown some hostility to the United States" (U.S. Senate, Committee on Pacific Islands and Porto Rico 1914, 17–18). Garrison favored individual voluntary citizenship and wanted only those Puerto Ricans with U.S. citizenship to vote and to hold public office in Puerto Rico. Those Puerto Ricans who opted not to apply for U.S. citizenship would be disenfranchised in their own country. In order to prevent a reoccurrence of the 1909 imbroglio Garrison requested that the governor have absolute veto over separate items in the appropriation bills. The centralization of power in the BIA was essential according to Garrison "because of the remoteness of the island and to meet conditions existing in the island" (20).

Congress wanted to clarify one significant legal conundrum before acting on the grant of US citizenship: Did U.S. citizenship constitutionally obligate Congress to territorially incorporate Puerto Rico? Garrison instructed BIA legal officer Frankfurter to examine this issue. Frankfurter informed the Senate committee that "citizenship does not defeat the conscious purpose against incorporation"; he also saw citizenship "as a means of removing the great source of political unrest in the island" (U.S. Senate, Committee on Pacific Islands and Porto Rico 1914, 23). Frankfurter reasserted that Congress had complete plenary powers, which meant that Puerto Rico's future rested solely in its hands. Puerto Rico's relationship was "a political question intrusted by the Constitution to unlimited congressional control" (22). He concluded, "If Congress chooses to grant citizenship without incorporation, the Supreme Court will respect such exercise by Congress of its political function" (24).

The proposed legislation was anathema to the Unión. Its response to the measure constituted a forceful statement on the Puerto Rican people's right to self-determination. Each point of the proposed law that circumscribed the role of Puerto Ricans in the policy process was repudiated by the UP. It continued to reject U.S. citizenship unless it was linked to greater powers of self-government. The provisions that reserved for Congress the power to annul the laws of Puerto Rico without judicial review and that conferred on the governor the power of absolute veto were particularly objectionable. The UP especially rejected the latter provision, "which places an appointee of the President over the 58 senators and representatives elected by the people" (U.S. Senate, Committee on Pacific Islands and Porto Rico 1914, 7). Vice President Frank Martínez warned Congress to heed the Unión's recommendations, since the party had "won the last five elections; carrying every district in the island in the last four elections" and told them that "our views, under the democratic principles, are the views of Puerto Rico" (26). Muñoz Rivera testified that "the immense majority of my constituents aspire to their national independence as an ultimate solution" (6). Fernández García echoed this theme: "Since the strong sentiment of the vast majority of Porto Ricans is for independence . . . the granting of American citizenship would . . . bar the aspiration of Porto Ricans" (9).

House Speaker José de Diego ridiculed the BIA's rationale that citizenship would ameliorate the insular discontent. He asserted that "The sentiment of American citizenship for Porto Rico is neither in you nor in us." The reason Puerto Ricans were in "constant protest," De Diego testifies, was "the absurd form of government that you imposed on us without our consent" (U.S. Senate, Committee on Pacific Islands and Porto Rico 1914, 51). U.S. citizenship was rejected as a ploy to alter the island's internal political dynamic. Muñoz Rivera cautioned that "the majority of Porto Ricans think that conferring of American citizenship in any form whatever would interfere with the future declaration of the status of the inhabitants of the island" (8). Fernández García told Congress that U.S. citizenship was meaningless, since Americanization had failed to achieve any substantive changes. He reminded Congress that Puerto Rico, "is a country thickly settled by a people of a different race and origin from that of the United States . . .

manners, customs and habits and language, overall cannot be changed by civil laws. . . . The population of the rural districts of the island does not know to-day, after 15 years of American influence, a single English word" (10).

On March 12, 1914, The House of Delegates sent a fiery message to the Senate denouncing the proposed legislation. The delegates asserted, "It imposes upon the people of Puerto Rico a government without their consent and taxation without representation" (U.S. Senate, Committee on Pacific Islands and Porto Rico 1914, 52). Charles Hartzell, a practicing attorney in Puerto Rico who was a consultant to the Senate Committee, warned against the BIA proposal to vest the governor with unprecedented powers. Hartzell recommended substantial modifications in the law and warned of the "tremendous feeling of opposition in this island to the fact that it is being governed by the War Department. There is an inherent feeling that we are under practically a military government" (41).

Despite overwhelming opposition from Puerto Ricans, the president endorsed the measure. He was convinced that "the failure thus far to grant American citizenship continues to be the only ground of dissatisfaction." But he cautioned, "it should be remembered that the demand must be . . . entirely disassociated from any thought of statehood" (U.S. House 1912, 11). The House bill never became law. The logic behind the BIA's support for the measure—to contain the rising chorus of discontent by giving the governor virtually dictatorial powers—was disconcerting to a number of Senators. This uneasiness, together with the UP's highly contentious behavior, may have caused the Senate not to act on the measure.

Potential Unity and Fragmentation

After a decade of U.S. rule under a "temporary government" and intensive Americanization, Puerto Ricans were still judged by the colonizers as incapable of self-government. Even the Republicans, notwithstanding their zealous pro-U.S. posture, were becoming increasingly impatient with Washington's refusal to reform the colonial regime and the Senate's opposition to granting Puerto Ricans U.S. citizenship. The manifestations of Puerto Rican dissatisfaction and dissent were numerous and no doubt troubling to U.S. officials.

The budget crisis of 1909 was a watershed. In the same year the leaders of the Republican and Unión Parties, José Celso Barbosa and Luis Muñoz Rivera, pledged in a joint public declaration to collaborate to repeal the most obnoxious sections of the Foraker Act (Golding 1973, 120). In 1912 Matienzo Cintrón and Luis Lloréns Torres, both influential UP delegates to the lower house, abandoned the organization and established the Independence Party of Puerto Rico (Díaz Soler 1960, 1:513–547). However, the party failed to generate the support its leaders had expected, and after a disastrous showing in the 1912 elections it ceased its activities (Pagán 1972, 1:149). These developments strengthened the independence faction of the UP, one of whose most effective spokespersons was José de

Diego. De Diego pressured the Unión's older leadership to incorporate an independence plank in the party platform. In 1913 de Diego addressed the Lake Mohonk Conference. "The present political situation in Puerto Rico is absolutely untenable"; so began de Diego's address. He announced, "The admission of our Island into your sisterhood of States . . . is impossible; neither you nor we desire it, nor de we believe it possible" (de Diego 1913, 154–155). In the same year the UP removed statehood from its platform and demanded the establishment of an independent republic as a protectorate of the United States or full self-government (Pagán 1972, 1:156).

Even the loyalist Republicans began to see the potential danger of unchecked foreign corporate expansion for the small and medium-sized landowners and wanted a policy role in shaping the trajectory of capitalist expansion. Barbosa warned in 1910, "The real danger is in those industrial corporations, sugar, tobacco and later, coffee, [that] could be controlled by those large corporations; small landowners could be turned into servants" (quoted in Meléndez 1988, 46). In 1913 the Republican Party of Puerto Rico revoked its affiliation with the U.S. Republican Party, noting its sense of betrayal by the Republican-dominated Congress in failing to pass a bill granting U.S. citizenship to Puerto Ricans (for text see Bothwell González 1979, 1:337). The next year Puerto Rico's Republican Party called on the United States to implement "genuine American constitutional principles and to satisfy the just aspirations of the Puerto Ricans." The party proposed extensive amendments to the Foraker Act including the separation of executive and legislative functions (Pagán 1972, 1:158). In 1915 UP and Republican delegates in the house unanimously approved a joint resolution declaring, "It is intolerable that the provisional government established by the Foraker Act should be prolonged any longer," and called on the President to reform the colonial government by ceding significant powers of home rule to the Puerto Ricans (text of statement in Trías Monge 1980, 2:61).

Congress Attacks the Sugar Trusts

Antiprotectionist Democrats, who dominated both houses of the sixty-third Congress, passed the Underwood Tariff of 1913. After their overwhelming electoral victory, the Democrats claimed they had a mandate to dismantle the tariff that favored the sugar trusts and made imported foods more costly (Taussig 1931, 411). From the vantage point of export-dependent firms, the United States needed to expand global trade and penetrate European and Latin American markets, which necessitated the reduction or elimination of tariffs (Lake 1988a, 155–157). The Underwood Tariff permitted duty-free entry of all sugar into the United States as of May 1, 1916. It represented a complete reversal of the protection accorded to Puerto Rican sugar by previous Republican administrations and made evident the vulnerability of the insular economy to the vagaries of Congress.

But the Underwood Tariff only served to intensify the anxiety and growing sense of frustration of Puerto Rico's Republicans. Just the year before, on the eve of the 1912 elections, *El Tiempo* had proudly informed its readers, "The Republican Party is the only political party in Puerto Rico that is genuinely friendly toward Americans and the interests and rights of Americans in this country" (Quoted in Vélez Aquino 1968, 112–113). Puerto Rican sugar producers lacked representation in Congress and felt betrayed by the elimination of one of the key props of the industry. They were convinced that the tariff would cripple, if not destroy, Puerto Rico's industry.

The UP, despite its association with the coffee growers, did have prominent sugar planters in the organization. Resident commissioner Muñoz Rivera reproached Congress for enacting a law that threatened destruction of Puerto Rican agriculture (Capó Rodríguez 1921, 547; Trías Monge 1980, 2:50). The Association of Sugar Producers, chaired by Puerto Rican sugar magnate and UP official Eduardo Giorgetti, sent a commission to Washington to lobby Congress to retain the restrictions on imported sugar (Fernández García 1923, 567; Verrill 1914, 135). Muñoz Rivera and Tulio Larrinaga were members of this commission of notable Puerto Ricans(Fernández García 1923, 565). Frustrated with Congress's apparent willingness to enact a measure that could have devastated the sugar industry, the Republicans became more active proponents for fundamental changes in the Foraker Act.

Even before the duty-free sugar clause went into effect, it precipitated a major cutback in investments. Governor Yager blamed the Underwood Tariff for the dramatic decline in sugar exports: "Amongst the general causes for business disturbance those that affected Porto Rico most were the new tariff law of the United States" (USDW Annual Report 1914, 3). Yager reported that the bill "tends to intensify the discontent and dissatisfaction with American Government which exists in the island" (U.S. Senate, Committee on Pacific Islands and Porto Rico 1914, 4). The free-trade provision for sugar was rescinded on April 27, 1916, four days before it was to go into effect, as a result of the Democrats' defeat in the midterm elections and subsequent loss of their overwhelming majority in Congress. Moreover the Democratic proponents "could no longer ignore the strenuous faction in their own ranks who fought against free sugar" (Taussig 1931, 427).

Although opposition appeared to be spreading, Puerto Ricans were too divided along class and ideological lines to mount a unified campaign to force Congress to amend the Foraker Act. Moreover, by 1914 the UP experienced a reversal in its electoral fortunes that hinted at its eventual political decline and weakened its ability to continue the battle for autonomy (Silén 1980, 218). Republicans outpolled the UP in three of the seven electoral districts and in twenty-four of the thirty-six *municipios*, and elected sixteen of the thirty-five House delegates (Pagán 1972, 1:164). In part the electoral reversal was the UP's own doing, since its legislators approved a change in the electoral laws that guaranteed minority party representation in the House. The election results did blunt Muñoz Rivera's bold declaration in 1914 before a Senate committee that "the immense majority of my constituents aspire to their national independence as an ultimate solution" (U.S. Senate, Committee on Pacific Islands and Porto Rico 1914, 6). On October 24, 1915, the UP held a convention and overwhelmingly resolved to "postpone all action looking toward the independence of Puerto Rico and to devote our entire efforts toward a steady activity in favor of self government" (*Cong. Rec.* 1916, 7469). The decision to adopt a reformist posture rather than agitate for independence may have been prompted by the UP's electoral reversals.

The United States was undoubtedly successful in establishing the foundations for a transition to capitalism and displacing Puerto Rico's political institutions without precipitating an insurrection. Nevertheless, it proved incapable of eliminating agitation and opposition to colonial rule and eradicating Puerto Rican aspirations for self-rule. Although Puerto Ricans did not forge a unified national movement of opposition to U.S. colonialism, neither did they meekly carry out the colonizer's instructions. Even supporters of U.S. colonial rule negotiated a complex political identity based on elements of the Puerto Rican political culture and what they had culled from the Americanization process.

Although the UP leaders were unable to halt the colonial juggernaut launched by the United States, they did prove resourceful and resilient in impeding its progress. The governor and the Executive Council often seemed to be caught up in an incessant campaign to evade the UP's legislative machinations. The colonial government was reviled for its cavalier, and often arbitrary, dismissal of modest legislative measures to provide a modicum of self-government and protection to farmers. The relentless agitation to amend the Foraker Act was a perennial source of consternation for colonial officials. Even the loyal Republicans were splintered because of the unyielding posture of the colonial authorities. The colonizing mission of the United States was hampered to the extent that these actions of resistance, which were also acts of national affirmation, resonated with a large portion of the subject population.

6

A New Beginning and
the Growing Crisis of Legitimacy

I really think it is a misfortune for the United States to take that class of people into the body politic. . . . I think we have enough of that element in the body politic already to menace the Nation with mongrelization.

—*Senator James K. Vardaman, 1916*

We have developed in the course of centuries a personality, a collective personality, with its own characteristics formed by reason of racial origin, geographical situation, sources of our culture, and other circumstances.

—*Manuel Rodríguez Serra, 1916*

The Jones Act:
Tinkering with the Colonial Formula

On March 2, 1917, President Wilson signed into law the Jones Act, which was "An act to provide a Civil Government for Porto Rico and for other purposes." The Jones Act conferred collective U.S. citizenship on Puerto Ricans and legally terminated Puerto Rican citizenship.[1] But the act did not alter Puerto Rico's territorial status. After nineteen years of U.S. sovereignty Puerto Rico was still in a state of political limbo—neither part of the United States nor apart from it.

Citizenship: The Tie That Binds

Since 1910 the BIA had attempted to amend the Foraker Act and convince Congress to grant Puerto Ricans U.S. citizenship. The recalcitrance of the House of Delegates, the growing sentiment for independence within the UP, the militancy of the workers, and the apparent disunity within the Republican Party convinced the War Department of the need to amend the Foraker Act. The aborted Olmstead Act of 1910 was the first of these efforts. The grant of U.S. citizenship was proposed as a gambit to abate Puerto Rican dissatisfaction with the colonial regime, quiet political agitation for independence, and serve to permanently bind the country to the United States. Nothing in the grant of U.S. citizenship would constitutionally alter the country's status as an unincorporated territory. However, the War Department was convinced that citizenship would politically strengthen the annexationist forces and psychologically tighten the colonial links.

In 1911, War Secretary Henry Stimson called for U.S. citizenship and apprised Congress that "the connection between Porto Rico and the United States is permanent and has been from the beginning regarded as permanent" (quoted in Cabranes 1979, 70). According to BIA chief McIntyre, "The definite continuance of United States control in the island has never been seriously questioned." However, in order "to remove the cause of political unrest . . . such Puerto Ricans as desire and may be regarded as entitled to it should, by definite congressional action, be admitted to citizenship in the United States"(USDW BIA 1911, 17–18). The following year the BIA repeated the theme that "the subject of citizenship of Porto Ricans is the underlying cause of whatever political and social unrest there is in the island" (USDW BIA 1912, 25–26). President Wilson endorsed U.S. citizenship with the understanding that "the failure thus far to grant American citizenship continues to be the only ground for dissatisfaction." But he warned that it "must be . . . entirely disassociated from any thought of statehood" (U.S. House 1912, 11).

Putting a Stop to Independence

The UP endorsed U.S. citizenship, but only as one element of a broader legislative initiative to liberalize the colonial regime. In the absence of such legislation, Muñoz Rivera was hostile to the proposal. He testified before Congress, "if we can not be one of your States; if we can not constitute a country of our own, then we will have to be perpetually a colony, a dependency of the United States. Is that the kind of citizenship you offer us? Then, that is the citizenship we refuse" (quoted in Cabranes 1979, 76). In March 1914, the House of Delegates passed a resolution declaring that "we firmly and loyally maintain our opposition to being declared in defiance of our express wish or without our express consent, citizens of any country whatsoever other than our own beloved soil" (quoted in Gatell 1960, 9).

As the war in Europe entered its third year and as pressure for the United States to enter the conflagration increased, the Unión continued to agitate for reforms. Concern about possible German adventurism in the Caribbean only served to intensify U.S. desire to impose stability in the Caribbean (see Challener 1973; Grenville 1979). Muñoz Rivera played to these fears by continuing to warn that "there exists in Puerto Rico a well-defined aspiration to the ultimate independence of the country" (quoted in Cabranes 1979, 74). By the end of 1915 government leaders were virtually certain the country would be drawn into the European war. It was therefore strategically important to mollify the voices of discontent in the colonial possessions and to eradicate any thought of independence. In his 1915 annual message President Wilson prepared the nation for the possibility of war and called on Congress to authorize a significant expansion of the country's military capability. He also informed the legislators that "our policy towards the Philippines and the people of Porto Rico" was a matter "very intimately associated with the question of national safety and preparation for defense" (*Cong. Rec.* 1915, 98).

In 1915 Muñoz Rivera's leadership was challenged by José de Diego and others who were frustrated after years of U.S. refusal to amend the Foraker Act. Martín Travieso, who was an advocate for Americanization and a member of the Executive Council, also challenged Muñoz Rivera. Governor Yager was eager to resolve the differences between Muñoz Rivera and Travieso in order to isolate the independence faction that was led by José de Diego. Muñoz Rivera was able to defeat the independence platform and marginalize the faction led by de Diego (see Gatell 1960). After his success Muñoz Rivera cabled McIntyre to announce the UP "officially expresses its willingness to maintain the most cordial relations with the executive authorities in the Island and Washington." He told the BIA chief, "The party shall confine its activities to demanding home rule leaving the independence plank in its platform simply as an ideal until some future convention shall determine the date on which the said plank shall be considered a party issue" (Quoted in Gatell 1960, 15).

Although Muñoz Rivera beat back the independence challenge, this was at the price of having to adopt a more militant autonomist posture (see Gatell 1960). He continued to demand that Congress grant Puerto Rico autonomy: "There is no reason which justifies statesmen in denying self-government to my country and erasing from their programs the principles of popular sovereignty" (*Cong. Rec.* 1916, 7471). After Muñoz Rivera's victory, Washington appeared ready to enact new colonial legislation. President Wilson informed Congress in December 5, 1916, "The present laws governing the Island and regulating the rights and privileges of its people are not just. . . . There is an uneasiness among the people of the Island and even a suspicious doubt with regard to our intentions concerning them" (*Cong. Rec.* 1916, 17).

As the war continued to rage in Europe the BIA became ever more insistent on obtaining U.S. citizenship for Puerto Ricans. McIntyre asserted that its denial "has become an humiliation to some Porto Ricans and a basis for agitation on the part of others." He reaffirmed that "the people of Porto Rico should be made citizens of the United States to make clear that Porto Rico is to remain permanently connected with the United States." McIntyre also called on Congress to make it "plain that the Constitution and general statutory laws of the United States were not extended to Porto Rico and that there was no direct or implied promise of statehood" (USDW BIA 1916, 18). Governor Yager repeated this idea in a *New York Times* interview: "I know of no gift that would go so far toward removing dissatisfaction and difficulties in Porto Rico as a simple grant of United States citizenship " (December 9, 1916, 4:10).

The European War and Puerto Rico's Political Status

U.S. citizenship and permanent colonialism were the essential components of the Jones Act. Congress finally acted when U.S. entry into the European war was imminent. On the opening day of debates on the Jones-Shaforth Bill, Minnesota representative Miller announced his support for the measure, including U.S. citizenship, "so . . . that the independence propaganda be discontinued, and that our sovereignty remain there permanently." He warned that "agitation for independence in Porto Rico must come to a decided and permanent end." To thundering applause he affirmed that "Porto Rico will never go out from under the shadow of the Stars and Stripes" (*Cong. Rec.* 1916, 7473). The House Insular Committee chair instructed Muñoz Rivera that "the people of the United States desire that Puerto Rico remain as a permanent possession of the United States . . . this talk of independence is an idle dream of the Unionist Party" (quoted in Wagenheim and Wagenheim 1994, 124). Yager testified that Puerto Rico "will always be part of the United States, and the fact that we now after these years, make them citizens of the United States simply means . . . that we have determined practically that the American flag will never be lowered in Porto Rico" (quoted in Cabranes 1979, 82).

The grant of citizenship was proposed as measure to dampen support for independence and to demonstrate U.S resolve to retain Puerto Rico as a colony. However, there was no congressional sympathy for statehood. Senator William A. Jones was unequivocally opposed to statehood: "If Porto Rico were admitted to statehood there would be two senators and at least half a dozen Porto Rican representatives; and the fear exists that they might exercise a decisive influence in the United States Congress and practically enact laws for the government of the United States. For this reason I believe there is no opinion favorable in the United States" (Quoted in Barceló 1928, 30).

The importance of preserving Puerto Rico as a stable and loyal bastion in a volatile Caribbean region during these years cannot be overemphasized. Representative William Green of Iowa emphasized Puerto Rico's importance for U.S. regional security: "While we hold it, it is an outpost for defense of the Panama Canal; held by any other nation it becomes a point of attack in war and danger in peace. For their own good and our good we must retain some kind of control over Porto Rico" (*Cong. Rec.* 1916, 7487). Representative Miller told his colleagues that "Porto Rico is necessary to the United States as a key defense of the whole American continent against aggression from Europe" (*Cong. Rec.* 1916, 7473). Representative Cooper endorsed U.S. citizenship for Puerto Rico in terms of national security: "We are never to give up Puerto Rico for, now that we have completed the Panama Canal, the retention of the island becomes very important to the safety of the Canal, and in that way to the safety of the nation itself. It helps to make the Gulf of Mexico an American lake" (quoted in Maldonado-Denis 1972, 106).

While the European powers were engaged in the bloodiest war the world had known, the United States consolidated its Caribbean defense perimeter (Turk 1978, 201).[2] Interventions ordered by Presidents Roosevelt, Taft, and Wilson, during the war and immediately thereafter, made evident their resolve to employ military might to preserve order and protect U.S. interests in a region considered an area of vital strategic importance (Challener 1973, 408). Puerto Rico figured prominently in this strategy of consolidating U.S. military hegemony in the region. Control of the Mona Passage between Puerto Rico and Haiti was of particular strategic significance for planners (Bradford 1899, 739). Barely a week before the Jones Act was signed into law the *New York Times* reported, "Every effort is being made to place West Indies affairs in as settled a condition as possible, not only to discourage insurrections which might distract the attention of this government at a critical time, but also in some measure to prevent breeding places for possible plots against the Panama Canal" (February 21, 1917, 6:3).

Ms. O. H. Belmont, president of the Congressional Union for Women's Suffrage, told a *Times* reporter that President Wilson "has announced his desire for immediate action on the bill giving self-government to the Porto Ricans as a war measure. The imminence of war makes it wise, the President thinks, to insure the loyalty of the Porto Ricans" (February 22, 1917, 20:4).

Soon after the declaration of war against Germany, Congress extended the selective draft laws to Puerto Rico. Puerto Ricans were required to register for the compulsory military service on July 5, 1917. In 1917 the Puerto Rican regiment was brought up to its authorized strength of 1,969 men and transferred to Panama, where it was stationed from May 1917 to March 1919 (Cabranes 1979, 15; Negroni 1992, 374). By the end of the war, over 4,000 Puerto Ricans were stationed in Panama to guard the canal (Clark 1975, 37). By October 26, 1918, about 241,000 Puerto Rican men had registered for military service, 17,855 of whom were inducted into the army (Capó Rodríguez 1921, 545; Clark 1975, 37).

Puerto Rican males were conscripted into military service but denied any representation in the government that had sent them to war. For some Puerto Ricans compulsory military service was "a blood contribution, a terrible taxation, to be levied on . . . Puerto Rico's manhood, for the purpose of raising a large national army, in an equal proportion with every one of the States" (Capó Rodríguez 1921, 545). It was precisely these concerns that provoked Governor Yager to report that he "feared that compulsory service coming so soon after the enactment of the Jones bill, might bring on a campaign of misrepresentation of the motives of the American government in granting citizenship, and that the natural desire of many persons to escape the draft might lead them to renounce American citizenship under the first proviso of section 5 of the Jones Bill" (USDW Annual Report 1918, 2). However, the opposition never materialized, and, in fact, U.S. citizenship was not a prerequisite for conscription into the armed forces (See Cabranes 1979, 16).

For Unión Puertorriqueña there was no contradiction between patriotism toward the United States and its aspirations for territorial autonomy. In August

1917, José de Diego, speaker of the House, wrote to President Wilson, "The House also resolved to express to the people of the United States that the people of Porto Rico were ready to contribute with their blood, under the glorious flag of the United States to the triumph of democracy throughout the world and demand from the United States the completion of its work in Porto Rico by granting to our people the full right of self government" (*New York Times*, August 15, 1917).

On the eve of U.S. entry into the war the military encountered an unanticipated irony of colonialism. It learned that its proposal to organize a National Guard unit in Puerto Rico was unconstitutional, because the country was an unincorporated territory. The BIA reported that "existing law . . . had rendered impossible in the past the creation of national guard organizations in Puerto Rico." To overcome this prohibition, the army included a clause in the National Defense Bill of 1916 that "the word Territory as used in this act" relating to the National Guard "shall apply to Puerto Rico" (USDW BIA 1916, 19). Puerto Rico was an incorporated territory for the purposes of its militarization.

You Don't Really Want to Vote, Do You?
Restricting the Male Working-Class Vote

The BIA wanted Congress to rescind the provision in the Foraker Act that authorized the legislature to establish voting requirements. According to Muñoz Rivera, the BIA-drafted bills presented by Shafroth and Jones were "ultraconservative, and do not respond to the desires of our people, nor . . . to the just demands of our party, especially with regard to citizenship" (Gatell 1960, 9). Puerto Ricans directed their ire with the BIA's regressive proposal at Congress. Given the intensity of the opposition, Congress chose not to link U.S. citizenship with the more centralized and less participatory colonial administration proposed by the Bureau of Insular Affairs. Gaining the disgruntled acquiescence of Puerto Rico's established political leadership was preferable to feeding their simmering hostility at this critical juncture.

The voting requirements were the most controversial and strenuously debated provision of the proposed Jones Act. The House version rescinded the universal male voting provisions that had been in place for sixteen years by substituting property and literacy requirements. Illiterate males or men not able to pay three dollars in annual insular taxes would be deprived of the right to vote (*New York Times*, May 6, 1916). Moreover, the BIA insisted that only male property-owners be eligible to hold legislative office. Governor Yager purportedly called for the restrictive provisions because he was certain that corporations controlled the votes of large numbers of their male employees. Allegations of electoral fraud and the presumption that an uneducated male voting population was incapable of acting in a politically responsible manner were the alleged rationale for disenfranchising about three quarters of the male votes. A *New York Times* editorial endorsed the position: "We desire to place the local government in the hands of intelligent persons and also to prevent dissatisfaction and hostility among the islanders" (Dec. 26, 1916, 10:03).

These restrictive provisions were strenuously debated in both the House and Senate and were ardently resisted by Puerto Rico's political parties (see Ringer 1983, 997–1028). Iglesias Pantín demanded that "property should never be a reason to deprive the citizens of Puerto Rico of the political and civil rights" (Iglesias Pantín 1958, 399). He called the measure "a dangerous proposition," and warned, "To give to only those with property qualification the right to control the affairs of the people of the island will have a tendency to strengthen and encourage the agitation and propaganda of those who are already spreading anti-American sentiments and striving for the independence of the island" (U.S. Senate Committee on Pacific Islands and Porto Rico 1916, part 3, p. 137).

Muñoz Rivera criticized those members of Congress who were prepared to disenfranchise 70 percent of the quarter million male registered voters because they did not satisfy certain academic and financial qualifications (*Cong. Rec.* 1916, 7472). Cayetano Coll y Cuchi could not understand why men who had responsibly exercised their right to vote for fourteen to fifteen years should be disqualified from voting, without any valid justification for the denial of these civil rights (U.S. Senate Committee on Pacific Islands and Porto Rico 1916, part 1, p. 66). Representative Meyer London, of the Socialist Party, admonished Congress that if it approved the controversial proposal it would "reestablish the principle that property is entitled to a vote and not the human being" (*Cong. Rec.* 1916, 7477). He rationalized that the disenfranchised voters "will have the right to use the revolver, and will have the right to use violence, and will have the right to kill Governors. Do you deny to a man the right to express his views through civilized methods, through the medium of the ballot? He has the right to use every weapon, at his command and every protection" (*New York Times*, May 16, 1916, 9:3).

The storm of controversy convinced the Senate Committee to liberalize the male suffrage requirements by waiving the restrictions for ten years "for all legally qualified electors of Porto Rico at the last general elections." The committee felt that "within the next 10 years those for whom this exception is made will be able to qualify under one of the alternative conditions of voting" (quoted in Ringer 1983, 1014). However, this proposal only made sense in the context of a functioning educational system. But such a system did not exist. John Lennon, a member the U.S. Committee on Industrial Relations, reported that the public education system was in crisis and that approximately 200,000 children were not receiving any educational instruction (U.S. Senate Committee on Pacific Islands and Porto Rico 1916, part 2, p. 125). Citing government deficits Yager reduced the 1914 budget for public education by $700,000.

According to Samuel Gompers, because of the failure of public education hundreds of thousands of Puerto Ricans, through no fault of their own, would be denied their civil rights to select their representatives. He pointed out that "the literacy qualifications are raised for voters although those responsible have denied, refused, failed to give the children an opportunity to obtain even a rudimentary education" (U.S. Senate Committee on Pacific Islands and Porto Rico 1916, part 2, p. 123).

The *New York Times reported* that the Senate passed the Jones Act only after a provision for women's suffrage was dropped in order to prevent a filibuster by those who opposed the provision (February 21, 1917). By a vote of eighty to fifty-nine the House had earlier defeated an amendment to the Jones act that would have granted women the vote (*New York Times,* May 24, 1916). The final bill essentially preserved universal male suffrage, imposed an age requirement of twenty-one years or over, and mandated that all electors and candidates be U.S. citizens. Congress also allowed the Puerto Rican legislature to prescribe additional qualifications, but prohibited property qualifications for any male voters. The BIA was forced to abandon its excessively restrictive suffrage proposal, which would have empowered only a small, conservative sector of the male population to participate in the political process.

The New and Improved Colonial State

The Jones Act preserved intact the colonial structure through which the metropolitan state continued to control and monitor activities in Puerto Rico. It established a measure of equilibrium between expanding the scope of Puerto Rican participation in colonial administration and subjecting this participation to closer regulation by the central authorities. The law did not affect Congress's plenary powers over Puerto Rico. Congress could still amend or annul insular legislation or apply federal legislation. Although Puerto Ricans had requested the transfer of jurisdiction from the War Department to another executive agency, Congress ignored these requests and reaffirmed the role of the BIA in conducting Puerto Rican affairs.

However, Congress did significantly expand Puerto Rican involvement in the legislative sphere. The Jones Act included a bill of rights partially modeled on that of the United States, but did not extend constitutional protection to the colony. It modified the colonial administration, but retained the executive-centered republican form of government established under the Foraker Act. The governor was granted greater powers to appoint officials without executive and congressional supervision. He exercised a conditional veto, which could be overturned with a two-thirds vote of both houses. However, the governor was required to transmit legislation that he did not approve to the president, who could veto the legislation or sign it into law. Congress established separate legislative and executive branches by rescinding the legislative functions of the Executive Council. The council was replaced by a cabinet of six executive departments, including the newly established Department of Agriculture and Labor and the Department of Health. The Finance and Interior Departments were retained.

Because of their centrality to the Americanization process, the commissioner of education and attorney general continued to be appointed by the president of the United States. In the opinion of federal court judge Peter Hamilton, "The public school and the Federal Court are the two educational forces for Americanization on the island" (quoted in Fram 1986, 113). Senator Jones insisted that, with respect to language policy, "It would be better to have the matter under the control of the commissioner of education appointed by the president, so as to insure the continued teaching of English in the public schools" (quoted in Ringer 1983, 1012). The commissioner had specific powers: He approved all disbursements, prepared rules governing the selection of teachers by local school boards, and prepared all courses of study.

The attorney general also had great authority and supervised the operation of the insular judicial system in accordance with the norms and practices of the federal courts. Puerto Rico was incorporated into the first circuit of the U.S. District Court, and the decisions of the Puerto Rican Supreme Court were subject to review by the U.S. Supreme Court. Puerto Ricans had repeatedly argued against the extension of the district court system to Puerto Rico because it was the mechanism through which federal laws were enforced in the colony. According to attorney Charles Hartzell, who served as a consultant to the congressional committees, the district "court was established very largely for the purpose of affording the administration of law in such a manner as to induce the development of the country and the investment of American capital" (U.S. Senate Committee on Pacific Islands and Porto Rico 1916, part 1, p. 30). Manuel Rodríguez Serra, spokesperson for the Civic Association and other political organizations, summarized the Puerto Rican view on the U.S. District Court: "It establishes a difference in the manner of distributing justice repugnant to our people and not understood by them. The comparatively few Americans who are in business in the island have not one single reason to doubt the ability, integrity and impartiality of the Porto Rican courts. Only an unjustified prejudice could create such doubt" (U.S. Senate Committee on Pacific Islands and Porto Rico 1916, part 1, p. 37).

The office of the auditor was an independent agency whose director was appointed by the president and accountable only to him. According to the Brookings Institute, through this office "Congress has the means of assuring itself that the affairs of the Island, from the financial standpoint at least, are being honestly conducted" (Clark 1930, 112). The auditor interpreted existing law in deciding whether to approve or deny disbursements of funds to finance projects approved by the legislature. According to legal scholar Trías Monge this was a "grave infringement on the functions of the legislature," which violated the principle of separation of power by shifting a legislative responsibility to the executive branch (Trías Monge 1980, 2:95). The Jones Act established a fully elective legislature consisting of an upper and lower house. The upper house consisted of nineteen male senators, and the lower house, or Cámara de Representantes, consisted of thirty-nine males.

Sections of the Foraker Act that were favorable to U.S. corporate investments were retained. However, Congress did include two provisions that were eventually to develop into fiscal tools for financing capitalist development. All bonds issued by the government of Puerto Rico would be exempted from federal, state, and municipal taxes. No duties would be imposed or collected on Puerto Rican exports, and its internal revenue laws could be applied to articles imported from the United States on a nondiscriminatory basis. These measures were designed to stimulate the inflow of capital into the colony, increase the revenue base of the colonial state, and expand the volume and range of trade. With the elimination of the Executive Council the power to grant franchises was transferred to a public service commission consisting of a president and two associates appointed by the governor. The franchises needed gubernatorial approval, and Congress had the power to annul or modify all franchises granted.

The Jones Act also listed the order in which funds would be disbursed if revenues were insufficient to meet the colonial state's financial obligations. The "first class" disbursements were for the expenses of the executive, judicial, and legislative branches; in addition, Congress stipulated that "interest on any public debt shall first be paid in full." The second class appropriations were for all institutions "where the inmates are confined involuntarily." Expenses for education and charities ranked third.

The Jones-Shafroth Act preserved the highly centralized structure of decision-making that was established by the Foraker Act. The act embodied the prevailing congressional attitude that justified depriving Puerto Ricans of a decisive role in their own government. Congress remained content in its belief that continued U.S. tutelage and education of the colonial subjects was necessary. Governor Yager candidly expressed these views: "The intention of Congress was to proceed with due caution . . . and to reserve to the national government for a considerable period all of the checks and restrictions upon the local administration" (quoted in Clark 1975, 28). Matters of defense, immigration, tariff and monetary policy, and communications were under federal jurisdiction. Nothing in the act modified the plenary powers of Congress to legislate for Puerto Rico, nor did it change the country's constitutional status as an unincorporated territorial possession. Little had changed in terms of the extraordinary powers reserved for the colonial regime to continue the process of transforming Puerto Rico's economy into a foreign branch of metropolitan sugar and tobacco trusts. By denying Puerto Rico control over all areas that are within the sovereign right of a nation, the metropolitan state reaffirmed the island's colonial status.

The Jones Act established additional agencies and, unlike the Foraker, had their powers set by federal law. Once the powers were codified in federal law, the Puerto Rican legislature could not redefine the responsibilities of the executive agencies without an act of Congress. The structure of colonial administration could only be altered by Congress. The legislature was effectively denied the power of the purse, since the governor was given a line-item veto. In effect, the governor had the authority to dictate the colony's budget without being held accountable, since he had the authority to arbitrarily strike out appropriations items he objected to (Capó Rodríguez 1919, 581). The governor's broad appointive powers not only deprived elected representatives of patronage powers, but denied the electorate any voice in selecting officials who had an immediate and direct impact on their lives.

Nonetheless, the Jones Act did represent a partial defeat for the BIA. Congress did give in to certain demands by Puerto Ricans, including the separation of executive and legislative functions, and an upper and lower legislative house. Puerto Ricans persuaded Congress to modify the proposal for investing the governor with an absolute veto over legislation. Congress did not accept the bureau's request for increasing the limitations on corporate landholdings to three thousand acres. Nor did it, in the end, respond favorably to the bureau's recommendations for voluntary as opposed to collective citizenship. Congress also dismissed the BIA's request for a highly limited electoral franchise that would have disenfranchised a large portion of the male population. It also rejected the BIA's recommendation for even greater appointive powers of the governor and for vesting the governor with absolute veto powers.

Given the influence of the BIA and its long experience in territorial management, it is interesting to speculate as to why Congress decided to reject some of its most significant recommendations. Some members of Congress considered that the restrictive citizenship and franchise requirements were excessive and antidemocratic constraints on political behavior. After seventeen years of relatively constructive relations with Puerto Rico, which were in marked contrast with the experience in the Philippines, Congress felt that the measures proposed by the BIA were unjustified. Congress doubted Puerto Rico would prove more manageable under the autocratic system the BIA envisioned than under the more liberal measures it proposed. The extraordinary efforts by Puerto Rico's political leadership, particularly the Unión Puertorriqueña, to reform the colonial regime were undoubtedly also a significant factor that influenced congressional thinking on Puerto Rico.

Although Puerto Ricans did attain their long cherished goal of becoming U.S. citizens, it was a second-class citizenship. Supreme Court justice William Taft observed, "What additional rights did it give them? It enabled them to move into the continental United States and becoming residents of any State there to enjoy every right of any other citizen of the United States, civil, social and political" (quoted in PRFAA 1988, 139). The hopes of the Republican Party that citizenship would finally initiate a process culminating in statehood were dashed. Congress made explicit its intention to divorce citizenship from territorial status, and for the first time it granted citizenship to a people without the explicit condition of eventual statehood (Cabranes 1979, 99). Puerto Ricans were not entitled to constitutional guarantees as long as they resided in the colony, nor did they have a voting representative in Congress.

Republicans and Unionists alike declared the Jones Act a significant victory. On August 14, 1917, the Cámara de Representantes unanimously agreed to send President Wilson a message of "gratitude to the American people for the law which in part has satisfied the legitimate aspirations of the Puerto Rican people" (quoted in Bothwell González 1979, 2:309). For Muñoz Rivera the Jones Act was "a step forward on the right road and a reform that will prepare the way for another, more satisfactory one, which will come a little later, provided that my fellow countrymen can demonstrate their ability to govern themselves." However, the other prominent Unionist, José de Diego, believed the Jones Act was passed "for the one and only purpose of assuring a despotic government for Puerto Rico and for no other reason" (quoted in Maldonado-Denis 1972, 110).[3] The Republicans waxed triumphant, since they proclaimed, mistakenly, that with the grant of citizenship the United States had effectively incorporated Puerto Rico.[4]

Republicans and Unionists did not wait long before calling for changes to the Jones Act. In their party platform the Republicans called for statehood when the illiteracy rate had declined to 29 percent. They called on Congress to designate Puerto Rico an incorporated territory, and repeated their long-standing demand to eliminate the U.S. district court system and transfer its functions to the insular court system. The annexationist position then, as now, was that the United States had only two viable options for Puerto Rico: statehood or independence. The Republicans declared, "If the people of the United States do not wish to admit us into the family of states, no other solution is open than to grant us independence, also we protest any colonial plan" (quoted in Pagán 1972, 1:183). The Unión continued to adhere to the ideal of autonomy and "reaffirmed its purpose of continuing the struggle for the establishment of a complete democratic regime, that will give our people the power to legislate without restrictions, over all matters that affect their life and rights, and to elect all the officials in the public administration" (quoted in Bothwell González 1979, 2:357).

The colonial state was empowered with the policy tools and personnel to promote a pattern of unjust economic growth and political exclusion that would generate new challenges to its rule. Twelve years after the Jones Act was passed, Resident Commissioner Córdova Dávila continued to criticize the bill. In Elmira, New York, in 1929, Córdova told his audience that "the Governor of Puerto Rico, appointed by the President, enjoys extraordinary powers." The legislature "can be converted by the executive into a mere debating society as he has the absolute power of veto." Córdova observed that since the governor's decisions are "final, he practically makes the budget and controls all the finances of the government of Puerto Rico." He concluded that Puerto Rico did not a have republican form of government, since "the supreme power does not reside in the whole body of the people and it is not exercised by representatives elected by them" (Córdova Dávila 1929, 10–11).

Women and the Vote:
Making Universal Suffrage Really Universal

The political entity, the people of Puerto Rico, is a conglomeration of men and women, but the anomaly exists that only the former have the right to become involved in the affairs of the country.

—Liga Femínea, 1917

While the Unión Puertorriqueña waged a campaign for autonomy, Puerto Rican women fought to gain the right to vote. Women not only confronted male opposition, but had to wrestle with class, ideological, and social differences that inhibited the formation of a unified women's suffrage movement. Moreover, Puerto Rico's colonial status imposed unique legal dimensions to the suffrage movement. Suffrage leaders argued that Puerto Rican men were demanding autonomy to conduct the affairs of government as they wished, but were ignorant of the needs and aspirations of women, who constituted approximately half the population. In 1920 the United States enacted the Nineteenth Amendment to the Constitution, which gave women the vote. Puerto Rico's status as an unincorporated territory armed the opponents of women's suffrage with a convenient legal argument to deny women the vote. In 1920 the BIA's judge advocate, citing the Insular Cases, calmly reported that "an axiom of government of our dependent peoples is that a prerequisite to efficiency is adherence to the doctrine of the non-applicability of the Constitution as a body of organic law to the outlying possessions of the United States" (Clark 1975, 43).

In 1908 women labor leaders persuaded House delegate Nemesio Canales to introduce the first woman's suffrage bill (Azize Vargas 1987, 20). Between 1908 and 1929 approximately one dozen bills to confer the vote to women were introduced in the Puerto Rican legislature, but each failed to pass (USDW Annual Report 1927, 64).The legislature ignored the recommendations of Governors Montgomery Reilly in 1921 and Horace Towner in 1927 to grant women the right to vote (Clark 1975, 44). Only after the U.S. Congress threatened in 1929 to amend the Jones Act to give women the vote, did the legislature approve a women's suffrage bill. Registered voters who had voted in the general election of 1928, and every man or woman who was twenty-one years or over on the day of the election and who could read and write would be eligible to vote starting in the 1932 general elections. The public schools were authorized to certify the literacy of all eligible voters. In 1935 the literacy requirements were eliminated. The legislature decided to finally act because women had brought the battle to the U.S. Congress. In this crusade U.S. women's organizations worked closely with Puerto Rican suffrage activists.

The struggle for women's political rights was split into two major strains that reflected the distinct social class orientations and material interests of working women and women from the middle and upper strata of society. One current originated from the organized labor movement, almost exclusively from the FLT. A second current emerged from associations that represented professional women and women from economically privileged sectors (Colón, Mergal, and Torres 1986, 41). In Puerto Rico, as in the U.S., class and ideological divisions diluted the strength of the suffrage movement, which conveniently permitted the colonial legislature to procrastinate in its response to women's demands for political inclusion. As late as 1926 the working-class women and suffragettes attempted to organize a united front, but the efforts failed because some suffragettes rejected the demand for universal female suffrage (Azize Vargas 1987, 21).

Ana Roqué de Duprey and Mercedes Solá founded Liga Femínea Puertorriqueña, which was one of the earliest suffrage organizations. In 1917, as the Jones Act was being debated, the Liga Femínea sent a provocative memorial to the Puerto Rican legislature asserting, "There is no just reason to continue to sustain the political inferiority of the woman, a humiliating status that we refuse to validate any longer with our silence" (quoted in Azize 1979, 83). The Liga Femínea was reorganized as Liga Social Sufragista. This was one of the most prominent organizations of women from higher socio-economic categories and claimed to represent "the most intellectual feminine element of Porto Rico" (Clark 1975, 40). Liga Social wanted the vote for literate women who were at least twenty-one years old—an extremely small percentage of the female population. Roqué de Duprey, one of the founders of the Liga Social, had a long and respected history of engagement in women's issues and was a journalist and founder of a number of periodicals and magazines, including the historically significant *La Mujer del Siglo XX* (Serrano 1986; Solá 1923, 823). Carlota Matienzo and Angela Negrón Muñoz also emerged as leaders and joined Roqué de Duprey in directing the Liga Social Sufragista (Silvestrini and Luque de Sánchez 1990, 419). In 1921 the league was reorganized and abandoned the literacy requirement as a condition for the female vote (Colón, Mergal, and Torres 1986, 42). In 1925 the Liga Social Sufragista, now under the leadership of Dr. Marta Robert de Romeu, conducted a survey of all Puerto Rican legislators to determine whether they endorsed suffrage for women, and if so whether it should be restricted by literacy (Bothwell González 1979, 2:369). The same year she and Isabel Andreu de Aguilar broke from the Liga Social because of its growing association with the Socialist Party, and established the Asociación Puertorriqueña de Mujeres Sufragistas, which wanted the vote confined to literate women (Colón, Mergal, and Torres 1986, 43).

Other suffrage organizations also waged the battle for women's inclusion in the political process. Among these were the Liga Sufragista Democrática, which was established in 1925 and was led by Milagros Benet de Mewton, and the Asociación Pan Americana de Mujeres (1923). These organizations were nonpartisan and carried on their political campaigns to obtain the vote for women in the United States as well as Puerto Rico. They were established principally by educated women from the middle sectors. Initially only interested in getting the vote for literate women, these organizations later emerged as advocates for universal suffrage, and in the process drew closer to the ideals of the working-class women in the FLT and the Socialist Party (Azize Vargas 1987, 21; Colón, Mergal, and Torres 1986, 43).

With the advance of capitalism women were rapidly absorbed into emerging industries. The material conditions under which they labored and the duality of their identity, as material and reproductive beings who lived in a patriarchal system, were powerful factors that politically radicalized women. The quest for political equality among many working women was the outgrowth of a struggle for economic equality in the workplace. Luisa Capetillo and Juana Colón emerged as national labor leaders. They were controversial figures of the moment: theoretically sophisticated and politically adventuresome, and in the vanguard of political and social currents of the time.

Legions of radicalized female workers who were members of the Federación Libre de Trabajadores and the Socialist Party pushed forward with a broad agenda of economic justice and universal suffrage. Puerto Rican working-class women took the battle for political rights to the legislature before middle-class women had organized the suffragette groups (Azize Vargas 1987, 20; Scarrano 1993, 652). In 1908 the FLT approved a resolution calling on the legislature to enact universal female suffrage. A decade later, in 1919, during the first congress of Mujeres Trabajadoras, the membership approved a resolution calling for the "establishment of equal rights and privileges for women as well as for men in the social, political and economic order." The Mujeres Trabajadoras called for female suffrage without restrictions and demanded that women be permitted in the legislature (Colón, Mergal, and Torres 1986, 42; Silvestrini and Luque de Sánchez 1990, 451). The 1919 program of the Socialist Party also demanded "universal and secret suffrage for men and women" (quoted in Quintero Rivera 1976, 110). The Socialists were opposed to the literacy requirement, since it disenfranchised a large number of female party members. By restricting the vote only to literate voters, the Union and the Republicans hoped to increase their electoral base among middle-class and educated urban dwellers. The Socialists, whose membership was comprised of campesinos and manufacturing workers, many of whom were deprived of an education, would not be able to expand their electoral base (Colón, Mergal, and Torres 1986, 43).

In 1924 two working women brought suit to force the election board to register them for the forthcoming elections. The board refused, and the women appealed to the Supreme Court of Puerto Rico. The court ruled that since the U.S. Constitution did not automatically extend to the unincorporated territorial possession of Puerto Rico the women's right to vote was not protected by the Nineteenth Amendment (House 1928, 14). According to Governor Towner, "This decision would appear to leave this important question to the action and control of the Legislature of Puerto Rico" (USDW Annual Report 1924, 72).

After repeated rebuffs by the legislature, the suffrage organizations went to Washington to petition the U.S. Congress to amend the Jones Act. They obtained the support of their sister organizations in the United States. The Liga Social became affiliated with the National Party of Women, and the Asociación Puertorriqueña de Mujeres joined with the National Association of Voting Women (Colón, Mergal, and Torres 1986, 44). In 1926 Senator Bingham, whose committee had jurisdiction over Puerto Rico, introduced a bill to confer the vote on women. But the measure included a punitive clause that would further curtail the Puerto Rican legislature's already limited authority over budgets and appropriations. The Puerto Rican Senate sent a resolution to Bingham protesting the bill because it aimed at "amending the organic Act, which are matters of local interest and should remain within the exclusive jurisdiction of the legislature." Ricarda Ramos, president of the Liga Social Sufragista, and Milagros B. Mewton, president of the Pan American Association of Women, responded by immediately sending Congress cablegrams endorsing the Bingham bill (*Cong. Rec.* 1928, 4058). The Bingham bill died in committee.

Representative Edgar Kiess, chair of the Committee on Insular Affairs, introduced a bill (H.R. 7010) to amend the Jones Act to provide for universal suffrage. His measure prohibited property qualifications as a condition for voting and provided that "the right to vote shall not be denied or abridged on account of sex." Mary Caroline Taylor of the U.S.—based National Woman's Party introduced the Puerto Rican suffragists at the April 30, 1928, hearings (U.S. House 1928a, 2). Marta Robert, secretary of the Liga Social Sufragista and director of the Maternity Hospital, testified that her organization was "discouraged at the long delays that we have suffered in our efforts to effect the passage of this bill." She called on Congress to give "the women of Puerto Rico the right to vote in their own country. We would like to have the same rights enjoyed by the women of the United States" (2). Robert reminded Congress that "the right to vote . . . is inherent in our citizenship." It was ludicrous, she pointed out, that Puerto Rican women could migrate to the United States and after meeting state residency requirements could vote for "any of you Congressmen, but we have not the right to vote for anybody in Puerto Rico." Robert concluded by telling the committee, "Your laws seem to think she ["woman"] is competent to choose the lawmakers of the country, yet when she remains in Porto Rico it is said tacitly, that we do not know how to choose our representatives, and the men must do that for us. . . . This is something that is against all reason and principles" (5).

Rosa Emanuelli, a schoolteacher from San Juan, testified that, since the vast majority of teachers were women, "so long as we have been intrusted with the education of children to be good American citizens we ought to have the right to vote" (6). She reminded Congress that even though Puerto Rican women owned property and paid taxes, they were not permitted to select their representatives. "It is, in fact, taxation without representation". She, like Robert, astutely deflected criticism from Puerto Rican male legislators, by informing the members of Congress that "we would never come and ask the Congress of the United States to take away from the Legislature of Porto Rico the rights now vested in it." Puerto Rican women were simply doing "the same as the women in the United States" who had come to Congress after "the States had failed to grant suffrage, to vote" (6).

The Republican-Socialist Coalición cabled the president of the Senate to call for passage of the woman's suffrage bill. The Coalición observed that "opposition due to local rights legislature is less important" than passage of the measure (*Cong. Rec.*, 3191). In contrast, the Unión Puertorriqueña opposed congressional action on the grounds that it constituted interference in local matters. UP president Barceló argued that the "extension of the franchise is a matter for Puerto Rico itself to determine" (U.S. House 1928a, 22). José de Diego opposed female suffrage, and arrogantly asserted that Puerto Rican women did not need more rights than those they already enjoyed (Colón, Mergal, and Torres 1986, 41). Resident Commissioner Córdova Dávila, while testifying that he was "strongly in favor of women's suffrage," was opposed to the legislation because "the Puerto Rican Legislature should be left to decide questions of a local nature and not leave them for determination by the American Congress" (U.S. House 1928, 11). He testified that the House of Delegates did not act on the measure because "there was opposition to the bill in Porto Rico from the Socialist Party on account of the literacy test" (11). He repeated his long-standing call for self-government for Puerto Rico. Ana Veléz, president of the Asociación Puertorriqueña de Mujeres Sufragistas, wrote Córdova Dávila to "energetically protest your attitude against women suffrage" (*Cong. Rec.* 1929, 3192).

Mary Caroline Taylor countered that "in connection with this question of self-government, . . . one-half of the citizens of Porto Rico have no self-government" (U.S. House 1928a, 13). She assured Congress that the proposed "amendment to the organic act of Porto Rico does no violence whatever to Porto Rican affairs or Porto Rican independence, because as it stands now the legislature is made up of only one-half of the citizenship who have a right to legislate for the other half" (9). The former attorney general of Puerto Rico, George C. Butte, supported the measure: "I really feel that the women of Porto Rico, having made such long efforts to get the ballot from their own people, and having failed owing to local conditions, have a right to come before the Congress of the United States and petition for that amendment of the organic act" (16).

The Committee on Insular Affairs favorably reported the bill and wrote that "the people of Porto Rico are full citizens of the United States and [the] committee sees no reason why the right to vote should be denied to the women of Porto Rico" (U.S. House 1928b). The Senate Committee on Territories and Insular Possessions also favorably reported the bill, although a minority was opposed. The minority report observed, "There was opposition to the bill in Porto Rico from the Socialist Party, on account of the literacy test, and I believe that is the reason that this bill did not pass the House" (*Cong. Rec.* 1929, 3192).

The Senate floor debate engaged proponents of states' rights against advocates of universal suffrage. Senator Tydings, a states' rights proponent, argued that Puerto Rico's legislature had the authority to confer suffrage on women, "if it sees fit to do so, without any help or action at all on the part of the Federal Congress." He asked Senator Bingham, "Does not the Senator think that the people of Porto Rico are competent to handle their own affairs down there without coercion or guidance from the Federal Government in this purely local matter?" (3191). Senator Hayden wrote to Ana Velez that he did not want to act "until after the Legislature of Porto Rico has had every reasonable opportunity to solve the problem in its own way" (3192). He was insistent, however, that the suffrage bill should contain a literacy requirement, because he believed "that ballots in the hands of ignorant voters are much more to be dreaded than the arms of invading armies, I am also a firm supporter of an educational qualification for voters." If the Puerto Rican legislature did not enact universal suffrage, Hayden said that he would introduce an amendment to H.R. 7010 that "no person shall have the right to vote who . . . shall not be able to read the Constitution of the United States in the English or Spanish language" (3192).

The pressure on the Puerto Rican legislators to act was mounting, and it was evident they could not continue to deny women the right to vote. On February 11, 1929, as the Senate debated the measure, Governor Towner warned the legislature, "Action on the question of Woman Suffrage in Porto Rico should no longer be delayed by the Legislature. The Congress of the United States has the matter under consideration, but if you take prompt action here at this time your judgment will be respected and Congress will not be called upon to act" (quoted in Clark 1975, 45). On April 16, 1929, Republican senator Manuel A. García Méndez introduced an act to amend the election law. The bill conferred the vote to women who could read and write and required that all male voters not previously registered be similarly qualified. The bill was passed by both houses, although Iglesias Santiago Pantín, the Socialist senator, criticized the measure because the literacy requirements prohibited over 300,000 women and 150,000 men from voting (Silvestrini and Luque de Sánchez 1990, 420).

Despite these reservations the Socialists, who had been severely criticized for voting against a literacy-based franchise for women, voted for the measure. Legislation was also enacted to organize a literacy campaign in order to increase the number of eligible voters (USDW Annual Report 1929, 91). In 1935 the voting requirements were liberalized so that all Puerto Ricans over twenty one who were U.S. citizens and were not convicted felons could vote. According to Governor Roosevelt, in 1932 the number of "women voters was beyond expectation, 120,955 women having registered" (USDW Annual Report 1932, 33). Women immediately became political players; in 1932 the Liberty Party nominated Isabel Andreu for the Senate and Adela Ramírez for the House of Delegates. The UP successfully ran María Luisa Arceley as the representative from Mayagüez. In addition, about 304 women were nominated for municipal posts (Silvestrini and Luque de Sánchez 1990, 421).

Puerto Rican women waged an effective struggle to gain the right to vote. After having exhausted all legitimate channels in the colony, the suffrage organizations established alliances with their counterparts in the United States. They successfully petitioned Congress and almost achieved its approval of an amendment to the Jones Act. The suffrage organizations presented compelling arguments that simply demolished the logic employed by the Puerto Rican legislature to deny women the vote. However, the measure enacted in 1932 privileged Puerto Ricans who had certain educational requirements, requirements that officials knew would not be met by the majority of voting-age Puerto Ricans because of the deplorable system of public education. Puerto Rico's legislature chose in 1935 to reinstate the more liberal voting requirements.

The Political Party System:
The Politics of the Impractical

Nor is it unreasonable to suggest that the people of Porto Rico, who are part of the people of the United States, will progress with the people of the United States rather than be isolated from the source from which they have received practically their only hope of progress.

—*Calvin Coolidge, 1928*

Between 1917 and 1932 the colonial experiment gradually but irresistibly began to unravel. By the time Franklin D. Roosevelt came to power, Puerto Rico was on the verge of social collapse, and the proponents of independence and radical nationalism were gaining adherents. Although Puerto Rico was a remarkably profitable investment zone for U.S. corporations, it had also been converted into a Caribbean sweatshop with its attendant social ills and political difficulties. The obscenity of a society mired in disease and poverty serving as a cornucopia of wealth and privilege for absentee capitalists and a few domestic firms was not unnoticed by colonial managers. Yet little was done to effectively mitigate the scope of immiseration; the few meager efforts to ameliorate such inequality were ineffectual.

Governors Theodore Roosevelt Jr. and James B. Beverley alerted their superiors in Washington to the country's desperate living conditions. Muñoz Marín observed that Roosevelt "probably presented the case of Porto Rico to the American people, both in its immediate and far reaching aspects, more completely than any other American or Porto Rican has done" (Muñoz Marín 1931, 22). Roosevelt's tenure in Puerto Rico was brief, and he was unable to reverse the country's continuing social and economic decline. One of the hallmarks of this period of colonial rule was the absence of political will by Puerto Rico's electoral parties to enact laws to achieve a rational reallocation of the country's resources. Muñoz Marín observed, "There is plenty of money—the commercial development has been truly astounding—but there is no economic compulsion to share it with the population" (Muñoz Marín 1931, 21).

The elected and appointed political leadership proved singularly unwilling to make the hard decisions needed to reverse the colony's deterioration. A political symbiosis had been formed among profit-hungry foreign corporations, a colonial state steeped in paternalism and distrustful of the capabilities of the subjects under its rule, and a complacent local political leadership wanting to protect their class prerogatives. While the Socialists cannot be accused of such overt class collaboration, they ultimately became proponents for the metropolitan state's colonizing mission in Puerto Rico, and through inaction were silent partners in a political economy steeped in human immiseration. Once the uncompromising enemy of the "bourgeois" political parties, the Socialists devised an electoral modus vivendi with the Republicans, the statehood party. In 1932, the legislature came under the control of political parties zealous to demonstrate how "Americanized" they had become and unwavering in their commitment to Puerto Rico's annexation as a state.

From 1917 to 1932 Puerto Rico was racked by political party turbulence, as the parties underwent a seemingly continuous process of dissolution and recomposition. Politically expedient alliances and pacts were readily formed, only to be dissolved. Often these alliances represented nothing more than tactical maneuvers to promote the political ambitions of entrenched leaders, although they were always justified in eloquent nationalistic rhetoric. Unlikely alliances emerged as temporary responses by groups that felt threatened by the unpredictable economic and social changes befalling the island. Since most political alliances were created to promote reform of the colonial formula, it is not surprising that the parties often lacked a coherent ideology and concrete programs for economic and social reconstruction. For the political leadership, resolution of the status issue was the panacea for the country's woes.

By the early 1920s, Puerto Rico's elected officials were well aware that the United States was not about to transform the nonegalitarian social and economic order, nor effect any meaningful change in its political status. Since the metropolitan state had effectively resisted any attempt to limit Congress's plenary powers over Puerto Rico, much of the leadership seemed to accept the inevitability of some kind of permanent association with the United States. This reality, in turn, had its effect on the aspirations and strategies of Puerto Rico's leadership.

Politics in the Puerto Rico of the 1920s took on the flavor and smell of the tawdry patronage politics of the big cities in the United States. The mendacity of much of local politics was papered over by the speeches of seasoned and gifted political orators. Yet the United States always held Puerto Ricans to higher standards of political responsibility and performance than it did its own politicians. A frustrating and humiliating reality of the colonial condition was the supercilious bearing of U.S. officials who depicted Puerto Ricans as if they were genetically incapable of self-rule. But this defamation of a national character was often motivated by nothing more than crass aspirations of U.S. officials to preserve the colony's patronage plums for mainland carpetbaggers (Mathews 1960, 23).

The governorship of Puerto Rico was a rich plum in U.S. politics. Governors were not appointed because of their expertise in management of colonial affairs or because they were familiar with the culture and language of the colonial subjects they were appointed to rule. In fact, such familiarity would have been a liability, since the governors were entrusted with overseeing the "Americanization" of Puerto Rico. Indeed, Puerto Rico was a political resting place for many colonial officials and its "governorship was a pawn of Washington politics" (Lewis 1963, 119). According to Muñoz Rivera, Puerto Rico had become a carpetbagger's paradise and for this reason alone Congress would not cede more authority to Puerto Ricans. "There is a reason and only one reason—the same sad reason of war and conquest which let loose over the South after the fall of Richmond, thousands and thousands of office seekers, hungry for power and authority, and determined to report to their superiors that the rebels of the South were unprepared for self government" (*Cong. Rec.* 1916, 7470).

The Jones Act was not the culmination of the Unión Puertorriqueña's quest for autonomy. With its grant of U.S. citizenship it was an expedient administrative adjustment designed to muffle growing commotion against colonial rule. But the country's political status remained judicially unresolved. Did U.S. citizenship open the door for Puerto Rico to become an incorporated territory and thus eventually for statehood? Was it still an unincorporated possession and capable of either gaining its independence or some form of quasi-sovereign tutelage? Puerto Rico's ambiguous and unresolved territorial identity conveniently allowed the political parties to divert their energies into the sterile politics of status. Even the Socialist Party, which earlier had reviled the bourgeois parties for their obsession with political status, succumbed to the myth that economic benefits would flow from a change in status.

By 1932 politics had become a perennial contest between elite political organizations whose goals were increasingly divorced from the everyday struggles of the vast majority of Puerto Ricans. Political parties were fixated on resolving the county's political status. The political parties diverted their energies and talents to often futile campaigns to extract minor concessions from the metropolitan power. Puerto Rico's legions of impoverished and working poor were routinely instructed that the country's economic ills were a function of its colonial status. The outcome of all this, of course, was that the political parties eventually lost much of their broad representative function and became the conduits through which the dominant economic and social sectors promoted their interests. By fostering the myth that economic salvation depended on a resolution of the status issue, the political parties essentially avoided responsibility for the colony's calamitous conditions.

The UP's leadership persisted in blaming Congress for Puerto Rico's endemic factionalism and fixation on political status. According to Córdova Dávila, Puerto Ricans could not be held accountable for their obsession with colonial reform. Córdova Dávila pleaded before Congress, "We are not to be blamed for the different views that are striking our minds. It is not our fault. If there is any fault at all it belongs exclusively to the doubtful position we are left in through the failure of the American Congress to define our status" (*Cong. Rec.* 1928, 6332). In this, as in virtually all other failings in the colony, Puerto Rican politicians were quick to blame the United States.

The Decline of the Unión Puertorriqueña and the Rise of the Alianza Puertorriqueña

The Unión Puertorriqueña was victorious in the 1917 general elections, the first held under the Jones Act. The party gained thirteen of the nineteen senatorial seats and twenty-four out of the thirty-nine House seats, and sent Félix Córdova Dávila once again to Washington as the resident commissioner. The Socialists had an impressive showing, obtaining 13 percent of the votes cast, and electing one representative and one senator (Pagán 1972, 1:185). In the subsequent elections of 1920, about the same percentage of the voters cast their ballots for the UP, but it gained two additional Senate and five House seats. The Socialists continued to register more impressive gains; they almost doubled their electoral support to 23 percent, reelected Santiago Iglesias Pantín to the Senate, and elected four of their candidates to the House (Pagán 1972, 1:199).

Despite its impressive showing, the period of unquestioned UP dominance was coming to an end. The political forces favoring statehood had emerged as a permanent feature of the political landscape. The growing strength of forces opposed to the UP was directly related to the changing occupational and class structure. By the mid–1920s Puerto Rico's class structure had been fundamentally transformed by a system of monopoly capitalism that was dominated by foreign corporations. The nature of the economy and its role in the metropolitan network of production and consumption would not change until the late 1940s. Until then, the occupational and class categories associated with the export-dependent agricultural economy controlled by U.S.-based firms would not be materially altered. The political parties became the primary vehicles through which these sectors advanced their interests, and these interests shaped the insular political discourse and strategies of the period.

On February 11, 1922, the Unión Puertorriqueña abandoned independence as a goal, called for the establishment of "an Association of a permanent and indestructible character, between the Island and the United States of America," and declared that "the creation of the Free Associated State of Puerto Rico is from this day on, the Program of the party" (Fernández García 1923, 195). The surprising announcement was made after Representative Philip P. Campbell had introduced a bill in mid-January to significantly liberalize the colonial regime. The measure, written by UP leader Miguel Guerra Mondragón, called on Congress "to declare the purpose of the people of the United States as to the political status of the people of Puerto Rico, and to provide an autonomous government for said island, creating the free associated state of Porto Rico" (quoted in Clark 1975, 83). On February 3, Democratic Senator King introduced an analogous bill to provide complete autonomy for Puerto Rico, "placing it politically on the same basis as a State in the Union with a governor and legislature elected by the people" (*New York Times*, February 11, 1922). The bill provided for an elected governor and enhanced the powers of the legislature.

UP president Barceló claimed that "Porto Rican opinion, as expressed through all parties, is agreed on the absolute necessity for the life of the islanders as a free people, that Porto Rico be associated permanently with the great republic" (Barceló 1925, 515). For this reason, the UP developed the "Free State plank." By proposing the "free associated state," or *Estado Libre Asociado*, Puerto Rico's beleaguered and battered bourgeoisie was relinquishing the goal of independence in the hope that the United States might bestow on the island more powers of self-government. Instead of independence, the UP now called for harmonious relations with the metropolitan state and cooperation with U.S. capital. This conciliatory posture reflected internal party dynamics that were heavily influenced by powerful landowners and prominent businessmen and lawyers. These individuals had decided to steer the party away from independence and towards self-government and permanent association (Mathews 1960, 30). The Puerto Rican Republican Party had strenuously resisted the measure, known as the Campbell-King bill, fearing that it would become the basis for Puerto Rico's eventual separation from the United States (Pagán 1972, 1:212; Trías Monge 1980, 2:123).

Other factors also help explain the UP's decision to abandon independence. During 1920–1921 Governor E. Mont Reilly instituted a virtual witch hunt for *independentistas* in government. In August 1921 Reilly informed Barceló, president of the Senate at the time, that "while discussing appointments I want you fully to understand that I shall never appoint any man to any office who is an advocate of independence." He warned Barceló, "When you publicly renounce independence and break loose from some of your pernicious and un-American associates, then I will be glad to have your recommendations" (*New York Times*, August 18, 1921). Reilly accused Barceló of "being a dictator who is using his great influence to thwart the beneficent efforts of the Governor" (*New York Times*, 12 December 1921).

Reilly's contempt for independence and its adherents may also have deepened the schism between the autonomists and *independentistas* within the UP. The governor's overt hostility motivated the independence forces to repudiate the accommodationist posture the party leadership had decided to adopt (Ferrao 1990, 39). When the UP leadership renounced independence, the simmering contention between the autonomist and independence/nationalist factions solidified into an irreconcilable fissure. The decision provoked members of the Asociación Nacionalista of the Unión Puertorriqueña to bolt the party, and to set up the Nationalist Party on September 17, 1922. The Nationalist Party was formed from the merger of the Juventud Nacionalista and city-based nationalist associations. José Coll y Cuchi was elected president, and José Alegría, vice-president. Other prominent leaders included Rafael Díaz de Andino and Julio César. They called for the immediate independence of Puerto Rico and the establishment of a free and sovereign republic (Fernández García 1923, 101). By 1933 the Nationalist Party had approximately twenty thousand members and sympathizers (Johnson 1980, 20).

In his first message to the Puerto Rican legislature Governor Towner referred approvingly to the UP's renunciation of independence. Towner told the legislator's that "independence has disappeared as an issue from the party platforms." He declared that "all who have given the subject consideration realize that Porto Rico is permanently a part of the United States" (*New York Times*, June 21, 1923, 18). In 1924 Antonio Barceló and José Tous Soto, president of the Republican Party, signed a joint manifesto that called for an electoral alliance between their respective political parties. The Alianza Puertorriqueña, as this electoral pact was known, reconfigured Puerto Rico's political party system and provoked an eventual crisis. According to Barceló and Tous Soto, "the question of Puerto Rico's final status was not an issue, for now." Puerto Rico, they explained, was "an organized territory, that was not incorporated into, although it was permanently associated with, the United States through the indissoluble ties of citizenship." After years of intense political rivalry, Barceló and Tous Soto "had finally found a point of contact, a common idea that would unite their aspirations": self-government and national "sovereignty within the sovereignty of the United States" (quoted in Bothwell González 1979, 1:427).

The genesis of this unlikely alliance may be traced to the UP's decision to jettison independence from its platform, and to the Republican Party's failure to establish a durable electoral coalition with the Socialists. Without such an alliance the Republicans could not hope to pose a viable electoral threat to the UP. The Alianza was proposed immediately after Congress refused in 1924 to amend the Jones Act. Specifically, Congress's decision not to expand the colony's self-governing powers and its staunch opposition to statehood for the foreseeable future gave impetus to the alliance. In refusing to amend the Jones Act Congress had chosen to reject the political status objectives that the Republicans and the UP were officially founded to carry out.

The Republican Party included among its leadership many of the largest domestic sugar concerns (Quintero Rivera 1974, 278). José Tous Soto, president of the party, was a prominent lawyer for the sugar corporations. The Alianza may have been a last-ditch, and futile, effort, by disparate sectors of the Republican bourgeoisie and remnants of the Unionist *hacendado* class (those sectors that had not made an accommodation with U.S. capital and were threatened by it) to develop a unified front in defense of their common interests (Meléndez 1985, 16). It is not coincidental that the alliance was formed during the early 1920s, precisely when U.S. sugar corporations were beginning to acquire domestic sugar firms and their holdings. This aggressive corporate acquisition campaign was a threat to domestic sugar growers, and it made their association with other Puerto Rican men of property and wealth likely.

Trying to Change the Colonial Formula

In July 1923 the Socialists, Republicans, and Unionists issued a joint resolution calling for reform of the Jones Act and for improvements in the country's social and economic situation. The parties sent a commission, which included Governor Towner, to Washington to pressure Congress into enacting these changes. (Trías Monge 1980, 2:124). On February 12, Córdova Dávila introduced a bill in the House calling for changes to the Jones Act, including popular election of the governor to go into effect for the 1928 elections, gubernatorial appointment of the heads of the executive departments, and the establishment of a department of labor. A comparable bill was introduced in the Senate.

Governor Towner spoke in favor of the bill, telling the committee that "the eyes of the world are upon us in regard to our record in the government of what are called dependencies. . . . We proclaim belief in self-government, as part of our American system, and we ought to practice self-government whenever and wherever justified. For these reasons I believe Porto Rico should be granted the right to elect their government" (House Committee on Insular Affairs 1924, 11). Towner said, "They want to continue as part of our territory; so their desire for extension of self-government is not for the purpose of becoming an independent republic. That is not in their minds. . . . To grant their prayer will bind Porto Rico closer to us as a friendly neighbor" (*New York Times*, 30 March 1924, 16).

Towner argued that Puerto Rico was not ready for statehood, since it "would not be economically independent." He also believed that Puerto Rico should reduce its illiteracy rate to 20 percent before it could be considered ready for statehood (U.S. House Committee on Insular Affairs 1924, 13). Secretary of War John Weeks opposed both statehood and increased local powers. He testified, "I do not think the time has come from the standpoint of the people of Porto Rico, to pass this bill." Like Towner, Weeks felt that the high rate of illiteracy was an obstacle (Trías Monge 1980, 2:127). BIA chief McIntyre supported the measure because it would undermine both the independence and the statehood forces: "It would seem wise to take advantage of this unanimity of opinion in Porto Rico, and thus prevent, if possible, the spasmodic talk, on the one hand of independence, and, on the other hand of an incorporated Territory and statehood—requests which could not be seriously considered" (U.S. Senate 1924, 1).

Ultimately the Senate and House committees voted favorably on the measures. The Senate committee confidently reported, "There is no disposition on the part of the people of Porto Rico to secure independence and separation from the United States. The whole trend of the testimony upon this point is to the effect that the Porto Ricans are proud of their American citizenship and desire to continue indefinitely as a part of the United States" (U.S. Senate 1924, 3). Although the Senate voted in favor of the bill, the full House failed to consider the measure. Puerto Ricans had to wait almost another quarter century for the privilege of electing their governor.[5] The hearings revealed just how entrenched congressional opposition was to any changes in the colonial formula.

The Alianza: An Improbable Alliance

During the congressional hearings the Republicans came to the harsh realization that Congress was not prepared to grant statehood anytime soon. On the return trip from Washington Barceló and Tous Soto drafted the famous manifesto calling for a political alliance between their respective parties (Pagán 1972, 1:227). On April 19, 1924, a joint commission met to negotiate the program of the alliance, the Alianza Puertorriqueña. Less than a month later, on May 4, the Republicans convened their assembly to approve the proposed alliance and to renounce electoral alliances with the Socialists (USDW Annual Report 1925, 67). This development was unexpected, given that Republican Party president José Tous Soto had sought to establish an electoral alliance with the Socialists that very year (Meléndez 1988, 49; Pagán 1972, 1:236). Indeed, as early as 1920 the Republicans and Socialists had worked to establish electoral alliances to defeat the UP.

However, the War Department was adamantly opposed to any Republican-Socialist alliance at this time. The Republicans were warned that U.S. officials would not approve any legislation that could result in a role for the Socialists in the administration (Meléndez 1985, 48). Tous Soto told his followers, "If the Republican-Socialist coalition were to triumph, the victory would be a sterile one for the coalition, since the government in Washington would not recognize it as having the right to participate in the executive and judicial functions" (quoted in Bothwell González 1979, 1:436). Despite the BIA warning, Tous Soto's decision to renounce an electoral alliance with the Socialists in favor of the Unionists provoked incredible dissension. A majority of the infuriated Republicans abandoned their party.

Rafael Martínez Nadal, one of the dissident leaders, wanted to preserve the ties with the Socialists and pointed to the widespread public support for a pact with them. He was convinced that a coalition with the Socialists would erode the UP's electoral strength. Martínez Nadal was also quick to brand Tous Soto a "man at the service of the corporations in Puerto Rico, who treacherously stabbed to death" the Republican Party (Bothwell González 1979, 1:442; quoted in Meléndez 1985, 51). These dissident Republicans established the Historical Constitutional Party, or as it was popularly known, the Pure Republicans. The Pure Republicans represented the small-scale producers, landowners, and "petty bourgeois sectors" who wanted to formulate an electoral coalition with the Socialists (Meléndez 1985, 17–18). The group of Republicans that established the alliance with the UP consisted of large-scale landowners and merchants linked to the sugar economy.

Political Party Realignments

For the 1924 elections an informal coalition of Socialists and Pure Republicans fielded the same slate of candidates on both ballots. The Alianza Puertorriqueña employed the same electoral arrangement, including a preelection deal to divide the elected offices between them (USDW Annual Report 1928, 88). The Alianza won the elections of 1924. However, the results were ominous for the Republicans, who experienced a net loss of 33,500 votes. The Republican Party under Tous Soto polled 30,286 votes, while the dissident Pure Republicans obtained 34,576 votes. The Socialists, with 56,103 votes, came in second to the Unionists, who obtained 132,755 votes (USDW Annual Report 1925, 68).

Immediately after its electoral victory the Alianza requested changes to the Jones Act. In 1925 U.S. Representative Edgar Kies introduced another elective governor bill, which was drafted by the Alianza. But the measure was never enacted into law. The Alianza persisted and introduced similar bills in 1927 and 1928 (Pagán 1972, 1:249; Trías Monge 1980, 2:129). During hearings on these bills Córdova Dávila warned Congress that if it refused to grant self-government, "you will compel us to take the stand of asking for independence as the only way left to secure the happiness of our country" (quoted in Trías Monge 1980, 2:130). Congress ignored these threats and chose not to amend the Jones Act.

The 1928 elections proved to be the beginning of the end for the Alianza, which barely defeated the Pure Republican-Socialist coalition. Although the Alianza obtained 132,826 votes, the coalition garnered a surprising 123,415 votes (USDW Annual Report 1929, 83). After the disastrous electoral results, Barceló withdrew his Union from the Alianza in 1929 and with his followers established the Liberal Party. The Union's political troubles could be traced in part to Barceló's decision to join Tous Soto in supporting a new corporate tax proposed by Governor Towner in 1925. Both foreign and domestic corporations had always proven remarkably hostile to any attempts to increase their tax burdens (Clark 1975, 112–113). In this case the corporations roundly criticized Barceló and the Union for abridging the favorable corporate and property tax laws. Although the assault by the corporate sector was aimed at the Alianza, it seemed that the electorally powerful Union was the prime target. Frustrated with the corporations' attempt to impede the task of government, Barceló and Tous Soto wrote to President Coolidge that "our past financial difficulties were due entirely to the concerted movement on the part of certain capitalist interests to embarrass our Government" (quoted in Barceló 1928, 10).

It was the growing fiscal crisis of the colonial state and the Union's willingness to work with the governor to resolve it that precipitated the party's political decline. In 1925 Governor Towner reported that government receipts for the preceding two years had fallen below revenues, and that he had to resort to debt financing. He proposed a new tax law that included an excess profits tax of up to 30 percent on all corporate incomes above $10,000 (USDW Annual Report 1925, 4). In a special message to the legislature, Towner reported that "as is well known, property taxes in Porto Rico are very low as compared with such taxes imposed elsewhere." Puerto Rico's tax laws "are so open to attack that they were almost an invitation to opposition and resistance to payment." According to Towner, New York had an $18 annual per capita expenditure for education, and $8 per capita for health and sanitation. Puerto Rico's expenditures were $3 and "less than one dollar," respectively (Puerto Rico Governor 1925, 9–10). The treasurer justified the new tax law: "The higher the profit the higher the tax; . . . it would be unfair to have the greater number of the smaller taxpayers pay proportionately a higher tax than the more fortunate ones" (USDW Annual Report 1925, 148).

According to Governor Towner the financial situation after 1924 had became even more precarious as a consequence of "a concerted movement of large taxpayers to contest the validity of the tax laws and to refuse payment of their taxes. . . . It was necessary to borrow money to meet the regular and ordered demands of the government" (USDW Annual Report 1925, 29). In 1925 the corporations attempted to intimidate Towner and the Alianza-controlled legislature by organizing a tax boycott. Towner reported that the protest took the "form of litigation contesting the validity of the taxes levied and a many great injunctions" issued by the United States district court (USDW Annual Report 1925, 4). As a result of the litigation a large part of the government's revenues were tied up court. Unable in the short term to counter this effective tactic, Towner relented and lowered the tax. He did so even though he complained that the corporations had no justification for their actions, since the Puerto Rican "taxes were small as compared with those imposed" by the states or the federal government (USDW Annual Report 1925, 5).

Towner's attempt to generate revenue by issuing insular bond was challenged in the courts by a citizens' committee that accused Towner of maladministration. The group, which included UP leader Coll y Cuchi, petitioned President Coolidge not to permit the issuance of the bonds. They protested, "No bonds should be sold, no more debts should be incurred by the island until our claims are heard and investigated. This criminal expenditure of the people's money should be promptly ended" (*New York Times*, December 21,1924, 15).

The Politics of the Coalición

In March 1932 the Pure Republicans and Tous Soto's Alianza Republicans were reunified and established the Republican Union Party (PUR) (see Bothwell González 1979, 1:495–507, for the PUR's program). In the November 1932 elections the PUR established the long awaited coalition with Socialist Party. This Coalición was a formidable organization that came to dominate the political process for the rest of the decade.

A clear economic logic promoted the alliance between class enemies. The Republican Party was convinced that it had to moderate the intensity of labor opposition to U.S. corporations. It was prepared to broker a social pact between capital and labor as a way of imposing labor peace (Meléndez 1988, 48). The deteriorating state of industrial labor relations was one of the considerations motivating the colonial state to establish a mediation and arbitration bureau in 1919. During the time that Tous Soto and the Republicans were seeking a modus vivendi with the Socialists, Governor Reilly reported, "When I arrived in Porto Rico I found labor and capital cross-wise, unable to agree, and I made it my first important work to try to settle the differences without further bloodshed or strike. I found five strikes running in full blast and the outlook was discouraging" (USDW Annual Report 1922, 35). Such a conflictual state of labor industrial relations could not help eroding a favorable investment climate and threatening continued foreign investments. By forging an agreement with the Socialists, the Republicans hoped to mitigate the intensity of labor strife, which was interfering with investments and profits.

Despite profound ideological differences, the territorial aspirations of the Republicans and the Socialists were identical. Both wanted Puerto Rico to be annexed as a state of the Union. According to Iglesias Pantín, the Coalición's

> main object is the establishment and organization in the Island of a government capable of safeguarding the fundamental principles and ideals of a true American democratic and republican form of government in the Island and which may be prepared to undertake the solution of the vital economic problems to bring about the complete rehabilitation of the island. (Quoted in Mathews 1960, 31)

By the late 1920s the Socialists were shedding their radical critique of capitalism and were directing their wrath against absentee corporations. They declared in their 1932 party platform, "that the economic industrial system that prevails in this island, is directed and dominated by egoistic and wicked absentee and resident monopoly capitalists" (quoted in Bothwell González 1979, 1:508).

Governor Colton had earlier reaffirmed the importance of the FLT and AFL as agents for Americanization: "The organized labor movement of Porto Rico has been patriotic and one of the most effective factors in Americanizing the people of the island" (U.S. House Committee on Insular Affairs 1924, 82). Their decision to lash out against the absentee foreign corporations and the remnants of the *hacendado* class cast the Socialists in a new light. They were not calling for class warfare against capital, nor were they repudiating colonialism. This more tempered philosophy tended to modify the intensity of bourgeois, as well as metropolitan state, opposition to the party. The coalition was also motivated by the Republicans' support of the socioeconomic reforms the Socialists were advocating (Silvestrini and Luque de Sánchez 1990, 414). Other purely electoral considerations were also important. With their combined electoral strength the Republican-Socialist coalition could unseat the dominant UP.

The Republicans were the dominant local force behind the Americanization of the country, which they saw as necessary for Puerto Rico's eventual absorption as a state. Tous Soto conveyed these assurances to a congressional committee: "We have already assimilated the American institutions . . . and in fact, the entire political and administrative system prevailing here and that process of assimilation has been carried out with the approval of the people and by the people itself" (U.S. House Committee on Insular Affairs 1924, 51). The Socialist Party also ardently advocated Americanization. According to Iglesias, "Its fundamental goal is permanent association with the people of the United States" (Quoted in Mathews 1960, 31). In the 1924 congressional hearings, Santiago Iglesias Pantín explained, "We would like to have the extension of the Constitution of the United States because we and the workingmen are claiming that we have the right to ask for that, since we are American citizens. We believe that it has been providential for us that the American ideals and institutions went to the island" (U.S. House Committee on Insular Affairs 1924, 58).

The Union Returns to Independence

At the 1930 Nationalist Party convention, Barceló made a public confession that he was deeply committed to the ideal of independence. He declared that the Unión Puertorriqueña would pursue the independence of Puerto Rico. Barceló thundered, "I feel among you as if I were in my own house, because I am in the midst of those who sustain the ideal of independence of the fatherland above everything" (quoted in Diffie and Diffie 1931, 195). The former Unionists established the Liberal Party of Puerto Rico in 1932. The party asserted that "its purpose is to demand the immediate recognition of Puerto Rico's sovereignty" and to "establish the absolute independence of Puerto Rico" (Pagán 1972, 2:23). Among the leading sectors of the Liberal Party were the aging *hacendados*, some of whom maintained a fragile hold over their land and others who had been displaced by U.S. corporations. By gaining Puerto Rico's independence and dominance over its internal affairs they hoped to reclaim their lands (Silvestrini and Luque de Sánchez 1990, 482).

Luis Muñoz Marín, the son of Muñoz Rivera, returned to Puerto Rico from self-imposed exile in 1931 and quickly established himself as a key propagandist and strategist for the Liberal Party. Muñoz Marín was convinced that independence was necessary for Puerto Rico's economic salvation (Bothwell González 1979, 2:406). He wrote his friend Eleanor Roosevelt that the Liberals would address Puerto Rico's problems "not with doles but with social justice, operating within an economy that shall be as far as possible planned and autonomous" (quoted in Lewis 1963, 126). To Ruby Black, another close friend, Muñoz wrote, "We are opposed to begging money from the American taxpayers and instead claim the right to have our own tariff, to get rid of the coastwise shipping laws, and to be empowered to regulate absentee ownership" (quoted in Mathews 1960, 30). Although Barceló had written Franklin D. Roosevelt that the Liberals wanted "as a political solution the independence of Puerto Rico," the BIA considered Muñoz merely "a highly vocal, but not entirely consistent advocate of independence" (quoted in Mathews 1960, 28). Governor Beverley reported that "a considerable element of this party . . . favors an autonomous form of government under the American flag rather than independence" (USDW Annual Report 1932, 32).

The 1932 elections were a contest between the formidable Coalición and the Liberal Party. The elections sealed the fate of the Liberals. The total combined vote for the Coalición surpassed the Liberals' vote tally: The Republican Union Party obtained 100,794 votes, while the Socialists garnered 97,438 and the Liberals 170,168 (Pagán 1972, 2:45). The electoral power of the Unión's successor, the Liberal Party, had fallen victim to an unlikely alliance of the party of capital and the party of labor. The Nationalist Party participated for the first and only time in electoral politics and nominated Pedro Albizu Campos for senator at large.

Pedro Albizu Campos, a Harvard-trained attorney and former U.S. army officer, served as president of the Nationalist Party. Albizu was a former member of the UP and one of the leading critics of Barceló's 1922 plan for an alliance between the UP and the Republican Party. After failing to prevent the merger, he abandoned the UP and in 1924 joined the Junta Nacionalista de Ponce (Marí Bras 1984, 68). According to Governor Beverley the Nationalist Party "favors immediate independence at all costs." He noted that the party was small and correctly predicted that it would not elect any candidates to public office (USDW Annual Report 1932, 32).

Albizu Campos repudiated the established political parties and lashed out against the colonialism that shackled his country. In 1926 he accused Barceló, "supreme chief of the Alianza, and Santiago Iglesias Pantín, owner of the Republican-Socialist Coalition, of having arrived at a harmonious understanding to share the political booty" (Albizu Campos 1979, 43). Albizu imbued the nationalist movement with radicalism that resonated with ever growing contingents of

Puerto Ricans. He did not believe the United States would easily relinquish its sovereignty over Puerto Rico. Albizu Campos declared,

> North American interests occupy a great part of our lands and are owners of almost eighty percent of the total wealth of the country, by virtue of this forced feudalism the majority of the electorate of this country are made dependent on its will. All the political parties with the only exception of the Nationalist Party, have been able to obtain . . . the good will of these powers. (Albizu Campos 1930, 15)

Albizu Campos accused large U.S. corporations of subsidizing the electoral campaigns of the dominant political parties. Once in office politicians did "not dare touch any of the powerful octopus," but indeed were indebted to them (Albizu Campos 1930, 16). The anti-imperialist Albizu Campos declared, "Under the harsh yoke of North American colonialism from a nation of proprietors we have changed into a mass of peons, a rich economic mine for exploitation by the capitalist invader" (quoted in Maldonado-Denis 1972, 118). In 1930 the Nationalists called for higher taxes on foreign corporations in order to "destroy the system of latifundias", for revision of the tariff which "exclusively benefits the invader," and for other measures to promote domestic industries and banks (Bothwell González 1979, 1:468–69). They condemned the economic system dominated by foreign corporations and denounced "absentee ownership as one of the greatest evils which prey on the national wealth of Puerto Rico" (quoted in Diffie and Diffie 1931, 193).

Under Albizu Campos leadership the Nationalist Party was a militant, overtly patriotic political organization committed to the realization of Puerto Rico's independence. He elevated the anti-imperialist campaign to a crusade of national identity (See Alvárez Curbelo 1993, 27). In its 1930 general assembly, the Nationalist Party declared: "We hereby solemnly swear that we will defend the ideal of independence and that we will sacrifice our goods and if necessary our lives, for the independence of our country" (quoted in Diffie and Diffie 1931, 195).

The Republican Union Party provided the Nationalist Party with the organizational and financial support to get its candidates on the ballot (Mathews 1960, 35). The Nationalists never evolved into a mass party, and Beverley's predictions were accurate, for they obtained only 5,275 votes, even though Albizu garnered over 11,882 votes in his campaign for the Senate. Yet their impact on Puerto Rico's political development and anticolonial struggles far outweighed their paltry electoral showing.

Mitigating the Effects of the Depression

Although U.S. colonial officials knew of the deplorable colonial conditions, they did little to improve the situation. At best essentially anemic measures were enacted that masked the symptoms instead of eradicating the causes of the social breakdown. Through 1928 the colonial officials enacted a number of desultory measures that did mitigate the misery for some of the most destitute sectors of the population. But only after the hurricane of 1928 did the War Department and Congress begin to gradually accept the idea that the United States bore some responsibility for the misery that prosperity had brought its colonial ward. With rare exception the colony's political leadership displayed a callous disregard for the despondency that engulfed the lives of the populace.

Governor Theodore Roosevelt Jr. was one of the few governors who attempted to educate U.S. officials and the public about the plight of the Caribbean possession. He sought to invest metropolitan policymakers with a sense of moral responsibility for the victims of colonialism. Roosevelt recollected in his memoirs that "poverty was widespread and hunger, almost to the verge of starvation, common. . . . Every city or large town had its slum, where the squalor and filth were almost unbelievable. . . . The island was disease ridden. Tuberculosis had reached an astonishingly high rate" (Roosevelt [1937] 1970, 108). Roosevelt agreed that it was "perfectly proper" for Puerto Ricans to be concerned over the country's future territorial status and form of government. But according to Roosevelt, "At this moment, however, our first consideration, one that overshadows all others in importance, is economic rehabilitation. All other matters are secondary at this time" (USDW Annual Report 1930, 9).

Roosevelt demonstrated an unusual public sensibility, although, like all the imperial proconsuls that preceded him, he viewed Puerto Ricans with characteristic paternalism. Roosevelt's administration developed small-scale programs to tackle the problems of landlessness, disease, malnutrition, and unemployment in Puerto Rico (Clark 1975, 138–139; Roosevelt [1937] 1970, 111–112, 121–122). The governor took particular pride in the Homestead Commission, which distributed land to landless farmers and was a precursor of the more ambitious agrarian programs of the 1940s. Roosevelt and his wife proved particularly adept at persuading U.S. charitable institutions to dispense some of their funds in Puerto Rico (Mathews 1960, 18). The largest charitable organizations promised to spend $7.3 million over a five-year period to eradicate the scourges that extinguished the vitality and life of so many Puerto Ricans (USDW BIA 1930, 11).

Although his intentions were laudable and his actions undoubtedly saved lives, Roosevelt could not initiate structural changes to rectify the magnitude of human immiseration. According to Muñoz Marín, Roosevelt's efforts were "palliatives based on philanthropy" (Muñoz Marín 1931, 22). In turning to the U.S. charities, Roosevelt was actually adhering to a long-standing and official practice of generating private funds to provide care for the sick and indigent (see McCune Lindsay 1904). The state was not in the business of providing for the well-being of those individuals who could not survive the rigors of the market. Roosevelt was irritated by Muñoz Marín's criticism, and he wrote in his 1931 report that "our policies have as their aim solutions, not merely palliatives" (USDW Annual Report 1931, 1).

Indeed, Roosevelt was acutely aware of the need to diversify the economy and promote industrialization. The Bureau of Commerce and Industry, with branches in Washington, DC, and New York, was established during his administration. The bureau's mission was to stimulate demand for Puerto Rican products, promote the development of new industries on the island, and carry out a publicity campaign to stimulate tourism. The Department of Labor was also established during Roosevelt's administration, because "as we are of a necessity building up our industries on the island, the labor problem becomes increasingly important as the years pass" (U.S. Senate Committee on Territories and Insular Affairs 1931, 1). During his administration the Congress approved a federal vocational education and civilian rehabilitation program for Puerto Rico.

The secretary of war believed that the federal aid programs were "an appropriate relief measure for the people of Porto Rico," and recommended a $120,000 appropriation for fiscal 1932. Yet he warned, "The duplication or paralleling in Porto Rico, by agencies of any Federal executive department, of functions which lie within the proper scope of action of the insular government . . . is undesirable" (U.S. Senate Committee on Territories and Insular Affairs 1931, 2). One consequence of Puerto Rico's social disaster was growing suspicion about the BIA's ability to manage the colony. During President Hoover's term, interest in creating a special insular bureau rematerialized (Pomeroy 1944, 527). In 1929, the BIA took the unusual measure of explaining its responsibilities toward the insular possessions and its ability to carry them out. Bureau chief Brig. General F. LeJ. Parker reported, "The War Department is believed to be, as a result of its organization and past duties particularly well prepared to perform, with efficiency and economy, the functions involved in the administrative supervision of insular possessions" (USDW BIA 1929, 2).

Parker went on to explain that the Department of War was equipped "with every agency necessary to handle efficiently the supervision of any Territory that may be brought under its control." He emphasized that it "would be difficult, if not wholly impracticable to secure similar conditions" with civilians and would be more costly (2). The White House was not persuaded, and on May 29, 1934, President Franklin Roosevelt issued an executive order establishing the Division of Territories and Island Possessions in the Department of the Interior. He ordered that "all the functions of the Bureau of Insular Affairs, Department of War" together with all its resources "pertaining to or connected with the administration of the government of Puerto Rico" be transferred to this new division (U.S. House 1934, 2). The Bureau of Insular Affairs was finally abolished in 1939 (Pomeroy 1944, 529).

Roosevelt accepted the appointment as governor of the Philippines before many of his programs in Puerto Rico could take effect. However, he left in place a novel, although uncertain, strategy to halt Puerto Rico's descent into poverty and squalor. Roosevelt not only alerted the metropolitan state to the looming social catastrophe, but proposed a relatively cost-efficient strategy consisting of modest reforms that mitigated the intensity of human suffering wrought by unregulated capitalist development. Roosevelt obtained funding from major philanthropies, successfully lobbied for inclusion of Puerto Rico in certain federal programs, promoted Puerto Rican commerce, and used public resources to create jobs and implement agrarian reform on a limited scale. This approach provided a model of colonial management that emerged as the standard for Puerto Rico through the 1940s.

Despite his public aura of confidence and optimism, Roosevelt was no idealist. He confided to his friend (and successor to the governorship) James Beverley that "There seems really to be a very hopeless prospect ahead for Porto Rico, even under the regime that you and I were trying to follow" (Clark 1975, 147). Beverley was ideologically in tune with his predecessor. He wrote that since he "was closely associated with" Roosevelt, "every effort has been made to continue the policies previously undertaken . . . and to attempt to bring them to their proper fruition" (USDW Annual Report 1932, 14). According to Beverley, Puerto Rico was spared the impact of the worldwide depression, but nonetheless "the amount of poverty, malnutrition and unemployment has been distressing" (USDW Annual Report 1932, 7). Puerto Rico's situation became ever more precarious after another devastating hurricane hit the island on September 26, 1932. The BIA reported that the hurricane, "laying waste approximately one half the island, had far reaching effects upon agriculture, banking, and government finance, and especially upon the conditions of the laboring classes." Over two-thirds of the municipalities sustained serious damage, resulting in the deaths of 257 people (USDW BIA 1933, 18).

Roosevelt left his reformist imprint on the minds of policymakers; during the rest of the decade the metropolitan state enacted a variant of the New Deal in Puerto Rico and pumped millions of dollars into the economy. But his dire assessment that conditions could not be fundamentally altered with the kinds of programs he instituted was borne out. Economist Harvey Perloff wrote of the New Deal in Puerto Rico, "The conclusion cannot be avoided that the federal contributions as a whole did little more than mitigate suffering and fill empty stomachs. They were essentially relief handouts. They did little permanently to strengthen the foundations of the economy or to solve the underlying economic problems" (Perloff 1950, 32).

By the end of 1932 the conditions for virtual disintegration of the colonial experiment were present. The established political parties had essentially abandoned the working class and the landless farmers. These men and women constituted the vast majority of Puerto Rico's population, and their voice was effectively muffled. The ideal of attaining either autonomy or independence via a peaceful electoral process was systematically rejected by the metropolitan state. Statehood and independence were also rejected. Congress was not willing to dismantle the colony. Despite steadfast U.S. refusal to alter the island's territorial status, Puerto Rico's political parties were undeterred and relentless in pursuit of this goal. But in the process they allowed a profoundly destabilizing political situation to unfold. By the mid–1930s Puerto Rico confronted a crisis of political representation and experienced loss of legitimacy in its key institutions (Baldrich 1981, 125).

The tactics and policies of colonial managers exacerbated schisms among Puerto Rico's political and economic elites. The old *hacendado* class, as well as transitional and intermediary elites linked to the sugar economy and metropolitan firms, was unresponsive to the needs of the vast majority of workers and poverty-stricken farmers. Those who labored for meager wages were seen as a greater threat to Puerto Rico's dominant classes than the imperialist nation that had invaded their land and whose firms were aggressively appropriating the country's land and human resources. Puerto Rico's landowning class cynically manipulated the ideal of independence in an unsuccessful ploy to extract concessions from the metropolitan state. This approach served only to alienate the poor and working sectors of the population, who eyed skeptically the machinations of a corrupt political leadership. By the early 1930s, in the throes of its most violent political period, Puerto Rico was devoid of political organizations with the capability, unity, and vision to propose viable development options.

Notes

1. The citizenship section of the bill included a proviso permitting Puerto Ricans to decline U.S. citizenship by making a declaration before a court within six months of the date the Jones-Shafroth Act was signed into law. The names of 289 Puerto Ricans who declined U.S. citizenship are listed in Bothwell González 1979, 2:310–313. Under another proviso, 800 people born in Puerto Rico of foreign parents obtained U.S. citizenship (Capó Rodríguez 1919, 573).

2. The possibility of war with Germany was ever present. The German Kaiser approved a plan for Germany to seize and retain Puerto Rico, particularly the island of Culebra, in the event of war with the United States. U.S. navy planners anticipated a German attack on Hispaniola and the Danish West Indies because of their proximity to the U.S. naval stations in Culebra and Guantánamo (Turk 1978, 188–189). The United States purchased the Danish West Indies because it feared that Germany might conquer Denmark and acquire the island, and thus gain a foothold in the Caribbean (Challener 1973, 400).

3. On the eve of his death Muñoz is quoted as having said that "the Jones Bill is the first step in our evolution. It is not the exact bill that we wanted, but after it is installed if our people demonstrates the will, surely a series of more liberal reforms will follow" (quoted in Pagán 1972, 1:178).

4. A district court decision in 1917 initially affirmed that Puerto Rico was an incorporated territory and that all federal legislation applicable to the territories was in effect in the country. In 1918, however, the U.S. Supreme Court reversed the lower court ruling and reaffirmed Puerto Rico's status as an unincorporated territory not subject to the full protection of the Constitution (Clark 1975, 26). The significance of the decision is analyzed in Torruella 1985, 96–100.

5. The House hearings provided an early glimpse of the role of U.S. resident Puerto Ricans in the legislative process. The standing of a Mr. Torres Mazorana, who claimed to represent the Porto Rican Civic Club of New York, was challenged by Córdova Dávila. Torres Mazorana was also disavowed by the Porto Rican Democratic Club of Brooklyn and the Porto Rican Democratic Federation of America. The accusation was made that he was "a radical anti-American and has endeavored to preach that sentiment among the members of the Porto Rican colony of the city of New York" (U.S. Senate 1924, 99).

7

The FLT,
the Socialists,
and the Crisis in
Colonial Management

The organized labor movement of the United States has been the most effective factor in Americanizing the people of Porto Rico.

—Governor George R. Colton, 1916

The Beginnings

By the turn of the century many artisans and craftspeople—painters, carpenters, cigar makers, dock workers—were members of mutual benefit and cooperative associations, *gremios*. The Spanish, always leery of insurrection, had barred the *gremios* from operating as labor unions (Galvin 1976, 35). Shortly after Spain evacuated Puerto Rico, the *gremios* coalesced into the Federación de Gremios, which elected as its president Santiago Iglesias Pantín, a Spanish anarcho-sindicalist who had moved to Puerto Rico. The Federación formed the core of Puerto Rico's first national labor organization, the Federación Regional de Trabajadores (Silvestrini de Pacheco 1979, 17).

From its inception the Federación Regional was subjected to the political influence of the Republican Party. In 1899 a group of workers defected and set up the Federación Libre de Trabajadores (FLT), to "combat the machinations of Barbosa and the Republican caciques" (quoted in Silén 1980, 205). The FLT, seeking to fortify is tenuous position in the contentious political landscape of Puerto Rico and desperately in need of organizational resources and an influential patron to promote its cause in Congress, became affiliated to the American Federation of Labor (AFL) (Iglesias Pantín 1958, 199). Iglesias waged an energetic campaign to generate support for the affiliation: "Let us, the Porto Rican laborers, join together, and join the AFL, with the object of mutually protecting ourselves and to improve our conditions and acquire gradually the immense progress of the American organization" (quoted in Whittaker 1968, 385). The FLT asserted that it would defend the economic interests of its members and that it had the "identical principles and goals" as the American Federation of Labor (Silvestrini de Pacheco 1979, 18). At the turn of the century Puerto Rico's rural labor force was quickly being transformed into a wage-earning proletariat. As Puerto Rico evolved into a sugar-exporting island-factory, the numbers of these workers increased rapidly, and so did their organizational capacity and willingness to challenge the corporations.

Two-Track Strategy: Economic and Political Arenas

Although the struggle for fair pay and working conditions was waged primarily on the shop floor and in the fields, workers were determined to gain representation in government. From almost the moment the United States acquired sovereignty of Puerto Rico, its workers attempted to escape the hegemony of the bourgeois parties by establishing their own independent political organization. In June 1899 the FLT established the Partido Obrero Socialista, which represented labor's interests in the political arena. In 1917 its successor, the Socialist Party, was able to finally elect its first candidate to the House of Delegates. Under U.S. sovereignty workers were legally entitled to organize into unions and form political parties. New electoral laws, the elimination of restrictions on union organizing, and the collapse of the restrictive Spanish legal and political order were all factors that militated in favor of building a working-class party.

The FLT pursued a two-track strategy of labor militancy and electoral politics. It organized workers, recruited independent labor organizations as affiliates, organized and financed strikes, and directly confronted management to extract collective bargaining rights. It also sent representatives to Washington to inform Congress of the plight of the Puerto Rican worker. Some of the largest and most militant strikes in Puerto Rico's history involved the FLT. During the first two decades of colonial rule growing numbers of the proletariat waged economic battle against the unified power of foreign and national capital, and confronted an obdurate colonial state that proved unsympathetic to its concerns.

The FLT was convinced that under U.S. sovereignty, even as a colony, Puerto Rican workers had a greater likelihood of improving their material conditions than under an independent republic dominated by national capital. In a 1901 address to the legislature, Governor Hunt reinforced this view: "There is no room for lawlessness in Porto Rico, but the right to organize to secure better wages by peaceable measures is perfectly lawful and consistent with good government. Ambition to better one's condition is intensely American and oftentimes only gratified through organized effort" (quoted in Whittaker 1968, 391).

Nonetheless, U.S. officials were determined to prevent the emergence of a unified labor movement that could disrupt the smooth functioning of the economy. Government officials overlooked the heavy-handed tactics the corporations often employed against workers to break up strikes. Moreover, the governor frequently called out the insular police to guard the property of U.S. firms and to protect strikebreakers. The Unión, and its rival Republican Party, supported the use of force to suppress worker militancy. From 1906 through 1916 the House of Delegates, under the control of the Unión, was the bastion of the local landowners. From this forum the Unión continued to launch an ideological attack against the FLT.

The decision to establish an independent political party under the auspices of the FLT provoked heated discussion within the organization. Iglesias and the AFL opposed the FLT's involvement in electoral politics. Iglesias Pantín also opposed FLT affiliates running candidates for municipal offices, but he backed down when challenged by the rank and file (García and Quintero Rivera 1982, 80; Silvestrini de Pacheco 1979, 21). Despite this opposition the rank and file reaffirmed its resolve to sustain an electoral organization that was independent of the bourgeois parties. Samuel Gompers and the AFL quickly came to understand that the political and economic conditions in the colony differed fundamentally from conditions in the metropole. The AFL ultimately chose to endorse a strategy in which Puerto Rican workers should "find the appropriate local remedies to obtain legislation that would improve the working conditions and life of the workers" (quoted in Pagán 1972, 1:169). According to labor historian William Knowles, "Gompers himself defended the union-party alliance in Puerto Rico and argued that pure and simple unionism was impossible under the circumstances" (quoted in Galvin 1979, 66).

The FLT followed a complex and shifting strategy: It arranged tenuous alliances with its class enemies in the hope of obtaining seats in the House of Delegates, supported local unions in electoral campaigns to elect their candidates to municipal offices, and fielded candidates for elective posts. As early as 1900 the Partido Obrero Socialista sought to elect its members to municipal posts. Even after the municipal reform law of 1901 stripped the *municipios* of much of their autonomy and resources, they were the focus of the workers' early electoral struggles. But Partido Obrero candidates were unsuccessful against the Republican and Federal Parties, leading the FLT by 1904 to abandon the political party (Mejías 1946, 73). In 1904, the FLT faced formidable impediments to building a workers' party that was capable of mounting an effective challenge to the bourgeois parties. The highly restrictive franchise in effect until 1904 prevented the Partido Obrero Socialista from developing a districtwide electoral base that could elect delegates to the House. Since they lacked their own organization, workers were deprived of a role in defining labor policy. Workers were essentially compelled to cede to the Republicans and Federals the legislative terrain from which they could subvert progressive labor legislation.

Alliance between Class Enemies

Throughout its history the FLT pursued sometimes contradictory maneuvers to assert its presence in the political arena. After suffering electoral defeats in 1904 the FLT entered into an agreement with the UP. In return for the UP listing six Partido Obrero candidates in its electoral slate (five of whom were subsequently elected), the FLT agreed to endorse the Unión platform and called on its members to vote for the UP (Iglesias Pantín 1958, 331; Pagán 1972, 1:113, 119). What explains this unlikely electoral alliance between the workers and the party of *hacendados*, their traditional class enemies? The UP was an alliance of the *hacendados* and nationalistic sectors of the professional strata. From the perspective of the FLT the latter, many of whom had ties with the labor movement, could conceivably mitigate the landowners' strident opposition to organized labor. When the alliance was forged in 1904, the UP supported statehood and endorsed U.S. citizenship for Puerto Ricans, positions that leading sectors of the FLT endorsed. The Republican Party was a proven opponent of the FLT, it had co-opted the leadership of the rival Federación Regional, paid the salaries of its officers, and attempted to usurp the Partido Obrero. The Republicans were accused of shooting up FLT headquarters and assaulting its members during the period of the *turbas republicanas* (Negrón Portillo 1990, 80–82; Quintero Rivera 1975, 57; Whittaker 1968, 396).

Despite this propitious set of circumstances, the UP unilaterally chose to terminate the alliance in 1906 (Silén 1978, 67; Iglesias Pantín 1958, 374). The UP claimed that the legislative activity of the labor delegates was in direct opposition to the interests of the landowners. Labor representatives introduced a number of projects, including an eight-hour workday, payment of wages in cash as opposed to *vales* (tokens redeemable for merchandise), and an institute for worker education. The House of Delegates condemned the measures as "socialistic and anarchistic and disruptive of public peace" (U.S. House 1913, 4). The UP leadership accused Partido Obrero member Ramón Romero Rosa of submitting projects "which have made us look like socialists before the American government," which "is prejudicial for the country, and certainly for the Unionist Party" (quoted in Quintero Rivera 1976, 53; Silén 1980, 210).

Violent clashes between workers and the owners of capital marked the first years of U.S. colonialism. In 1903, railroad workers in Ponce and tobacco workers in a number of cities organized important strikes. Particularly militant confrontations involving truckdrivers took place in 1905 and 1906. Sugar workers in Ponce and Guayama struck in 1905, paralyzing production in 38 sugarcane plantations and 140 smaller farms (Córdova 1993, 106). In the Ponce and Arecibo strikes, secretary of Puerto Rico Charles Hartzell obtained federal injunctions against the strike leaders and the FLT (Iglesias Pantín 1958, 339). The strikes, some of which the FLT organized, also doomed the alliance between the Partido Obrero and the UP. The activities of striking sugar workers were particularly obnoxious to the UP, which had among its leaders some of the most prominent Puerto Rican sugarcane landowners (Negrón Portillo 1981b, 55; Quintero Rivera 1988, 170). The FLT's shaky electoral ally, alarmed by these threats to capital, wanted state protection of the sugar owners' property and waged a bitter editorial campaign against Iglesias (García and Quintero Rivera 1982, 53; Iglesias Pantín 1958, 388; Pagán 1972, 1:169).

Antipathy between the FLT and the UP as well as the Republicans intensified, as these parties sought to convert the rank and file to their cause, endorsed the repressive measures of the colonial authorities, and thwarted labor's efforts to enact favorable legislation. The FLT went to Washington and condemned the UP not only as "enemies of the working class" but as aristocratic reactionaries and traitors to the principles of justice and liberty (Iglesias Pantín 1958, 388). The FLT newspaper, *Unión Obrera*, reviled the UP for buying the votes of impoverished workers (Córdova 1993, 109).

For the Puerto Rican men of property who controlled the UP the proletariat was a greater danger than the foreign corporations. The FLT's open contempt for the Union only served to convince party officials that the proletariat, rather than foreign capital, was the class enemy of the UP. The party did not intend to nurture a coalition with the FLT, given the latter's relentless quest to improve the salary and conditions of rural workers at the expense of the beleaguered *hacendados*. According to Gordon Lewis "the colonial bourgeois class" waged battle on two fronts: against U.S. colonial and economic power, and against the organized proletariat (Lewis 1963, 116).

Americanization and the Political Process

The FLT ridiculed the UP and Republicans for being obsessed with reforming the Foraker Act. Iglesias Pantín denounced the political parties' campaigns as "conventional lies that divide the workers, and distract the people from urgent political and social necessities" (quoted in Pagán 1972, 1:171). He wrote to President Taft that he opposed self-government because it would result in "slavery, ignorance, and disgrace to 90 percent of the population" (quoted in Morales Carrión 1983, 182–183). Labor leader Eduardo Conde affirmed, "It is not necessary to argue whether the Americans in power are worse or better than the Puerto Ricans, for at least with them we are free to protest their errors, which we cannot do with Puerto Ricans, because in so attempting they will beat in our ribs and we will lose our liberty" (quoted in History Task Force 1979, 102). Iglesias asserted that with self-government the capitalists would inescapably "come to have in their hands greater power to continue their work of popular repression." He pointedly asked, "What practical benefits will the workers obtain from putting their energies and their influence to the test in order to deposit in the hands of the elites of Puerto Rico the absolute and unhindered direction of the political, administrative and judicial matters of Puerto Rico?" (Quoted in Galvin 1976, 28–29).

After the aborted alliance with the UP the FLT tenaciously fought to prevent the *hacendados* from reclaiming their earlier social and political influence. The UP represented a discredited social order based on hierarchy and the workers' submission to the *hacendados*. The FLT repudiated the hierarchical social order personified by traditional landed interests. The workers rejected the UP's call for resuscitating the *gran familia*. In turn, the economic objectives and political posture of the FLT were mortal threats to the UP and made any rapprochement between the national bourgeoisie and the working class impossible. As the FLT waged war against the bourgeois political parties, Iglesias Pantín claimed that as the AFL representative he would promote Americanization of Puerto Rico: The FLT was an agent in this process as well (Galvin 1976, 29). Iglesias Pantín argued that "our objective is . . . not to combat the American system, no; we want to demonstrate a condition . . . that is incongruent with the American principles of representative government" (Iglesias Pantín 1958, 325). Iglesias Pantín met regularly with BIA chief Edwards, since the "battle camp" for the FLT was the bureau (Iglesias Pantín 1958, 389).

The FLT's conversion into a proponent of Americanization and economic modernization has been widely attributed to the influence of Gompers and the AFL (Galvin 1976; Galvin 1979, 64; Lewis 1963, 105; Mattos Cintrón 1980, 65; Whittaker 1968). Samuel Gompers himself boasted, "There is no factor that has been of such value in Americanizing the people of Porto Rico as the American labor movement, the American Federation of Labor" (U.S. Senate Committee on Pacific Islands and Porto Rico 1916, part 2, p. 113). The AFL provided financial support and strike funds to its Puerto Rican affiliate. Through its congressional allies the AFL introduced favorable labor legislation for Puerto Rican labor. Gompers introduced Iglesias Pantín to policy makers in Washington (including President Taft), intervened in insular politics on behalf of the FLT, and regularly informed the Congress of the Puerto Rican workers' plight. According to Iglesias, the FLT "was practically under the protection and auspices of the AFL" (Iglesias Pantín 1958, 202).

The metropolitan state supported the AFL in its efforts to influence the conduct of Puerto Rico's independence-minded and independent labor movement at the turn of the century (García and Quintero Rivera 1982, 40; Mattos Cintrón 1980, 62–63). Iglesias Pantín declared that the FLT had an important role in the Americanization process. He wrote to Samuel Gompers: "The labor movement in Porto Rico has no doubt been, and is the most efficient and safest way of conveying the sentiments and feelings of the American people to the hearts of the people of Porto Rico. If the people of Porto Rico should really become Americans, the AF of L would be the only institution to be held responsible for it" (quoted in Morales Carrión 1983, 182).

The FLT leadership made a distinction between the corporate sector and the colonial regime on the one hand, and the metropolitan government on the other hand, which it felt was more permeable and potentially responsive to the workers. Iglesias Pantín and other FLT leaders believed that under U.S. sovereignty workers' rights would be legally protected and the economy industrialized. The FLT did not oppose U.S. institutions and the republican form of government.

Quite the contrary, it argued that unions were proponents for political and economic modernization. The FLT reviled the UP's paternalistic local leadership as
political relics who impeded the establishment of genuine republication institutions. In this the FLT echoed Gompers's own campaign in the United States to
present the labor movement as "the embodiment of democracy" (Tomlins 1985,
60–67).

From the turn of the century until the 1920s, the FLT leadership guided the
labor movement into ever more conventional modes of interaction with business
and the colonial state. The FLT was established by urban artisans and tobacco
workers who advocated a form of anarcho-syndicalism that projected the state
and capital as oppressors, and called for an independent workers' republic (Quintero Rivera 1983). Santiago Iglesias Pantín was himself a product of southern European anarcho-syndicalism, and during his early years in the movement was a
proponent of radical change. Yet under his stewardship the FLT evolved into a
conservative labor confederation that turned to government to control the excesses of capital. Interestingly, the AFL was undergoing a similar conservative
transformation during the early part of the century. By the early 1900s Gompers
had relinquished the idea that through voluntary association and collective bargaining labor could achieve the social and political transformation of the United
States. The AFL increasingly relied on "mechanisms for the improvement of
material conditions within the political and industrial framework of the new corporate economy" (Tomlins 1985, 74). In Puerto Rico, Gompers opposed the minimum wage, and he warned the workers if such legislation were enacted the colonial government "might find it convenient to enforce compulsory service to labor
at the wage set by law" (Gompers 1914, 384).

The Repressive State and the FLT

Capitalist expansion generated profound social inequities and dramatically
transfigured the nature of work and the composition of the labor force. The
major strikes that frequently erupted revealed the socially destructive effect of the
new economic order. Colonial state policy toward organized labor reflected the
same imperial attitude typified in its relations with the political parties and
Puerto Rican society. On one hand the colonial authorities sought to discredit the
FLT and employed the insular police and courts to suppress the most militant
strikes. On the other hand these officials recognized the need for protective labor
legislation and became intermediaries in capital-labor conflict. This role required
changing the antiquated labor laws, which were "ill-defined and permissive of
virtually any judicial interpretation" (Whittaker 1968, 389).

The UP-controlled legislature opposed protective labor legislation. The local
courts were also hostile to organized labor. They issued injunctions against
strikes and routinely upheld the arrest and incarceration of union organizers.
The courts in Puerto Rico, as in the United States, were a major impediment to

the organizing activities and political development of the early labor movement. Iglesias Pantín himself was convicted by the District Court of San Juan soon after the change in sovereignty for conspiring to raise the price of labor through his organizing activities (Pagán 1:1972, 165). At that time colonial officials viewed organized labor's challenge to the industrial order with increasing alarm and were determined to assert their role in protecting private property.

The colonial state's relations with the FLT varied. Governor Colton's relations with the federation were a marked improvement over those of his predecessor, Regis Post. Colton issued a decree "reaffirming the right of workers to peacefully meet with the purpose of protesting and to discuss issues of interest to them." His administration also enacted social legislation for the "protection of the masses of workers" (Iglesias Pantín 1958, 86–87). However, the situation deteriorated with the appointment of Arthur Yager, who refused to acknowledge a role for the FLT. According to Iglesias Pantín, "the general attitude assumed by the administration of Governor Yager was reactionary," and he "demonstrated a manifest prejudice and hostility to the labor movement" (Iglesias Pantín 1958, 96, 170). Yager proved to be singularly antagonistic toward the FLT and Iglesias Pantín. In an effort to discredit the FLT Yager testified before a Senate committee, that it was "so completely under the domination of a few leaders who seem to be rather neglectful of the real interests of the laborers and inclined to look to their personal interests, so that I do not believe that any opposition from them would be important or useful as a guide to the committee" (U.S. Senate 1916, part 3, p. 146).

In his 1913 message to the legislature, Yager refused to endorse protective labor legislation introduced by the FLT (Córdova 1993, 121). The governor also sought to remove Socialists from elective office. In 1915 Yager used the pretext of administrative irregularities to dismiss the Partido Obrero officials elected the year before to the municipal government of Arecibo (García and Quintero Rivera 1982, 81). Yager rejected the FLT's grievances and claimed that the strikes that paralyzed the district of Arecibo were cynical political maneuvers by the Partido Obrero Socialista. He reported to President Wilson that "the so-called labor leaders and agitators of the strike in Arecibo are in reality political leaders of a recently organized socialist party and are playing a game for political control of the municipality" (quoted in Clark 1975, 16).

On October 14, 1913, approximately two thousand cigarmakers in Caguas struck. Workers in the Porto Rican-American Tobacco Company went on strike the following February. Soon the strike spread, and approximately seven hundred cigarmakers and about an equal number of tobacco strippers and other workers became engaged (PR. Bureau of Labor 1914, 19; USDW Annual Report 1914, 442). In 1915 workers mounted a campaign of sustained strike activity that continued through part of 1916. Although the insular police provided protection, workers torched many sugar cane fields and destroyed corporate property. The director of the Bureau of Labor reported to Governor Yager in 1915 that "the strike of agricultural workers from January to March 15, has been considered the most important in Porto Rico since the American occupation . . . fires occurred and other kinds of damage were done all over the island" (USDW Annual Report 1915, 424, 425).

The colonial authorities operated with impunity and readily called out the insular police, which had a proclivity for intimidating workers. Given the collusion of the colonial authorities and business, the FLT turned to the AFL for assistance. The FLT wanted Congress to know that "under the American flag there is a suffering people who are exploited, and gunned down when they protest" (Iglesias Pantín 1958, 178). Iglesias Pantín appealed to Congress and reported that Governor Yager "turned over to the police the whole rural region. So practically a species of martial law was declared by the police and attacks upon strikers were very common" (U.S. House 1916, 8140) Supported by the AFL, the FLT called on Congress to initiate an investigation of conditions in Puerto Rico.

The AFL obtained the support of Representative Keating of Colorado, who alerted Congress to the violence workers faced, the denial of their basic civil rights, and the collusion between the colonial regime and the corporations in suppressing the strikes. Keating presented an amendment to an early version of the Jones Act to declare that "the right of workers to organize for the purpose of securing better wages, shorter hours and improved working conditions shall never be questioned" (U.S. House 1916, 8409, 8412). Muñoz Rivera opposed the measure and informed Congress it was unnecessary, since "in no instance have the officials of Porto Rico opposed the organization of the laboring classes." He justified the use of the police to suppress strikes "when they disturbed the public order and public peace," and argued that the governor "has been obliged to compel them to respect order" (U.S. House 1916, 8409, 8412). Congress did not adopt the amendment. The failure to obtain congressional support for its cause convinced the FLT it would have to elect its own representatives to the House of Delegates. Manuel Rojas, a top party official, declared, "Economic independence cannot be realized through struggle only in the economic arena. . . . We have to change the laws of privilege into the laws of universal protection, and for this we have to elect our own representatives" (quoted in Quintero Rivera 1975, 62). Moreover, labor militancy had been proven ineffectual in materially improving the lot of most of Puerto Rico's laborers.

The FLT confronted a formidable tripartite alliance consisting of the colonial state, foreign capital, and the insular bourgeois parties. In its 1915 convention the FLT adopted the 1899 program of the Partido Obrero and resurrected the Socialist Party (Quintero Rivera 1975, 67–70; Silén 1978, 77; Silvestrini de Pacheco 1979, 22). Although administratively independent, the FLT and the Socialist Party were essentially one organization because they shared the same leadership. Membership in the FLT was a condition for joining the Socialist Party (Knowles 1966, 318; Silvestrini de Pacheco 1979, 22–23). The FLT established the party in the context of mounting pressure on the United States to reform Puerto Rico's civil government. The prospects that Congress would set up an elected bicameral legislature, along with more liberal voting requirements for males, looked favorable. Collective U.S. citizenship seemed a virtual certainty, and with it, the FLT assumed, the full application of the Constitution. The new political environment would significantly improve the opportunities for the Socialist Party to elect representatives to the expanded legislature. What the FLT had failed to obtain in the fields and shops for its workers, the Socialist Party sought to attain through legislation.

During the years leading to the passage of the Jones Act, the Socialist Party denounced the "capitalist parties and its leaders as the chief accomplices in this great economic crime that is maintained in Puerto Rico" (quoted in Bothwell González 1979, 1:365). Characteristically the FLT denounced House Speaker José de Diego's call for independence as motivated by an "aspiration and thirst for dominion over the producing masses, to secure places and to strangle in the throat of the people the blessed freedom" the United States had provided (U.S. House 1913, 9). The FLT and the Socialists also aired a withering critique of the corporate order. It called for nationalization of key sectors of the economy. However, despite its rhetoric the party did not block the process of capitalist expansion; instead, it called for the enactment of legislation to curtail the excesses of absentee corporations and domestic landowners, and to provide workers with fair treatment and decent wages (Anderson 1965, 34–35; Galvin 1979, 66–70; Silvestrini de Pacheco 1979, 23–24).

Although it was prone to employ revolutionary rhetoric, the FLT aspired to the same economic and political goals as its parent organization, the AFL: collective bargaining, voluntary arbitration, educational programs, the right to strike, and salary increases (Pagán 1972, 1:170; Silén 1978, 77; Silvestrini de Pacheco 1979, 20). The Socialist Party and the FLT attempted to abate the most nefarious social and human consequences of rampant and uncontrolled capitalist growth, and they fought to overthrow the electoral power of the paternalistic political parties. Such political participation channeled the FLT's interactions with capital into the nonconflictive procedural arenas. The Socialists endorsed U.S. citizenship as a stage in Puerto Rico's evolution toward statehood and called for the protection of individual rights and further expansion of U.S. democratic institutions (Pagán 1972, 1:175).

By the 1920s the inflammatory rhetoric, which no doubt accurately reflected the beliefs and aspirations of much of the rank and file, was profoundly at variance with the conciliatory attitude of the FLT hierarchy toward the colonial regime. Although the Socialists espoused a militant anticapitalist critique, many of its top leaders endorsed colonial rule and defined the FLT's objectives primarily in traditional trade union economic terms. The more radical elements of the Socialist Party were marginalized. Many workers and local unions still adhered to the original ideology of the Partido Obrero Socialista and called for revolutionary class struggle and resistance to imperialism. This simmering difference within the labor movement eventually erupted into a rupture between the leadership of the FLT and the Socialist Party and the affiliated unions. By the end of the first two decades of U.S. occupation the Socialist Party was evolving into a stabilizing agent in the colonial calculus. It dispensed with earlier calls for the establishment of a socialist republic and emerged as a vocal proponent of Americanization and annexation.

The Socialist Party mounted effective electoral challenges in the UP's traditional strongholds after 1916 (Quintero Rivera 1988, 146ff). Muñoz Rivera knew the UP's political fortunes depended on gaining the support of labor, and he had feared substantial losses to the Socialists in the 1917 elections. He cautioned Antonio Barceló, "Capital wants it all and takes it all from the workers. We are its accomplice through our inexcusable silence. We should adopt measures that will salvage the Unionista responsibility" (quoted in Pagán 1972,1:170). However, the UP could not prevent the Socialist Party from gaining significant electoral support from the workingmen of Puerto Rico. Although Muñoz's predictions regarding the magnitude of the Socialists' victory were off the mark, the Socialists did obtain 14 percent of the vote, elect one senator and one delegate to the new insular legislature, and win the elections in six *municipios* in the 1917 elections (Pagán 1972, 1:185). The electoral achievements of the Socialist Party injected a new dynamic into the political process.

The process of class decomposition and reformulation rapidly transfigured Puerto Rico's political landscape. Angel Quintero Rivera posits the formation of *la política triangular* during the first two decades of colonial rule. Political conflict revolved around three poles, the organized proletariat, the landed oligarchy (*hacendados*), and the "metropolitan power and classes and social sectors in the colony whose interests were identified with its policy" (Quintero Rivera 1975, 74). The process of social class recomposition and political struggle did not occur in a vacuum. It was mediated through the colonial state, which functioned as a political institution of external domination that also transfigured the nature of class conflict. Colonial officials took an early and active role in diverting class conflict into forums they regulated and sought to erode the legitimacy of the FLT as a vehicle for the expression of working-class aspirations for social justice and material improvement.

The Bureau of Labor

U.S. officials could not ignore the growing discrepancy between private material gain by U.S. citizens and widening social immiseration. The Bureau of Labor reported that "wages are extremely low; the extent of unemployment is, at present, at least, appalling" (Puerto Rico. Bureau of Labor 1914, 112). Low wages, unemployment, and the forced reliance on costly imported food were creating deplorable conditions for the majority of Puerto Rico's people, which threatened the colonial enterprise. During the first decade of U.S. rule the Puerto Rican working class had demonstrated a solidarity and capacity for militancy that exploded any misconceived notions as to its docility. It was willing to disrupt the productive process in apparent disregard for the violence it would confront or the persecution of its leaders. Colonial officials decided to establish the Bureau of Labor in the hope of ameliorating the conflictual state of labor industrial relations. The FLT had proposed a bureau or department of labor in 1903, but the Executive Council rejected the measure. However, nine years later, on March 14, 1912, the governor signed the law that established the Bureau of Labor (Córdova 1993, 101). According to Iglesias Pantín the Puerto Rican legislature decided to act because Congress was about to establish a Department of Labor for the possession and the legislature "feared that its authority would suffer in as much as this would be the creation of an agency devoted to the defense of the working-men by the United States Congress" (U.S. Senate 1916, part 3, p. 149). But the local legislature did not adequately fund the bureau nor did it provide it with the legal authority to enforce its decisions.

The bureau was to study the conditions of labor, compile statistics, "attend to the enforcement of laws enacted for its protection, exercise its good offices for the maintenance of satisfactory relations between employers and employees, and to suggest such legislation as its investigations may indicate to be necessary" (USDW Annual Report 1912, 21). The bureau published reports on the conditions of the working class, established a free employment agency, advocated for workers' disability compensation and for legislation to regulate the employment of women and child labor, and obtained the legal authority to prosecute employers for defrauding workers of their wages. Bureau chief J. C. Bills reported that the aim of the Bureau of Labor "is to promote the welfare of the laboring classes, to protect them from exploitation or unjust treatment by their employers or by other persons of capital, such as their landlords, and to promote better relations between laborers and employers" (Puerto Rico Bureau of Labor 1914, 9).

Bills, however, was careful to point out that the bureau would "keep to a middle line between the conflicting interests" of laborers and employers and would not endorse actions that he thought would injure the employers. Gompers faulted Bills for wanting "to be perfectly impartial as between the employers and employees" (Gompers 1914, 385). According to Iglesias Pantín the Bureau of Labor had a decided "inclination toward favoring the capitalists." He accused officials of the Bureau of Labor of being "hostile to organized labor and [having] neither the sympathy nor confidence in or for the laborers" (U.S. Senate 1916, part 3, p. 150).

The reports issued by the Bureau of Labor through 1917 highlight the concerns of the colonial government with unemployment and landlessness. Landlessness, reported the bureau, and "the present systems of paying land rent without a lease or of occupying land at the will of the landowner are alike stunting the development of our laboring classes." The bureau estimated that 600,000 Puerto Ricans living in the rural areas were landless (Puerto Rico Bureau of Labor, 1914, 108). According to the bureau director, unemployment "is not only a labor question, but a social one as well, which demands prompt action" (USDW Annual Report 1913, 427). By 1914, approximately 800,000 people, or 75 percent of the population, were "absolutely landless" (USDW Annual Report 1914, 443). The bureau director reported in 1915, "It may be said beyond any doubt that the most serious labor problem of Porto Rico . . . is unemployment. . . . It is absolutely necessary to take some steps . . . to diminish the great evils of unemployment" (USDW Annual Report 1915, 428). But after two years of operations the bureau concluded,

> It may be said that the laboring conditions of our island have not improved during the last two years. Unemployment has increased to proportions which nobody can imagine. The cost of living is higher every day. The employment of children has increased in spite of the law and in spite of the suggestions made to employers to minimize it, inasmuch as they know how important it is to reduce the alarming number of men who are without work. (USDW Annual Report 1915, 423)

The bureau urged that some form of land distribution be enacted, arguing that "the ownership of land, even though it be a small lot to build a hut upon, has important sociological as well as economic influence" (USDW Annual Report 1914, 443). The bureau was also actively engaged in mediating labor-management disputes as it sought the "reestablishment of industrial peace" (USDW Annual Report 1918, 550). In 1914 the Bureau of Labor mediated a strike by cigar workers against the Porto Rican-American Tobacco Company. During the first two months of the strike the bureau "was unable to accomplish anything because of the refusal of the officials of the company to negotiate or confer with the cigar makers." Only after the governor intervened was the strike settled two months later (USDW Annual Report 1914, 442). As strike activity increased, the bureau intervened with increasing frequency in managing industrial relations. "A great part of the time of the personnel of the bureau was devoted to an endeavor to effect a compromise of the differences between the owners of the sugar mills and the agricultural laborers, which culminated in the big strike declared in January and ended in March, 1915. This strike has been the most important one ever declared in Puerto Rico" (USDW Annual Report 1915, 36).

The bureau reported that in the most important strike of 1916, which involved forty thousand agricultural workers, "the workers were fully justified in asking for an increase," given the high cost of food and with "sugar selling at a price never dreamed of by the employers" (USDW Annual Report 1916, 442). Of particular concern to the colonial authorities was the longshoremen's strike of September-November 1916, which "was one of the most important ever occurring in Porto Rico up to the present time" (USDW Annual Report 1917, 550). The bureau director noted that conflict occurred in those regions where the owners refused to negotiate with the strikers. Strikes continued through 1917, prompting the secretary of the agriculture and labor to report, "In connection with controversies, disputes and strikes occurring during this year, the bureau of labor has been called upon to perform its most important functions, being forced to devote to such work the greatest part of its activities" (USDW Annual Report 1917, 550).

The Bureau of Labor's reports documented the deplorable working conditions, low pay, and arbitrary and often illegal actions by management and landowners. It called on the legislature to enact protective labor laws, and cautioned that callous disregard for the plight of Puerto Rico's poor and unemployed could precipitate a problem of colonial management. The bureau assumed an important practical and symbolic role in mediating labor disputes and sought to channel potentially disruptive conflict to the negotiating table. Its staff not only studied the sources of labor strife and mediated industrial conflict, but formulated legislation to ameliorate the rising turmoil in the sugar fields, tobacco factories, and docks (Mixer 1926, 313).

As the level of industrial strife intensified and employers proved ever more recalcitrant to grant wage increases, the Executive Council began to introduce protective labor legislation. A number of key measures were passed in 1913, including an act to regulate the work of women and children, "and protecting them against dangerous occupations," an act to regulate the number of hours that laborers paid by the state could work on public works projects, and an act to provide for the safe construction and maintenance of scaffolds (Puerto Rico Bureau of Labor 1914, Appendix). In April 1916 a workmen's relief commission was established "for the purpose of providing for the relief of such workmen as may be injured or of the dependent families of those who may lose their lives while engaged in different trades and occupations" (USDW Annual Report 1918, 37).

Capitalist expansion, unplanned and unregulated, intensified the level and intensity of class conflict and complicated the task of colonial management. Continuous labor-capital confrontations and use of the police to protect private property and to intimidate served to erode the legitimacy of U.S. rule. Moreover, this instability placed at risk the metropolitan state's wider regional aspirations, including its ability to manage economic modernization. In this context of turbulent political and economic change, the Bureau of Labor emerged as an important practical and symbolic institution. It acquired a comprehensive understanding of the state of industrial relations throughout the country, and could monitor and strengthen the colonial state's capacity to guide development. To the degree that it was able to persuade corporations to accede to some of the demands of striking workers, the Labor Bureau undermined the role of the FLT and unaffiliated unions. No doubt the effect of the bureau's intervention was to counteract the unmitigated greed of absentee and domestic corporations that was placing at risk Puerto Rico's Americanization. The Bureau of Labor was a policy tool that was used to manage a conflict-ridden and chaotic system of industrial relations. The bureau intervened on a number of occasions on the side of striking workers, and while the consequences were not necessarily favorable to the particular firm the bureau's actions were in the interests of capital in general by preserving a stable social order.

Yet, despite its implicit critique of the corporations, the bureau blamed overpopulation as the primary factors for poverty and unemployment. In 1929, the commissioner of labor observed that "overpopulation is one of the great obstacles encountered by our laborers in their struggle for higher wages." He went on to report that since "the country lacks sufficient number of industries to employ the oversupply of labor, the situation of the workers is a difficult one." The commissioner called for emigration to solve the unemployment problem (USDW Annual Report 1929, 736–737).

The Socialist Party saw the Bureau of Labor as another agency which the bourgeois parties would use to suppress the workers. This view was forcefully expressed in its newspaper, *La Unión Obrera:* "The labor office in the consolidated department will be an office manipulated by the politics of the country, the objects of which will be to favor no other than its own interest. The labor class has gained nothing in the passage of this bill by the legislature, which places the fate of the laborers in the hands of the caciques" (Quoted in Mixer 1926, 48).

Nevertheless, the Bureau of Labor did not become an instrument of the local bourgeoisie and did take controversial and principled positions. The bureau reported that "employers are paying good premiums to accident insurance companies and lawyers are earning fees, but injured laborers are receiving practically nothing" (USDW Annual Report 1914, 443). The bureau urgently called for workmen's compensation legislation, only to have the UP vote against the measures it introduced in 1913, 1914, and 1915 (Córdova 1993, 115) For the UP the Bureau of Labor was no doubt another policy instrument of the colonial state that would further restrict the domestic landowners' control over the country's human and material resources. Although the Bureau of Labor was deprived of the funds to adequately enforce protective measures, its actions were symbolically important for Puerto Rico's workers. The bureau was portrayed in official reports as working to ameliorate the dreadful social and economic conditions of the laboring classes. Such action by the governmental authorities was unprecedented in Puerto Rico's history, and no doubt served to reinforce popular notions as to the colonial state's commitment to the rule of law.

By taking these positions the Bureau of Labor served an important ideological function, portraying the colonial state as standing above capital-labor conflict. The bureau seemingly retained its independence from the bourgeois political parties. However, the bureau was not intended to function, and in fact did not function, as an advocate for the working class. Its function was to moderate the most nefarious and damaging consequences of capitalist expansion. By diverting working-class attention from the labor unions and political parties, it may also have served to erode the intensity of electoral support for these political organizations. The Bureau of Labor evolved as another bureaucratic agency whose primary function was to preserve a measure of social stability and regulate the behavior of the colonial subjects; ultimately it was another agency for Americanization.

Private Wealth, Social Poverty, and Policy Crisis

Puerto Rico [is] a land of beggars and millionaires. More and more it becomes a factory worked by peones, fought over by lawyers, bossed by the absent industrialists. It is now Uncle Sam's second largest sweat shop.

Luis Muñoz Marín, 1929

After World War I ended, U.S. capital poured into sugar and tobacco, two sectors of the economy that promised great profitability. Investors purchased and leased land, built railroads, warehouses, and ports, imported cutting-edge technology, and, most important, purchased the cheap and abundant labor power of hundreds of thousands of Puerto Rican men, women, and children. Puerto Rico's land, water, and human resources were mobilized in an effort to make the United States self-sufficient in sugar. In 1930 Governor Roosevelt reminded U. S. investors that Puerto Rico had "the most important raw material that exists, namely, abundant, intelligent and industrious labor. This labor is capable of learning quickly what may be required and of applying it" (USDW Annual Report 1930, 13). But more to the point, these resources were placed at the service of investors who bought hundreds of millions of dollars worth of the stocks tendered by the great sugar and tobacco corporations that dominated the island-nation's economy.

In 1920 Governor Yager gushed with enthusiasm as he reported, "Commercial business was active and growing throughout the year. . . . The increase in money value of both exports and imports was so extraordinary that it seems incredible" (USDW Annual Report 1920, 3). Four years later Governor Towner confidently reported, "The financial condition of the island is good . . . the island may look forward to years of financial progress and stability" (USDW Annual Report 1924, 4). In 1927 BIA chief McIntyre echoed the theme of growth and development: "This year in Porto Rico has been one of marked progress, notably in education, in health and sanitation, in public and private building, and markedly in agriculture" (USDW BIA 1927, 4). Two decades after it lost its Spanish sovereign, Puerto Rico had been transformed into a modern agricultural export economy. Decades of capitalist development had been condensed into a brief historical moment, and centuries—old international networks of trade and commerce were abruptly and irrevocably terminated.

Yet beneath this official euphoria another reality afflicted Puerto Rico's people. The Evangelical Union of Puerto Rico reported in 1928:

During the past 25 years at least one third of the small farms have passed into the hands of the corporations or have been added to the larger farms. . . . It is a recognized fact that the large majority of the people of Porto Rico is undernourished. Wages are exceedingly low, and, owing to seasonal employment in the island, many of the people work only a part of the year. The number of unemployed is always large. Such a condition can not continue indefinitely. (U.S. Senate–U.S. House 1928, 36)

Capitalist development had generated a profound deterioration in the conditions of Puerto Rican society. The profits that accrued to absentee capitalists were repatriated and either invested or consumed in the United States. Companies sought to maximize their gains by introducing labor-saving machinery, extracting more value out of workers by lowering wages, or shifting different productive functions to the mainland. Given the dynamics of corporate operations in Puerto Rico, colonial authorities could do little to improve the material and social conditions of the colonial subjects. They cautioned that without some improvements Puerto Rico faced a social disaster that would threaten U.S. objectives in the region. In 1940 the White House Interdepartmental Committee on Puerto Rico described the paradox of U.S. colonial rule:

The first fifteen years following American occupation of Puerto Rico were a period of rapid economic development. Since the Great War of 1914–1918, however, the optimism engendered by the closer commercial relationship between Puerto Rico and the Mainland, and by the initial influx of American capital, has been slowly fading. In its stead, doubt has arisen as to the basic soundness of the earlier economic expansion. (USICPR 1940, 3)

During the late 1920s, Puerto Rico's economy degenerated into a morass of poverty and social immiseration that demonstrated the failure of the United States, despite its great wealth, to provide its colonial ward with economic security and social justice. The federal government was acutely aware of the unfolding social crisis in the island. Colonial officials repeatedly commented on the depressed wages that kept workers at barely subsistence levels and worried that unregulated market forces would create an unmanageable social crisis. Unemployment and underemployment were widespread. The Census Bureau reported that 69.5 percent of males ten years or older and 22.9 percent of females ten years or older were gainfully employed in 1930. Governor Theodore Roosevelt Jr. reported in 1930, "More than 60 percent of our people are out of employment, either all or part of each year." He commented that, "Hundreds come to the government offices weekly with but a single request—work." Roosevelt wrote that these hungry workers did not "ask for a dole, merely the opportunity to earn a livelihood" (USDW Annual Report 1930, 2). Congressmen Johnson alerted his colleagues in 1930 that "the distress in Porto Rico among those citizens of ours is almost beyond words to express. More than 600,000 people of Porto Rico are woefully undernourished. . . . They work when they can, but there is so little work at so little pay—pennies not dollars" (*Cong. Rec.* 1930, 11345). Carlos Chardón, secretary of agriculture and labor, warned that "the ever-growing surplus of workers seeking jobs is reaching a dangerous limit" (USDW Annual Report 1930, 61).

Even for those lucky enough to find work the wages were often too low to meet their minimum needs. Governor Towner reported in 1925 that "since 1915 the cost of the sugar laborer's diet has increased 48.6 percent, while his wages have increased but 26.5 per cent. . . . The fact remains that for agricultural laborers the wages paid have not increased as rapidly as the cost of living" (USDW Annual Report 1925, 35). In 1928 Towner complained, "Employers who refuse to pay a living wage are following a short-sighted policy . . . it is clear that the wages paid in Porto Rico are too low" (USDW BIA 1928, 35). Puerto Rico's working population was not only poor, but sickly and malnourished. Governor Theodore Roosevelt Jr. reported on the disheartening situation, "Our death rate in this disease [tuberculosis] was higher than that of any other place in the Western Hemisphere, and four and one-half times the death rate in the continental United States" (USDW Annual Report 1930, 1). In 1932 the BIA cautioned that Puerto Rico's deplorable health and sanitary conditions were directly related to the poor economic conditions and lack of employment (See USDW BIA 1933, 25). Governor Beverley reported that hookworm was as widespread in 1932 as it was in 1918 and that malaria control was not successful. He observed that all major health problems were "closely allied with the economic condition of the Island and the standard of living of the people" (USDW Annual Report 1932, 12–13).

Representative Fiorello LaGuardia, who was later elected New York City's populist mayor, condemned the practices of the absentee sugar corporations for the conditions afflicting Puerto Rico's people. He told his colleagues in Congress, "Most of the invested capital belongs to nonresident stockholders who drain the island every year, taking out from this country in the form of profits and dividends over two thirds of the product of labor and leaving there only the meager wages paid for long hours of labor" (*Cong. Rec.* 1930, 11348). Resident Commissioner Dávila pressed the attack against the corporate-dominated sugar economy. He told Congress that "heads of these corporations have no interest whatever in the development and progress of the people of Puerto Rico. Their goal is to amass wealth, and they apply themselves to this end with whole-hearted interest." Córdova Dávila deplored the massive repatriation of profits to U.S. resident stockholders and estimated that "two thirds of the benefits accruing from the sugar industry are received by absentee owners" (*Cong. Rec.* 1928, 6328).

A devastating hurricane that struck Puerto Rico in 1928 preceded the massive depression that hit the United States. It seemed as though the economy and nature had conspired to plunge Puerto Rico into an unprecedented human calamity. Hurricane San Felipe struck on September 26, 1928. According to the BIA "the ravages of this hurricane were the most devastating known to Puerto Rico" (U.S. Senate Report of the Central Survey Committee 1928, 73). Governor

Towner advised Washington that "before the storm Porto Rico was well described as a luxuriant, flowered paradise. After it the beautiful island was likened to the war-devastated areas of France and Belgium" (USDW Annual Report 1929, 635, 2). San Felipe was significantly more violent than San Ciriaco and caused much more property damage, but because of an improved advance warning system deaths were kept to approximately one-tenth the number of people killed by San Ciriaco. Although less deadly in the short term, San Felipe seriously undermined the fragile health and sanitary system and left a terrible legacy of disease. The death rate increased dramatically, from 21.9 deaths per 1,000 inhabitants before the hurricane struck to 35 deaths per 1,000 by December 1929, and continued at this elevated rate for some time (USDW BIA 1930, 13).

Hurricane San Felipe was also a watershed in U.S. colonialism. Congress received a crash course on the human and material conditions of its colonial possession. It learned of a colonial economy that generated great wealth for investors and profound human immiseration for those who were the source of that wealth. Puerto Rico had been abandoned to the fate of market forces and a colonial administration dominated by the sugar and tobacco corporations and their local allies. The hurricane precipitated a review of U.S. colonial policy and ushered in a new period of increased metropolitan state vigilance and benevolence.

The poverty, hunger, and disease attributable to the operation of the market-driven monoculture economy, dominated by absentee corporations, compelled the metropolitan state to become more engaged in social and economic management of its colonial ward. It embarked on a program of material assistance to its colonial ward to counteract the crisis in colonial management the market driven economy had created and to impose stability. In 1931 federal agricultural legislation was made applicable to Puerto Rico and included appropriations "on the same terms and conditions as similar appropriations for the various states" (USDW BIA 1931, 9). The War Department reported that federal agricultural legislation would "be extended to Porto Rico, therefore enabling the island to obtain its share of the money spent by Congress in fostering agriculture throughout the nation" (USDW Annual Report 1931, 87). In 1933 the BIA chief summarized the changing role of the federal government:

> Following the disastrous hurricane of September 1928 the Congress authorized special appropriations for hurricane relief in the form of both direct monetary aid to the insular government and loans to agriculturists. During the next few years, other appropriations for the extension to Puerto Rico of various Federal services (such as agricultural extension work, vocational education, etc.,) were authorized. (USDW BIA 1933, 17)

Puerto Rico was a federal recipient of public relief, direct cash grants for reconstruction, and loans and credits to small and medium-sized farmers. Eventually dependency on federal largesse to sustain the colony became the most important, although unanticipated, legacy of the early Americanization campaign. The 1930s spectacle of massive wealth driven by profit-repatriating corporations on one hand, and a toiling, poor, and politically powerless working class on the other, continues to be an accurate portrayal of Puerto Rico's colonial experience. Similarly, it is significant to recall that almost a hundred years after the United States forcibly established its sovereignty over Puerto Rico, Puerto Ricans are still perceived as a Spanish-speaking, Latin American people whose country is unfit for statehood. This perception indeed might be the most telling indictment of the failure of the hundred-year-old U.S. campaign of Americanization.

References

Adams, T. S. 1901a. First Porto Rican Legislature. *The Nation* 72 (March):191–192.

_____. 1901b. The Financial Problems of Porto Rico. *Annals of the American Academy of Political and Social Science* 17 (July 1):444–453.

Albizu Campos, Pedro. 1930. *Comercio, Riqueza y Soberania.* San Juan, PR: Editorial Nacionalista.

_____. 1979. *La conciencia nacional puertorriqueña.* Vol. 1. 1979. Mexico City: Siglo Veintiuno Editores.

Alfonso, Oscar M. 1970. *Theodore Roosevelt and the Philippines,* New York: Oriole Editions, Inc.

Allen, Charles H. 1901. See U.S. Department of State. 1901.

_____. 1902. How Civil Government Was Established in Porto Rico. *North American Review* 174 (February):159–174.

Alvárez Curbelo, Silvia. 1993. La conflictividad en el discurso político de Luis Muñoz Marín. In *Del nacionalismo al populismo: cultura y política en Puerto Rico.* Ed. Silvia Alvárez Curbelo and María Elena Rodríguez Castro. Río Piedras, PR: Ediciones Huracán.

American Academy of Political and Social Science. Notes on Colonies and Colonial Government. *The Annals of the American Academy of Political and Social Science* 19 (1902): 162–164.

Ames, Azel. 1900. The Effect of the Proposed Porto Rican Tariff. *The Independent* 52:637–641.

Anderson, Robert. 1965. *Party Politics in Puerto Rico.* Stanford: Stanford University Press.

Azize Vargas, Yamila. 1979. *Luchs de la mujer en Puerto Rico: 1898–1919.* San Juan, PR: Litografia Metropolitana.

_____. 1987. *La mujer en Puerto Rico.* Río Piedras, PR: Ediciones Huracán.

Baerga, María del Carmen, ed. 1993. *Género y Trabajo: La Industria de la Aguja en Puerto Rico y el Caribe Hispánico.* San Juan, PR: Editorial de la Universidad de Puerto Rico.

Baldrich, Juan José. 1981. Class and the State: The Origins of Populism in Puerto Rico, 1934–1953. Ph.D. diss., Yale University.

_____. 1988. *Sembraron la no siembra.* Río Piedras, PR: Ediciones Huracán.

Barbosa, José. C. 1939. *Orientando al pueblo: 1900–1921.* edited by P. Barbosa de Rosario, San Juan, PR: Imprenta Venezuela.

Barceló, Antonio. 1925. American Rule in Porto Rico, 1899–1924. *Current History* 21 (January):511–517.

_____. 1928. *In Defense of Porto Rico: Letter addressed by Messrs. Antonio R. Barceló and Jose Tous Soto to the Resident Commissioner for Porto Rico in Washington,* San Juan, PR: Bureau of Supplies, Printing, and Transportation.

Barón Fernández, José. 1993. *La guerra hispano-norteamericana de 1898*. Moret, Spain: Edicios de Castro.

Bayron Toro, Fernando. 1989. *Elecciones y partidos politicos en Puerto Rico*. Mayagüez, PR: Editorial Isla.

Beale, Howard K. 1962. *Theodore Roosevelt and the Rise of America to World Power*. New York: Collier Books.

Beard, Charles A. 1955. Territorial Expansion Connected with Commerce. In *American Imperialism in 1898*, edited by T. P. Greene. Lexington, MA: D. C. Heath and Company.

Beard, Rev. A. F. 1901. Education in Porto Rico. Lake Mohonk Conference, 19th Annual Conference.

Becker, William H. 1973. American Manufacturers and Foreign Markets, 1870–1900: Business Historians and the "New Economic Determinists." *Business History Review* 47 (Winter):467–481.

_____. 1982. *The Dynamics of Business-Government Relations*, Chicago: Chicago University Press.

Beisner, Robert L. 1968. *Twelve Against Empire: The Anti-Imperialists, 1898–1900*. New York: McGraw-Hill Book Company.

_____. 1986. *From Old Diplomacy to the New, 1865–1900*. 2nd ed. Arlington Heights, IL: Harlan Davidson, Inc.

Bemis, Samuel F. 1955. The Great Aberration of 1898. In *American Imperialism in 1898*, edited by T. P. Greene. Lexington, MA: D. C. Heath and Company.

Benner, Thomas A. 1929. American Difficulties in Porto Rico. *Foreign Affairs* 8 (4):609–619.

_____. 1965. *Five Years of Foundation Building: The University of Puerto Rico, 1924–1929*. Piedras, PR: University of Puerto Rico.

Berbusse, Edward J. 1966. *The United States in Puerto Rico: 1898–1900*. Chapel Hill, NC: The University of North Carolina Press.

Bergad, Laird W. 1978. Agrarian History of Puerto Rico. *Latin American Research Review* 13 (3):63–94.

_____. 1983. *Coffee and the Growth of Agrarian Capitalism in Nineteenth-Century Puerto Rico*. Princeton, NJ: Princeton University Press.

Bothwell González, Reece B. 1979. *Puerto Rico: cien años de lucha política*. 2 Vols. Río Piedras, PR: Editorial Universitaria.

Bowers, Claude G. 1932. *Beveridge and the Progressive Era*. New York: Houghton Mifflin Company.

Boyce, William D. 1914. *States Colonies and Dependencies*. New York: Rand McNally and Company.

Bradford, Royal. 1899. Coaling Stations for the Navy. *The Forum* 26 (February):732–747.

Braeman, John. 1971. *Albert J. Beveridge: American Nationalist*. Chicago: University of Chicago Press.

Brands, H. W. 1992. *Bound to Empire: The United States and the Philippines*. New York: Oxford University Press.

_____.1995. *The Reckless Decade: America in the 1890s*. New York: St. Martins.

Brumbaugh, Martin G. 1904. Problems in the Beginning of American Government in Porto Rico. Lake Mohonk Conference, 22nd Annual Meeting.

_____. 1907. An Educational Policy for Spanish-American Civilization. *Annals of the American Academy of Political and Social Science* 30 (July):65–68.

_____ 1911. The Beginnings of Education Under Civil Law in Porto Rico (1900–1902). Lake Mohonk Conference, 29th Annual Meeting.

Bryan, William Jennings. 1900. *Bryan on Imperialism: Speeches, Newspaper Articles and Interviews.* Chicago: Bentley and Company.

Burch, Henry R. 1902. Conditions Affecting the Suffrage in the Colonies. *Annals of the American Academy of Political and Social Science* 19 (3):408–431.

Burgess, Larry E. 1975. *The Lake Mohonk Conference of Friends of the Indian: Guide to Annual Reports.* New York: Clearwater Publishing Company, Inc.

Butler, Benjamin F. 1903. Notes on Colonies and Colonial Government: The Elections in Porto Rico. *Annals of the American Academy of Political and Social Science* 21 (2):186–190.

Cabranes, José A. 1967. The Status of Puerto Rico. *International and Comparative Law Quarterly* 16:531–536.

_____. 1979. *Citizenship and the American Empire.* New Haven, CT: Yale University Press.

Callcott, Wilfred Hardy. 1942. *The Caribbean Policy of the United States, 1898–1920.* Baltimore, MD: Johns Hopkins University Press.

Campbell, C. S. 1976. *The Transformation of American Foreign Relations.* New York: Harper & Row, Publishers.

Capó Rodríguez, Pedro. 1916. The Relations Between the United States and Puerto Rico. *The American Journal of International Law* 10:312–327.

_____. 1919. Some Historical and Political Aspects of the Government of Porto Rico. *The Hispanic American Historical Review* 2 (4):543–585.

_____. 1921. Colonial Representation in the American Empire. *American Journal of International Law* 15 (4):530–551.

Carr, Raymond. 1984. *Puerto Rico: A Colonial Experiment.* New York: Vintage.

Carroll, Henry. 1899. *Report on the Island of Puerto Rico.* Washington, DC: Government Printing Office.

Castañer Casasnovas, Pedro. 1909. *La crisis política y económica de Puerto Rico: Apuntes sobre la actual situación.* Aguadilla, PR: Tipografía El Griollo.

Catholic Association for International Peace. Committee on U. S. Dependencies. 1931. *Porto Rico and the United States.* New York: Paulist Press.

Chadwick, French E. 1911. *The Relations of The United States and Spain.* Vol. 2. New York: Charles Scribner's Sons.

Challener, Richard. 1973. *Admirals, Generals and American Foreign Policy, 1898–1914.* Princeton, NJ: Princeton University Press.

Clark, Truman. 1973. "Educating the Native in Self-Government": Puerto Rico and the United States, 1900–1933. *Pacific Historical Review* 42 (May):220–233.

_____. 1975. *Puerto Rico and the United States, 1917–1933.* Pittsburgh, PA: University of Pittsburgh Press.

_____. 1969. President Taft and the Puerto Rican Appropriations Crisis of 1909. *The Americas* 46 (October):152–170.

Clark, Victor S. 1930. *Porto Rico and Its Problems.* Washington, DC: Brookings Institution.

Clarke, G. S. 1898. Captain Mahan's Counsels to the United States. *The Nineteenth Century* 43 (February):292–300.

Coletta, Paolo. 1957. Bryan, McKinley and the Treaty of Paris. *Pacific Historical Review* 26 (May):131–146.

Coll Cuchi, C. 1909. A Defense of Porto Rico. 174–180. Lake Mohonk Conference, 27th Annual Meeting.

Collin, Richard H. 1990. *Theodore Roosevelt's Caribbean: The Panama Canal, the Monroe Doctrine, and the Latin American Context.* Baton Rouge, LA: Louisiana State University Press.

Colón, Alice, Margarita Mergal, and Nilsa Torres. 1986. *Participación de la mujer en la historia de Puerto Rico.* Río Piedras, PR: Centro de Investigaciones Sociales, University of Puerto Rico.

Conant, Charles A. 1898. The Economic Basis of Imperialism. *North American Review* 167 (September):326–340.

Congressional Record. 1900–1901, 1915–1916, 1928–1930.

Córdova Dávila, Félix. 1929. Porto Rico's Anomalous Political Status. Paper read at Conference on International Relations, at Elmira, NY.

Córdova, Gonzalo F. 1993. *Resident Commissioner Santiago Iglesias and his Times.* Río Piedras, PR: Editorial Universitaria de Puerto Rico.

Cosmas, Graham A. 1994. *An Army for Empire: The United States Army in the Spanish American War.* Revised ed. Shippensburg, PA: White Mane Publishing Co.

Coudert, Frederic. 1926. The Evolution of the Doctrine of Territorial Incorporation. *The American Law Review* 60 (November-December):801–864.

Crampton, Charles A. 1899. The Opportunity of the Sugar Cane Industry. *North American Review* 169 (March): 276–284.

Cremer, Henry. 1932. Spanish and English in Porto Rico. *School and Society* 36 (924):338.

Crist, Raymond. 1948. Sugar Cane and Coffee in Puerto Rico, parts 1–3. *The American Journal of Economics and Sociology* 7 (2–3):175–184, 321–327, 469–474.

Crow, Ben, Mary Thorpe, et al. 1988. *Survival and Change in the Third World.* New York: Oxford University Press.

Cuesta, José Enamorado. [1929] 1975. *Porto Rico, Past and Present: The Island After Thirty Years of American Rule.* Reprint New York: Arno Press.

Curtis, Thomas D. 1966. *Land Reform, Democracy and Economic Interest in Puerto Rico.* Tucson, AZ: University of Arizona.

Dana, A. G. 1928. *Porto Rico's case, outcome of American sovereignty.* New Haven, CT: The Tuttle, Morehouse & Taylor Company.

Dávila Colón, Luis. R. 1979. The Blood Tax: The Puerto Rican Contribution to the United States War Effort. *Revista de Colegio de Abogados de Puerto Rico* 40 (4): 603–640.

Davis, Brigadier General George W. 1900. Our Policy Toward Puerto Rico. *The Independent* 52:161–162.

_____. Porto Rico—Its Present and Future. Lake Mohonk Conference, 27th Annual Meeting.

de Diego, José. 1913. The Problem of Porto Rico. Lake Mohonk Conference, 31st Annual Meeting.

Delgado Cintrón, Carmelo. 1988. *Derecho y Colonialism: La trayectoria historia del derecho puertorriqueño.* Río Piedras, PR: Editorial Edil.

Dexter, Edwin G. 1908. Education in Porto Rico. Lake Mohonk Conference, 26th Annual Conference.

_____. 1911. Present Educational Conditions in Porto Rico. Lake Mohonk Conference, 29th Annual Conference.

Di Venuti, Biagio. 1950. *Money and Banking in Puerto Rico.* Río Piedras, PR: University of Puerto Rico Press.

Díaz Soler, Luis M. 1960. *Rosendo Matienzo Cintrón.* 2 Vols. Río Piedras, PR: Ediciones del Instituto de Literatura Puertorriqueña.

Dietz, James. 1986. *Economic History of Puerto Rico.* Princeton, NJ: Princeton University Press.

Diffie, W., and Justine Whitfield Diffie. 1931. *Porto Rico: A Broken Pledge.* New York: The Vanguard Press.

Dinwiddie, William. 1899. *Puerto Rico: Its conditions and possibilities.* New York: Harper & Bros.

Domínguez, Jorge V. 1915. The Language Problem and Political Relations with the United States. Lake Mohonk Conference, 33rd Annual Conference.

Eblen, Jack Ericson. 1968. *The First and Second Empires: Governors and Territorial Government, 1784–1912.* Pittsburgh, PA: University of Pittsburgh Press.

Edwards, Colonel Clarence R. 1904. The Work of the Bureau of Insular Affairs. *The National Geographic Magazine* 15 (6):239–255.

Eichner, Alfred S. 1969. *The Emergence of Oligopoly: Sugar Refining as a Case Study.* Westport, CT: Greenwood Press.

Estades Font, María Eugenia. 1988. *La presencia militar de Estados Unidos en Puerto Rico 1898–1918.* Río Piedras, PR: Ediciones Huracán.

Falkner, Roland P. 1905. Porto Rican Problems. Lake Mohonk Conference, 23rd Annual Conference.

_____. 1908. Progress in Puerto Rico. Lake Mohonk Conference, 26th Annual Conference.

_____. 1910. Citizenship for the Porto Ricans. *American Political Science Review* 4:180–195.

Faulkner, Harold U. 1951. *The Decline of Laissez-Faire: 1897–1917,* New York: Rinehart and Company, Inc.

Fernández García, E., ed. 1923. *El Libro de Puerto Rico.* San Juan, PR: El Libro Azul Publishing Co.

Ferrao, Luis Angel. 1990. *Pedro Albizu Campos y el Nacionalismo Puertorriqueño.* Río Piedras, PR: Editorial Cultural.

Figueroa, C. A. 1925. La odisea del cafe. *Revista de Agricultura de Puerto Rico* 15 (3):95–99.

Figueroa, Loida. Breve História de Puerto Rico. Vol. 2. Río Piedras, PR: Editorial Edil, 1971.

Fisher, Horace N. 1899. *The Principles of Colonial Government.* Boston, MA: L. C. Page and Company.

Fitzgibbon, R. H. 1964. *Cuba and the United States: 1900–1935.* New York: Russell and Russell.

Fleagle, Fred K. 1917. *Social Problems in Porto Rico.* New York: D.C. Heath & Company.

Foner, Philip S. 1972. *The Spanish-Cuban-American War and the Birth of American Imperialism.* New York: Monthly Review.

Foraker, Joseph B. 1900. The United States and Puerto Rico. *The North American Review* 170:464–471.

Forbes-Lindsay. C. H. 1906. *America's Insular Possessions.* Vol. 1. Philadelphia, PA: The John C. Winston Company.

Foreign Policy Association. 1929. The Problem of Porto Rico. *Information Service* 4 (23):435–456.

Frieden, Jeffry. 1988. Sectoral Conflict and U. S. Foreign Economic Policy, 1914–1940. *International Organization* 42 (1):59–90.

_____. 1989. The Economics of Intervention: American Overseas Investments and Relations with Underdeveloped Areas, 1890–1950. *Comparative Studies in Society and History* 31 (1):55–80.

Galvin, Miles. 1976. The Early Development of the Organized Labor Movement in Puerto Rico. *Latin American Perspectives* 3(10):17–35.

_____. 1979. *The Organized Labor Movement in Puerto Rico.* Rutherford, NJ: Fairleigh Dickinson University Press.

Gannon, Peter Steven. 1978. The Ideology of Americanization in Puerto Rico in 1898–1909: Conquest and Disestablishment, Ph.D. diss., New York University.

García, Gervasio L., and Angel G. Quintero Rivera. 1982. *Desafío y solidaridad.* Río Piedras, PR: Ediciones Huracán.

García-Muñiz, Humberto. 1997. The South Porto Rico Sugar Company: The History of a U.S. Multinational Corporation in Puerto Rico and the Dominican Republic, 1900–1921. Ph.D. diss, Columbia.

Gatell, Frank Otto. 1960. The Art of the Possible: Luis Muñoz Rivera and the Puerto Rican Jones Act. *Americas* 17 (July):1–20.

Giddings, Franklin H. 1898. Imperialism? *Political Science Quarterly* 13 (4):585–605.

Godkin, E. L. 1899. The Conditions of Good Colonial Government. *Forum* 27 (April): 190–203.

Golding, Morton J. 1973. *A Short History of Puerto Rico.* New York: New American.

Gompers, Samuel. 1914. Porto Rico: Her Present Condition and Fears for the Future. *American Federationist* 21:377–389.

González, Lydia Milagros. 1993. La Industria de la aguja en Puerto Rico. In *Género y Trabajo: La Industria de la Aguja en Puerto Rico y el Caribe Hispánico*, edited by María del Carmen Baerga. San Juan, PR: Editorial de la Universidad de Puerto Rico.

Gould, Lyman Jay. 1958. The Foraker Act: The Roots of American Colonial Policy, Ph.D. diss., University of Michigan.

Gould, Lewis L. 1982. *The Spanish American War and President McKinley.* Lawrence, KS: University of Kansas Press.

Graffam, Richard. 1986. The Federal Courts' Interpretation of Puerto Rican Law: Whose law is it, anyway? *Revista del Colegio de Abogados de Puerto Rico* 47:111–142.

Grenville, J. A. S. 1968. American Naval Preparations for War with Spain. *American Studies* 2 (1):33–47.

_____. 1979. Diplomacy and War Plans in the United States, 1890–1917. In *The War Plans of the Great Powers, 1880–1914*, edited by P. M. Kennedy. Boston, MA: George Allen & Unwin.

Grenville, J. A. S., and G. B. Young. 1966. *Politics, Strategy and American Diplomacy.* New Haven, CT: Yale University Press.

Guerra y Sánchez, Ramiro. 1961. *La expansión territorial de los Estados Unidos: A expensas de España y de los países hispanoamericanos.* Havana, Cuba: Editora del Consejo Nacional de Universidades.

Guerra-Mondragón, Miguel. 1972. The Legal Background of Agrarian Reform in Puerto Rico. In *Portrait of A Society,* edited by E. Fernández Méndez. Río Piedras, PR: University of Puerto Rico Press.

Halstead, Murat. 1899. *Our New Possessions. Natural Riches, industrial resources.* Chicago: The Dominion Co.

Hanna, Philip C. 1899. Conditions in Porto Rico. In *Consular Reports: Commerce, Manufacturers, Etc.* Washington, DC: Government Printing Office.

Healy, David. 1963. *The United States in Cuba: 1898–1902.* Madison, WI: University of Wisconsin Press.

———. 1970. U. S. *Expansionism: The Imperialist Urge in the 1890s.* Madison, WI: University of Wisconsin Press.

———. 1988. *Drive to Hegemony: The United States and the Caribbean: 1898–1917.* Madison, WI: University of Wisconsin Press.

Henry, Guy V. 1899. Americanizing Porto Rico. *The Independent* 51:1475–1477.

Herrero, José A. Working Paper. 1971. La mitología del azúcar: Un ensayo en la historia ecónomica de Puerto Rico, 1900–1970. Río Piedras, PR: Centro de Estudios de la Realidad Puertorriqueña.

Herwig, H. H., and D. F. Trask. 1979. Naval Operations Plans Between Germany and the USA, 1898–1913, A Study of Strategic Planning in the Age of Imperialism. In *The War Plans of the Great Powers, 1880–1914*, edited by P. M. Kennedy. London: George Allen and Unwin.

Higgs, Robert. 1971. *The Transformation of the American Economy, 1865–1914, An Essay in Interpretations.* New York: Wiley and Sons.

Hill, Howard C. 1965. *Roosevelt and the Caribbean.* New York: Russell and Russell.

History Task Force. 1979. *Labor Migration Under Capitalism: The Puerto Rican Experience.* New York: Monthly Review Press.

Hitchcock, Frank. H. 1898. *Trade of Puerto Rico.* Bulletin 13, Division of Foreign Markets. Washington, DC: U.S. Department of Agriculture.

Hobsbawm, Eric. 1989. *The Age of Empire: 1875–1914.* New York: Vintage.

Hoffman, Charles. 1970. *The Depression of the Nineties: An Economic History.* Westport, CT: Greenwood Publishing Company.

Hofstadter, Richard. 1992. *Social Darwinism in American Thought.* Rev. ed. Boston, MA: Beacon.

Hollander, J. H. 1901. The Finances of Porto Rico. *Political Science Quarterly* 16 (4): 553–581.

Hunt, Major I. L. 1913. The Bureau of Insular Affairs. Lake Mohonk Conference, 31st Annual Meeting.

Hunt, William H. 1901. The Results of Civil Government in Porto Rico. *The World's Work* 2 (September):1170–1174.

Iglesias Pantín, Santiago. 1958. *Luchas Emancipadoras: Cronicas de Puerto Rico.* Vol. 1. San Juan, PR: Imprenta Venezuela.

Independent. 1900. Congress and Porto Rico. 52: 559–561.

Ireland, Alleyne W. 1898. The Government of Tropical Dependencies. *Handbook of the American Academy of Political and Social Science* (May):60–65.

James, Arthur. 1927. *Thirty Years in Porto Rico: A Record of the Progress Since American Occupation.* San Juan, PR: Porto Rico Progress.

Jessup, Philip C. 1938. *Elihu Root.* 2 vols. Dodd, Mead and Company, Inc.

Johnson, Roberta A. 1980. *Puerto Rico: Commonwealth or Colony.* New York: Praeger.

Jones, Lloyd Chester. 1916. *Caribbean Interests of the United States.* New York: D. Appleton and Company.

Judson, W. W. 1902. Strategic Value of Her West Indian Possessions to the United States. *Annals of the American Academy of Political and Social Science* 12:383–391.

Kennan, George F. 1951. *American Diplomacy*. Chicago: University of Chicago Press.

Kidd, Benjamin. 1898. The United States and the Control of the Tropics. *The Atlantic Monthly* 82:721–727.

Kidder, Frederick Elwyn. 1965. The Political Concepts of Luis Muñoz Rivera. Ph.D. diss., University of Florida.

Kirkland, Edward C. 1961. *Industry Comes of Age: Business, Labor and Public Policy 1860–1897*. New York: Holt, Rinehart and Winston.

Knowles, William. 1966. *Unionism and Politics in Puerto Rico*. in U. S.-Puerto Rico Commission. *Selected Background Studies*. Washington, DC: Government Printing Office.

LaFeber, Walter. 1962. A Note on the "Mercantilist Imperialism" of Alfred Thayer Mahan. *Mississippi Valley Historical Review* 47:674–685.

_____. 1963. *The New Empire: An Interpretation of American Expansion: 1860–1898*. Ithaca, NY: Cornell University Press.

_____. 1971. Election of 1900. In *History of American Presidential Elections*, edited by A. Schlesinger.

Lake Mohonk Conference of Friends of the Indian and Other Dependent People. Proceedings of nineteenth through thirty-fourth conferences, Lake Mohonk, NY, 1901–1916.

Lake, David. 1988a. *Power, Protection and Free Trade: International Sources of U.S. Commercial Strategy, 1887–1939*. Ithaca, NY: Cornell University Press.

_____. 1988b. The State and American Trade Strategy in the Pre-hegemonic Era, in *The State and American Economic Policy*, edited by J. G. Ikenberry, D. A. Lake, and M. Mastanduno. Ithaca, NY: Cornell University Press.

Larrinaga, Tulio. 1905. Conditions in Porto Rico. *Annals of the American Academy of Political and Social Science* 16:55–56.

_____. 1907. Porto Rico's Attitudes Toward the United States. Lake Mohonk Conference, 25th Annual Meeting.

Latané, John Halladay. 1907. *America as a World Power: 1897–1907*. New York.

Leibowitz, Arnold H. 1989. *Defining Status: A Comparative Analysis of United States Territorial Relations*. London: Martinus Nijhoff.

Leuchtenburg, W. E. 1952. Progressivism and Imperialism: The Progressive Movement and American Foreign Policy, 1898–1916. *Mississippi Valley Historical Review* 39:483–504.

Lewis, Gordon K. 1963. *Puerto Rico: Freedom and Power in the Caribbean*. New York: Monthly Review Press.

Lindsay, Samuel McCune. 1906. What Porto Rico can do for the United States. Lake Mohonk Conference, 24th Annual Meeting.

Link, A. S., and W. M. Leary, eds. 1970. *The Diplomacy of World Power: The United States, 1889–1920*. New York: St. Martin's Press.

Livezey, William. 1980. *Mahan on Sea Power*. Revised ed. Norman, OK: University of Oklahoma Press.

Lodge, Henry Cabot. 1899. *The War With Spain*. New York: Harper & Brothers Publishers.

Long, Chester Isaiah. 1900. *Revenue for Porto Rico and the Philippines: Speech of Hon. Chester I. Long, of Kansas, in the House of Representatives, Wednesday, February 21, 1900*. Washington, DC.

Lord, Everett W. 1908. Some Educational Experiments in Porto Rico. Lake Mohonk Conference, 26th Annual Meeting.

Lowell, A. Lawrence. 1898. The Government of the Dependencies. *Handbook of the American Academy of Political and Social Science* May:45–59.

_____. 1899. The Colonial Expansion of the United States. *Atlantic Monthly* 83:145–157.

Luque de Sánchez, María Dolores. 1980. *La ocupación norteamericana y la Ley Foraker*. Río Piedras, PR: Editorial Universitaria.

_____. 1983. Las franquicias: instrumento de penetracion económica en Puerto Rico, 1900–1905. In *Politics, Society and Culture in the Caribbean*, edited by B. G. Silvestrini. San Juan, PR: Universidad de Puerto Rico y Asociación de Historiadores del Caribe.

Lyle, E. P. 1906. Our Experience in Puerto Rico. *World's Work* 11 (January):7082–7094.

Mahan, Alfred T. 1890. *The Influence of Sea Power Upon History, 1669–1783*. Boston, MA: Little, Brown and Company.

_____. 1897. The Strategic Features of the Gulf of Mexico Caribbean Sea. *Harper's New Monthly Magazine* 95:680–691.

_____. 1899. *Lessons of the War with Spain and Other Articles*. Boston, MA: Little, Brown and Company.

Maldonado-Denis, Manuel. 1972. *Puerto Rico: A Socio-Historic Interpretation*. New York: Vintage.

Marcus, Joseph. 1919. *Labor Conditions in Porto Rico*. Washington DC: Government Printing Office.

Marí Bras, Juan. 1984. *El Independentismo en Puerto Rico*. Santo Domingo, DR: Taller.

Martínez-Fernández, L. 1994. *Torn between Empires: Economy, Society and Patterns of Political Thought in the Hispanic Caribbean, 1840–1878*. Athens, GA: The University of Georgia Press.

Mathews, Thomas. 1960. *Puerto Rican Politics and the New Deal*. Gainesville, FL: University of Florida Press.

Mattos Cintrón, Wilfredo. 1980. *La política y lo político en Puerto Rico*. Mexico: Ediciones Era.

May, Glenn Anthony. 1980. *Social Engineering in the Philippines: The Aims, Execution, and Impact of American Colonial Policy, 1900–1913*. Westport, CT: Greenwood Press.

McCormick, Thomas J. 1962. Commentary on John W. Rollins, "The Anti-Imperialists and Twentieth Century Foreign Policy." *Studies on the Left* 3 (1):12–32.

_____. 1963. Insular Imperialism and the Open Door. *Pacific Historical Review* 32:155–169.

McCune Lindsay, Samuel. 1904. The Public Charities of Porto Rico. *Annals of the American Academy of Political and Social Science* 23 (January-June):502–513.

McIntyre, Frank. 1932. American Territorial Administration. *Foreign Affairs* 10 (January):293–303.

Mejías, Félix. 1946. *Condiciones de vida de las clases jornaleras de Puerto Rico*. Río Piedras, PR: Junta Editora de la Universidad de Puerto Rico.

Meléndez, Edgardo. 1985. La estadidad como proyecto histórico: del anexionismo decimonónico al proyecto republicano. *Hominoes* 8 (2):9–29.

_____. 1988. *Puerto Rico's Statehood Movement*. Westport, CT: Greenwood Press.

Meléndez Ortiz, Miguel. 1949. The Government and the Coffee Industry. *Revista de agricultura de Puerto Rico* 40 (2):193–207.

Merk, Frederick. 1963. *Manifest Destiny and Mission in American History*. New York: Alfred A. Knopf.

Miles, Nelson A. 1911. *Serving the Republic: Memoirs of the Civil and Military Life of Nelson A. Miles*. New York: Harper & Brothers.

Mixer, Knowlton. 1926. *Porto Rico: History and Conditions.* New York: The Macmillan Company.

Morales Carrión, Arturo. 1981. Puerto Rico and the United States; A Historian's Perspective. *Revista del Colegio de Abogados de Puerto Rico* 42:585–603.

_____. 1983. *Puerto Rico: A Political and Cultural History.* New York: W. W. Norton and Company.

Morgan, Senator John T. 1898. What Shall We Do With the Conquered Islands? *North American Review* 499:641–649.

Morgan, W. H., ed. 1965. *Making Peace with Spain: The Diary of Whitelaw Reid.* Austin, TX: John Wiley and Sons, Inc.

Mullins, Jack Simpson. 1964. The Sugar Trust: Henry O. Havemeyer, and the American Sugar Refining Company. Ph.D. diss., University of South Carolina.

Muñiz Varela, Miriam. 1981. El capital monopólico en la formación al capitalismo en Puerto Rico. *Revista de Ciencias Sociales* 23 (3–4):445–495.

Muñoz Marín, Luís. 1931. T.R. of P.R. *World's Work* 60 (July):21–24.

Muñoz Morales, Luis. 1910. Collective Citizenship for Porto Ricans. Lake Mohonk Conference, 28th Annual Meeting.

Muñoz Rivera, Luis. 1899. The Needs of Porto Rico. *The Independent* 51:1284–1287.

_____. 1911. Political Conditions in Porto Rico. Lake Mohonk Conference, 29th Annual Meeting.

Neale, R. G. 1966. *Great Britain and United States Expansion: 1898–1900.* Ann Arbor, MI: Michigan State University Press.

Nearing, Scott, and Joseph Freeman. [1925] 1966. *Dollar Diplomacy, A Study in American Imperialism.* Reprint New York: Monthly Review.

Negrón de Montilla, Aida. 1977. *La americanización de Puerto Rico y el sistema de instrucción pública, 1900–1930.* Río Piedras, PR: Editorial Universitaria.

Negrón Portillo, Mariano. 1972. El liderato anexionista antes y despues del cambio de soberania. *Revista del Colegio de Abogados de Puerto Rico* (October): 369–391.

_____. 1978. Conflictos legislativos en Puerto Rico. *La Toga* 10 (1).

_____. 1981a. *El autonomismo puertorriqueño: Su transformación ideológica, 1985–1914.* Río Piedras, PR: Ediciones Huracán.

_____ 1981b. *Reformismo liberal, reformismo conservador: dos etapas del autonomismo puertorriqueño (1895–1914).* Río Piedras, PR: Centro de Investigaciones Sociales, Universidad de Puerto Rico.

_____. 1990. *Las turbas republicanas: 1900–1904.* Río Piedras, PR: Ediciones Huracán.

Negroni, Héctor Andrés. 1992. *Historia Militar de Puerto Rico.* Spain: Sociedad Estatal Quinto Centenario.

New York Times. 1916. , December 9, 1916. 1923., September 18, 1923, 12:1.

Notes on Colonies and Colonial Government. 1902. *Annals of the American Academy of Political and Social Science.* 19 (1):326–327.

Ober, Frederick A. 1899. *Puerto Rico and Its Resources.* New York: D. Appleton and company.

Offner, John. L. 1992. *An Unwanted War: The Diplomacy of the United States and Spain Over Cuba, 1895–1898.* Chapel Hill, NC: University of North Carolina.

O'Leary, Daniel Hugh. 1936. The Development of Political Parties in Puerto Rico Under American Occupation. Ph.D. diss. Boston College, Boston, MA.

Osborne, John Ball. 1904. The Americanization of Porto Rico. *The World's Work* 8:4759–4766.

Osuna, Juan José. 1949. *A History of Education in Puerto Rico.* Río Piedras, PR: Editorial de la Universidad de Puerto Rico.

Pagán, Bolívar. 1972. *Historia de los partidos políticos puertorriqueños.* 2 vols. San Juan, PR: Campos.

Parrini, Carl.1993. Charles A. Conant, Economic Crisis and Foreign Policy. In *Behind the Throne: Servants of Power to Imperial Presidents, 1898–1968,* edited by T. J. McCormick and W. LaFeber. Madison, WI: University of Wisconsin Press.

Parsons, Herbert. 1907. A Bureau of Information and Report for the Insular Possessions. *Annals of the American Academy of Political and Social Science* 30 (1):123–128.

_____. 1910. The Olmstead Bill and Its Provisions. Lake Mohonk Conference, 28th Annual Meeting.

Pedreira, Antonio Salvador. 1974. *Bibliografia puertorriqueña (1493–1930),* New York: Franklin Reprints.

Pérez, Louis A. 1983. *Cuba Between Empires: 1878–1902.* Pittsburgh: University of Pittsburgh Press.

Perkins, Whitney T. 1962. *Denial of Empire: The United States and Its Dependencies.* Leyden: A. W. Sythoff.

Perloff, Harvey S. 1950. *Puerto Rico's Economic Future.* Chicago: University of Chicago Press.

Pettus, Edmund W. 1900. The Porto Rican Bill. *The Independent* 52:637–641.

Picó, Fernando. 1987. *La guerra después de la guerra.* Río Piedras, PR: Ediciones Huracán.

_____ 1988. *Historia General de Puerto Rico.* Río Piedras, PR: Ediciones Huracán.

Pletcher, David M. 1984. 1861–1898: Economic Growth and Diplomatic Adjustment. In *Economics and World Power: An Assessment of American Diplomacy Since 1789,* ed. William H. Becker, Jr., and Samuel F. Wells. New York: Columbia University Press.

Pomeroy, Earl S. 1944. The American Colonial Office. *Mississippi Valley Historical Review* 30:521–532.

Pratt, Julius. 1932. The "Large Policy" of 1898. *Mississippi Valley Historical Review* 19:219–242.

_____. 1939. *The Expansionists of 1898: The Acquisition of Hawaii and The Spanish Islands.* Baltimore, MD: The Johns Hopkins Press.

_____. 1951. *America's Colonial Experiment: How the United States Gained, Governed and In Part Gave Away a Colonial Empire.* New York: Prentice-Hall.

Puerto Rico Federal Affairs Administration. 1988. *Documents on the Constitutional Relationship of Puerto Rico and the United States.* Ed. M. R. Lavandero. Washington, DC: PRFAA.

Puerto Rico. Bureau of Commerce and Industry. 1931. *Report of the Bureau of Commerce and Industry for Fiscal Year Ended June 30,1931,* San Juan, PR: Bureau of Supplies, Printing and Transportation.

_____. Commission for the study and treatment of "Anemia" in Puerto Rico. 1904. *Report Submitted to the Honorable Beekman Winthrop,* San Juan, PR: Bureau of Printing and Supplies.

_____. Bureau of Labor. 1914. *Second Annual Report of the Bureau of Labor to the Legislature of Porto Rico,* San Juan, PR: Bureau of Supplies, Printing and Transportation.

_____. Bureau of Labor. 1918. *Special bulletin of the Bureau of Labor on strikes in Porto Rico during fiscal year 1917–1918 and appendix of labor laws approved from 1916 to March, 1918. June 1, 1918.* San Juan, PR: Bureau of Supplies, Printing and Transportation.

_____. Governor. 1925. *Special Message of the Governor of Porto Rico,* Eleventh Legislature: first session.

_____. Legislature. 1928. See Barceló, Antonio. 1928.

_____. Office of the Secretary. 1905. *Register of Porto Rico for 1905.* San Juan, PR: Bureau of Printing and Supplies.

_____. Office of the Secretary. 1911. *Register of Porto Rico for 1910.*, San Juan, PR: Bureau of Supplies, Printing and Transportation.

Puerto Rico. Policy Commission. 1934. *Report of the Puerto Rico Policy Commission (Chardon Report),* San Juan, PR.

Pumarada O'Neill, L. 1990. *La industria cafetalera de Puerto Rico, 1736–1969.* San Juan, PR: Oficina Estatal de Preservación Histórica.

Quintero Rivera, Angel. 1974. La clase obrera y el proceso político en Puerto Rico. *Revista de Ciencias Sociales* 18 (1–2):147–197.

_____. 1975. El Partido Socialist y la lucha politíca triangular de las primeras décadas bajo la dominación norteamericana. *Revista de Ciencias Sociales* 19 (1):49–97.

_____. 1976. *Worker's Struggle in Puerto Rico: A Documentary History.* Translated by Cedric Belfrage. New York: Monthly Review Press.

_____. 1977. *Conflictos de clase y política en Puerto Rico.* Río Piedras, PR: Ediciones Huracan.

_____. 1980. Background to the Emergence of Imperialist Capitalism in Puerto Rico. In *The Puerto Ricans: Their History, Culture and Society,* edited by Adalberto López. Cambridge, MA: Schenkman Publishing Company.

_____. 1983. Socialist and Cigar Maker: Artisans' Proletarianization in the Making of the Puerto Rican Working Class. *Latin American Perspectives* 10 (Spring-Summer):19–38.

_____. 1988. *Patricios y plebeyos: burgueses, hacendados, artesanos y obreros.* Río Piedras, PR: Ediciones Huracán.

Raffucci de García, Carmen I. 1981. *El gobierno civil y la ley Foraker: Antecedentes Históricos.* Río Piedras, PR: Editorial Universitaria.

Ramos, Aarón Gamaliel. 1987. *Las ideas anexionistas en Puerto Rico bajo la dominación norteamericana.* Río Piedras, PR: Ediciones Huracán.

Ramos de Santiago, Carmen. 1970. *El gobierno de Puerto Rico.* Río Piedras, PR: Editorial Universitaria.

Ramos Mattei, Andres. 1974. Las inversiones norteamericanas en Puerto Rico y la Ley Foraker, 1898–1900. *Caribbean Studies* 14 (3):53–69.

_____. 1988. *La sociedad del azúcar en Puerto Rico: 1870–1910,* Río Piedras, PR: Editorial Universidad.

Reinsch, Paul S. 1900. *World Politics: At the End of the Nineteenth Century.* London: The Macmillan Company.

_____. 1908. Can the United States Americanize Her Colonies?. *The World Today* 950–953.

_____. 1911. *Colonial Government: An Introduction to the Study of Colonial Institutions.* New York: Macmillan.

Ribes Tovar, Federico. 1973. *Historia cronologica de Puerto Rico.* New York: Plus Ultra Educational Publishers.

Richardson, James D. 1900. Is Porto Rico a Part of the United States?. *The Independent* 52:467–469.

Rigual, Néstor. 1967. *Reseña de los mensajes de los gobernadores de Puerto Rico 1900–1930.* Río Piedras, PR: Editorial Universitaria.

Ringer, Benjamin B. 1983. *"We the People" and Others: Duality and America's Treatment of its Racial Minorities.* New York: Routledge.

Rivera Quintero, Marcia. 1980. Educational Policy and Female Labor. In *The Intellectual Roots of Independence: An Anthology of Puerto Rican Political Essays,* edited by Iris M. Zavala. New York: Monthly Review Press.

Rivera Ramos, Efrén. 1996. The Legal Construction of American Colonialism: The Insular Cases (1901–1922). *Revista Jurídica Universidad de Puerto Rico* 65 (2):226–328.

Rodríguez Beruff, Jorge. n.d. *Imperialism and Militarism: An Analysis of the Puerto Rican Case.* Mimeo.

Rodríguez Fraticelli, Carlos. 1991. Colonial Politics and Education: The Pan-Americanization of the University of Puerto Rico, 1923–1929. *Historia y Sociedad* 4:138–166.

Rodríguez-Serra, Manuel. 1908. The Aspirations of the Porto Ricans. Lake Mohonk Conference, 26th Annual Meeting.

Roosevelt, Theodore. [1937] 1970. *Colonial Policies of the United States.* Reprint. New York: Arno Press and the *New York Times.*

Root, Elihu. 1916. *The Military and Colonial Policy of the United States.* Edited by R. Bacon and J. B. Scott. Cambridge, MA: Harvard University Press.

———. 1917. *Latin America and the United States: Addresses by Elihu Root.* Edited by R. Bacon and J. B. Scott. Cambridge, MA: Harvard University Press.

———. 1917. *Miscellaneous Addresses.* Cambridge, MA: Harvard University Press.

Rosario, José C. Home Economics in the Rural Schools. *Bulletin of the Pan American Union* 61:685–692.

Rosario Natal, Carmelo. 1989. *Puerto Rico y la crisis de la guerra hispano-americana, 1895–1898.* Río Piedras, PR: Editorial Edil.

Rosenberg, Emily S. 1993. *Spreading the American Dream: American Economic and Cultural Expansionism, 1890–1945.* New York: Hill and Wang.

Rosenn, Keith S. 1963. Puerto Rican Land Reform: The History of An Instructive Experiment. *The Yale Law Journal* 73:334–356.

Rowe, Leo S. 1901a. The Significance of the Porto Rican Problem. *The North American Review* 173:35–39.

———. 1901b. The Supreme Court and the Insular Cases. *Annals of the American Academy of Political and Social Science* 17:226–250.

———. 1901c. Military Training as a Factor in the Civic Restoration of Porto Rico. *The American Monthly Review of Reviews* 23:334–335.

———. 1902. Political Parties in Porto Rico. *Annals of the American Academy of Political and Social Science* 19:351–369.

———. 1904. *The United States and Porto Rico.* New York: Longmans, Green and Co.

———. 1905. The Reorganization of Local Government in Cuba. *Annals of the American Academy of Political and Social Science* 25 (Jan.-June):311–321.

Samonte, Vedasto Jose. 1925. *The American System of Colonial Administration.* Iowa City, Iowa: The State University of Iowa.

Santiago-Valles, Kelvin A. 1981. Algunos aspectos de la integración de Puerto Rico al interior del estado metropolitano norteamericano: Los orígenes de la nueva estructura estatal colonial (1898–1929). *Revista de Ciencias Sociales* 23 (3–4):297–346.

_____. 1984. La concentracion y la centralizacion de la propiedad en Puerto Rico (1898–1929). *Hominoes* 8 (1, January-July):129–156.

_____. 1994. *"Subject People" and Colonial Discourses: Economic Transformation and Social Disorder in Puerto Rico, 1898–1947.* Albany, NY: State University of New York Press.

Scarrano, Francisco A. 1993. *Puerto Rico: Cinco Siglos de Historia.* Mexico DF, Mexico: Mc-Graw-Hill.

Schurz, Carl. 1955. American Imperialism: An address Opposing Annexation of the Philippines, January 4, 1899. In *American Imperialism in 1898*, edited by T. P. Greene. Lexington, MA: D. C. Heath and Company.

Schwartz, Stuart B. 1992. The Hurricane of San Ciriaco: Disaster, Politics, and Society in Puerto Rico, 1899–1901. *Hispanic American Historical Review* 72 (3):303–334.

Seager, Robert. 1953. Ten Years Before Mahan: The Unofficial Case for the New Navy, 1880–1890. *Mississippi Valley Historical Review* 40:491–512.

Serrano, Helga. 1986. El legado de Ana Roque de Duprey. *Hominoes* 10 (2):498–499.

Silén, Angel Juan. 1978. *Apuntes para la historia del movimiento obrero puertorriqueño.* Río Piedras, PR: Editorial Cultural.

_____. 1980. *Historia de la nación puertorriqueña.* Río Piedras, PR: Editorial Edil.

Silvestrini, Blanca G., and María Dolores Luque de Sánchez. 1980. The Needlework Industry in Puerto Rico, 1915–1940: Women's Transition from Home to Factory. Paper read at Twelfth Conference of the Association of Caribbean Historians.

_____. 1990. *Historia de Puerto Rico: Trayectoria de un pueblo.* San Juan, PR: Ediciones Cultural Panamericana.

Silvestrini de Pacheco, Blanca. 1979. *Los trabajadores puertorriqueños y el Partido Socialista.* Río Piedras, PR: Editorial Universitaria.

Sklar, Martin J. 1959. The NAM and Foreign Markets on the Eve of the Spanish American War. *Science and Society* 23:133–162.

_____.1988. *The Corporate Reconstruction of American Capitalism, 1890–1916.* New York: St. Martin's.

_____. 1992. *The United States as a Developing Country.* New York: Cambridge University Press.

Sloan, Harold S. 1929. Tariff as a Cause of Porto Rican Poverty. *Current History* 29 (March):993–998.

Smith, George H. 1900. Puerto Ricans and the Constitution. *The Arena* 13(June):626–634.

Snow, Alpheus H. 1902. *The Administration of Dependencies.* New York: G.P. Putnam's Sons.

Society for the Advancement of Education. 1931. The Vocational Education Program of Porto Rico. *School and Society* 33 (862):558–559.

Solá, Mercedes. 1923. Women's Aspirations. In *El Libro de Puerto Rico.* Ed. E. Fernández García, San Juan, PR: El Libro Azul Publishing Co.

Solomon, A. 1898. Porto Rico as a Field for Investors. *The Independent* 50:903–905.

Stead, W. T. 1902. *The Americanization of the World.* New York: Garland Publishing, Inc.

Stephanson, Anders. 1995. *Manifest Destiny: American Expansionism and the Empire of Right.* New York: Hill and Wang.

Stern, C. A. 1971. *Protectionist Republicanism: Republican Tariff Policy in the McKinley Period.* Ann Arbor, MI: Edwards Brothers.

Sumner, William G. 1899. The Conquest of the U. S. by Spain. *Yale Law Review* 8 (163–193).

"Survey of the World. Puerto Rico's Tariff." 1900. *Independent* 52:517–518.

Taussig, F. W. 1931. *The Tariff History of the United States*. 8th ed. New York: Capricorn Books.

Thompson, Winfred Lee. 1989. *The Introduction of American Law in the Philippines and Puerto Rico 1898–1905*. Fayetteville, AR: University of Arkansas Press.

Thorpe, F. N. 1903. *The Government of the People of Porto Rico*. Philadelphia, PA: Eldredge & Brother.

Todd, Roberto. 1939. *La invasion americana: como surgio la idea de traer la guerra a Puerto Rico*. San Juan, PR: Cantero Fernández.

———.1943. *Desfile de Gobernadores de Puerto Rico: 1898 a 1943*. San Juan, PR: Impreso en Casa Baldrich.

———. 1953. *Estampas coloniales*. San Juan, PR: Biblioteca de autores puertorriqueños.

Tomlins, Christopher L. 1985. *The State and the Unions: Labor Relations, Law and the Organized Labor Movement in America, 1880–1960*. New York: Cambridge University Press.

Tompkins, E. Berkeley. 1970. *Anti-Imperialism in the United States: The Great Debate, 1890–1920*. Philadelphia, PA: University of Pennsylvania Press.

Torruella, Juan R. 1985. *The Supreme Court and Puerto Rico: The Doctrine of Separate and Unequal*. Río Piedras, PR: Editorial de la Universidad de Puerto Rico.

Tous Rodríguez, José M. 1977. *El desarrollo historico-politico y juridico del estado libre asociado de Puerto Rico*. San Juan, PR.

Trask, David F. 1981. *The War With Spain in 1898*. New York: Macmillan Publishing Company.

Trías Monge, José. 1980. *Historia Constitucional de Puerto Rico*. Vols. 1 and 2. Río Piedras, PR: Editorial Universitaria.

———. 1991. *El choque de dos culturas juridicas en Puerto Rico*. Austin, TX: Equity Publishing Company.

Tugwell, Rexford G. 1945. *Puerto Rican Papers of R. G Tugwell*. San Juan, PR: Service Office of the Government of Puerto Rico.

———. 1976. *The Stricken Land: The Story of Puerto Rico*. New York. Greenwood Press.

Turk, Richard W. 1978. Defending the Empire, 1900–1914. In *In Peace and War: Interpretations of American Naval History, 1775–1978*, edited by K. J. Hagan. Westport, CT: Greenwood Press.

U. S. Bureau of the Census. 1932. *Fifteenth Census of the United States, 1930. Outlying territories and possessions*. Washington, DC: Government Printing Office.

U. S. Department of Commerce and Labor. 1907. *Commercial Porto Rico in 1906*.Washington, DC: Government Printing Office.

U. S. Department of State. 1901. *First Annual Report of the Governor of Porto Rico*. Washington, DC: Government Printing Office.

———. 1903–1909. *Annual Reports of the Governor of Porto Rico*. Washington, DC: Government Printing Office.

U. S. Department of the Treasury. 1898. *Report on the Industrial and Commercial Condition of Porto Rico*. Special Commissioner to Porto Rico. Washington, DC: Government Printing Office.

U. S. Department of War. Division of Customs and Insular Affairs. 1899a. *Puerto Rico, Embracing the Reports of Brig. Gen. Geo. W. Davis, Military Governor*. Washington, DC: Government Printing Office.

_____. United States Insular Commission. 1899b. *Report of the United States Insular Commission Upon Investigations made into the Civil Affairs of the Island of Porto Rico*, Washington, DC: Government Printing Office.

_____. 1899c. *Amended Customs Tariff and Regulations for Ports in Porto Rico*, Washington, DC: Government Printing Office.

_____. Division of Insular Affairs. 1900a. *Report of Brig. Gen. George W. Davis on Industrial and Economic Conditions of Puerto Rico.*, Washington, DC: Government Printing Office.

_____. 1900b. *Report of Brig. General George W. Davis on Civil Affairs of Puerto Rico, 1899*, Washington, DC: Government Printing Office.

_____. 1901. Military Government of Porto Rico from October 18, 1898 to April 30, 1900. *Appendices to the Report of the Military Governor. Epitome of Reports of the Superior Board of Health*, Washington, DC: Government Printing Office.

_____. Bureau of Insular Affairs. 1902. *Reports on the Law of Civil Government in Territory Subject to Military Occupation by the Military Forces of the United States*, Charles E. Magoon. Washington. DC: Government Printing Office.

_____. *Annual Report of the Governor of Porto Rico*. 1909–1933. Washington, DC: Government Printing Office.

_____. Bureau of Insular Affairs. 1909–1933. *Report of the Chief of the Bureau of the Bureau of Insular Affairs*. Washington, DC: Government Printing Office.

U.S. House. 1901. *Message from the President of the United States. Agricultural Resources and Capabilities of Porto Rico*, House Doc. 171. 56th Cong., 2d sess.

_____. 1912. *Message of the President of the United States on Fiscal, Judicial, Military and Insular Affairs*, House. Doc. 1067. 62nd Cong., 3d sess.

_____. 1913. *The Tyranny of the House of Delegates of Porto Rico: An Address by the Free Federation of Laborers of Porto Rico*, Doc. No. 1415.

_____. 1917. *Civil Government for Porto Rico*. House Report 1546. 64th Cong., 2d. sess.

_____. 1934. *Executive Order Establishing the Division of Territories and Island Possessions in the Department of the Interior.* House Doc. 390. 73rd Cong., 2nd sess.

_____. 1924. Committee on Insular Affairs. *The Civil Government of Porto Rico: Hearings on H.R. 4087 and H.R. 6583*. February 13 and 14, 1924. 68th Cong., 1st sess.

_____. 1924. *Amend the Organic Act of Porto Rico: Hearings on H.R. 6583*. February 26, 1924. 68th Cong., 1st sess.

_____. 1928a. *Suffrage for Porto Rico: Hearings on H.R. 7010*. 30 April 1928. 70th Cong., 1st sess.

_____. 1928b. *Confer the Right to Vote to Women of Porto Rico: Report to Accompany H.R. 7010*. 70th Cong., 1st sess. Report No. 1895.

U. S. Interdepartmental Committee on Puerto Rico. 1940. *Staff Report to the Interdepartmental Committee on Puerto Rico by Erich W. Zimmermann*, Washington, DC: Unpublished Mimeo.

U. S. Office of the President. 1899. Customs Tariff and Regulations for Ports in Porto Rico. Washington, DC: Government Printing Office.

U.S. Senate. Committee on Pacific Islands and Porto Rico. 1914. *A Bill to Provide a Civil Government for Porto Rico: Hearings on S. 4604*. 63rd Cong., 2d sess.

_____. Committee on Pacific Islands and Porto Rico. 1916 *Government for Porto Rico: Hearings on S. 1217, Pts. 1–3*. 64th Cong., 2nd sess.

_____. 1924. Committee on Territories and Insular Possessions. *To Amend the Organic Act of Porto Rico: Report to Accompany S.2448.* Report No. 356: 68th Cong., 1st sess.

_____. Committee on Pacific Islands and Porto Rico. 1928. *Hearings on Government for Porto Rico: Part 1.*

_____. 1928. Committee on Territories and Insular Possessions. *Hearings on Woman Suffrage in Porto Rico.* April 25, 1928. 70th Cong., 1st. sess.

_____.1928. *Report of the Central Survey Committee.* 70th Cong., 2d sess. S. Doc. 180.

_____. 1931. Committee on Territories and Insular Affairs. *Department of Labor for Porto Rico Report No. 1294.* 71st Cong., 3d sess.

Valle Ferrer, Norma. 1990. *Luis Capetillo: Historia de una mujer proscrita.* San Juan, PR: Editorial Cultural.

Van Alstyne, Richard. 1960. *The Rising American Empire.* New York: W. W. Norton.

Van Buren, James H. 1913. Problems in Porto Rico. Lake Mohonk Conference, 31st Annual Meeting.

Vatter, Harold G. 1975.*The Drive to Industrial Maturity: The U.S. Economy, 1860–1914,* Westport, CT: Greenwood Press.

Vélez Aquino, Luis Antonio. 1968. Puerto Rican Press Reaction to the Shift from Spanish to United States Sovereignty, 1898–1917. Ph.D. diss., Columbia.

Verrill, Hyatt A. 1914. *Porto Rico: Past and Present and San Domingo of Today.* New York: Dodd, Mead and Company.

Viallate, Achille. 1923. *Economic Imperialism and International Relations During the Last Fifty Years.* Freeport, NY: Books for Libraries Press.

Wagenheim, Kal, and Olga Jiménez de Wagenheim. 1994. *The Puerto Ricans: A Documentary History.* Princeton, NJ: Markus Weiner Publishers.

Ward, George Cabot. 1908. The Rural Population of Porto Rico. Lake Mohonk Conference, 26th Annual Meeting.

Weibe, Robert H. 1967. *The Search for Order: 1877–1920.* New York: Hill and Wang.

Wells, Henry. 1971. *The Modernization of Puerto Rico: A Political Study of Changing Values and Institutions.* Cambridge, MA: Harvard University Press.

Weston, Rubin Francis. 1972. *Racism in U.S. Imperialism: The Influence of Racial Assumptions on American Foreign Policy, 1893–1946.* Columbia, SC: University of South Carolina Press.

White, Gerald T. 1982. *The United States and the Problem of Recovery after 1893.* University, AL: The University of Alabama Press.

White, Trumbell. 1938. *Puerto Rico and Its People.* New York: F.A. Stokes.

Whittaker, William G. 1968. The Santiago Iglesias Case, 1901–1902: Origins of American Trade Union Involvement in Puerto Rico. *The Americas* 25 (4):378–393.

Widenor, William C. 1980. *Henry Cabot Lodge and the Search for an American Foreign Policy.* Berkeley, CA: University of California Press.

Wilkins, M. 1970. *The Emergence of Multinational Enterprises.* Cambridge, MA: Harvard University Press.

Williams, William Appleman. 1952. Brooks Adams and American Expansion. *The New England Quarterly* 25:217–232.

_____. 1969. *The Roots of the Modern American Empire.* New York: Random House.

Willis, H. Parker. 1903. Reciprocity with Cuba. *Annals of the American Academy of Political and Social Science* 22 (July-Dec.):129–147.

Willoughby, William F. 1902. Two Years Legislation in Porto Rico: The Work of the First
    Legislative Assembly of Porto Rico, 1900–1902. *The Atlantic Monthly* 90:34–42.
_____. 1905. *Territories and Dependencies of the United States: Their Government and Ad-
    ministration.* New York: The Century Co.
_____. 1907. The Executive Council of Porto Rico. *American Political Science Review.*
    1:561–582.
_____. 1909. The Problem of Political Education in Porto Rico. Lake Mohonk Confer-
    ence, 27th Annual Meeting.
Wilson, Edward S. 1905. *Political Development of Porto Rico.* Columbus, OH: Fred J. Heer.
Wood, Leonard, William Taft, and Charles Allen. 1902. *Opportunities in the Colonies and
    Cuba.* New York: Lewis, Scriber.
Yager, Arthur. 1915. "Fundamental Social and Political Problems of Porto Rico." Lake Mo-
    honk Conference, 33rd Annual Meeting.
Zeitlin, Maurice, and Richard Earl Ratcliff. 1988. *Landlords and Capitalists: The Dominant
    Class of Chile.* Princeton, NJ: Princeton University Press.
Zinn, Howard. 1992. *A People's History of the United States.* New York: HarperCollins.

Index

Accountability, 117, 127, 166, 185
Acuña, Francisco de P., 51
Adams, Brooks, 24
Advisory Board of Insular Policy, 92
Advisory boards, 60–61, 62, 81, 92
AFL. *See* American Federation of Labor
Africa, 16
Agriculture, 44, 65, 74, 92, 94, 112, 136, 173, 177, 186
    cash-crop farming, 73, 74
    exports, 4, 20, 21, 68–71
    machinery for, 74
    tax on agricultural lands, 76–77. *See also* Taxation, land/property
Albizu Campos, Pedro, 228
Alcaldes (mayors), 174, 175
Alegría, José, 221
Allen, Charles, 101, 118, 126, 145, 154, 155, 163, 164, 166, 167, 168, 171, 172, 173, 175, 176, 184
Alianza Puertorriqueña, 221, 223–224
Amadeo Antonmarchi, Luis, 179
Amended Customs Tariff and Regulations for Ports, 72
American Academy of Social and Political Science, 179, 181
American Beet Sugar Company, 97
American Cigar Company, 20
American Cigar Workers Union, 96
American Federation of Labor (AFL), 5, 96, 158, 159, 226, 235, 237, 240, 243
Americanization, 4–5, 9, 10, 11, 16, 47, 51, 60, 66, 82, 83, 84, 106, 117, 118, 120, 152, 163–164, 177, 182, 183, 187, 189, 193, 206, 217, 218, 239–241, 245, 250, 254
    and the courts, 154–155
    through education, 54–58, 128, 130, 132, 133, 134
    and Executive Council, 122–126, 161
    and labor movement, 226–227
    of laws, 153–154
    and Republican Party, 169–171
American National Hymn, 133

American Railroad Company, 151, 159
American Sugar Refining Company, 97, 102, 110, 111
American Tobacco Company, 20, 97, 159
Ames, Azel, 102
Anarcho-syndicalism, 241
Andreu de Aguilar, Isabel, 211, 215
Anemia, 141
Annexation, 8, 16, 25, 32, 33–40, 89, 107, 110, 245
    in lieu of reparations, 37
    logic of, 37–40
    as serendipitous, 34
    and statehood, 86
Anti-Imperialist League, 38
Appointments, 115–116, 166, 175, 184, 188, 193, 206, 218, 220
Arceley, Maria Luisa, 215
Arecibo, 238, 242
Arrests, 53, 57, 158
Arroyo, 147
Ashford, Baily K., 141
Asia, 16, 18, 26, 40
Asociación Pan Americana de Mujeres, 211
Asociación Puertorriqueña de Mujeres Sufragistas, 211, 213
Association of Sugar Producers, 196
Attorney general, 152, 155, 159, 191, 206
Austria, 107
Autonomic Charter, 29, 42, 45–46, 50, 52, 66, 71, 165, 173, 177
Autonomist Party of Puerto Rico, 6, 7
Autonomy, 7, 8, 67, 120, 164, 174, 175, 183, 185, 186, 187, 196, 200, 202, 209, 218, 220, 233. *See also* Autonomic Charter; Self-government

Bacon (U.S. Senator), 98
Bainter, Edward, 135
Balearic Islands, 29
Banditry, 55. *See also Partidas sediciosas*
Bankruptcies, 74
Banks, 19, 74, 185, 188
Barbosa, José Celso, 7, 163, 170, 171, 177, 191, 194